PETER BROOK

Contemporary Theatre Studies

A series of books edited by Franc Chamberlain, University College Northampton, Northampton, UK

Please see the back of this book for other titles in the Contemporary Theatre Studies series

PETER BROOK

OXFORD TO ORGHAST

Edited by

Richard Helfer

and

Glenn Loney

 harwood academic publishers
Australia • Canada • China • France • Germany • India
Japan • Luxembourg • Malaysia • The Netherlands • Russia
Singapore • Switzerland • Thailand

Amsteldijk 166
1st Floor
1079 LH Amsterdam
The Netherlands

British Library Cataloguing in Publication Data

Peter Brook: Oxford to Orghast. – (Contemporary theatre
  studies; v. 27)
  1. Brook, Peter, 1925– Criticism and interpretation
  I. Helfer, Richard   II. Loney, Glenn, 1928–
  792'.023'092

  ISBN   90-5702-208-7 (softback)

Cover illustration: Peter Brook. Photo: Glenn Loney

CONTENTS

INTRODUCTION TO THE SERIES

Contemporary Theatre Studies is a book series of special interest to everyone involved in theatre. It consists of monographs on influential figures, studies of movements and ideas in theatre, as well as primary material consisting of theatre-related documents, performing editions of plays in English, and English translations of plays from various vital theatre traditions world-wide.

Franc Chamberlain

PREFACE

As instigator of the project, I would like to relate how it came about. Of course Peter Brook's name—along with those of Antonin Artaud, Bertolt Brecht, Jerzy Grotowski, and Jan Kott—was very well known in avant-garde and counter-culture theatre circles, beginning in the 1960s. His deeply disturbing London production of *The Persecution and Assassination of Marat as Performed by the Inmates of the Asylum of Charenton under the Direction of the Marquis de Sade*—better known as *Marat/Sade*—which bowed on Broadway at the Martin Beck, in 1965, made many aware of his brilliance and of his interest in exploring new forms of theatre.

Those Broadway regulars who loved the spritely Parisian musical, *Irma La Douce* (1960), could scarcely believe that the two shows had been staged by the same director. They might have had some intimation of Brook's evolution in his craft, had they seen and pondered his spare, anguished, cruel *King Lear* in 1964, as it officially opened the New York State Theatre in Lincoln Center, at the end of a world tour. Even today, there are still senior theatre-lovers who will shake their head as they consider: "What a loss it was to the commercial Broadway/West End theatre, when Peter Brook turned his back on it."

But, because most of Brook's British stagings of the 1940s and 1950s were never seen in New York—or anywhere else in the United States, for that matter—few Americans at that time had any idea of his protean, innovative talents. The charming, but very light-weight Parisian sex-farce, *The Little Hut* (1953), could scarcely have prepared them for the *Marat/Sade* a decade later, though Brook's stunning and shocking production of Friedrich Dürrenmatt's *The Visit*, starring Alfred Lunt and Lynn Fontanne (1958) might have warned them that Brook had a darker side. In the original German, *Der Besuch der alten Dame—The Visit of the Old Lady*—a bitter satire on family and community values, was judged so strong that it had to be diluted for the Lunts, as well as for their adoring fans. Even in a gelded version, it was still seen as too potent to première in London, which saw it only after its Broadway success.

As a theatre student at UC/Berkeley, I had heard of Brook's work in England even in the late 1940s, especially the "scandal" of his Covent Garden production of *Salome* in 1949. Even then it was clear to me from thoughtful reports that this man was an extraordinary talent, a director one would want to watch. On the West Coast, however, there was unfortunately no opportunity to do that literally. My first experience of a Brook production came, oddly enough, in Venice, after I had moved to Europe to teach. I had planned to visit, among other Venetian landmarks, the historic Teatro Fenice, hoping for a Goldoni play, but willing to settle for Pirandello. Imagine my disappointment when the hotel concierge told me they currently had some English play on view. Perhaps one could see the inside of the theatre on a daytime tour, I thought, so I went there, only to discover that the English play was *Titus Andronicus*, with Laurence Olivier, Vivien Leigh and Anthony Quayle, among others, on tour. I hardly noticed that it had been staged by Peter Brook. What I had thought of as a blood-and-thunder Elizabethan melodrama—on a par, say, with Kyd's *The Spanish Tragedy*—had been transformed into something theatrically marvelous, but spiritually frightening. From that time on, whenever I could get to London or Stratford, I made a point of seeing Brook's work. Since then—with the exception of works created in Paris which have not toured to the United States—I must have seen them all.

But this book is not a record of my memories of Brook's productions—though there is some of that too. Rather, it is intended only as a research resource, to be of use to students, scholars, and critics who would like to know more about Brook's career before he moved definitively to Paris to found his International Center for Theatre Research. That work has been amply and excellently documented in France—in the series called *Recherches Théâtrales*—and in Britain and America.

As soon as it became known in New York that Peter Brook was going to bring his epic production of *The Mahabharata* to the Brooklyn Academy of Music, Dr. Marvin Carlson, head of the City University Graduate Center's Theatre Ph.D. Program, suggested that I offer a seminar on the Hindu epic itself and on Brook's reworking of it. This I was eager to do, but in preparing materials for the sessions, I thought it might be helpful to survey Brook's career from its beginnings, compiling the chronology of plays, operas, films and television productions presented in this volume. I was myself amazed at the range and variety of his interests as a director. Sorting individual productions I had seen into this sequence brought Brook's development as a director and his evolution as an experimenter and theoretician in the theatre into much sharper focus.

It appeared that the occasional light comedy or musical Brook staged were not only ways to pay the bills, but also stages in his growth. Just as some critics are fond of pointing out that Picasso first had to learn to draw a tree before he could cube the *Demoiselles* of Avignon, so also was Brook's apprenticeship in the commercial theatre a valuable preparation for going far beyond it, in a dedicated effort to renew a morbid, lackluster art. To rediscover the essence of theatre in its beginnings; to find its powers to speak to and to move Mankind in a desperate, dangerous time in the world's long history: that is only part of Peter Brook's gift to us.

My intent was to concentrate largely on Brook's early career, lest it be forgot, especially by theatre students who were themselves somewhat expert on his Paris productions and his theories. In fact, his early work was news to many. Some found it difficult to believe that the guru who wrote *The Empty Space*, or the genius who staged the *Marat/Sade*, could also be the man who directed *The Little Hut*. Some could not credit the fact that Brook had been eager to reform opera-staging, or that he was still interested in finding new resonances in old "war-horses" of the operatic repertory. There is, after all, a long-standing prejudice among some theatre-people regarding opera: that it is not real theatre at all, or that, it is a grotesque perversion of it.

So there were many discoveries to be made: not least that Brook had also done interesting and innovative work in film and television. My idea was that the seminar members could explore the early work and share their findings with us, possibly compiling enough of value to assemble into a research reference, largely on Brook's pre-Paris work. As I had the opportunity over the years—not only to study various Brook stagings, but also, on occasion, to interview him and discuss them—I proposed to share some of this archival material. We would also take advantage of City University of New York's mid-town Manhattan location to invite people who had worked with Brook on past projects to review their experiences. At the same time, we would discuss *The Mahabharata* in depth, see it several times, invite cast-members to talk to the seminar, and have Peter Brook himself generously discuss his work and theories.

This book is the result.

Glenn Loney

*   *   *

This project started with the Production Chronology, which was developed in a seminar at the Graduate Center of the City University of New York, and some of the entries are the work of students in that class—of which I was a member. In the manuscript's later stages, several other students at CUNY were invited to write about individual productions. Following are the names of those writers and the particular entries for which they are responsible: Ramon Albino, 49; Zsuzsa Berger, 48, 58; J. K. Curry, 11, 13, 47; Eva Dorsey, 57; Steven Fechter, 63, 66; Jason Goldsmith, 28, 66; Susana Powell, 37; Cecelia Riddett, 38; Martin Russell, 43, 46, 50, 56; Barbara Saltzman, 27, 36; Linda Gale Sampson, 28, 51, 55, 61, 62; Jim Seymour, 40, 41, 42; Sarah Standing, 21; Lydia Stryk, 29 and Shauna Vey, 9, 12. Because of the changes this book went through, some productions were covered by more than one person, in which case I must bear blame for any problems resulting from putting the various versions together, as I am also responsible for the various changes required to convert all entries into a uniform style.

Special thanks to Susana Powell for the arrangements made in Britain and to Peter Hodges, present by his absence, in that he discovered that some material did *not* belong in the book. Thanks also to both of them for assistance in editing.

Thanks to Peter Hollins and to Diane Arnold of the Birmingham City Council Central Library and to Gabrielle Heller of the International Theatre Institute, Paris, as well as to the Museum of Television and Radio and the Library of the Performing Arts (a branch of the New York Public Library) in New York, and to the British Film Institute and the BBC in London.

When we first knew we were going to be using the interviews, we thought we would order them chronologically according to the productions covered in the interview. We soon saw that almost all of them ranged over so broad a territory as to make this approach impractical. The interview section now starts with Dr. Loney's *Myth and Music*, as an overview, and the others are chronological according to the date of the interview.

Finally, this book is titled *Peter Brook, Oxford to Orghast*, since its first part (the Chronology) covers the earlier half of his career. It must be admitted that the "Oxford" part is not as complete as the editors had hoped it would be, the records of the earliest productions largely having vanished, despite searches in both Britain and the United States. Two of Brook's British television productions have undergone the same fate, as has his production in Brussels of *Death of a Salesman* (#23) and his later Oxford production of *The Perils of Scobie Prilt* (#54). While these cannot be considered significant—indeed, their lack of significance is the main reason records have been apparently lost—if any reader has access to information about them, the editors would appreciate notification, and acknowledgement will be made in future editions.

Richard Helfer

Production Chronology
Oxford to Orghast

LIST OF PETER BROOK'S PRODUCTIONS
(1942–1971)

1942

1
Doctor Faustus
London: Torch Theatre

1943

2
A Sentimental Journey
Oxford: The Oxford Union

1945

3
The Infernal Machine
London: Chanticleer Theatre

4
The Barretts of Wimpole Street
London: "Q" Theatre

5
Pygmalion
National Tour
(Entertainments Natl. Service
Assn.)

6
August 14
Man and Superman
Birmingham Rep

7
October 16
King John
Brimingham Rep

8
November 20
The Lady from the Sea
Birmingham Rep

1946

9
April 26
Love's Labour's Lost
Stratford: Sh. Mem. Th.

10
June 4
The Brothers Karamazov
London: Lyric Hammersmith

11
July 16
Vicious Circle (Huis Clos)
London: Arts Theatre Club

1947

12
April 5
Romeo and Juliet
Stratford: Sh. Mem. Th.

13
> July 17
> *Men without Shadows &*
> *The Respectable Prostitute*
> London: Lyric Hammersmith

12a
> October 6
> *Romeo and Juliet*
> London: His Majesty's

1948

Xa
> From January 1948
> The Covent Garden Operas

14
> May 12
> *Boris Godunov*
> London: Royal Opera,
> Covent Garden

15
> October 15
> *La Bohème*
> London: Royal Opera,
> Covent Garden

1949

16
> January 22
> *The Marriage of Figaro*
> London: Royal Opera,
> Covent Garden

17
> March 9
> *Dark of the Moon*
> London: Lyric Hammersmith

18
> September 29
> *The Olympians*
> London: Royal Opera,
> Covent Garden

19
> November 11
> *Salome*
> London: Royal Opera,
> Covent Garden

1950

20
> January 26
> *Ring Round the Moon*
> London: Globe

21
> March 9
> *Measure for Measure*
> Stratford: Sh. Mem. Th.

22
> August 23
> *The Little Hut*
> London: Lyric

23
> Exact date unknown
> *La Morte d'un Commis Voyageur*
> Brussels: Théâtre d'l'Monnaie
> (and Oxford)

1951

21a
> *Measure for Measure*
> European Tour

24
March 1
A Penny for a Song
London: Haymarket

25
June 27
The Winter's Tale
London: Phoenix
(and Edinburgh Festival)

26
Filmed 1951
(Televised 1957)
Heaven and Earth

27
December 13
Colombe
London: New

1952

1953

28
February 25
Box for One
British Television

29
May 5
The Beggar's Opera
London: ("private showing")
general opening June 5

30
May 15
Venice Preserv'd

London: Lyric Hammersmith

22a
October 7
The Little Hut
New York: Coronet

31
October 18
King Lear
New York: CBS TV

32
November 16
Faust
New York: Metropolitain Opera

1954

33
April 30
The Dark is Light Enough
London: Aldwych

34
June 9
Both Ends Meet
London: Apollo

35
December 30
House of Flowers
New York: Alvin

1955

36
May 11
The Lark
London: Lyric Hammersmith

Xb
> July 22
>
The Birthday Present
BBC Television
(wrote script)

37
> August 16
>
Titus Andronicus
Stratford: Sh. Mem. Th.

38
> November 24
>
Hamlet, Prince of Denmark
Moscow: Vakhtangov Theatre
(after Brighton)

39
> Late 1955
>
Report from Moscow
BBC Television

1956

40
> April 5
>
The Power and the Glory
London: Phoenix

41
> June 7
>
The Family Reunion
London: Phoenix

42
> October 11
>
A View from the Bridge
London: Comedy/Club Theatre

43
> December 18
>
La Chatte sur un Toit Brulante

Paris: Théâtre Antione

1957

37a
> July 1
>
Titus Andronicus
World Tour

44
> August 13
>
The Tempest
Stratford: Sh. Mem. Th.

45
> October 28
>
Eugene Onegin
New York: Metropolitain Opera

Xc
> December 24
>
Time and Again
Brighton: Theatre Royal
(see #47 - *The Visit*)

(26)
> Shown 1957
> Filmed 1951
>
Heaven and Earth
BBC Television

1958

46
> March 11
>
Vu du Pont
Paris: Thèâtre Antoine

47
> May 5
>
The Visit
New York: Lunt-Fontanne

48
> July 17

Irma La Douce
London: Lyric

1959

49
> December 8

The Fighting Cock
New York: ANTA

1960

50
> March 19

Le Balcon
Paris: Théâtre de Gymnase

51
> May 24

Moderato Cantabile
Cannes

47a
> June 23

The Visit
London: Royalty

48a
> September 29

Irma La Douce
New York: Plymouth

1961

1962

52
> November 6

King Lear
Stratford: Sh. Mem. Th.

1963

Xd
> January 7

The Hollow Crown
Washington DC: National

53
> January 9

The Physicists
London: Aldwych

Xe
> April 2

The Tempest
Stratford: Sh. Mem. Th
(co-direct)

54
> June 12

The Perils of Scobie Prilt
Oxford: New Theatre

55
> August 20

Lord of the Flies
New York

56
> October 10

La Danse de Sergent Musgrave
Paris: Théâtre de l'Athenée

Xf
> December 10

Le Vicaire
Paris: Théâtre de l'Athenée
(co-direct)

1964

57
January
The Theatre of Cruelty
London: RSC/LAMDA

52a
February 11
King Lear (RSC)
World Tour, inc. NY in May

58
August 20
Marat/Sade
London: Aldwych

53a
October 13
The Physicists
New York: Martin Beck

1965

59
October 19
The Investigation
London: Aldwych

58a
December 27
Marat/Sade
New York: Martin Beck

1966

60
October 13
US
London: Aldwych

1967

61
February 22
Marat/Sade (Film)
New York

1968

62
February 17
Tell Me Lies
New York

63
March 19
Oedipus (Seneca)
London: Old Vic

64
July 18
The Tempest
London: The Round House

1969

1970

65
August 27
A Midsummer Night's Dream
Stratford: (RSC)

66
November 22
King Lear (Film)

65a
December 4
A Midsummer Night's Dream
London: Aldwych
        also (from Jan 20 '71)
US tour

1971

1972

65b

67

August 8

August 28

A Midsummer Night's Dream

Orghast at Persepolis

London: Aldwych

Persepolis

and World tour

DESCRIPTIONS OF PETER BROOK'S PRODUCTIONS (1942–1971)

1942

1

Doctor Faustus
by Christopher Marlowe

London: Torch Theatre

1943

2

Late 1943

A Sentimental Journey
from the novel by Lawrence Sterne

Oxford: the Oxford Union

January 17, 1944
London: The Torch Theatre

Like many geniuses, Peter Brook has his share of nerve. While a student at Oxford, he had worked his way into being President of the University Film Society—which he had himself revived—and became Britain's youngest film director. J. C. Trewin describes what happened:

He had chosen a full-length treatment of Laurence Sterne's "traveling fancy," *A Sentimental Journey Through France and Italy*. Sacha Guitry's mimeodramatic technique in *Le Roman D'un Tricheur* had impressed him, so the script had no dialogue, merely a commentary extracted from the book and spoken as if by Sterne himself, with a background of eighteenth century music. [This is also, it should be noted, a good idea for making a film on a severe budget, live sound being much more expensive.] Character parts, as in Russian films, were played by ordinary folk recruited from Oxford pubs and haunts. Improvising gallantly on a budget of £250—the unit had to take a garden truck as a trolley—Brook shot his exteriors in Oxford and the nearby country, at Abingdon, and at Woodstock in Blenheim Park. The problem of interiors he solved after going to see John Gielgud's Haymarket revival of *Love for Love*. Calling at Gielgud's dressing-room, he asked tentatively if he might use the set for his film, Gielgud agreed, and the unit came into the theatre for some rapid work. Unhappily, because the film was made on short lengths of raw 16 mm stock, [there were wartime restrictions on such things] each roll of which reacted to printing in a different way, *A Sentimental Journey* could not be shown in an ordinary cinema, and when it had its premiere at the Oxford Union, the hall was the wrong size, diminishing the images while disconcertingly magnifying the sound. Still, within two months, the film had a London showing at the Torch.

What is even more amazing, the film was actually reviewed in advance by the *Times*, though the tone of the review—not helped by the problems with the film processing—might have made Brook wish otherwise.

> *This film, which was made by Oxford undergraduates at a cost of a £250, shows how thorny and difficult is the task of the amateur director. It should, theoretically, be easy enough for a man with a good camera and a knowledge of what he wants to produce a film which will be aesthetically and intellectually satisfying and not fall too far short of the technical standards of the commercial cinema. Apparently it is not.*
>
> *A* Sentimental Journey, *since it keeps close to the pattern of Sterne—there is no dialogue and gramophone records of passages from the book recited by Mr. Frederick Hurdis supply the commentary—doubtless has aesthetic and intellectual virtues, but it is hard to discern through the murk in which the action takes place. The camera seems to find the lighting provided by our weather altogether too much for it, and the variable noises of the gramophone combined with the uncertain photography on the screen continually get between the audience and a sincere effort to transcribe Sterne faithfully into terms of visual acting. The cast, in spite of the wigs, can hardly help looking its youth, and A* Sentimental Journey *must be regarded as a brave attempt at an objective which, in the event, proved too difficult.*
>
> *The film begins a week's run at the Torch Theatre on Monday.*

1945

3

February 3 to 18, 1945

The Infernal Machine

by Jean Cocteau
Translated by Carl Wildman

London: The Chanticleer Theatre Club

Production by . . . . .Peter Brook
Scenery Painted by . . . . Corinne Cooper

CAST

The Young Soldier . . . . *Roger Trafford*
The Soldier . . . . *Frank Tregear*
The Chief . . . . *Ronald Long*
Jocasta, the Queen, widow of Laius . . . . *Sigrid Landstad*
Tiresias . . . . *Robert Marsden*
The Sphirx . . . . *Joy Harvey*
Anubis . . . . *Joan Veale*
A Theban Matron . . . . *Betty Linton*
Oedipus, son of Laius . . . . *Frederick Horrey*
Creon, brother of Jocasta . . . . *Roger Trafford*
The Messinger from Corinth . . . . *Ronald Bowman*
The Shepherd of Laius . . . . *Ronald Long*

Censorship forced the Chanticleer into being a theatre club for the short run of this incest-themed play. In a short review, the unnamed critic for *The Evening Standard* said, "I believe that in young Peter Brook we have a producer who may develop into something first class." Then, after telling of Brook's career, including *A Sentimental Journey*, comes the following:

> *He contived to give a sense of space even to the miniature stage at the Chanticleer and drove his actors to a splendid emotional climax. Mr. Brook has a rare combination of gifts, inasmuch as he is a sensitive artist and something of a thruster. He gave me no peace until I went to see Infernal Machine, and I am grateful for his pertinacity.*

J. C. Trewin, in *The Observer*, did not go into Brook's (short) history, and did not much like the play, but found "its pretence is masked by the fantastic direction of Mr. Peter Brook. He has done nobly on his two-by-four stage with a play that needs all the batteries of theatrical effect."

4

July 3 to 8, 1945

The Barretts of Wimpole Street
by Rudolf Besier

London (Knightbridge): The "Q" Theatre

Produced by . . . . Peter Brook

CAST

Doctor Chambers	*Arthur Burne*
Elizabeth Barratt Moulton-Barrett	*Mary MacKenzie*
Wilson	*Mary Vernon*
Henrietta Moulton-Barrett	*Violet Loxley*
Arabel Moulton-Barrett	*Rita Daniel*
Octavius Moulton-Barrett	*Dennis Fraser*
Charles Moulton-Barrett	*Jack Notley*
Septimus Moulton-Barrett	*Donald Webster*
Henry Moulton-Barrett	*Allan Barnes*
George Moulton-Barrett	*Frederick Hill*
Edward Moulton-Barrett	*James Dale*
Bella Hedley	*Pamela Stirling*
Henry Bevan	*John Burch*
Robert Browning	*Geoffrey Wardwell*
Doctor Ford Waterlow	*John Burch*
Captain Surtees Cook	*Allan Barnes*
Flush	*Rhett Maillard*

5

Pygmalion
by George Bernard Shaw

Entertainments National Service Association tour of England

Entertainments National Service Association was a huge organization created when it was realized that entertainment was not just a luxury in wartime, but was a necessity for the morale of soldiers and civilians alike. There were other productions, like Brook's *Pygmalion*, meant for domestic consumption, but the bulk of its activity was intended for troops in the field and overseas; the books covering its history do not even mention Brook.

The production, said to have been faithful, straight, and lively, had its dress rehearsal backstage at Drury Lane, which sounds impressive until it is noted that during this period the Drury Lane was used as ENSA headquarters, so that most productions used it in some capacity. Nevertheless, it was fortunate for Brook, for William Armstrong, the head of the Liverpool Repertory Theatre, saw the rehearsal and mentioned it to Barry Jackson, director of the Birmingham Rep, who had been wanting to do *Man and Superman*.

6

August 14, 1945

Man and Superman

by George Bernard Shaw

The Birmingham Repertory Theatre

Director . . . . Peter Brook
Settings . . . . Paul Shelving

CAST

Roebuck Ramsden . . . . *Herbert Vanderfelt*
Parlormaid . . . . *Patricia Meakin*
Octavius Robinson . . . . *John Harrison*
John Tanner . . . . *Paul Scofield*
Mrs. Whitefield . . . . *Maud Gill*
Anne Whitefield . . . . *Barbara Lott*
Miss Ramsden . . . . *Mabel France*
Violet Robinson . . . . *Joy Parker*
Henry Straker . . . . *Duncan Ross*
Hector Malone, Junior . . . . *Stanley Baker*
Hector Malone, Senior . . . . *Hugh Barnet*

For his first production at the Birmingham Rep, Peter Brook cut the entire third act of Shaw's classic, eliminating *Don Juan in Hell*, but leaving what was described by the critics as a more-or-less straightforward comedy-drama, sufficiently provocative and entertaining to give the play, "more piquancy than most period pieces," according to the *Birmingham Mail*.

The *Birmingham Gazette* said that it was one of the most noteworthy presentations of Shaw that the Birmingham Rep had done, brilliantly acted, but M. F. K. Fraser of the *Dispatch* described the acting as rather lightweight, apart from Scofield's "finely flowing and rhetorical" John Tanner (despite an irritating accent). Although some actors "rattled off their lines with machine-gun rapidity," T. C. K. of the *Birmingham Post* still felt the pace was slow and anti-Shavian, but on the whole praised Brook's direction as sensitive and discerning, playing for subtlety.

All four critics mentioned delightful costumes and an excellent set, the villa at Granada being an "architectural gem." It is worth noting that all four also misspelt Brook's name as "Brooke." It was not a mistake they would make again.

7

October 16, 1945

King John

by William Shakespeare
The Birmingham Repertory Theatre

Director..Peter Brook
Settings and Costumes.....................................Paul Shelving

CAST

King John . . . . *David Read*
Elinor . . . . *Mabel France*
Earl of Pembroke . . . . *Hugh Barnet*
Earl of Sussex . . . . *Eric Syree*
Earl of Salisbury . . . . *Herbert Vanderfelt*
Lord Bigot . . . . *Stanley Ellison*
Hubert de Burgh . . . . *John Harrison*
Chatillon . . . . *Alun Owen*
Philip, The Bastard . . . . *Paul Scofield*
Faulconbridge . . . . *Denis Quilley*
Lady Faulconbridge . . . . *Maud Gill*

James Gurney . . . . *Trevor Barker*
King of France . . . . *Michael Madell*
Dauphin . . . . *Duncan Ross*
Duke of Austria . . . . *Stanley Baker*
Constance . . . . *Eileen Beldon*
Arthur . . . . *Herman Martyn*
Melun . . . . *Denis Quilley*
Blanch of Castile . . . . *Patricia Brewer*
Citizen of Angiers . . . . *Bertram Tyrell*
Cardinal Pandulph . . . . *Scott Sutherland*
Executioner . . . . *Stanley Baker*
Peter of Pomfret . . . . *Alun Owen*
Prince Henry . . . . *Trevor Barker*

Soldiers, Monks, Attendants
Robin Griffin, Eric Syree, Denis Quilley,
William Morgan, Stephen Brewer, Michael Forman,
Jay Appleton, Barbara Ormerod, Evanne Salt,
Ida Reddish, Lysbeth Harley, Brenda Barrie

At first glance, *King John* seems a typical Brook choice of an unusual Shakespeare offering. But it had, in fact, been a popular play during the Second World War, the mood matching that of the beseiged Londoners during the Blitz. In immediate postwar England, the critics found the Birmingham Rep production equally apt, linking the barbarism and concern for expediency with the politics of the war's aftermath.

The review in the *Birmingham Mail* noted that Stanley Baker played a Goering-like Duke of Austria and that the same mad world and mad humans that inhabit the play "still bend the knee to that same 'smooth faced gentleman, tickling commodity'." But the review also complained that the players lacked "authentic direction," that Eileen Beldon's Constance was a "second mad Ophelia," and felt that Sunderland's melancholic and Calvinistic Cardinal was an anachronism.

W. H. Bush in the *Gazette*, on the contrary, thought Brook's imaginative production enriched the text and recommended it "on moral grounds to those who are now re-shaping the world." In the *Dispatch*, M. F. K. Fraser also praised Brook, whom he called the hero of the much-awaited production. Minor quibbles with the grotesque interpretation of Austria and the "royal fishwives" Elinor and Constance did not detract from "the magnitude of Mr. Brook's achievement. That is terrific."

The acting of David Read as King John and Paul Scofield as the Bastard was uniformly praised, Read for his excellent voice and suave dignity,

Scofield for his lightness and lyricism. Two of the critics noted that Brook opened the production with mime. Though Bush of the *Gazette* thought the stylized pictures and lighting effects matched the mood of Shakespeare's scenes, the *Post* reviewer disputed the "fussiness of the bacchanal," though he liked the tragic tableau behind the bastard's final speech.

One thing not commented on was Brook's cutting, rearranging and even adding to the text. The major addition was a line added to the beginning of the Bastard's great "commodity" speech at the end of Act II, scene 1. Feeling the speech was at the center of the meaning of the play, and knowing that the modern meaning of "commodity" would be read into it, Brook started the passage with, "Commodity, which some do call expedience."

The titles of the Birmingham reviews reflect the fact that Brook was already en route to a career of making classics relevant in his own mode. "Repertory producer's 'Occasion'" (the *Dispatch*); "A Tract for the Times" (*Gazette*). He was seen as a director to be reckoned with, and everybody got his name right.

8

November 20, 1945

The Lady from the Sea
by Henrik Ibsen
Translated by William Archer

The Birmingham Repertory Theatre

Director . . . . Peter Brook
Set Designer . . . . Paul Shelving
Costumes . . . . Edith Hirons

CAST

Ballested . . . . *Michael Madell*
Boletta . . . . *Monica Stutfield*
Lyngstrand . . . . *Denis Quilley*
Hilda . . . . *Diana Houlston*
Dr. Wangel . . . . *Paul Scofield*
Arnholm . . . . *John Harrison*
Ellida Wangel . . . . *Eileen Beldon*
A Stranger . . . . *Duncan Ross*

Of all Brook's Birmingham Rep productions, reviewers were most critical of his *The Lady From the Sea*. They were unhappy with the choice of the play, the translation (listed in the reviews as being by *Mrs.* William Archer) and the directorial concept. In an article titled "Ennui and Sea Spray," the writer in the *Birmingham Mail* suggested that the Rep had selected the play as an antidote to the farces running at the other Birmingham theatres; he pronounced the play "dead" and the production a "mere exercise in stylised dramatics." "T. C. K." of the *Birmingham Post* complained about the slow pace, and Thomas Olsen of the *Gazette* wondered what Ibsen would have thought about Ellida's ocean passage being backed by "The Skater's Waltz."

It is difficult to form an opinion of Brook's work in this production, for the critics were so mixed on substansive matters that it is difficult to get a clear picture of just what was happening on stage. Paul Scofield's Dr. Wangel (looking dangerously like Dr. Crippen) was judged underplayed by two critics, full of pathos by a third, and excellent by the fourth. Eileen Beldon as Ellida was praised for keeping the audience's attention through long silences, but also criticised as sinking "to a nagging wife who deserves spanking." Fraser, of the *Dispatch*, said she played the part with terrific abandon, but his compatriot at the *Mail* saw this as overplaying, leaving no emotion unturned. All agreed that the entrance of the much- awaited Stranger was a complete anti-climax. "There are other songs to sing to-day," sighed the *Mail*, "—and the Rep should be singing them to us."

1946

9

April 26, 1946

Love's Labour's Lost
by William Shakespeare

Stratford-upon-Avon: Shakespeare Memorial Theatre

Presented by The Shakespeare Festival
Under Sir Barry Jackson
In repertory through 9/21/46

Director . . . . Peter Brook
Scenery and Costumes . . . . Reginald Leefe
Music . . . . Allan Gray

CAST

Ferdinand, King of Navarre . . . . *Paul Stephenson*
Berowne . . . . *David King-Wood*
Longville . . . . *John Harrison*
Dumaine . . . . *Donald Sinden*
Boyet . . . . *John Ruddock*
Don Adriano de Armado . . . . *Paul Scofield*
Sir Nathaniel, a curate . . . . *Dudley Jones*
Dull, a constable . . . . *William March*
Holofernes, a schoolmaster . . . . *Hugh Griffith*
Costard, a clown . . . . *Dudley Jones*
Princess of France . . . . *Valerie Taylor*
Rosaline . . . . *Ruth Lodge*
Maria . . . . *Joy Parker*
Katherine . . . . *Muriel Davidson*
Marcade, a messenger . . . . *?*

9a

Production revived April 14, 1947
In repertory through August

Cast changes for second season

Berowne . . . . *Lawrence Payne*
Holofernes . . . . *John Blatchley*
Princess of France . . . . *Veronica Turleigh*
Rosaline . . . . *Helen Burns*

"An extravaganza of admirable lightness," *Punch* wrote of Brook's 1946 *Love's Labour's Lost*, later labeled "his first professional work of genius," by the *Picture Post*. This first Stratford production by the twenty-one-year-old director animated an unpopular play and became a surprise hit for the Shakespeare Festival, which revived it the following season.

The production opened with a dumbshow prologue showing the tearful women of Navarre reading the king's proclamation from a scroll on the palace gates. When this painted drop was removed, the court was a vision out of Watteau. Critics were stunned by the delicate interplay of color, shadow and groupings. While elsewhere Brook had been taken to task for distracting audiences with visual effects, here "the constant excitement of the eye is at one with the play, buoying its nonsense and carrying us on delightedly," according to *Punch*.

Most commented upon was the moment late in the play when a messenger comes with news that the King of France is dead. Brook brought the black-clad figure over a rise at the back of the stage and faded the lights during a long silence preceding his speech. Writing later, Brook connected his Watteau imagery with this mood-changing character.

> He came into an artificial world to announce a piece of news that was real . . . the reason the Watteau Age of Gold *is so particularly moving is that although it's a picture of springtime, it's an autumn springtime, because every one of Watteau's pictures has an incredible melancholy . . . there is somewhere in it the presence of death . . . usually a dark figure somewhere. The man in black came onto a very pretty summer stage, with everybody in pastel Watteau and Lancret costumes.*

Critics felt this abrupt shift in mood was handled with brilliant simplicity, noting how the end threw a surprising amount of depth backward onto a play usually felt to be nothing but fluff.

Brook also succeeded in mixing periods and genres, broad comedy with pastels. The lovers were dressed in early eighteenth-century styles, while Constable Dull wore a Victorian helmet and carried a truncheon and a string of sausages. The Princess was followed by a mute attendant in chalk-face and white clothes. Paul Scofield, who earned praise for his wordy splendor as Don Armado, was dressed out of Velazquez, and Costard used a water pistol. The anachronistic concoction—still somewhat avant-grade—was successful. *Punch* raved: "Mr. Peter Brook has contrived to blend delicate satire and gusty humor without any sense of strain or pretentiousness." The *Times* concluded that the production was "from first to last, consistent with itself."

As Berowne and the Princess, David King-Wood and Valerie Taylor were approved as suitably romantic, as were Lawrence Payne and Veronica Turleigh the following season. The comedy of this production was consistently praised with Scofield, Dudley Jones and the "riotously wry" Hugh Griffith the standouts. One critic summed up the general response: "But when all the credit has been given to a keen young cast at the top of their form, the main triumph remains with Mr. Brook."

10

June 4, 1946

The Brothers Karamazov

From the novel by Dostoevsky
Adapted by Alec Guiness

London (Hammersmith): Lyric Theatre
(39 performances)

Director . . . . Peter Brook
Producer . . . . The Company of Four
Set design . . . . Gurschner

for the Company of Four

Manager . . . . Lovat Fraser
Stage Director . . . . Reginald Grosse
Stage Managers . . . . Jean Ingram, Kay Bradley
Asst. Stage Managers . . . . Betty Woolfe, Sheila Spence

CAST

Smerdyakov . . . . *James Donald*
Father Zossima . . . . *Ernest Milton*
Nastasya . . . . *Marriott Longman*
Prohorovna . . . . *Meg Maxwell*
Woman with a Baby . . . . *Betty Woolfe*
Madame Hohlakov . . . . *Veronica Turleigh*
Lise . . . . *Dorothy Gordon*
Alyosha Karamazov . . . . *Pierre Lefevre*
Karamazov . . . . *Frederick Valk*
Miusov . . . . *Douglas Bradley-Smith*
Father Paissy . . . . *Laurier Lister*
Ivan Karamazov . . . . *Raymond Jaquarello*
Father Librarian . . . . *Roderick Walker*
Mitya Karamazov . . . . *Alec Guiness*
Grigory . . . . *Aubrey Richards*
Katerina . . . . *Hazel Terry*
Grushey . . . . *Donald Pleasance*
Police Captain . . . . *Rhoderick Walker*
Monksnka . . . . *Elizabeth Sellars*
Trifon . . . . *Victor Clarke*
Mavrik, Peasants . . . . *Bernard Bennett*
                                                                                Michael Byrne
                                                                                Douglas Danvers
                                                                                Gordon Pullar
                                                                                Sheila Spence

The critics scolded Guiness and Brook for attempting the impossible—putting a full length Russian novel on the stage. Yet, their effort, while predictably unsuccessful as a complete work, was considered a valiant one and quite effective in parts. The play featured key scenes from the novel connected with narration delivered by a performer stepping temporarily out of character. The result was many powerful scenes that did not quite add up to a play, and apparently a bit of confusion for some of the audience members who were not familiar with the novel. In the *Sunday Times*, James Agate described the event as "one of those colossal mistakes which are tremendously worth while." Brook, who shocked the audience into attention by firing pistols, was consistently praised for his ability to create moving stage pictures. Trewin commented: "One remembers the *Karamazov* principally for its production; for its atmospherics, its grouping, the painting of the scene around Father Zossima outside the monastery, the curious rapture of Zossima's death, the sweeping lights of the nightmare." Besides Guiness, actors receiving favourable notice included Frederick Valk as the vulgar old father, Ernest Milton as the priest, and Veronica Turleigh as Madame Hohlakov.

11

July 16, 1946

Vicious Circle
(Huis Clos)
by Jean-Paul Sartre
Translation by Marjorie Gabain and Joan Swinstead

The Arts Theatre Club, London
limited 27 performance run through August 8

Director . . . . Peter Brook
Producer . . . . Peter Brook
Set Designer . . . . Rolf Gérard

CAST

Garcin . . . . *Alec Guiness*
The Attendant . . . . *Donald Pleasance*
Inés . . . . *Beatrix Lehmann*
Estelle . . . . *Betty Ann Davies*

Sartre's drama, known to American audiences as *No Exit*, offers a vision of hell composed of three people locked forever in a single room, their flaws while alive promising that they shall be each other's tormenters throughout eternity. Brook's production was the first presentation of the drama in England and it was given an ostensibly private production to avoid censorship—one of the women is a lesbian. It seems Brook's greatest innovation was selecting the play, which J. C. Trewin thought "has something of the fever chills of the better Guignol, a pit and pendulum horror." Though Trewin found Brook's production "admirably precise," there is little critical comment available on it. An unsigned review in the *Times* thought the play had not touched Brook's imagination and found the picture of hell a bit too cozy.

1947

12

April 5, 1947

Romeo and Juliet
by William Shakespeare

Stratford-upon-Avon: Shakespeare Memorial Theatre

Presented by The Shakespeare Festival
Sir Barry Jackson, Director

Director . . . . Peter Brook
Scenery and Costumes . . . . Rolf Gérard
Music . . . . Roberto Gerhard
Fight Arrangers . . . . Rex Rickman and Patrick Crean

CAST

Chorus . . . . *John Harrison*
Escalus, Prince of Verona . . . . *Robert Harris*
Paris . . . . *Donald Sinden*
Montague . . . . *Michael Golden*
Capulet . . . . *Walter Hudd*
Romeo . . . . *Lawrence Payne*

Marcutio . . . . *Paul Scofield*

Benvolio . . . . *John Harrison*

Tybalt . . . . *Myles Eason*

Friar Lawrence . . . . *John Ruddock*

Lady Montague . . . . *Gwen Williams*

Lady Capulet . . . . *Veronica Turleigh*

Juliet . . . . *Daphne Slater*

Nurse . . . . *Beatrice Lehmann*

Balthasar . . . . *William Avenell*

Sampson . . . . *William March*

Gregory . . . . *Anthony Groser*

Peter . . . . *Leigh Crutchley*

Abraham . . . . *George Cooper*

An Apothecary . . . . *Douglas Seale*

and

Joss Ackland, Julian Amyes, David Hobman, Maxwell Jackson,
John Mayer, David Oxley, Lennard Pearce, John Randall,
Richard Renny, Herbert Roland, Duncan Ross, John Wormer,
Kenneth Wynne, Helen Burns, Margaret Courtnay, Anne Daniels,
Elizabeth Ewbank, Margaret Godwin, Lois Johnson,
Joanna Mackie, Diana Mahoney, Irene Sutcliffe, Beryl Wright

12a

October 6, 1947

London: His Majesty's Theatre
11 performances in repertory through October 24

Cast change for London performances

Lady Capulet . . . . *Muriel Davidson*

Riding on the success of *Love's Labour's Lost*, Brook made bold choices for the Festival's 1947 *Romeo and Juliet*. The critics reponded with attacks on the casting, the set design, the cuts, the music, and the sword fights. However, the *Daily Worker* pointed out that "Undoubtedly it was living Shakespeare—to be argued about and discussed." Even the *Times* had to admit that "its realistic crowd scenes and elaborate dueling pleased festival audiences and . . . became the most popular thing of the year." At the end of the season, it was brought down to London, but only for a short time.

Before rehearsals, Brook consulted George Bernard Shaw, who advised him to accentuate the youth of the lovers and the vigor of the fights. Accordingly, Brook cast eighteen-year-old Daphne Slater as Juliet. The *Times* called her "childlike and nothing more," and the *Observer* spoke of her "untutored prattling." To the *Sunday Times*, she seemed like "a precocious child babbling of things she doesn't understand," while the *Daily Mail*, Lionel Hale declared, "It is far from enough to be agreeably puppying." Lawrence Payne, as Romeo, fared only slightly better. Hale's highest praise was "handsome and clear-spoken." Harold Hobson, in the *Sunday Times*, sighed: "I can do no more than recall that Irving also failed in the part," while Ivor Brown labeled Payne a good character actor "wrongly cast, worse directed, and nonsensically enscened."

The "nonsensical scene" was inspired by a single line of the play: "These hot days is the mad blood stirring." It was Brook's intention to eradicate the sweetly sentimental and replace it with "the violence, the passion, and the excitement of the stinking crowds, the feuds and the intrigues. To recapture the poetry and the beauty that arise from the Veronese sewer." The *Times* called his vision "recklessly spectacular." In the *Daily Worker*, Philip Bolsover described "a great blaze of colours. Costumes of crimson and gold and blue; fierce lighting that caught the glare of an Italian summer." Hobson observed "All the life of this production is packed into the burning pavements under the glaring sun."

Above was a great expanse; circling the scene was a short, partial wall. "It is a play of wide open space," wrote Brook, "in which all scenery and decoration becomes an irrelevance." This was too revolutionary a concept for most critics. Ivor Brown wrote in the *Observer*: "Surely children imply homes, walls, . . . But at Stratford a vast cold, blue cyclorama, with fragmentary scenery in front, suggests chiefly that the play is happening among a few megaliths and air-raid ruins . . . . I never had the slightest sense of . . . an Italian city. We seemed to be outside the walls, not within them." Most felt that the heart of the play had been sacrificed to visual effects and echoed Hale, who called the production "a highly coloured job which appeals only to the eye and which is strikingly short of the poetic or dramatic interests."

Critics also felt these interests were not served by Brook's cuts. The scene in which Juliet obtains the poison was missing, as was the reconciliation of the sorrowful parents over their children's graves. The first, considered vital to the plot's logic, was reinserted for London, but the other remained out, and the critics unanimously howled. The Prince's final speech was given to John Harrison as the Chorus. Generally the press was pleased by Harrison's moment at the start of the play, which began in startling silhouette. Brook's crowd scenes also earned grudging praise, although most felt they overwhelmed the play's focus. Hale wrote: "Much of the treatment belongs to ballet, alive with colour and movement. Indeed, it turns out to be a contest of Ballet versus the Bard, with the Bard an easy loser." The sword fights were thrilling, although too long for some. Costumes were "oddly assorted." Brook was given credit for action and color, and was blamed for all that was lacking in the performances.

Aside from the young lovers, the press was divided about the acting. *Punch* and the *Times* agreed that Paul Scofield made a good Mercutio, but the *Sunday Times* and the *Observer* thought he was miscast or ineffective. As Capulet, *Punch* judged Walter Hudd fussy and overdone, while the *Times* and the *Observer* found him amusing. Beatrice Lehmann as the Nurse was variously described as "something between the Red Queen and a Picadilly flower-woman," "something like a Tenniel drawing," [probably the Red Queen again] and "almost a cartoon."

Punch and the *Times* both had good things to say about Myles Eason as Tybalt, and Harold Hobson went even further, devoting his entire *Sunday Times* column to praising the characterization: "frail and dark and evil; he is thin-lipped and looks as cruel as the sea." Veronica Turleigh was also generally lauded as Lady Capulet.

This *Romeo and Juliet*, problematic as it was, added to Brook's reputation, for even critics who felt that he had "made a gallant mess of things," admitted his genius and blamed only his youth. Sixteen years later, in an article covering Scofield's career, Clive Barnes remembered it:

> Not much liked by the critics of the day, Peter Brook's Romeo and Juliet was, I suspect, a turning point in the history of the British theatre. It approached Shakespeare with few preconceptions; it tried to treat the text as if it were living theatre, and proved in the process that it was. The production had little style, but the fight scenes were magnificent and the actors did not speak Shakespeare as if they wanted to spit the plum-stones out. Its qualities misunderstood, its mistakes battened upon, Brook's production merely went to add to the store of trouble he was accumulating for himself by his opera productions at Covent Garden. But without his Romeo, I have a feeling that the British theatre would have been a very different place in 1963. If we ever get a national theatre, I will always think of Brook's Romeo as its first production.

13

July 17, 1947

Men Without Shadows
and
The Respectable Prostitute
by Jean-Paul Sartre

Translation/adaptation by Kitty Black

London (Hammersmith): Lyric Theatre
(51 performances)

Director . . . . Peter Brook
Producers . . . . H. M. Tennent Ltd.
The Company of Four
Peter Brook
Set design . . . . Rolf Gérard

for The Company of Four

Manager . . . . Lovat Fraser
Stage Director . . . . Alison Covil

Men Without Shadows

CAST

Francois, Lucie's Brother . . . . *Aubrey Woods*
Sorbier . . . . *John Byron*
Canoris, the Greek . . . . *Lyn Evans*
Lucie . . . . *Mary Morris*
Henri . . . . *Hector MacGregor*
Jean . . . . *David Markham*
Landrieu . . . . *Philip Leaver*
Pellerin . . . . *Sidney James*
Clochet . . . . *Denis Carey*
Militiamen . . . . *Alan Tilvern*
Derek Ensor

The Respectable Prostitute

CAST

Lizzie . . . . *Betty Ann Davies*
The Negro . . . . *Orlando Martins*
Fred . . . . *David Markham*
John . . . . *Alan Tilvern*
James . . . . *Dale MacDonald*

The Senator . . . . *Hugh Griffith*
Townsfolk . . . . *Mary Shaw*
Derek Ensor
Alan Tilvern

This double bill was a financial failure, and the critical reception was much less positive than for Brook's production of Sartre's *Vicious Circle* in the same theatre a year earlier. *Men Without Shadows* is a grim piece focusing on the torture of members of the French Resistance. Most critics and audience members seem to have been simply repulsed by the horrible spectacle. Ivor Brown wrote: "The continuing sight of physical beastliness is nauseating, except, presumably, for sadists, and impedes any of the emotions likely to be stirred by imaginative art." *The Respectable Prostitute*, set in the American South, is a darkly comic attack on racial prejudice and patriotic indoctrination. In this play a Negro is wrongly accused of raping a white woman, a prostitute being coerced by a Senator and others to back the accusation. This play was somewhat more popular than the first. All reviews commented on the slowness of Brook's direction, possibly because of his great concern for details. About *Men Without Shadows*, Harold Hobson wrote: "Whatever may be the legitimate limits of realism on the stage, the first of M. Sartre's plays transgresses them. Presenting murder, rape, torture, and sadism, it achieves about as much aesthetic effect as a street accident." Concerning *The Respectable Prostitute* he wrote: "Everything is right about Mr. Peter Brook's production except its pace, which is that of a middle-aged snail with a sleeping draught." Ivor Brown wondered whether *The Respectable Prostitute* was "good enough to make up for the wearisome horrors of the first piece . . . . Must Sartre's lines be spoken as though handed down from heaven?"

1948

Xa

1948–1950
BROOK AT COVENT GARDEN

Those productions, starting with *Boris Godunov*, over which Brook had total control will be discussed in their proper order, but it should be noted that all through this period he had the official (self-created) title of "Director of Production," and thus had a hand or a finger in *all* performances. The following are the operas for which he was listed as Director of Production but not as Producer. Since no change was noted in those productions premiered before he was appointed, the date is of the first performance, *not* the first performance that listed him; the titles, some translated and some not, are given as they were actually listed by Covent Garden.

1/14/47 **Carmen**: Georges Bizet
1/30/47 **Manon**: Jules Massenet
3/20/47 **The Magic Flute**: Wolfgang Amadeus Mozart
4/22/47 **Der Rosenkavlier**: Richard Strauss
6/23/47 **Il Trovatore**: Giuseppi Verdi
10/31/47 **Rigoletto**: Giuseppi Verdi
11/6/47 **Peter Grimes**: Benjamin Britten
1/21/48 **The Mastersingers**: Richard Wagner
2/19/48 **Tristan und Isolde**: Richard Wagner
3/3/48 **The Valkyrie**: Richard Wagner
4/6/48 **La Traviata**: Giuseppi Verdi
9/29/48 **Aida**: Giuseppi Verdi
11/11/48 **Siegfried**: Richard Wagner
12/9/48 **Fidelio**: Ludwig von Beethoven
5/12/49 **Das Rheingold**: Richard Wagner
5/25/49 **Gotterdammerung**: Richard Wagner
12/15/49 **Lohengrin**: Richard Wagner

14

May 12, 1948

Boris Godunov

Composed by Modeste Mussorgsky
Text by the composer, after Pushkin
English text by M. D. Calvocoressi

London: The Royal Opera House, Covent Garden

Director . . . . .Peter Brook
Costumes and Scenery . . . . Georges Wakhevitch

CAST (opening night)

Nikitich . . . . *Ronald Lewis*
Mitiukha . . . . *Hubert Littlewood*

Andrei Shchelkalof .... *Rhydderch Davies*

Boris Godunov .... *Paolo Silveri*

Feodor .... *Barbara Britton*

Xenia .... *Jean Carpenter*

Pimen .... *David Franklin*

Grigory, the Pretender .... *Edgar Evans*

Hostess .... *Edith Coates*

Varlaam .... *Howell Glynne*

Missail .... *David Tree*

Police Officer .... *Geraint Evans*

Xenia's Nurse .... *Beatrice Gibson*

Boyar .... *Emlyn Jones*

Prince Shuisky .... *Hubert Norville*

Marina Mnishek .... *Constance Shacklock*

Rangoni .... *Tom Williams*

The Boyar Khrushchof .... *Thomas Fletcher*

Lavitsky .... *Rhydderch Davies*

Chernikofsky .... *Ronald Lewis*

The Simpleton .... *Richard Lewis*

Conductor: Karl Rankl

Like everything else, Opera had suffered during World War II, and there was an extensive period of reconstruction. Covent Garden, the theatre, had long been the main opera house in London, but it had been used by one impresario after another. The new National Opera Company, with the stated mission of performing in English, had only just formed at the end of 1946, with Frederick Ashton listed as "Production Consultant." Tyrone Guthrie also directed two productions in this early period, but he estranged the musicians with his comments and the critics with what they felt was his not always musically-informed direction. Brook was to last longer, but not have much better luck.

By the end of 1947, he had replaced Ashton and had the title "Director of Productions." He helped "clean up" a revival of *The Magic Flute* in February, but *Boris* was the first production that was his alone. Because so much that is planned in an opera house has to be divided among those in charge of the music, the staging, and the financing, the choice of opera was probably not Brook's alone, but it would fit his Russian heritage and his taste for the surprising. *Boris Godunov* was accepted as a masterpiece, but very rarely seen in London. It is a work on the largest scale, and demands an excellent chorus—indeed, some critics have called the chorus the hero of the opera. This was a point in its favor in 1948, when the Covent

Garden chorus was good, but the general standard of the soloists could be problematic. Another surprising element was the choice of edition. *Boris Godunov* was left in several versions at Mussorgsky's death, and the usual performing version was the one completed by Rimsky-Korsakov. This is indeed brilliant in sound, but it is now felt that this very brilliance goes against the somber character of the opera itself. Rimsky-Korsakov also re-ordered the scenes, ending the opera with the death of Boris—focusing on the tragedy of one man—rather than ending with the forest scene and the lament of the fool, which makes the opera the tragedy of an entire people. The conductor, Karl Rankl, might have been the one who chose to use the Mussorgsky original, but it fit Brook's tendencies. As with most elements of the production, the critics were divided on this: the *Times* felt this meant it was not an exaggeration to say *Boris* was being presented "for the first time in this country," but Arthur Notcutt, in the *Musical Courier*, said, "To conclude the opera with the Forest Scene, with the Idiot singing his plaintive phrases, was a complete anti-climax after the tremendous death scene of Boris and his farewell to his son. Those who had not heard the opera before were obviously puzzled."

The result was lavish for the time; it cost somewhere between £10,000 and £18,000, and there were many extra rehearsals. The *Times* not only loved the edition: it was enthusiastic about the whole production.

> Boris *demands production on a grand scale and its crowd scenes (in which the excellent chorus of the Royal Opera excelled itself) put even the central figure into the second place. They were devised by Mr. Peter Brook, whose first operatic production this was, with such resource that they made a thundering dramatic impact, sustaining even the anti-climax of the final scene. One stage picture succeeding another with mounting effect added further impetus to an opera in which structure and dramatic sequence are not strong points. Two* motifs *persisted, tall icons and various suspensions, bells, lamps, a pendulum, a swing. Out of this grew an elaboration of magnificence, conceived with a grand imaginative sweep and executed without a flaw or a hitch.*

The two most commented-on examples of this magnificence were Brook's staging of the coronation scene, with the front of the stage as a giant belfry (the actual bells were pre-recorded), and Boris' death scene. Charles Stuart, in the *Observer* faulted the production as a whole for "over-lavishness," and thought the coronation scene was "sumptuousness for its own sake," but he found Boris' death "a solid half-hour of genius."

> *The elaborate technical means here used by Peter Brook (producer) and Wakhevitch, his designer, instead of swaddling and smothering, enhance the musico-dramatic end. Harried by self-torment, Boris comes panting and reeling to his death scene down an endless corridor, with doors sliding silently behind him, sealing off light, air, and sanity. The ultimate door, when its wings meet, forms a giant image of the Christ, dark-bearded and Byzantine, with piercing eyes. Those luminous eyes are the last thing we see as the curtain falls on a darkened stage: the imperial corse is folded in the blackness and forgotten.*

Other reviewers felt the production was over-done, but it is rather a shock to turn to Ernest Newman of the *Sunday Times*, whose various books on music and opera are still read:

> Boris Godunov *on Wednesday evening touched, for the most part, the lowest depth to which the new Covent Garden has yet fallen. Most of the solo singing and acting did no more than awaken nostalgic memories of greater days. Some of the settings were excellent, and the chorus was always good; but the greater part of the production went beyond all permissible limits of the ludicrous.*

As the single most important critic at the time, and as a representative of the old guard, this negative notice was an ominous indication of what Brook was going to face.

15

October 15, 1948

La Bohème

Composed by Giacomo Puccini
Text by Giuseppe Giacosa and Luigi Illica
English version by W. Grist and Percy Pinkerton

London: The Royal Opera House, Covent Garden

"The Covent Garden production, revised by Peter Brook"

CAST

Marcel	*Paolo Silveri*
Rudolph	*Rudolf Schock*
Colline	*David Franklin*
Schaunard	*Geraint Evans*
Benoit	*Grahame Clifford*
Mimi	*Elizabeth Schwartzkopf*
Parpignol	*Dennis Stephenson*
Musetta	*Ljuba Welitsch*
Alcindoro	*David Tree*
A Customs Official	*Hubert Littlewood*

Conductor: Karl Rankl

This caused much less comment than *Boris*, since it was less "new" because the scenery and costumes were from stock—indeed they were the sets from the 1901 London premiere! In the *Musical Courier*, Arthur Notcutt admired the care he felt was taken in rehearsal, saying "This was the *real Bohème*, and this reviewer, who has seen the opera countless times, has never enjoyed a performance more." The other critics were cooler, with a general feeling that Welitsch (a major artist, but not in Puccini) was hamming her Musetta. Brook's contribution was not singled out; several reviewers didn't even mention his name. One of those was Ernest Newman, who lamented a cast of mixed nationality singing an Italian work in English.

1949

16

January 22, 1949

The Marriage of Figaro

Composed by Wolfgang Amadeus Mozart

Text by Lorenzo da Ponte
After the play by Beaumarchais
English version by Edward J. Dent

Director . . . . Peter Brook
Costumes and settings . . . . Rolf Gérard

CAST (opening night)

Figaro . . . . *Geraint Evans*
Susanna . . . . *Elizabeth Schwartzkopf*
Doctor Bartolo . . . . *Howell Glynne*
Marcellina . . . . *Edith Coates*
Cherubino . . . . *Eugenia Zareska*
Count Almaviva . . . . *Hans Braun*
Don Basilio . . . . *Murray Dickie*
Countess Almaviva . . . . *Sylvia Fisher*
Antonio . . . . *Rhydderch Davies*
Don Curzio . . . . *David Tree*
Barbarina . . . . *Adele Leigh*
Bridesmaids . . . . *Irene Baldry*
Iris Kells

Conductor: Karl Rankl

Despite new decor, this too caused little comment and few surviving reviews. The *Times*, despite noticing "an irrelevant crowd of scullions at the end of act one," felt that Brook

> *was more than usually successful in making the intrigue clear and in preserving the sharp class distinctions on which it turns—Susanna, for instance, never forgot that she was a lady's maid. His lighting showed an improvement on Covent Garden's previous standards— the fourth act was especially well managed.*

But later the review mentions the decor as "sufficiently attractive to the eye without falling into the opulence that is Covent Garden's besetting vice." That, and the scullion comment, show that Newman was not the only critic feeling something was wrong in Covent Garden. A cast change in March prompted a short unsigned re-review mentioning that "the production is fussy where it need not be and unnecessarily bare in the third act."

17

March 9, 1949

Dark of the Moon

by Howard Richardson and William Berney

London (Hammersmith): Lyric Theatre
Production transferred for the Ambassadors Theatre
April 12, 1949
(103 performances)

Presented by
Tennent Production Ltd.
in association with
The Arts Council of Great Britain

A Company of Four Production

Director . . . . Peter Brook
Settings . . . . Gurschner and Stanley Moore

CAST

John . . . . *William Sylvester*
Conjur Man . . . . *Hugh Pryse*

Dark Witch . . . . *Mary Laura Wood*
Fair Witch . . . . *Sandra Dorne*
Conjur Woman . . . . *Joan Young*
Hank Gudger . . . . *Gordon Tanner*
Edna Summey . . . . *Gabrielle Blunt*
Mr. Summey . . . . *Bartlett Mullins*
Mrs. Summey . . . . *Joan MacArthur*
Atkins . . . . *Denis Shaw*
Uncle Smelicue . . . . *Gerald Lawson*
Floyd Allen . . . . *Peter George*
Bergen . . . . *Gaylord Cavallaro*
Mrs. Beregen . . . . *Edie Martin*
Burt Dinwitty . . . . *Donald Reed*
Mrs. Gorman . . . . *Evelyn Moore*
Mr. Biggs . . . . *John Murphy*
Hattie . . . . *Nina Polan*
Marvin Hudgens . . . . *David Greene*
Barbara Allen . . . . *Sheila Burrell*
Mrs. Allen . . . . *Joan Young*
Mr. Allen . . . . *John Kidd*
Preacher Hagglar . . . . *Craddock Munro*
A Man with a Guitar . . . . *Tommy Moddleton*
A Man with a Fiddle . . . . *Jack Thomas*

This was a solid success, probably all the more welcome because of the problems Brook had been having at Covent Garden. *Dark of the Moon* is an Appalachian folk tale, the story of Barbara Allen, who falls in love with a witch-boy, only to be ruined by prejudice and Fundamentalism. All critics commented on the American vitality and pace that Brook managed to draw from the actors, and on the ensemble work. J. C. Trewin, in the *Observer*, found Brook "uncannily inventive" in the grouping, movement, and lighting. There were several comparisons with *Oklahoma!*.

The *Times* review began with that comparison:

> Mr. Peter Brook's production is in the spirit of Oklahoma!. He drives his company at an exhilarating pace, but they are never allowed to get out of hand. When they have galloped through a comic passage they drop to the gentle trot becoming to romance and return at need with the utmost smoothness to the breakneck gallop. Nor do they cut their corners at this pace. Every twist and turn of the course is clearly taken. Mr. Brook obviously enjoys himself causing real mist to flood along the witch's mountain ridge and with curtains that allow for degrees of definition. Most of these tricks are justified by their imaginative quality, but what chiefly distinguishes this production is that even small characters are given a telling individuality.

In the *Sunday Times*, Harold Hobson took some offence at the revival scene, finding it blasphemous if taken seriously, but he still found the whole an unqualified success:

> *The piece is, in fact, something that must be seen, heard, and savoured. It is a mixture of folk legend, religious hysteria, bawdiness, dancing, Moody and Sankey, belly laughs and poetry which Mr. Howard Richardson and Mr. William Berney might have written if, after seeing Oklahoma!, they had spent a night in the [Isle of] Skye, with the winds howling in the valleys and the goblins creeping down the mountainsides. Mr. Peter Brook, in producing it, has magnificently ridden the whirlwind and directed the storm, making a large cast speak, sing, dance and roister superbly.*

18

September 29, 1949

The Olympians

by Arthur Bliss
(World Premiere)
Libretto by J. B. Priestley

London: The Royal Opera House, Covent Garden

Director . . . . Peter Brook
Scenery and Costumes . . . . John Bryan
Choreography . . . . Pauline Grant

CAST (opening night)

The Curé . . . . *Murray Dickie*
Madam Bardeau . . . . *Edith Coates*
Jean . . . . *Ronald Lewis*
Joseph Lavatte . . . . *Howell Glynne*
Hector de Florac . . . . *James Johnston*
Madeline . . . . *Shirley Russell*
Alfred . . . . *Rhydderch Davies*

THE OLYMPIANS, a troupe of strolling players

Mercury . . . . *Robert Helpmann*
Venus . . . . *Moyra Fraser*
Bacchus . . . . *Thorstenn Hannesson*
Mars . . . . *David Franklin*

Diana . . . . *Margherita Grandi*
Jupiter . . . . *Kenneth Schon*

Conductor: Karl Rankl

As the world premiere of a new English opera, this caused a great deal of comment, the recent success of Benjamin Britain's *Peter Grimes* (at Sadlers Wells, not Covent Garden) having raised hopes high. The reviews were long, but most of the space was on the work itself, rather than the production. Priestley's libretto for *The Olympians* is based on a "legend" (from where, he does not say) that the old Greek Gods, having lost their power, became a group of strolling players, who regain their powers for one night each century. At the start of the opera they come into a small town in 1838, knowing that night will bring their powers back. A girl of the town, Madeline, is in love with a poet against her parent's wishes. In the masque-like second act the restored Gods play "The Comedy of Olympus," in which their true natures are revealed and celebrated. In the third act, the Gods, now simple players again, leave, having solved Madeline's problem.

Reviews were mixed, those for the second act particularly so, and there was a general feeling that Brook was being too lavish. For instance, Edward Lockspeiser in *Musical America* noted:

> *The most spectacular part of the opera, the second act, is also the weakest dramatically, and the most superficial musically. The art of the producer, Peter Brook, is allowed to take precedence over the demands of the composer, whose fluency and melodic gift often descend here into mere facility.*

But Arthur Notcutt, of *Musical Courier*, thought the second act had "particularly fine writing for the chorus, worked up to a masterly dramatic climax," though even he found that here "even the large Covent Garden stage appeared somewhat overcrowded."

The *Times* said: "the plot allowed Mr. Peter Brook to indulge his taste for fireworks on the largest possible scale when Jove hurled his bolt, and the eye was not distracted but cooperated with the ear throughout, which is the final test for good operatic production."

As usual, Ernest Newman, in *The Sunday Times* was the most negative:

> *The production left a great deal to be desired. I find it difficult to imagine a worse handling of the second act. This was not the Olympus of the Gods, and, for a space, of mortals privileged to catch a glimpse of it, but something near a musical comedy. Regardless of expense, the stage was packed with people going through those fidgety evolutions that have contributed so much to our exasperation or amusement at Covent Garden during the last few years. When will Mr. Peter Brook realize that the opera producer's business is to give more power to the music's aim, not to hamper it? The more the eye is distracted by*

those stage fidgets the less we are able to concentrate on what the music is saying. The first thing that a theatrical producer has to do in an opera house is to learn his true place there.

It is difficult to tell how much of Newman's negativity was due to the musical standards of the house, which had suffered during the war, and how much was due to a conservative's dislike of Brook's methods. Certainly he was not alone. Whichever it was, the situation came to a head with the next production.

19

November 11, 1949

Salome

by Richard Strauss
From the play by Oscar Wilde

Director . . . . Peter Brook
Scenery, Costumes, Special Effects . . . . Salvador Dali

CAST (opening night)

Narraboth . . . . *Edgar Evans*
Page to Herodias . . . . *Jean Watson*
First Soldier . . . . *Norman Walker*
Second Soldier . . . . *Geraint Evans*
Jokannan . . . . *Kenneth Schon*
A Cappadocian . . . . *Kenneth Stevenson*
Salome . . . . *Ljuba Welitsch*
Herod . . . . *Franz Lechleitner*
Herodias . . . . *Constance Shacklock*
First Jew . . . . *Murray Dickie*
Second Jew . . . . *David Tree*
Third Jew . . . . *Dennis Stephenson*
Fourth Jew . . . . *Emlyn Jones*
Fifth Jew . . . . *Rhydderch Davies*
First Nazarene . . . . *Marian Nowakowski*
Second Nazarene . . . . *Thorstenn Hannesson*
Conductor: Karl Rankl

This production was generally considered to be on a high level musically, but with it, all of Brook's own problems with the critics came to a head as the combination of Wilde, Strauss, Brook and Dali proved too much. There were, indeed, some who liked, or, at least, didn't mind the end result. The *Times*, for instance, said:

> *The worst fears aroused by the announcement of Dali's name after he had shown what he can perpetrate in his* Mad Tristan *were fortunately not realized. Apart from some headresses that threatened decapitation to the wearers, the general effect was properly macabre, and the special effects, pomegranates, peacocks, and a pavillion, served to mask the drama without calling too much attention to themselves.*

Writing a month later in *Musical America*, Edward Lockspeiser first admitted that the production was "often deliberately disregardful of the composer's expressed directions," but still found that: "While such a production brings opera to the verge of cinema—a bewildering circumstance, certainly, after the civilized Glyndebourne productions of Carl Ebert—it does display a sense of adventure in English opera production that is not to be discouraged lightly."

The negative notices were more frequent and much stronger. The Earl of Harewood was fairly mild in *Opera*, when, after praising Brook's *Dark of the Moon*, he found *Salome* to be "the climax of a series of more or less unmusical productions at Covent Garden." In *Musical Courier*, Arthur Notcutt found that: "The production by Peter Brook was bizarre and ugly." Eric Blom in the *Observer*, after saying that the production was, "musically one of the best things done at the Royal Opera since its partial naturalization," felt that Dali's "many oddities fail to make either an interesting work of art by themselves or to suit the half-hearted perversities and whole-hogging opulence of the Straussian score—or, for that matter, to match the mastery of that score."

As usual, Ernest Newman, in the *Sunday Times* was strongly negative, and took two full weekly columns to say so. (It must also be noted that he was fighting not only Brook, but, along with the great conductor Sir Thomas Beecham, was fighting the musical hierarchy at Covent Garden as well). On November 20, 1949, he first devoted a column to "a few of the many sins of omission and commission . . . ":

> *Of the production in general it is difficult to speak in the restrained language appropriate to a Sunday paper.*
> *One absurdity followed fast on the heels of another: space fails me to deal with all of them. Jochanaan was conducted by the soldiers from the cistern to a sort of platform in the centre of the stage, there to harangue the audience full face . . . . The decapitated head looked like a large steamed pudding, though Salome's airy handling of it suggested that it was much lighter than this sort of pudding usually is . . . . The soldiers and others should remain in view all through Salome's final monologue; we should feel that, when Herod's maddened cry of "Kill that woman!" comes, that they are liberating their own reactions of disgust as well as his when they crush her under their shields. What we saw was a couple of soldiers emerging from somewhere or other with an apparatus that struck others besides*

myself as being the sister of the Iron Maiden of Nuremberg, which they proceeded to fit around the passive form of Salome in couturier fashion.

. . . at that climatic moment—towards which the whole opera has been steadily moving from the beginning—the moon comes out again, throwing a ghastly light on the ecstacy of madness in her face. Of all this co-operation of sound and sight and inner drama there was not a hint in the production: the moon, which had been absent without leave during the whole of the scene, suddenly took it into its head to make an ineffective and meaningless reappearance after *the crisis was over.*

The next week was an attack on Brook—though not mentioning his name—and a call for sweeping changes at Covent Garden.

. . . I merely ask the people responsible for these offences against opera and against us to take my word for it that we have had as much in the way of burlesque as we are prepared to put up with. We must ask ourselves once more how some of these people who are running opera in what is in fact, if not in mine, the British State Opera House . . . ever came to hold the positions they now do.

Brook did not let this and the other criticisms go by without comment. The following letter was printed in the *Sunday Times* two weeks later:

Sir,

The opera critics say that an opera production must be based on the music. I agree. They say that the stage picture, the scenic effects, the movements, must not distract from the music. I agree again. But what exactly is a "distraction"? Here we part company.

Isn't ugliness distracting? Isn't clumsiness distracting? I find the scenery of most traditional opera productions so hideous that I cannot listen. To me all the traditional paraphernalia of opera, the meaningless positions, the exaggerated agony, the stock-in-trade gestures, the out-of-date scenery, are so removed from the style of any great composer that they destroy all pretensions at drama.

A couple of years ago there was a production of Don Giovanni *that was played in a single stone set that resembled the Arc de Triomphe. The singers stood in grey costumes in static position, as though at a concert performance of* Elijah. *I remember critics praised this production, saying it hadn't distracted from the music. I was puzzled.* Don Giovanni *had always been my favorite opera; its composer labled it a* dramma giocosa. *Its music, to me, demands life, colour, movement, excitement; frozen immobility distracted me far more than the fussiest action could have done.*

My experience teaches me that simplicity can, at times, be more worrying than elaboration, and that elaboration can, at times, achieve great simplicity. The most complicated and unconventional stage effect that is dramatically relevant can give conviction to the picture, reality to the illusion, and thus increase one's receptivity to the music.

An opera producer must work entirely from what he finds in the score. He will be surrounded by good people who will tell him where the doors and windows have stood for generations, where, in fact, they must *stand for evermore. He will be told how it was all done in the past and how it is done in Milan today. He must, of course, listen. But then he must do exactly what the score seems to dictate to him and what he believes is right.*

This is a clear and forthright statement of certain principles, but avoids, deliberate or not, dealing with any of the specific charges that he indeed *was* ignoring what was in the score. Certainly some of the critics seemed to dislike his entire attitude, but there were many who seemed to be genuinely confused or irritated by elements in his Covent Garden operas, and this letter does not answer them. *Salome* was to be his last Covent Garden production.

1950

20

January 26, 1950

Ring Round the Moon
by Jean Anouilh
Translated by Christopher Fry

London: Globe Theatre
(678 performances)

Presented by
Tennent Productions Ltd.
In association with
The Arts Council of Great Britain

Director . . . . Peter Brook
Decor . . . . Oliver Messel
Music . . . . Richard Addinsell

CAST

Joshua . . . . *David Horne*
Hugo . . . . *Paul Scofield*
Frederic . . . . *Paul Scofield*
Diana Messerschmann . . . . *Audrey Fildes*
Lady India . . . . *Marjorie Stewart*
Patrice Bombelles . . . . *Richard Wattis*
Madame Desmortes . . . . *Margaret Rutherford*
Capulet . . . . *Daphne Newton*
Messerschmann . . . . *Cecil Trouncer*
Romainville . . . . *William Mervyn*
Isabelle . . . . *Claire Bloom*

Isabelle's Mother . . . . *Mona Washbourne*
A General . . . . *Mayne Lynton*
Footmen . . . . *Richard Scott*
David Phethean

Anouilh's fable of two identical rich brothers of very different personalities (played by the same actor) has always been one of his most popular in English. Brook seems to have played a large part in creating the proper atmosphere for the Christopher Fry translation. As the *Manchester Guardian* noted: "Undoubtedly much of the success is due to the animated production by Peter Brook, which is as dainty as a ballet . . . " The *Sunday Times* found: "There were several kinds of magic on the stage, that of the producer who took Mr. Scofield off into the wings at one moment and brought him on at the other side of the stage literally two seconds later, but above all the magic of the language, of the decor, and of the music." The *Times*, perhaps noting Brook's by now established reputation for doing things that were, depending on one's outlook, either innovative or strange, noted: "It is the more enchanting since Mr. Peter Brook's imaginatively deft contribution as producer betrays no possessive designs on the theme . . . "

21

March 9, 1950

Measure for Measure
by William Shakespeare

Stratford: Shakespeare Memorial Theatre

Director . . . . Peter Brook
Scenery and Costumes . . . . Peter Brook
Michael Northen
Kegan Smith
Music Adviser . . . . Leslie Bridgewater

CAST

Vincentio . . . . *Harry Andrews*
Escalus . . . . *Harold Kasket*
Angelo . . . . *John Gielgud*

Lucio . . . . *Leon Quartermaine*
First Gentleman . . . . *Robert Hardy*
Second Gentleman . . . . *Robert Shaw*
Mistress Overdone . . . . *Rosalind Atkinson*
Pompey . . . . *George Rose*
Claudio . . . . *Alan Badel*
Provost . . . . *Michael Gwynn*
Friar Thomas . . . . *Cyril Conway*
Isabella . . . . *Barbara Jefford*
Francisca . . . . *Romany Evens*
Elbow . . . . *Michael Bates*
Froth . . . . *Geoffrey Bayldon*
A Justice . . . . *Peter Norris*
Servant to Angelo . . . . *Timothy Bateson*
Juliet . . . . *Hazel Penwarden*
A Boy . . . . *Mairhi Russell*
Mariana . . . . *Maxine Audley*
Abhorson . . . . *Nigel Green*
Barnardine . . . . *Paul Hardwick*
Friar Peter . . . . *Peter Norris*

Citizens, Soldiers, Warders, Prisoners
Marjorie Steel, Felicity Barrington, Richard Dare,
John Dunbare, David Lytton, John Gay, Ronald Hines,
Peter Halliday, Michael Ney, Michael Atkinson,
Ward Williams, Peter Jackson, David Woodman,
Charles Lepper, Godfrey Bond, Edward Atienza,
Michael Ferry, John York, Brendon Barry, John Wright

(By the end of the season Andrew Cruickshank had replaced Gielgud in the role of Angelo.)

Measure for Measure is the most famous of Shakespeare's "Problem Plays," a term invented in Victorian times. These plays are problems in two ways. First, they seem to be dealing with social problems—for which reason Shaw championed them—in a more direct way than is normal for pre-modern plays, though the exact analysis and implied solutions are unclear. Second, they have problems in staging, those questions of analysis and attitude leading to problems in focus and unity. Brook's 1950 production was a landmark, and is still influential in the staging of this play.

   One thing Brook did was to cut. Some of the cuts were of the type of Jacobean comic word-play that befuddles or irritates a modern audience, but many were made that had the result of simplifying the characters. This did eliminate much of the ambiguity of motivation that some find pleasing, but it also had better effects. According to Brian Gibbons' introduction to the *New Cambridge Shakespeare* edition:

> Brook reinforced the admirable characteristics of Isabella and the Duke, and gave Angelo a context in which agonising struggle demonstrated his "twisted nobility," and he gave this area of the play a less devious plot. What Brook did to the scenes of low life was to make them a genuine counterweight; this demonstration of their power is of major importance, marking the modern rediscovery of the play's full design.

Measure for Measure opened at Stratford as the first play of the season, while the other offerings were being assembled. The play was not exactly a rarity, as the intensity of the central confrontations—the strongest outside of the formal "tragedies"—make the roles so strong that actors have always wanted to perform it, but the "problems" involved in interpretation had made literary critics deeply divided on its merits. The *Sunday Times*, for instance, said "*Measure for Measure* is hardly a good play: If it were the work of a young contemporary one would rate it as equally full of promise and mistakes . . . " but its short notice ended by saying "Mr. Brook swept the play along with a number of ingenious devices, some of which were appropriate and all exciting." Others commented on how the play, confusing in the study, seemed clear in performance, though some mentioned Brook's cuts, especially those which simplified the last act. In *The Observer*, for instance, J. C. Trewin noted it "is surely plain enough if we regard it as a piece designed for the Jacobean stage instead of something to be probed in the study." *The Times* found it "gains on the stage a simplicity which it seems to lack in the study."

In addition to the cuts, Brook seems to have approached the characters in a deliberately simple way, not bothering deeply to search for hidden psychology. Isabella's holding her viginity more important than her brother's life was merely a natural expression of genuine belief, and Gielgud's Angelo, according to Trewin, "does not fret the part into a pathological study: but his mind is clear before us." The result, according to the *Times*, was that:

> Mr. Brook reaps the reward of his faith: the effect of this treatment is to broaden our sympathy at the expense of our everyday antipathy, to win us to the dramatist's own extraordinary tolerance for bawds and cowards and fantastical dukes and women who may be saints but are so unamiable as to hold their chastity dearer than a brother. To like the play at all we must be made uncommonly generous in our acceptance of ugly facts, and it is the greatest virtue of Mr. Brook's production that it so clearly establishes that the play's philosophical lesson, far from being immoral, is in fact a fine expression of the morality that is above legal and hard and fast rules.

22

August 23, 1950

The Little Hut
by Andre Roussin
Adapted by Nancy Mitford

London: Lyric Theatre
(1260 performances)

Director . . . . Peter Brook
Decor . . . . Oliver Messel

CAST

Susan . . . . *Joan Tetzel*
Henry . . . . *David Tomlinson*
Philip . . . . *Robert Morley*
A Stranger . . . . *Geoffrey Toone*
A Second Stranger . . . . *William Chappell*

22a

October 7, 1953

New York: Coronet

CAST

Susan . . . . *Anne Vernon*
Henry . . . . *Colin Gordon*
Philip . . . . *Roland Culver*
A Stranger . . . . *John Granger*
A Second Stranger . . . . *Ray Gil*

Although it's recognized that many of Peter Brook's most important productions were done for various non-commercial companies, it still may be a surprise to know that his second longest run after *Irma La Douce*, was the London version of this little French farce, as translated by Nancy Mitford. The plot is equal parts *Private Lives* and *Gilligan's Island* before-the-fact. A husband and wife and their male friend are shipwrecked on a desert island—in formal wear; the boat sank at dinner time. After a while, the friend informs the husband that he and the wife have been lovers for some time and demands his share in her. She sets herself up in "the little hut," the men alternating their time with her. This arrangement winds up liberating the husband, while the lover becomes jealous and suburban. Things are complicated by a "native"—the shipwrecked cook in disguise—before all are rescued.

As might be expected for this type of well-done fluff, critical comment did not talk about the director so much as it summarized the plot and praised the actors and, especially, the colorful sets by Oliver Messel. In the *Observer*, J. C. Trewin found that:

> *Robert Morley is like a bland seal. David Tomlinson has some of Naunton Wayne's ruefulness, and Joan Tetzel as a blithe young woman with a past, is like a constantly fizzing drink. Peter Brook, the producer, juggles the whole thing delightfully against an exuberant Messel setting in tropical technicolor.*

Brook was not able to recreate that success with the American cast, despite the company rehearsing and trying out in Britain and Boston before the New York opening. John Chapman, in the *Daily News*, was enthusiastic, but most found something lacking. In *The Herald-Tribune*, Walter Kerr called it " . . . a tantalizing show. It looks wonderful, it sounds as if it were going to be wonderful; but it is just never wonderful enough." He found a lack of subtlety and variation in the acting: "Unhappily all three play at precisely the same pitch and the same rate. The style might be described as a sort of well bred gargle." John Gassner, in *The Educational Theatre Journal*, seemed to blame the American audiences, saying "In spite of the publicized sophistication of New York and its Broadway, we are, as a matter of fact, quite elephantine in managing this kind of continental make-believe . . . "

Richard Watts, of *The New York Post*, also saw a London—New York difference, but interestingly, laid the blame on Brook. After lamenting that we were not seeing the London cast, especially Robert Morely, he went on to say

> . . . *it is played with a sort of heavily realistic emphasis . . . Having seen with admiration Peter Brook's superb staging of* The Little Hut *and* Venice Preserv'd *in London, I know that Mr. Brook is one of the most brilliant directors in the contemporary Theatre, but I doubt if one could guess that fact from watching the present production of the Roussin comedy, and it is difficult to avoid the suspicion that he hasn't a high opinion of American audiences. He seems to have felt that everything had to be emphasized heavily for us and has laid on with a bludgeon.*

It's possible that this was the case, for Brook also seems to have had problems adjusting to America the next year, with the troubled rehearsals of *House of Flowers*.

23

Exact date unknown

La Morte d'un Commis Voyageur
(Death of a Salesman)
by Arthur Miller

Brussels: Théâtre de la Monnaie
(and Oxford)

(Neither the editors nor their various contacts in Europe can find records of this production, not even for the opening date)

1951

21a
Measure for Measure

European tour

24

March 1, 1951

A Penny for a Song
by John Whiting

London: Haymarket

Director . . . . Peter Brook
Decor . . . . Emett

CAST

William Humpage . . . . *George Rose*
Sir Timothy Bellboys . . . . *Alan Webb*
Samuel Breeze . . . . *Denis Cannan*
Lamprett Bellboys . . . . *Denys Blakelock*
Hester Bellboys . . . . *Marie Löhr*
Hallam Matthews . . . . *Ronald Squire*
Dorcas Bellboys . . . . *Virginia McKenna*
Pippin . . . . *Joy Rogers*

Edward Sterne . . . . *Ronald Howard*
A Small Boy . . . . *?*
George Selincourt . . . . *Basil Radford*
Joseph Brotherhood . . . . *Kenneth Edwards*
James Giddy . . . . *Peter Martyn*
Rufus Piggott . . . . *Alan Gordon*

John Whiting was to achieve success with *The Devils*, but this, his first West End production, was in a very different mood of farcical-poetic-historical comedy, which the *Times* compared to the work of Christopher Fry. Set in a small English Channel town in 1804, it plays a love story against an expected Napoleonic invasion, which, through various mistakes and misunderstandings, the eccentric characters believe is actually happening. The general response was that it was a nice attempt, but that the promising young author was trying too hard. As the *Times* said: "He may have fallen into go-as-you-please charade while trying for fantasy, but he has escaped pretentiousness . . . "

Ivor Brown, in the *Observer*, was reminded of "A Napoleonic sequel to 1066 and All that," and mentioned "a team of stars who, directed by the ever ingenious Peter Brook, are "simply bustin" out all over" in desperate attempts to be funny. (Perhaps the reference to the song from *Carousel* was meant to imply that the energetic effect was more American than English.) The *Times*, more pleased, felt: "They do it all very acceptably; and Mr. Peter Brook's whimsical production suits well Emett's whimsical setting."—which included the *Punch* cartoonist's idea of an 1804 fire engine.

25

June 27, 1951

The Winter's Tale
by William Shakespeare

London: Phoenix Theater
(212 performances)

Run interrupted for presentation at the Edinburgh Festival
Lyceum Theatre
August 27 to September 1

Tennent Productions, Ltd.
In association with
The Arts Council of Great Britain

Director . . . . Peter Brook
Settings and Costumes . . . . Sophie Fedorovitch
Music . . . . Christopher Fry
Dance arranged by . . . . William Chappell

CAST

Leontes	*John Gielgud*
Hermione	*Diana Wynyard*
Mamillius	*Robert Anderson*
Polixenes	*Brewster Mason*
Camillo	*Michael Goodlife*
Emilia	*Hazel Terry*
Second Lady	*Margaret Wolfit*
Antigonus	*Lewis Casson*
First Lord	*Hugh Stewart*
Second Lord	*John Moffatt*
Third Lord	*Kenneth Edwards*
Paulina	*Flora Robson*
Gaoler	*John Whiting*
Cleomenes	*Paul Hardwick*
Dion	*Michael Nightingale*
A Bear	*Churton Fairman*
A Mariner	*Michael Nightingale*
Old Shepherd	*George Howe*
Young Shepherd	*Philip Guard*
Time	*Norman Bird*
Autolycus	*George Rose*
Perdita	*Virginia McKenna*
Florizel	*Richard Gale*
Dorcas	*Joy Rodgers*
Mopsa	*Charlotte Mitchell*
Paulina's steward	*John Moffatt*

Lords, Ladies, Servants, Shepherds and Shepherdesses
Denys Graham, William Patrick, Churton Fairman,
Oliver Cox, Philip Pearman, Sarah Davies,
Frances Hyland, Charles Doran

The inspiration for this revival for the 1951 Festival of Britain was Gielgud's, who liked the idea of acting a classical part done seldom enough that he would not have the ghosts of a dozen other readings haunting his every line. It ended up being one of the hits of the season. Even the only negative notice to speak of, Harold Hobson's in *The Sunday Times*, included a long list of virtues before saying: "I should have to admit that I was not once moved throughout the performance." Brook got much praise for the appropriateness and—surprisingly for Brook, it was felt—for the simplicity of the production. As Eric Johns said in *Theater World*:

> Mr. Brook has swept away what Mr. Gielgud calls all the "familiar clichés" of Shakespearian production. Leontes, as King of Sicilia, has no fanfare or entrance music, nor does he glitter with jewels. The settings by Sophie Fedorovitch are the essence of attractive simplicity. The indoor scenes are without furniture, which means that the audience, instead of being distracted by the elaborate scenery favored by Charles Kean or Beerbohm Tree, is left undisturbed to appreciate the full beauty of the words. The production has both pace and simplicity, with one scene overlapping the other. Not since the days of Elizabeth has the stage been quite so empty, not the beauty of the play been allowed to emerge so unimpaired in all its verbal loveliness.

This was echoed by Ivor Brown, in the *Observer*, who said: "The decoration is unobtrusive, almost drab. Unobtrusive too, is Peter Brook's production, which leaves out Peter Brookishness and is admirably simple and quick, an actor's vehicle and not a producer's raree-show." *Theatre Newsletter* described it in greater detail, indicating the simplicity lay more in a lack of fussiness than in a spartan philosophy:

> Peter Brook's production (which will also be seen in Edinburgh later in the year) is a feather in his cap and in the cap of Tennent Productions, who continue to provide the best artistic fare in the West End. Set on a peep-show stage, the tragical-pastoral-comical plot is unfolded against a semi-permanent set, with, in Act 1, alcoves and side-galleries supported on some obtrusive pillars. We get a surrealist storm, with not only the dimmest of heavens, but also the most savage of clamors (and, alas, a brown bear) followed by a Father-Time complete with a (real) Victorian snowstorm.
>
> The stylised décor (by Sophie Fedorovich) of Acts 1 and 3 is divided by a rustic scene that might have served for a Philpotts Devonshire comedy, with the shepherds mumming away in mummersetshire, all but Perdita, whose accents and gait defy all modern theories of environmental influences.

As for the bear—and Brook's "Brookish" reputation after only five years in the public eye—*Theatre Newsletter* may have been disappointed that it was brown, but the *Times*, after saying: "It is a graceful, measured production, wholly free from personal capriciousness and remarkable for the quiet skill with which it imposes romantic unity on the bifurcated plot," noted that: "The bear that dines off the luckless courtier played by Sir Lewis Casson is a good Peter Brook bear, a bear of the prime."

26

Filmed 1951
(Broadcast 1957)

Heaven and Earth

Director . . . . .Peter Brook
Writers . . . . .Peter Brook
Denis Cannan

ACTORS
Paul Scofield, Lois Maxwell, Marjorie Stewart,
Peter Illing, Leo McKern, Richard Johnson,
Dorothy Bromiley, Thomas Heathcote, Michael Goodlife

Brook's other films are in the chronology by the date they were released, but this had such a long period between creation and showing that it seems more relevant to use the earlier date. Brook himself wrote the script with Denis Canaan, which was shot at Elstree in ten days for ITC. It was intended to be a theatrical release, but various contract complications kept it in storage.

The story was a modern version of the Jonah myth. An aircraft bound across the Atlantic for the Riveria is endangered when all four engines are in trouble; knowing disaster is near, and believing him to be the cause, the passengers jettison a young evangelist, handsome, haggard, and, owing to exceptional circumstances, full of whisky and remorse. A court of inquiry is held; just as the truth is emerging, he arives on crutches, miraculously saved.

The *Daily Telegraph* said, "Attention is sustained throughout an exceptionally smooth production. Its originality and action are worth at least another showing." The *News Chronicle* found it "full of good things rather than a completely successful production." thinking the dialogue the weak point and the performances, especially Scofield's, strong.

Although the showing passed without much comment, *Heaven and Earth* is interesting in being the first occasion on which Brook used *music concrète*. Feeling conventional music would be out of place in the tight quarters of the plane, he devised a score interweaving electronic tones with actual engine sounds. He was to continue this technique in several of his stage productions, especially *Titus Andronicus* and both the 1957 and 1963 versions of *The Tempest*.

27

December 13, 1951

Colombe

by Jean Anouilh
Adapted by Denis Cannan

London: New Theatre
Produced by Tennent Production, Ltd.
(123 performances)

Director . . . . .Peter Brook
Settings . . . . .Gurschner and Stanley Moore
Costumes . . . . .Motley
Music . . . . .John Hotchkis

CAST

Madame Alexandra . . . . *Yvonne Arnaud*
Julien, her son . . . . *Michael Gough*
Paul, her son . . . . *John Stratton*
Colombe . . . . *Joyce Redman*
Emile Robinet, a dramatist . . . . *Esme Percy*
Desfournettes, theatre director . . . . *David Horne*
Lagarde, an actor . . . . *Laurence Naismith*
Madame Georges, a dresser . . . . *Rosalind Atkinson*
Surette, a secretary . . . . *Eliot Makeham*
A Hairdresser . . . . *Vernon Greeves*
A Chiropodist . . . . *Billie Hill*
A Manicurist . . . . *Nancy Manningham*
Joseph, a stagehand . . . . *Peter Wigzell*
Leon, a stagehand . . . . *Timothy Forbes Adam*

Paris, at the turn of the century: Colombe is a charming and beautiful flower girl who has been living in poverty with her idealistic husband. He contrives to fling her on a Parisian stage, whose leading actress is very like the aging Bernhardt. There she discovers that love is no hardship, but a pleasure that constantly renews itself at the command of youth and beauty.

She becomes mistress of a jaunty gentleman, revels in the affections of the leading man, and in the gifts and supper parties of older men. She sees herself as a flower opening to the sun, but her gruff military husband sees her as a moth too close to the flame. He happens to be the neglected son of the older actress, who despises him as much as he does her. In the distress to which Colombe has brought him, he turns to her for comfort, but she tells him the cynical truth about love.

The particular romantic cynicism of Anouilh is attractive to English-speaking theatre people, but often runs into trouble with English-speaking audiences. This production was no exception to that rule. Many found the play more bitter than they wished, even though *Theatre World Annual* mentioned the adaption had "purged it of some of its cruelty." Ivor Brown, for instance, said in the *Observer*: "A dismal defeatist theme—this time that young love will never abide, which is as fatuous as to say that it always endures—is brushed with a period burlesque and larded over with a certain amount of surface gaiety."

Brook was not much mentioned. Two critics who did mention him, and were favorable, were Hobson in the *Sunday Times*, saying, "Anouilh's translator, Denis Cannan, and his producer, Mr. Peter Brook, put the gold in it." and W. Macqueen Pope in *The Morning Telegraph*, who said,

> There was another play by Anouilh, who is becoming the most prevalent dramatist in town and infests so many theaters. This time it was at the New Theatre and was called Colombe. Well adapted by Denis Cannan, and produced by Peter Brook, who specializes in Anouilh, it was a good production—a much better production than a play.

28

February 25, 1953

Box for One

British Television

Very litle survives on this production, evidently based on a Brook radio play of which even less survives. It dealt with a man desperately making phone calls from a public call-box to try to avoid the consequences of a crime. *The Listener* thought Robert Helpmann "sustained the visual side of it without flagging..." but felt the material worked better as a sound-only play, noting the large amount of threepences the plot required the character to have on hand.

29

May 5, 1953
London ("private showing")
General opening June 5

The Beggar's Opera

Warner Brothers

Director..Peter Brook
Producers.............................Herbert Wilcox, Laurence Olivier
Screenplay..Denis Cannan

(Adapted by Christopher Fry from the play by John Gay)

Music..Sir Arthur Bliss
Photography (color by Technicolor)..........................Guy Green
Dance Arrangements.......................................Frank Staff
Editing...Reginald Beck

CAST

Capt. Macheath .... *Laurence Olivier*
The Beggar .... *Hugh Griffith*
Polly Peachum .... *Dorothy Tutin*
Peachum .... *George Devine*
Mrs. Peachum .... *Mary Clare*
Mrs. Trapes .... *Athene Seyler*
Lockit .... *Stanley Holloway*
Lucy Lockit .... *Daphne Anderson*
Jenny Diver .... *Yvonne Furneaux*
The Actress .... *Margot Grahame*
The Footman .... *Denis Cannan*
Ist Turnkey .... *George Rose*

and
Cyril Conway, Edward Pryor, Felix Felton, Oliver Hunter
Sandra Dome, Eileen Harvey, Edith Coats
Kenneth Williams, Tamba Alleney, John Kidd
Joycelyn James, John Baker

The Beggar's Opera is Brook's first commercial film, produced when he was in his late twenties. It attempts to recreate John Gay's musical play on film. The result is a burlesque, but recognizable, play-within-a-play.

A begger is imprisoned for being a drain on society. He brings with him all he owns: his hopes, his dreams and his integrity. All are in a labor of love, an opera he has composed.

After being shunned initially as an intruder, whose scattered papers are considered garbage, he begins to weave a tale through which he instills hopes and dreams of freedom in his fellow cellmates. As they begin to sing his opera, they are transported outside, into the life of Captain Macheath, a prisoner in Newgate.

Macheath is himself a legendary figure, a dashing highwayman who loves the ladies. Lovely ladies are irresistible to him and their jealousies make him vulnerable. Ladies high and low weave a net to entrap him, in return for a £40 reward.

In the end, bolstered by the strength of their performance, the cellmates revolt, giving Macheath a chance to escape just as the prison guards come to take him to his execution.

Brook infuses his work with action, crowd scenes, and rebellious spirit. Vivid photography of settings, crowds, and close-ups interestingly forshadow techniques he uses in later productions. Nevertheless, the overall effect of the film is disturbingly jumbled. Most of the singing is dubbed; only Olivier and Holloway sing for themselves. Polly is sung by Adele Leigh, Lucy by Jennifer Vyvyan, and Mrs. Trapes by Joan Cross. While a bold attempt, *The Beggar's Opera* mainly appeals to the film enthusiast and was a failure at the box office.

Archer Winston of the *New York Times* was one of the more favorable critics. He felt it was generally a happy liaison between film and opera and a credit to both media, saying, "While it deviates from its original intent and now lampoons neither opera nor political personalities, it is still a spirited musical" and recognizing "a kaleidoscopic view of truly colorful facets of the London dear to Hogarth." He stressed that it was "a purposeful job of editing and blending" to bring "Gay's lusty and amorous characters" to life "on a variety of sprawling canvases." The most dramatic scenes are those at Newgate prison; dances in a tavern full of outlaws and cavorting women; the bustling gaiety of a rich gambling party; and a brawling, raucous mob following their hero, Macheath, as he waves to the crowd while being transported to the gallows on his coffin. They provide "movement and authentic color, attributes missing from most filmed operas."

He saw the snubnosed and petite Dorothy Tutin (Polly) as a charmingly innocent bride, Daphne Anderson (Lucy) as properly vengeful and contrite, and Stanley Holloway (Lockit) as broadly farcical, with a rich voice and a venal personality. Supporting actors were also good.

Olivier's Macheath was a problem. A reckless daredevil, a wily but manly lover and a fearless, brooding adventurer, Winston found his portrayal was endowed "with genuine abandon, stature, and feeling. However, he displays a pleasant, but airy and undistinguished baritone, which does not fit his acting portrayal." As a result, critics judged his entry into musicals unsuccessful, an inappropriate venue for his talents, and Brook got a roasting which made him choose not to make another studio film for years.

30

May 15, 1953

Venice Preserv'd
by Thomas Otway

London (Hammersmith): Lyric Theatre
(67 performances)

(Brighton: Royal Theatre, May 4)

Presented by
Tennent Productions, Ltd.
("John Gielgud's Season")

Director . . . . Peter Brook
Scenery and Principals' Costumes . . . . Leslie Hurry
Music arranged by . . . . Leslie Bridgewater

CAST

Priuli . . . . *Herbert Lomas*
Jaffier . . . . *John Gielgud*
Pierre . . . . *Paul Scofield*
Belvidera . . . . *Eileen Herlie*
Aquilina . . . . *Pamela Brown*
Renault . . . . *Eric Porter*
Spinosa . . . . *Paul Hardwick*
Eliot . . . . *Basil Henson*
Brabe . . . . *Peter Whitbread*
Durand . . . . *Geoffrey Bayldon*

Ternon . . . . *Nicholas Amer*
Retrosi . . . . *Peter Sallis*
Bramveil . . . . *Anthony Carrick*
Theodore . . . . *John Richmond*
Revillido . . . . *James Coats*
Bedamar . . . . *Brewster Mason*
Maid to Aquilina . . . . *Gillian Webb*
Antonio . . . . *Richard Wordsworth*
Duke of Venice . . . . *David Dodimead*
Second Senator . . . . *Edward Mulhare*
Officer . . . . *Geoffrey Taylor*
Friar . . . . *Norman Bird*

Footmen, Servants, Soldiers, Executioners
John Richmond, James Coats, Peter Sallis,
Anthony Carrick, Basil Henson, Nicholas Amer,
Paul Hardwick

John Gielgud's revival of Thomas Otway's 1681 tragedy was the first in thirty-three years. (The 1920 production had also been at the Lyric.) The play tells the story of the fanatical, brilliant Pierre, a young revolutionary in Venice, and his sensitive, romantic friend Jaffier, whom he convinces to join a band of conspirators intent on overthrowing the decadent Senate. Jaffier swears to take part, even though his beloved wife Belvidera is the daughter of a Senator. When she draws the secret out of him, she pleads with him to betray the conspirators before it is too late. He leaves her with them as a pledge of allegiance to the cause, only to learn on his return that she has barely escaped being raped by the conspirator left to watch over her. Now she is able to convince him to reveal the plot. In a series of climatic scenes, which some feel reach the melodramatic, Jaffier stabs Pierre to death at Pierre's request, to spare him the torture planned by the Senate, and then stabs himself to death out of anguish at his betrayal, leading Belvidera to madness and suicide.

Venice Preserv'd was the final production of a highly praised "Gielgud season," and his star far outshone Brook's in the reviews. It was definitely Gielgud's show in the critics' eyes: his company, his triumph, and under his "leadership." Brook's direction was praised in the same breath as the designer in brief mentions. But the very choice and effectiveness of the play is due to Brook, in large part. Brook has said that the production evolved from his, Gielgud's and Scofield's interest in reviving the play—a joint venture among friends. And, he had a "good group of actors" at his disposal in Gielgud's company.

As T. C. Worsley wrote in *The New Statesman and Nation*: "Mr. Peter Brook has once again shown us that he can discipline his exuberant imagination when this is called for and apply himself to giving us a straightforward faithful interpretation." And Kenneth Tynan said: "A prodigy has been brought to birth. By which I mean a pure, plain, clear classical production of the last great verse play in the English language."

This is not to say that Brook's unique theatricality was missing—note that already, in 1953, a critic can speak of his "exuberant imagination" as something taken for granted when he is under discussion. In *Plays in Performance*, J. W. Lambert mentioned that the audience "abandoned [itself] to a purely theatrical spell." And the visual aspects and staging were pleasurably noted by all. Tynan said that Brook's production "went straight to the atmospheric point," creating the feeling of being "trapped in a torch-lit vault." Nothing could have been more appropriate for a play about intrigue, secret oaths, plots, and entrapment. It shows that Brook knew just when fidelity to the period and style of the original would best bring the work to life, and that he was perfectly capable of supplying just what might have been expected—when the play itself was not overly familiar.

23a

October 9, 1953

The Little Hut

by Andre Roussin
Adapted by Nancy Mitford

New York: Coronet

31

October 18, 1953

King Lear

by William Shakespeare

as shown on

Omnibus

CBS Television

The Television and Radio Workshop of the Ford Foundation

Director (Staged by) . . . . Peter Brook
Executive Producer . . . . Robert Saudek
Director (for **Omnibus**) . . . . Andrew McCullogh
Music . . . . Virgil Thomson
Associate Producer . . . . Paul Feigay
Production Designer . . . . Henry May
Set Decoration . . . . Gene Callahan
"Artistic Consultant" . . . . Georges Wakhevitch

CAST

Lear . . . . *Orson Welles*
Cordelia . . . . *Natasha Parry*
Duke of Albany . . . . *Arnold Moss*
Kent . . . . *Bramwell Fletcher*
Oswald . . . . *David J. Stewart*
Regan . . . . *Margaret Phillips*
Goneril . . . . *Beatrice Straight*
Fool . . . . *Alan Badel*
Poor Tom . . . . *Michael MacLiammoir*
Gloucester . . . . *Frederick Worlock*
Cornwall . . . . *Scott Forbes*
France . . . . *Wesley Addy*
Burgundy . . . . *Fred Sadoff*
1st Gentleman . . . . *Lloyd Bochner*
1st Servant . . . . *Chris Gampel*
Doctor . . . . *Le Roi Operti*

This production—still available on kineoscope at the Museum of Television and Radio in New york—was one of the most elaborate ever done for the famous *Omnibus* series; *Variety* reported it cost over $150,000. It was one of the few times *Omnibus* had been devoted to a single work. Even with "the American video premier of Orson Welles," however, it was designed to fit into a 90 minute slot; the actual playing time is 74 minutes, with commercials held until the end.

Alistair Cook defended that in his introduction, reporting Brook saying that even if he had three hours, it would still run 74 minutes. The result is certainly good enough not to need much justification, but the justification that is made is questionable: Cook (and, through him, Brook) claiming that the average running time of an Elizabethan play was four hours and that the custom of the subplot developed so the lead actors wouldn't have to be on stage that entire time. Thus Brook cut the entire Gloucester-Edgar-Edmund subplot, leaving, basically, only Lear and his daughters.

All this works better than a purist might suppose, though there is a lack of breathing space—Lear seems rather quickly to start worrying about his sanity. The substitution of a real "poor Tom" for the disguised Edgar turns out to be surprisingly effective. Even the favorable *Variety* critic wondered if an intermission would have helped, assuming it would somehow not have commercials, and Jack Gould, in the *New York Times*, found the last half-hour almost incomprehensible.

The result is surprisingly fluid and cinematic, considering that it was done live. As *Variety* reported:

> For the delineation of one of the bard's greatest tragedies, Brook's staging did much to push back the walls of the television studio and permitted for a natural continuity from scene to scene—at all times superbly backed by flawless technical direction, cameras and lighting crews. The highly creative scenic designing transposed the time place and mood to the TV screen with sensitivity and strength. Lear's flight through the storm after his banishment from his daughter Regan's castle was a technical achievement that must have posed some intricate problems, yet it came off with a terrifying realism.

Ben Gross in the *Daily News* said:

> The scenery, the costuming, the lighting and the camera work were invested with the beauty of imagination. These merged into a spectacle which would have received critical acclaim in the Broadway theatre.

As he was to do later in the film of *Lear*, the opening scene is played formally—though here it comes after a sudden opening shot of a knife ripping through a map. The energy level of passion rises rapidly after that with a scene of Lear's knights carousing. The acting throughout is on a high level, with the possible exception of Badel's Fool, which gets somewhat lost in the crush. Even the *Times*, somewhat critical of the physical production as a whole, found Welles "caught the human qualities of the King and his agony and suffering," and that in the "tricky storm scene" he "did not allow himself to be carried away by Shakespeare's lines or his own emotions." Looking at first like the elderly Henry VIII, he achieves some beautiful moments and the end, as he drags the body of Cordelia in on a robe, fits what *Variety* called "the Bard's biggest weeper.'

It might have been interesting if they could have worked together again, but this meeting of two famous Boy Wonders, at least, has to be counted as a success.

32

November 16, 1953

Faust

Composed by Charles Gounod
Text by Jules Barbier and Michel Carré

New York: The Metropolitan Opera

(Original production, Paris, 1859)

Staged by . . . . Peter Brook
Decor and Costumes . . . . Rolf Gérard

CAST (opening night)

Faust . . . . *Jussi Bjoerling*
Marguerite . . . . *Victoria de los Angeles*
Mephistopheles . . . . *Nicola Rossi-Lemeni*
Valentine . . . . *Robert Merrill*
Siebel . . . . *Mildred Miller*
Marthe . . . . *Thelma Votipka*
Wagner . . . . *Laurence Davidson*

Conductor: Pierre Monteux

The opera retains the familiar plot of Goethe's *Faust, Part I*, but centers only on the love affair between Faust and Marguerite. This has enraged those who love Goethe's work for its philosophical depth, but the opera's strong melodic qualities have endeared it to generations of opera-lovers. (It is even popular in Germany, though there it is called *Marguerite* to avoid the blasphemy of claiming it as a serious treatment of the classic drama.) As with many operas, there can be a tendency to treat it as a mere vocal showpiece, ignoring the dramatic qualities it does indeed have. Peter Brook seems to have been determined to take it seriously on its own, non-Goethean, terms.

An extensive article in the *New York Times* Sunday Magazine explored the history of the production, which was expensive for the time, costing $85,000. The decision for a new production was Rudolph Bing's. He felt the old sets were beyond use and that such a popular opera should be kept in the repertoire. Bing had known Brook from England, where Bing had been director of the Glyndebourne Opera, and it was Bing's idea that Brook be asked, though he didn't know if Brook would be interested in directing such an old warhorse. (The old Met had played *Faust* so often that it was nicknamed "the Faustschpielhaus.")

As it turned out, Brook had also been thinking about *Faust* and was interested in a production. He didn't want to do anything too experimental or to change its construction, but he was interested in moving the period of the action up to that of the composer's own time. Nowadays this is not unusual, but in 1953 it was perhaps felt that it needed justification, for, both in this article and other newspaper reports, Brook gave the strange reason that:

> To my mind Faust *on the stage always suffers from the lack of relation between the style of the scenery and costumes and the absolutely characteristic nineteenth century idiom of the music. I feel the anachronism of realistically dressed medieval characters in the second act dancing a typical 1840 waltz, for instance, is the sort of thing that makes opera staging unconvincing.*

This seems to imply an imperfection in any work in which the medium is not of the same artistic period as the story, as if to say that Berlioz' *Les Troyans* should be set in 19th century Paris since it is not written in Greek modes.

Whatever the justification, the result was well enough received, though there were quibbles with individual moments. Mephistopheles had a black, red-lined opera cloak and top hat, and the rejuvenated Faust wore student clothes, with pearl grey slacks. Some reviewers missed the splendor of a *Faust* in full renaissance regalia, but most felt the result was appropriate. One thing in the staging that was criticised was the setting for the third act, normally a garden in front of Marguerite's house. Here it was more like a park or garden outside of the city, which some felt made Faust's aria *salude demure* (apostrophising Marguerite's dwelling) seem pointless and which made the traditional action at the end of the act—Marguerite, inside her house, throwing open the windows and singing to the night of her love—impossible.

Despite a certain amount of attention paid in print to Brook before the opening, the actual reviewers did not mention him much, concentrating instead on Rolf Gérard's designs, as if the designer was the only one who had anything to do with creating the new production. This might have resulted merely from the reviewers realizing that a director in an opera house such as the Met can find his own staging vanishing rapidly as new casts move in and as the production is revived in later years, but generally opera directors did not get much attention then unless they were trying something exceptionally strange. In the *Post*, Harriet Johnson found it "theatrically effective," and John Chapman, in the *Daily News*, thought it was "very good theatre."

Two reviewers went into slightly greater depth. In *The World Tele-gram and Sun*, Robert Bacar said:

> *Young Peter Brook, who staged the opera, shows a good deal of talent in the handling of crowds and also in making very effective groupings of small ensembles, such as the quartet in the garden scene. He likes movement, sparkle, excitement on stage and that, up to a point, is extremely pleasing to the eye. But then he permits too much freedom of action to single characters.*

In *The Herald Tribune*, Virgil Thomson, an esteemed composer as well as a music reviewer, felt the 19th century atmosphere was not consistent, but then went on:

> *Much of Mr. Brook's work was of the not very noticeable but ever so important kind which moves the principals around gently and expressively in their arias and duets. All this was clear, simple, distinguished. And the waltz scene was brilliant. Any one could see that it had been directed, not just thrown together.*

The production stayed in the repertoire for several years. It was replaced in the '65-66 season with sets more appropriate to the new house.

1954

33

April 30, 1954

The Dark is Light Enough
by Christopher Fry

London: Aldwych Theatre
(242 performances)

Director . . . . Peter Brook
Decor by . . . . Oliver Messel

CAST

Jakob . . . . *John Moffatt*
Belmann . . . . *Hugh Griffith*
Kassel . . . . *Peter Bull*
Stefan . . . . *Peter Barkworth*
Bella . . . . *Violet Farebrother*
Willi . . . . *David Spenser*
Gelda . . . . *Margaret Johnston*

Richard Gettner .... *James Donald*

Countess Rosmarin Ostenburg .... *Edith Evans*

Colonel Janik .... *John Glen*

Count Peter ZichyJack .... *Jack Gwillim*

Beppy .... *George Murcell*

Rusti .... *Peter Halliday*

1st Soldier .... *Peter Sallis*

2nd Soldier .... *Frederick Treves*

3rd Soldier .... *Churton Fairman*

During the 1848 Hungarian rebellion against the Austro-Hungarian Empire an elderly Austrian countess takes a difficult journey to rescue her former son-in-law, Richard Gettner, a deserter from the Hungarian army. She shelters him in her house, hiding him in the loft over the stables, and later, when the fortunes of the war turn, also shelters the man who has been pursuing him. Gettner is not a particularly good man—he is weak, drunken, and heartless—and the motivations of the Countess herself can be obscure; quiet as she is, "lives make and unmake themselves in [her] neighborhood as nowhere else." She married her daughter to Gettner knowing the chances the marriage would succeed were faint. It turns out she doesn't even like him particularly; to her he means: "Simply what any life may mean."

When her son finds that he is present and is still interested in his former wife, he challenges Gettner to a duel and is wounded. This causes an eventually fatal heart attack for the Countess, but beside her body, Gettner finds his courage.

As a new play by Christopher Fry, this caused quite a bit of comment, some finding it obscure, and many feeling there wasn't much of a play here, aside from a magnificent part written for Edith Evans, who got glowing notices. It was compared with Fry's other successes, *The Lady's not for Burning* and *Venus Observed*, with the more wintery tone of the new work being especially noted.

Brook was hardly mentioned in the criticism. *Theatre World Annual* thought it "the most satisfying theatre of the year" and chose it for its jacket and frontpiece. It mentioned the verse as being less rich than in Fry's earlier work, and then said: "But there is a pervading air of romance which tends to lull the consciousness of underlying subtleties, and Peter Brook's direction and the entrancing decor and costumes by Oliver Messel served to heighten this romantic aspect."

This may not be the best example of Brook's ability to work with actors. Edith Evans was consistently praised, but the quality of acting in the rest of the cast was generally felt to be inadequate. *Plays and Players*, in a June article on what was felt to be the poor quality of supporting performances in the West End, said: "But perhaps the most important example is in *The Dark is Light Enough*. Here, apart from Edith Evans and Margaret Johnson, the cast convey the impression that they are bored and do not understand the play." It is, of course, possible that the critics were blaming the actors for the obscurities of the play, which has not often been revived, but here Brook seems not to have inspired the cast to that type of performance which can cover up flaws by the energy of the presentation.

 The Sunday Times kept mention of him to the very end of the review, saying: "Not perhaps a major play but an immensely interesting one which owes much to the exactness of Mr. Peter Brook's direction." the *Guardian* spoke only of his "imaginative skill."

34

June 9, 1954

Both Ends Meet
by Arthur Macrae

London: Apollo Theatre

(284 performances)

Director . . . . Peter Brook
Setting by . . . . Alan Tagg

CAST

Mr. Wilson . . . . *Richard Pearson*
Margaret Ross . . . . *Brenda Bruce*
Tom Davenport . . . . *Arthur Macrae*
Clarissa Davenport . . . . *Jane Downs*
Edward Kinnerton . . . . *Richard Easton*
Jimmy Scott-Kennedy . . . . *Cyril Raymond*
Sir George Treherne . . . . *Alan Webb*
Lord Minister . . . . *Miles Malleson*

 This is a comedy about tax-fraud and how to get away with it. Tom Davenport is a writer who mistakes a tax official for a journalist and, before he realizes the mistake, has revealed several improprieties in the course of conversation. All becomes even more complicated when it turns out his niece's fiancé, also a tax official, has overheard. There are the expected complications as the writer tries to get out of the awful situation. By midplay, it turns out he has inherited a fortune from his late aunt, but that fails to clear the situation, as two elderly men turn up, claiming the estate as her former lovers. By the end, a bit of friendly blackmail solves all problems, as the writer is helped by his niece's fiancé, who is leaving his hated profession.

This production was a success despite cool reviews, but it can't be considered anything but a footnote in Brook's career, an interesting example of his ability to work in popular, commercial forms, which might allow him the right to work in less popular, more experimental forms. Reviewers concentrated almost entirely on the action and actors, most not mentioning the director at all. *The Times'* entire comment on him was: "The play is produced with pace and skill by Mr. Peter Brook." *Plays and Players* said: "Peter Brook's direction has been done with enormous skill, apart from the acting."

35

December 30, 1954

House of Flowers

New York: Alvin Theatre
(165 performances)

Book . . . . Truman Capote
Music . . . . Harold Arlen
Lyrics . . . . Capote and Arlen
Director . . . . Peter Brook
Sets and Costumes . . . . Oliver Messel
Dances and Musical Numbers . . . . Herbert Ross
Lighting . . . . Jean Rosenthal
Musical Director . . . . Jerry Arlen
Orchestrations . . . . Ted Royal

CAST

Tulip . . . . *Dolores Harper*
Gladiola . . . . *Ada Moore*

Pansy . . . . *Enid Mosier*
Do . . . . *Winston George Henriques*
Don't . . . . *Solomon Earl Green*
Mother . . . . *Miriam Burton*
Ottilie, alias Violet . . . . *Diahann Carroll*
Madame Fleur . . . . *Pearl Bailey*
Captain Jonas . . . . *Ray Walston*
Madame Tango . . . . *Juanita Hall*
Mamselle Ibo-Lele . . . . *Pearl Reynolds*
The Sisters Meringue . . . . *Leu Comacho*
                                                                                                   Margot Small
Mamselle Honolulu . . . . *Mary Mon Toy*
Mamselle Cigarette . . . . *Glory Van Scott*
Royal . . . . *Rawn Spearman*
The Champion . . . . *Geoffrey Holder*
Chief of Police . . . . *Don Redman*
Carmen . . . . *Carmen De Lavallade*
Alvin . . . . *Alvin Ailey*
Monsieur Jamison . . . . *Dino DiLuca*
The Houngan . . . . *Frederick O'Neal*
Baron of the Cemetery . . . . *Geoffrey Holder*
Duchess of the Sea . . . . *Miriam Burton*
Steel Band . . . . *Michel Alexander*
                                                                                                   Roderick Clavery
                                                                                                  Alphonso Marshall

Townspeople
Joseph Comadore, Hubert Dilworth, Phillip Hepburn,
Louis Johnson, Mary Louise, Audrey Mason, Arthur Mitchell,
Walter Nicks, Albert Popwell, Sabu, Herbert Stubbs

     House of Flowers is one of the legendary failures of the American Musical Theatre, with a fondly remembered score, a long list of performers who went on to fame, and a sadly confused book. Although Brook certainly worked with Truman Capote in turning his novella into a musical, was the director at the start of rehearsals and was listed as the director of record, he was replaced as director before the opening.

     Biographies of Capote and Bailey report on clashes between Brook and the cast in which Brook, apparently, was not innocent. One particular problem was Brook's not giving much "direction" at all, probably to let the actors discover their parts for themselves. This worked in classical drama, but these Musical-Comedy performers felt cut adrift. Bailey was especially upset, feeling that Brook was not available for character guidance; she said that she would be able to give the audience an entertaining evening, but that it would be closer to her night-club act than to what was really needed for the play. In *Not Since Carrie*, Ken Mandelbaum, after observing how Herbert Ross replaced the initially engaged George Balanchine as choreographer, continues:

> Ross had also replaced Brook—with whom Bailey had clashed violently—as director, although Brook retained program credit.
>
> During the run the second act was restructured... When Brook was called back to stage the second act revisions, Bailey announced to the press that as Brook had nothing to do with the show since the middle of the Philadelphia engagement, Ross was her director and she did not intend to cooperate with Brook.

At any rate, the critics raved about Messel's decor, admired the performers, and were split on Arlen's score, but the *Times*, the *Daily News*, the *Post*, the *Herald-Tribune* and *The New Yorker* all utterly failed to mention Brook.

1955

36

May 11, 1955

The Lark
by Jean Anouilh
Translated by Christopher Fry

London (Hammersmith) Lyric Theatre
(109 performances)

Presented by Tennent Productions Ltd.

Director . . . . Peter Brook
Scenery, Costumes based on designs by Jean-Denis Malclés

CAST

Beauchamp, Earl of Warwick . . . . *Richard Johnson*
Cauchon, Bishop of Beauvais . . . . *Laurence Naismith*
Joan . . . . *Dorothy Tutin*

Her Father . . . . *Peter Duguid*

Her Mother . . . . *Alexis France*

Her Brother . . . . *Barry MacGregor*

The Promoter . . . . *Leo McKern*

The Inquisitor . . . . *Michael Goodsmith*

Brother Ladvenu . . . . *Michael David*

Robert de Beaudricourt . . . . *David Bird*

Boudousse . . . . *Churton Fairman*

Agnes Sorel . . . . *Hazel Penwarden*

The Young Queen . . . . *Catherine Feller*

Charles, the Dauphin . . . . *Donald Pleasance*

Queen Yolande . . . . *Lucienne Hill*

Archbishop of Rheims . . . . *John Gill*

M. de la Tremouille . . . . *Peter Cellier*

Page to the Dauphin . . . . *David Spenser*

Captain La Hire . . . . *George Murcell*

The Hangman . . . . *Gareth Jones*

An English Soldier . . . . *Norman Scace*

The Lark, Anouih's version of the story of Joan of Arc, was first produced in 1953 at the Montparnasse Theatre in Paris, and was one of his greatest successes, running two seasons. English-speaking critics, as might be expected, compared it to Shaw's *Saint Joan* and usually found it a lesser work, but admirable nonetheless.

Most of the focus was on the play itself—the *Times* didn't even mention Brook—and where he was mentioned it was in connection with the material of the play rather than on what he as director might have added; one tends not to notice "director's touches" in works one hasn't seen before, ascribing such things to the author. In the *Sunday Times*, Harold Hobson, who alone of reviewers thought that it was "the best play about Joan of Arc which the English theatre has seen," had some problems with Brook's treatment of the ending, in which Anouilh, saying that the true nature of Joan's story ends happily, suddenly whisks away the stake and brings on the earlier glory of the coronation of the Dauphin. Here Hobson felt Brook muted the effect of the sudden change with too slow a pacing and too many "lugubrious prayers." He also disagreed with the final speech being given to Cauchon, rather than to the Dauphin, (though that was probably Fry's doing as translator). On the whole, however, he noted that "Peter Brook has directed it with a splendid sense of movement, and of the alternating play of light and darkness."

Xb

July 22, 1955

The Birthday Present
by Peter Brook

BBC Television

Director .... Tony Richardson

CAST

Husband .... *Michael Gwynn*
Wife .... *Yvonne Mitchell*
Doctor .... *Violet Farebrother*

It will be noted that this is not numbered in sequence, as Brook did not direct it, but wrote it. It is included here as a literary footnote to a directing career. The following review, apparently its only record, appeared in the *Times* on the next day:

> *Mr. Peter Brook's* The Birthday Present, *which was performed last night on television, is the kind of serious dramatic joke—one thinks of M. Jean Cocteau's* Théâtre de poche—*which to succeed must from the first wholly arrest the attention; and this, alas, it fails to do. Lasting only a quarter-of-an-hour, the piece tried to sketch with quick strokes the first meeting after seven years of a divorced couple. But neither the husband (Mr. Michael Gwynn) nor the wife (Miss Yvonne Mitchell) possessed sufficient character for the encounter between them—which as it turned out was cunningly staged by a lady psychiatrist (Miss Violet Farebrother)—to be more than merely pointless. It was not even embarassing. A solemn production by Mr. Tony Richardson, full of unusual angles and close-ups of wedding rings and tanks of tropical fish, only made one aware of the missing slight of hand in the writing of the play.*

37

August 16, 1995

Titus Andronicus
by William Shakespeare

Stratford: Shakespeare Memorial Theatre

Director . . . . Peter Brook
Designs and Music . . . . Peter Brook
Michael Northen
Desmond Heeley
William Blezard

CAST

Saturninus . . . . *Frank Thring*
Bassianus . . . . *Ralph Michael*
Marcus Andronicus . . . . *Alan Webb*
A Roman Captain . . . . *Michael Blakemore*
Titus Andronicus . . . . *Laurence Olivier*
Lucius . . . . *Basil Hoskins*
Quintus . . . . *Leon Eagles*
Martius . . . . *John McGregor*
Mutius . . . . *Ian Holm*
Tamora . . . . *Maxine Audley*
Alarbus . . . . *Michael Murray*
Chiron . . . . *Kevin Miles*
Demetrius . . . . *Lee Montague*
Aaron . . . . *Anthony Quayle*
Lavinia . . . . *Vivien Leigh*
Aemilius . . . . *William Devlin*
A Messenger . . . . *Bernard Kay*
Young Lucius . . . . *Meurig Wyn-Jones*
A Nurse . . . . *Rosalind Atkinson*
A Clown . . . . *Edward Atienza*
First Goth . . . . *Paul Hardwick*
Second Goth . . . . *David Conville*
Third Goth . . . . *Patrick Stephens*
Publius . . . . *Neville Jason*
Caius . . . . *Gordon Gardner*
A Roman . . . . *Hugh Cross*

Kinsmen of Titus, Priests, Judges, Soldiers, Huntsmen,
Citizens and Goths
Frances Leak, Ellen McIntosh, Moira Redmond,
Victoria Watts, James Greene, Terence Greenidge,
Alan Haywood, Ewan Hooper, Peter James,

George Little, Grant Reddick, John Standing,
Peter Whitbread, Ian White

Production revived July 1, 1957
Tour: Paris, Venice, Belgrade, Zagreb, Vienna, Warsaw

followed by
London: Stoll Theatre

Universally acknowledged as a landmark production, Brook's re-vival of Shakespeare's first tragedy was only the third in the twentieth cen-tury and set the stage for future directors to tackle this and other previously "unstageable" plays. Proclaimed a "director of genius," by Caryl Brahms in *Plays and Players*, Brook tamed the barbarism without losing its power, producing a result that was found full-bodied but bloodless. He avoided the gore of the multiple murders and mutilations through judicious edit-ing, off-stage action, and, above all, the use of symbolic rather than realistic techniques.

Brook's *Titus* was hailed by critics and audiences alike as a revelation of what a "lesser" Shakespeare tragedy might be, though some reviews regretted that Brook had banished scenes and butchered lines—especially graphic, symbolic, and poetic ones. Streamlining the script and speeding up the action cauterized the sensationalism of the four murders in the banquet scene: like the sudden deaths of the three sisters in Brook's film of *Lear*, the victims toppled like skittles. As, at times, did the audience. Despite the fact that he draped severed heads in black cloth tastefully arranged in baskets, and had Lavinia cradle her father's severed hand instead of dangling it from her teeth, St. John's Ambulance Brigade volunteers tended an average of three (and a record of twenty) spectators who passed out at every performance.

In his program notes, Brook described the play as "an austere and grim Roman tragedy, horrifying indeed, but with a real primitive strength, achieving at times a barbaric dignity." After the 1957 European tour, which culminated in a London run at the Stoll Theatre, Brook attributed the play's success to recognition of "the most modern of emotions—violence, hatred, cruelty, pain—in a form that, because *unrealistic*, transcended the anecdote and became for each audience *quite abstract and thus totally real.*"

Laurence Olivier's Titus was acclaimed as one of the highlights of his illustrious career, and his lightning-flash portrayal was often described as a crusty military forshadowing of *Lear* J. C. Trewin found it: "The quietness at the core of a hurricane, the storm wind of the equinox." Kenneth Tynan noted that in "an unforgettable concerto of grief," Titus is constantly compared to the sea, and Olivier "dredged from an ocean bed of fatigue... the noise made in its last extremity by the cornered human soul." Even those who disliked the production recommended the play for his operatic performance, for his stillness as well as his rage. Anthony Quayle's vigorous Aaron and Maxine Audley's vicious Tamora were also highly praised, especially after the maturing process of the European tour.

Vivien Leigh, as Lavinia, was credited with handling an impossible task well. Some reviewers made snide comments about the fact that she continued to be beautiful, with every hair in place, after rape and dismemberment, but this may have been merely the general affect of her great beauty—others mention her hair as being disordered. To Olivier's opera, Leigh played a silent ballet: Brahms found her "the Fonteyn of Drama, taking as a river takes rain and so absorbing it into her art that who is to know what she found in herself and what she has been lent." In the light of subsequent biographical information, it seems that the grueling role and the physical trial of the tour contributed to her later breakdown. *Theatre Notebook's* Muriel Byrne found her: "Fixed in despair, the very incarnation of woe." and Jan Kott—who considered the production one of the five most important of his life—was impressed by: "How much suffering she is able to convey, just by bending her body, by hiding her face."

As Brook had occasionaly done before, he conceived sets, costumes and music himself, with a resulting harmony that was hailed by all critics as "abstract symbolism" and "formalized ritual." He thrust great fluted pillars Trewin found to be "like a grove of organ pipes" on stage for his simple basic set, and lit it with what the *Manchester Guardian* described as a "terrifying tawney darkness" that allowed for quick changes. Evoking "brooding splendor" through "disciplined unobtrusiveness," according to J. B. Boothroyd of *Punch*, the inconspicuous subtleties of the lighting were declared by the *Times* "to carry on the process so far as mere staging can carry it." In the second half of the play, Brook plunged his actors into a blood-red interior, full of the shapes, shadows and smoke of a Websterian nightmare. Some, such as *The New Statesman & Nation's* T. C. Worsley, noted the influence of German expressionism: "that distorted mirror of half-madness... that fishy world of the unconscious [where] insensate cruelty has some vague kind of meaning."

The limited palette of colors: bile green, black, red, and the liver brown of congealed blood, extended from set to costumes. Eclectic and anachronistic, they called up a Renaissance idea of Romans straight out of the well-known sketch in Thomas Peachum's 1595 letter describing a *Titus* performance. Only Aaron stood out, in a blue, black, and gold costume after Rubens. Evelyn Waugh reported the effect as "Fourteenth-century justices and fourth-century legionaires mingled felicitously with visions from Bakst ballet."

The details most vividly etched on the minds of all viewers were the scarlet streamers, variously described as crimson ribbons and red scarves, which Brook borrowed from Korean masked dance-drama, to indicate the mutilated hands and torn tongue of the ravished Lavinia. This stage image, "right arm outstretched, head drooping away from it, left arm crooked with the wrist at her mouth, hair in disorder over face and shoulders." according to Richard David in *Shakespeare Survey*, (vol. 10) was devoid of stage blood, but flowed with bloody symbolism. As Lavinia changed from virginal white to funereal black, the scarlet ribbons of outrage were replaced by flowing white bandages.

Not content with dizzying visual images, Brook sought to compose a score for his concerto of grief that would underline the agony. With the collaboration of William Blezard, he developed a *music concrète* score including the clashing of pots and pans, pencils tapping on Venetian glass, the plucking of wire baskets, and distorting "real" instruments by speeding up the sound of a toy trumpet through an echo box, slowing down a contorted three-note dirge on recorders, and placing a microphone in a grand piano for two terrifying chords in endless alternation. Brook achieved his goal. He gave voice to the primal scream through wailing, thudding, and the slow plucking of harp-strings. A blood-lust rhythm at unbearable pitch.

Those lucky enough to have seen it still remember Brook's *Titus* as one of his greatest triumphs.

November 24, 1955

Hamlet, Prince of Denmark
by William Shakespeare

Moscow:Vakhtangov Theatre

(Provincial tour opened October 25, 1955
at the Theatre Royal, Brighton)
Production transferred December 8, 1955
London: Phoenix Theatre
(123 performances)

Director . . . . .Peter Brook
Scenery and Costumes . . . . Georges Wakhevitch
Music and Songs . . . . Thomas Eastwood

CAST

Bernardo	*Gareth Jones*
Francisco	*Michael Allinson*
Marcellus	*John Turner*
Horatio	*Michael David*
Ghost of Hamlet's Father	*John Phillips*
Hamlet	*Paul Scofield*
Claudius	*Alec Clunes*
Gertrude	*Diana Wynyard*
Polonius	*Ernest Thesiger*
Laertes	*Richard Johnson*
Ophelia	*Mary Ure*
Voltemand	*Peter Whitbread*
Cornelius	*Anthony Service*
Rosencrantz	*Gerald Flood*
Guildenstern	*David De Keyser*
Reynaldo	*Norman Scace*
First Player (Lucianus)	*Harry H. Corbett*
Second Player (Player Queen)	*Aubrey Woods*
Third Player (Player King)	*Anthony Service*
Fourth Player (Prologue)	*Norman Bird*
Fifth Player	*Gareth Jones*
Sixth Player	*John Turner*
Fortinbras	*Richard Pasco*
A Captain	*Michael Allinson*
A Messenger	*Anthony Service*
An Attendant to Horatio	*Norman Scace*
A Sailor	*Churton Fairman*
First Gravedigger	*Harry H. Corbett*
Second Gravedigger	*Aubrey Woods*
A Priest	*Norman Bird*
Osric	*Timothy Findley*
A Gentleman	*Robert Robinson*
Ladies in Waiting	*Beryl Andrews*
	Greta Watson
	Catherine Feller

Courtiers, Soldiers, Musicians, etc.

Peter Brook's *Hamlet* of 1955 was his sixth major Shakesperian production. It was a play Brook seemed destined to direct, as he had staged it in a toy-theatre for his parents the Christmas he was seven. (The version lasted six hours.) One of Brook's early notebooks has this entry: "*Hamlet by P. Brook and W. Shakespeare.*" Having scored great successes with *Titus Andronicus* and *Love's Labours Lost*, Brook decided to take on *Hamlet* and cast his frequent partner Paul Scofield, who had played to role in London seven years earlier. The production cannot count among the Brookian revelations, but is significant historically as the third longest run of *Hamlet* on the British stage, and, because of the Moscow tour, as the first significant British production in Russia since 1917.

It received a warm reception in Moscow, being presented to sold-out houses. There were twelve calls for the cast on opening night, which was attended by Chekhov's widow and many dignitaries. The Russians were surprised by the simplicity of the set and the speed of the production. Brook actually had to add intermissions because the three-and-a-half hour running time was considered too short an evening! *Pravda* praised Scofield, calling him a "positive dynamic hero," but disliked the female characters.

Ivor Brown, editor of *Theatre*, might have been correct when he said: "Give Peter Brook the impossible and he will solve your problem. But it would be unwise, I fancy, to trust him with safe jobs." Brook himself has stated that he felt he failed in this production because his approach was too academic and traditional.

The set by Georges Wakhevitch was very simple—an arched stone hallway with galleries and windows. There was little decoration except for cannons, red hangings, and some old piers which were used, along with the lighting, to indicate set changes. For the most part, the critics felt the sets were "imposing and simple," and the play was praised for its rapidity and movement. The *Times* noted "Mr. Brook's swift direction," W. A. Darlington acknowledged Brook's "usual dexterity," and Harold Hobson said, "It has a swift, confident rhythm, and an assured placing of detail." Kenneth Tynan also liked the flow of the production, but felt it moved rapidly without a purpose. Several critics praised Brook's crowd scenes, but the overall impression was that the production lacked passion. Another criticism was of a lack of humor. Tynan said:

> Broad fun was never Mr. Brook's strong suit. Hence Osric falls flat; Ernest Thesiger's praying-mantis Polonius is annoyingly restrained; and the gravediggers, despite the earthiness of Harry H. Corbett, miss their true galgenhumor.

In the same vein, Darlington remarked:

> Of all great tragedies ever written, Hamlet most clearly demonstrates the difference between seriousness and solemnity. Mr. Brook, it seems, does not feel that way about it, and has influenced Mr. Scofield to forget that he once did.

Critics noted two innovations: Brook gave the court musicians toy instruments, and Ophelia sang flamenco chants in her mad scene rather than the traditional songs. The toy instruments were meant to suggest the idea of the family question and parent-child relationships, but Tynan said of this: "When he seeks to play a trump . . . one is merely consious that he has revoked."

His handling of the actors got mixed notices. It was suggested in reviews that Brook concentrated on externals of character without sufficient concern for inner workings, but there is no evidence of that in interviews with Brook or the actors. Brook himself regretted his treatment of the Ghost in a naturalistic manner, saying he "fell headfirst into the trap of making the Ghost into a human figure . . . it was against the whole conception of ghost-ness and the scene just seemed drab and underplayed."

On the other hand, the interpretation of Claudius and Gertrude as passionate lovers was a clear success. Hobson remarked:

> It is an immense relief to find instead of the usual lugubrious couple couched in wickedness, a Gertrude and Claudius who really look as if they were enjoying their honeymoon, even if the demands of the plot make them spend it at home.

Clunes, who got excellent notices, did not play Claudius as a villain. Tynan noted that he "plays Claudius from Claudius' own point of view; as a man who committed a *crime passionnel* after an internal battle which has left scars on his conscience," and said, "Under his influence, *Hamlet* is the tragedy not only of a prince, but of a whole doomed family." This is a suggestion, perhaps, that Brook's idea of bringing out the "family question" did indeed have results, even if the toy instruments didn't work.

The overall feeling about the production was definitely mixed—and one should remember that "mixed reviews" does not mean that each reviewer gave a middling notice. Siriol Hugh-Jones described the production as "shining, taut, as urgent as a plucked string." Ivor Brown called it a "melancholy and soporific presentation." Kenneth Tynan summed it up:

> *Hamlet,* as his first attempt at a major tragedy, seems to have overawed him. In the crowd scenes—the play and the duel—he brings off grand slams, but elsewhere his direction is oddly tentative, with niggling cuts and ear-distressing transpositions.

Clearly this was not one of Brook's triumphs. Nonetheless, one can see an attempt to achieve simplicity, a desire to keep the action moving, and characterization based on a reading of the play rather on than tradition. These are the hallmarks of his greatest successes.

39

Late 1957

Report from Moscow

BBC Television

This is mentioned in the index to Trewin, but the editors have not been able to find material on it. It seems to have been Brook's own documentary about the preceeding production of *Hamlet*.

1956

40

April 5, 1956

The Power and the Glory

by Graham Greene
Adapted for the stage by
Denis Cannan and Pierre Bost

London: Phoenix Theatre
(68 performances)

Presented by
Tennent Productions Ltd.
(Paul Scofield–Peter Brook Season)

Director . . . . Peter Brook
Music . . . . Peter Brook
Decor . . . . Georges Wakhevitch

CAST

Tench . . . . *Brian Wilde*
The Chief of Police . . . . *Roger Delgado*
Diaz . . . . *Robert Robinson*
A Priest . . . . *Paul Scofield*
A Lieutenant of Police . . . . *Harry H. Corbett*
A boy . . . . *Meurig Wyn-Jones*
Maria . . . . *Patience Collier*
Brigitta, her daughter . . . . *Ann Cooke*
Francisco . . . . *Alex Scott*

Miguel . . . . *Oscar Quitak*
A Policeman . . . . *Churton Fairman*
Mestizo . . . . *Robert Marsden*
The Governor's cousin . . . . *Willoughby Goddard*
A drunken prisoner . . . . *John Turner*
Lopez, another prisoner . . . . *Gerald Flood*
A spinster . . . . *Henzie Raeburn*
The warder . . . . *Norman Scace*
A farmer's wife . . . . *Beryl Andrews*
Alvarez . . . . *John Turner*
Vittorio, a muleteer . . . . *Maurice Bannister*
A schoolmaster . . . . *David de Keyser*
Obregon, a storekeeper . . . . *Gareth Jones*
Obregon's wife . . . . *Veronica Wells*
Ramon . . . . *Barry Martin*
Lola . . . . *Ann Maureso*
An Indian . . . . *David Spenser*
A peasant woman . . . . *Catherine Willmer*
A villager . . . . *William Robertson*
An old villager . . . . *Norman Bird*
A young woman . . . . *Carmen Vickers*
A stranger . . . . *Oscar Quitak*

Townspeople, prisoners, etc.

Graham Greene focuses his story on the gradual degeneration of a Catholic priest in a Communist Mexico: his attempt to procure the wine for his sacraments for the poor, and his pathetic downfall in the face of a corrupt State. Demoralized and corruptible, this "whiskey priest" risks everything to celebrate these masses, while a Lieutenant attempts to win the friendship of his daughter, Brigitta, who despises the father she is seing for the first time. The priest is betrayed by Mestizo and sent to prison, but is released to escape the country. Enticed back to perform rites for a dying man, he is trapped and sentenced to death. A young priest appears at the end to continue the work.

Writing in the *Observer*, Kenneth Tynan was the most negative, confessing to a distaste for Greene's book, calling it "not so much a dark night of the soul as a lost weekend. Buy your martyr's kit here." He goes on to say: "when virtue is presented to me so whoreishly garlanded and vice is defined as the manure in which salvation flowers, I begin to suspect that I am in the presence of special pleading." Harold Hobson in the *Times* was more sympathetic, calling it "a quietly absorbing play which never once causes the pulse to lose a beat." As one who appreciated Greene's novel, he found merit in the priest who was "a slightly comic little man who gathers up what little physical courage he can claim and goes fearfully to his martyrdom at the hands of the firing squad." More or less agreeing with his peers, Philip Hope-Wallace, in *The Manchester Guardian*, said that "as a play it is lame; brave but limping."

All critics seemed have trouble accepting this man's story as tragic in any sense, Greek or modern. Hobson claimed that "the emotional impact of the poor little priest's death is not strengthened by the smung tones in which he justifies his life to his not unsympathetic captor," while Tynan observed that "we see his vocation leading him irrevocably to his death, and still, and yet, the tears will not come." Hope-Wallace was more positive, admitting that "even rationalists can share the idea that a worthless vessel may contain priceless elixir." He too, however, agreed that "what is strange is that it does not yield more which really touches or sways our heart, mind, or soul."

All three agreed that Paul Scofield was not to blame. Tynan called him "a prodigious success as the trudging, wizened hero-victim," but then noted that "part of the trouble lies in the difficulty of reconciling English accents with Mexican make-up." Hope-Wallace thought most of the cast "tend to mere vehemence and simple type-playing."

Brook's direction did not go unappreciated. Tynan stated: "The physical production is assuredly not at fault. Using a "sound track" of his own composition and five glorious settings by Georges Wakhevitch, Peter Brook plants us firmly in Mexico." Hobson agreed: "Mr. Peter Brook's production is wholly admirable, creating all the Mexican local color that is needed without fuss and handling the difficult prison scene with imaginative expertness."

41

June 7, 1956

The Family Reunion
by T. S. Eliot

London: Phoenix Theatre
(100 performances)

Presented by
Tennent Productions, Ltd.
(Paul Scofield–Peter Brook Season)

Director, designer . . . . Peter Brook
Decor . . . . Georges Wakhevitch

CAST

Amy, Dowager Lady Monchensey . . . . *Sybil Thorndike*
Agatha . . . . *Gwen Ffrangon-Davies*
Ivy . . . . *Nora Nilcholson*
Violet . . . . *Patience Collier*
The Hon. Charles Piper . . . . *David Horne*
Col. The Hon. Gerald Piper . . . . *Cyril Luckham*
Mary . . . . *Olive Gregg*
Denman . . . . *Catherine Willmer*
Harry, Lord Monchensey . . . . *Paul Scofield*
Downing . . . . *Harry H. Corbett*
Dr. Warburton . . . . *Lewis Casson*
Sergeant Winchell . . . . *Norman Scace*

Amy, the Dowager Lady Monchensey, has called her family together to mark the return home after a long absence of her son Harry. He is tormented by a sense of guilt and startles the family by admitting murder, thinking he has thrown his wife overboard. Aunt Agatha is the only one able to bring him to an understanding of himself, so he accepts his father as the true murderer, who attempted and failed to kill his mother. A program note explains: "The Furies (Erinyes) of Greek mythology, the avengers of crime against kinship, who appear during Act One, were propitiated, according to the Orestes legend, by the expiation of crime, and became transformed into the Kindly Ones (Eumenides)—the 'bright angels' of Act Two." In order to expiate his mother's moral responsibility for his father's sins, he renounces his heritage and embarks on a pilgrimage of atonement. Amy blames Harry's departure on Agatha and dies of a weak heart from the stress, thereby fulfilling the intentions of Harry's father.

Kenneth Tynan opened his notice in the *Observer* by bemoaning the plight of Paul Scofield, who, he said: "is now called on to impersonate a tormented pseudo-Greek." According to Tynan, he did it "yeomanly." Quoting Manes Sperber's essay on Freud, Tynan continued: "In the circle of his actions, the neurotic is as much in pursuit of the Furies as he is pursued." While Harold Hobson in *The Times* felt that the "failure to adjust the Greek myth with the modern situation divided and confused the sympathies of the audience," he couldn't help but praise Brook and Scofield for trying to "show that the play has virtues far outweighing the admitted defects and in a revival as good as we can ever expect to see they go a long way towards justifying their act of faith." Tynan took issue with what he felt was Eliot's obssesive guilt, but Hobson differed, observing that "Mr. Brook has also coped successfully with the hitherto unsolved problem of presenting Furies. There is no straining of the imagination to suppose them either Greek goddeses or modern spooks." He accepted Harry's dilemma as one "of universal significance," while Tynan stated "if Mr. Eliot had admitted that Harry was a rare and special case, all might have been well. Instead, he insists that we accept him as a timeless and universal symbol."

Paul Scofield was given much of the credit for the success of the production, as was Sybil Thorndike as the doomed matriarch and Gwen Ffrangcon-Davies as Agatha. Hobson noted that Thorndike "once again uses silence as the principal element in the making of yet another of her wonderful old ladies."

Tynan remarked: "This has-been, would-be masterpiece is magnificently revived by Peter Brook." Hobson went to great lengths to commend Brook for his work with the spoken text by:

> *passing from consciously 'played' conversation to the required degree of formality when the effect is choral. His reward is that all the talk falls into a clearly recognizable pattern in which all the subtle criss-crossings of design can be followed with an ease which delights and flatters the intelligence of the hearers.*

This production must surely be seen as an example of Brook's ability to work with actors—considering the difficulty of speaking Eliot's dialogue without making it stilted—and a chapter in his continuing search for contemporary applications of the tragic form.

42

October 11, 1956

A View from the Bridge
by Arthur Miller

London: Comedy Theatre
(220 performances)

Presented by
The New Watergate Theatre Club
Watergate Presentations, Ltd.

Director, Designer . . . . Peter Brook

CAST

Louis	*Richard Harris*
Mike	*Norman Mitchell*
Alfieri	*Michael Gwynn*
Eddie	*Anthony Quayle*
Catherine	*Mary Ure*
Beatrice	*Megs Jenkins*
Marco	*Ian Bannen*
Tony	*Ralph Nossek*
Rodolpho	*Brian Bedford*
First Immigration Officer	*John Stone*
Second Immigration Officer	*Colin Rix*
Mr. Lipari	*Mervyn Blake*
Mrs. Lipari	*Catherine Willmer*
A "Submarine"	*Peter James*

Eddie Carbone, a Brooklyn longshoreman, has given sanctuary to two illegal imigrants from Italy who are also working the docks. His adopted niece, Catherine, has taken a liking to the younger, Rodolpho, but Eddie becomes disturbed by this and tries to convince her that Rodolpho only wants her to gain citizenship. Unable to control his own affections for Catherine and unwilling to listen to his wife, who fears the worst, Eddie convinces himself that Rudolpho is a homosexual and breaks the rules of his people by informing on him, thereby bringing on his own death at the hands of Rudolpho's brother.

While critics from *The Times, The Guardian,* and *The Observer* agreed that the production was a worthy and healthy addition to the London season—especially since its performance had been banned by the Lord Chamberlain, causing it to be produced at a "private theatre club"—all three had reservations regarding Eddie's lack of self-knowledge and Miller's use of a chorus. Harold Hobson wrote in the *Times*: "Mr. Miller hangs a good picture in a pretentious frame." In a more enthusiastic notice, Kenneth Tynan in *The Observer* noted that: "An indispensable part of the tragic process is self-knowledge: and, although everyone else in the play knows himself inside out, Eddie never comprehends himself." The *Guardians's* Philip Hope-Wallace observed that: "with the handicap of inarticulateness in your leading character, it is probably necessary to ram the rawly compassionate moral home, but it would seem much nearer the fine modern tragedy that it so nearly passes muster as, if we could dispense with a 'compere,' however disguised." Hobson added, "They have violent passions, but the moral resistance they offer to these passions is not so strong as to produce a sense of inner conflict."

Considering these general reservations, other response was enthusiastic. Hope-Wallace wrote: "This is a fine specimen of the lurid, morally earnest soul-searching drama of the American school." Hobson concurred: "this one has sufficient imaginative power to justify the expedient of turning a West End theatre into a theatre club." Tynan praised Miller, finding the play the best of the season, and saying: "Eddie dies unforgiven, but not unpitied. The curtain falls, as in tragedy it should, on a great unanswered question: for this man what other way was possible?"

Anthony Quayle's performance was appreciated by all, but qualified by Tynan, who wrote: "I think he underlines the play's weakness. He plays Eddie as an obtuse and mumbling simpleton, a hurt animal dramatising its own pathos." Hobson noted that: "he might perhaps put a theatrically sharper edge on the man's toughness without any compromise of what is good natured and well meaning under the toughness." Hope-Wallace wrote that Quayle gave "an extraordinary power and even a heroic size to the poor, muddled brute." Equally high praise went to Mary Ure, whom Hobson said: "renders the innocent gaiety of the child who is the unwitting cause of the tragedy," and to Brian Bedford, whose efforts Tynan called: "the roundest performance . . . an ingenuous faun, all shrugs and snickers, who walks smiling into disaster."

For both his direction and his decor, Peter Brook went unchallenged. Tynan found it and the sound-effects: "strikingly original," while Hope-Wallace said the entire production was "brilliantly effective." Hobson wrote: "Peter Brook has directed skillfully and designed the scenery, which is sombre, ingenious, and servicable."

As the third and final production of his 1956 London season, *A View from the Bridge* would seem best to exemplify Brook's attempt to define a modern tragic figure. While *The Power and the Glory, The Family Reunion* and *A View from the Bridge* all had flaws, the critics found Brook's productions served these "tragedies" as well as one could expect.

43

December 18, 1956

La Chatte sur un Toit Brûlante (Cat on a Hot Tin Roof)

by Tennessee Williams
(adapted by André Obey)

Paris: Théâtre Antoine

Director, mise-en-scène . . . . Peter Brook
Costumes . . . . CHANEL

CAST

Margaret (Maggie)	*Jeanne Moreau*
Brick	*Paul Guers*
Docteur Baugh	*Georges Sellier*
Révérend Tooker	*Riandreys*
Edith	*Monique Mélinand*
Gooper	*Maurice Duléac*
Grand-Mère	*Jane Marken*
Grand-Père (Big Daddy)	*Balpêtré*
Lacey	*Ousseynou Fall*
Sookey	*Moréna Casamance*
Brightie	*Pierre Cocouri*

When Peter Brook was thirty-one, his work had already garnered sufficient praise and hostility for him to be considered the *enfant terrible* of the British theatre, but he had also had a close relation with France, as shown by his productions of Sartre and Anouilh. The four French premières that he directed over the ensuing eight years, 1956–1963, works by Tennessee Williams, Arthur Miller, Jean Genet, and John Arden, each milestones of postwar theatre, were to firmly establish his international reputation.

The headline: "PETER BROOK Praises the Parisian Public, and prepares to confront them one day" appeared in an advance piece from London on the theatre page of *Le Figaro* in November 1956. In that interview, Brook notes that one of the marvels of the Parisian theatre-going public was a primary concern for a well-written text and a willingness to come to an evening of theatre on the name of the author alone, unlike the London scene, where actors had long proved the principal draw; he also comments that one of his dearest ambitions was to present a play in Paris and that such a project might well be in the offing. These remarks were clearly not made lightly, for six weeks later Jeanne Moreau opened in Paris in the Broadway hit, *Cat on a Hot Tin Roof*.

"Strange show!" began the review of *Le Monde's* Robert Kemp, then a recently-elected member of the Académie Francaise; selecting a quote from Goethe's Mephistopheles: "Bestiality in all its candor." Then, arguing with an unidentified colleague who had classified the work as a tragedy, Kemp responded: "I am not persuaded. A crude, heavy drama of sexuality, that's what first leaps to the eye." After describing the play's narrative, Kemp returned to his central concern, "the beautiful Margaret," observing:

> *Here is a role in which Miss Moreau excels, she is a ravishing semi-nude, she cries out, weeps, begs, threatens, sometimes grovelling prostrate, sometimes legs in the air, . . . from beginning to end, the spirit of the play is drawn, fixed, focused, whatever else it does to think of other things, on the manifestations of physical love. The most brutal, the most animal . . . seasoned with allusions to perversions . . . Miss Moreau has given of herself as she should, from the voice, from the arms, from the shoulders, and from the legs. She was gay, chatty, voluble, shrill, melodious, appetizing, irritating, pitiful.*

Noting that Peter Brook had both designed and directed the play, and that "this director from the Old Vic" had been "lent by Laurence Olivier," Kemp closed his review, observing dryly, of Brook: "His reputation is not unwarranted. Strange show!"

In a brief, anonymous article, under the headline "With Critics Unimpressed," the Paris edition of *The New York Herald Tribune*, commented: "Tout Paris was on hand for the première." It noted that Brick was played by Paul Guers, "recently of the Comédie Francaise," and somewhat begrudgingly noted that Paul Gordeaux, of the powerful *France-Soir*, praised both actors and the direction by the English producer, Peter Brook, but called the famous *Cat* a 'confused tragedy, gross and heated, and very noisy.'

If Brook's Parisian debut had aroused the interest of the enamored academician, Kemp, and won the approval of Gordeaux, it caused an almost apoplectic Jean-Jacques Gautier to break out in a veritable plethora of question and exclamation marks in *Le Figaro*:

> *So this is what all America is running to see! A certain degree of bewilderment, disgust, and boredom almost prevents me from reacting. Stupefying magma of hideousness and obsessions. Is all of American theatre uniquely preoccupied with eroticism and hysteria?*

Punctuating his outline of the play with such phrases as "You think that's all? Then wait!" and "You think you'll get away that easily? Not at all, not yet!" Gautier dismisses the action of the play as "a nervous breakdown here, a striptease there," and describes the dialogue as "foulness vomited in the face"of the characters. In an extraordinary display of critical outrage, he finally explodes:

> *I can no longer remain silent: a frightful onslaught of lust amidst the yells, screams, howls, shrieks, moans and groans of an entire family freed, in the light of a death, of a hundred thousand pains. This is one of the most ugly and most tiresome scenes—for this display of filth is, nonetheless, dismally monotonous—that I have ever seen in the theatre...melodramatic filth.*
>
> *With this triumphal entry, Peter Brook est arrivé a Paris!*

1957

37a

July 1

Titus Andronicus
London revival and then world tour

44

August 13, 1957

The Tempest
by William Shakespeare

Stratford: Shakespeare Memorial Theatre

December 5, 1957
Production transfered to
London: Drury Lane Theatre
(61 performances)

Director . . . . Peter Brook
Designs and Music . . . . Peter Brook
. . . . Michael Northen
. . . . Kegan Smith
. . . . William Blezard
Choreography . . . . Raimonda Orselli

CAST

The Master of a Ship . . . . *Peter Palmer*
A Boatswain . . . . *Ron Haddrick*
Alonso . . . . *Robert Harris*
Antonio . . . . *Mark Dignam*
Gonzalo . . . . *Cyril Luckham*
Sebastian . . . . *Robin Lloyd*
Adrian . . . . *Tony Robertson*
Miranda . . . . *Doreen Aris*

Prospero . . . . *John Gielgud*
Ariel . . . . *Brian Bedford*
Caliban . . . . *Alec Clunes*
Ferdinand . . . . *Richard Johnson*
Trinculo . . . . *Clive Revill*
Stephano . . . . *Patrick Wymark*
Iris . . . . *Jane Wenham*
Ceres . . . . *Stephanie Bidmead*
Juno . . . . *Joan Miller*

Mariners, Nymphs, Reapers,
and others represented by Spirits,
Mavis Edwards, Elizabeth Evans, Pamela Taylor,
Eileen Atkins, Rex Robinson, Robert Arnold,
Thane Bettany, Anthony Brown, Derek Mayhew,
John Murry Scott, Barry Warren, Edward Caddick,
Simon Carter, John Davidson, Henry Davies,
William Elmhirst, Kenneth Gilbert, Julian Glover,
John Grayson, Norman Miller, John Salway, Gordon Souter,
Roy Spencer, Gordon Wright

This production got generally favorable press, and much notice was taken of its unique elements, but it cannot be counted as one of the revolutionary Brook-Shakespeare productions which changed the way the play itself was perceived.

As Caryl Brahms said in *Plays and Players*: ". . . we knew from the beginning that it is about as useful to go to a Peter Brook production with a preconceived idea of the play as it would be to go to a sack-race with an octopus." It opened in semi-darkness with the actors tossing as if on the tempest-tossed ship—nothing unusual there—but then a large lamp flat on the stage slowly rose and traveled from one side of the stage to the other in a huge semi-circle, that motion then being echoed by a smaller lamp at the back. Harold Hobson, in the *Sunday Times*, was moved: "Thus can the waste of waters put out the life of man." The set, though simple, produced: "a strange jungle-grown place where the sun never penetrates and life seems to have the suspended motion of a realm under water."

One aspect universally commented upon was Brook's use of *music concrète*; the score consisted of "plucked strings and clashing saucepan lids and resonant wood and echoes," according to Brahms, or "gong beats, hyaena cries and off-key chimes," according to Cecil Wilson. Brook was quoted: "This play can be ruined if it is done with a proper ballet and a proper orchestra and proper singing." Despite this, and *The Times* feeling that: "It is determined that the dramatic poem shall not become a glorified stage masque . . . ," W. A. Darlington, in the *Daily Telegraph*, felt that the literal masque to celebrate the betrothal of Ferdinand and Miranda was the high point of the evening.

> *Mr. Brook throws into it all of his resources, making the figures of the goddesses and the dancers seem to be silhouetted in fire and floating in air; so that when they are swept away by a wave of Prospero's wand John Gielgud's voice in "We are such stuff as dreams are made on" comes with an overwhelmingly moving effect.*
>
> *This is the great moment of production which at other times lays so much stress on atmosphere that the action seems sluggish and clogged.*

Several reviewers commented on the problems in interpretation of Prospero; how can dramatic suspense be sustained when the main character seems to be omnipotent? All admired Gielgud, but in rather differing terms. Wilson saw a man "genuinely embittered over the loss of his kingdom," Darlington found him "a vital figure of mysterious power," and J. C. Trewin in the *Birmingham Post and Gazette*, said: "I have never known a more wistful Prospero." Brahms said: " . . . we do not go to the Stratford *Tempest* in search of Shakespeare, but to enjoy Peter Brook's visual annotations to the text," and felt that "Prospero, our true host, was only intermittently in the house." ending with " . . . his *Tempest* is a play about two clowns ship-wrecked upon a music-vibrant island . . . "

The above, though a complaint, shows that Brook seems to have been unusually successful with the minor characters—Adrian and Francisco having been combined. The *Times* was alone in thinking that "the comic scenes are inclined to drag." Hobson was offended by some of the production's bawdry, but admitted its energy. Trewin followed up his review with a later column on the figure of Gonzalo in the production: "It is an experience that every Shakespearian must share: the flashing up of some personage that, before, has been merely so many lines, a stage cipher." He also remarked on Brook finding "two legitimate laughs in the usually blurred storm scene, "and not merely 'a confused noise within'."

All in all, Wilson summed up much of the reaction when he said, "The whole production, a regular Brook's Benefit, puts fantastic general effect before individual performance."

45

October 28, 1957

Eugene Onegin

Composed by Peter Ilitch Tchaikovsky

Text by the composer, Modest Tchaikovsky, and K.S. Shilkov
after the verse novel by Alexander Pushkin
English translation for this production by Henry Reese

(original production, Moscow 1879)

New York: The Metropolitian Opera House

Staged by . . . . Peter Brook
Sets and costumes . . . . Rolf Gérard

CAST (opening night)

Mme. Larina . . . . *Martha Lipton*
Tatyana . . . . *Lucine Amara*
Olga . . . . *Rosalind Elias*
Eugene Onegin . . . . *George London*
Lenski . . . . *Richard Tucker*
Prince Gremin . . . . *Giorgio Tozzi*
Fillipyevna . . . . *Belen Amparan*
A Captain . . . . *Louis Sgarro*
Zaretski . . . . *George Cehanovsky*
Triquet . . . . *Alessio De Paolis*
Conductor: Dimitri Mitropoulos

The story, adapted from Pushkin, is rather Chekovian—at least compared to many other operas—with a great deal of emotion beneath a quiet surface. Tatyana, a young girl, falls in love with the Byronic and blasé Eugene Onegin, a friend of Lensky, her sister's fiance. In an impassioned solo scene, she writes him a letter revealing her love, but he rejects her in an off-handed way. Later, Onegin attempts to irritate Lensky by dancing with his betrothed. This backfires as the quarrel escalates into a duel in which Lensky is killed. Six years later, Tatyana is married to an older man who dotes on her. Onegin meets her at a ball and realizes what he rejected, but Tatyana, though attracted to him, is determined to remain faithful.

That this opera, though not done with great frequency, can now be considered to be in the regular repetoire, is at least partly due to this production. The Metropolitan handled it with care, choosing a cast of singers known for good acting and using an English translation to help the audience enter the world of this unfamiliar but dramatically rather "realistic" work. The production was originally intended as a showpiece for Renata Tebaldi, but she turned down the role of Tatyana when she found it was to be sung in English rather than the Italian translation in which she had received good notices at La Scala. (It is now sung in the original Russian.) Lucine Amara, who replaced her, probably hurt the initial impression, as she had a good voice but lacked spark on stage.

Brook seems to have focused on realism and intimacy in his treatment of the opera. In an article in the *New York Times*, he stated:

> *When Rolf Gérard and I started work on "Onegin," we both agreed that we had no choice: the only legitimate manner in which we could stage this opera was precisely in accordance with...Russian tradition. It seemed to us that we needed the very elements that in other operas one so often deplores; we felt that it was through the old-fashioned technique of painted vistas and realistic scenes that we would arrive at the climate in which this opera belongs.*

Other than the use of English, the major changes were in the use of interludes, newly composed from themes in the opera, to cover scene changes—this at the order of Mitropoulos—and in setting the last scene outdoors rather than in a hall in Gremin's palace. In the *Times* article, Brook mentioned that this last scene is frequently, even in Russia, judged incomplete, lacking in atmosphere, and he hoped that placing it outside would strengthen it; the early scene in which Onegin rejects Tatyana, as leaves are falling, being paralled by the scene in which she rejects him as snow is falling.

Because of its novelty as an opera, the reviews were mainly focused on the work itself, rather than the production. The opera was found to be pretty rather than strong, and was even found to be weak in characterization, though that is now considered to be one of its strongest points. As usual, the reviewers concentrated on the sets and singers, not mentioning the director much. Howard Taubman wrote in the *New York Times*:

> *The Met's production . . . wisely accepts Tchaikovsky on his own terms. It has not attempted to magnify "Onegin" into a work filled with vital force. Realizing that the essential intimacy of the work could not be denied, the Met has stressed elements of time and place. It has caught admirably, despite the size of the theatre, the atmosphere of a period piece.*

But all he said of the actual directing was: "Peter Brook's staging is full of invention and has authentic atmosphere." Winthrop Sargent, in *The New Yorker*, said the production was:

> *. . . a triumph, but the triumph was scored by Rolf Gérard's scenery, Peter Brook's direction, Dimitri Mitropoulos' conducting, and the singing of an excellent cast in the face of certain difficulties presented by the work itself.*

Xc

December 24, 1957

Time and Again

*(see # 48, **The Visit**)*

(26)

?/?/ 1957

Heaven and Earth

BBC Television
(Filmed 1951)
(The editors have not been able to discover the exact date in 1957
that this was broadcast)

1958

46

March 11, 1958

Vu du Pont
(A View from the Bridge)

by Arthur Miller
"Adapted" by Marcel Ayme

Paris: Théâtre Antoine

CAST

Alfieri	*Henri Nassier*
Peter	*André Rousselet*
Mike	*Jacques Ferrières*
Eddie Carbone	*Raf Vallone*
Catherine	*Evelyne Dandrey*
Béatrice	*Lila Kedrova*
Tony	*Serge Dubos*
Marco	*Marcel Bozzufi*

Rudolpho . . . . *José Varela*

Premier Inspecteur . . . . *Jean Morel*

Deuxième Inspecteur . . . . *Pierre Pascal*

Troisième Inspecteur . . . . *Edmond George*

Lipari . . . . *Ernest Varial*

Le Neveu Lipari . . . . *Pierre Pillot*

La Femme Lipari . . . . *Maya Morani*

La Fille Lipari . . . . *Clara Lerins*

Primier Docker . . . . *Jean-Claude Hechinger*

Deuxiéme Docker . . . . *Alain Dal*

Troisiéme Docker . . . . *Jean-Paul Ferrari*

Le Figaro had a reporter and a photographer waiting at the stage-door of the Théâtre Antoine after a costume rehearsal of Brook's production of Arthur Miller's *A View from the Bridge*, a week before it opened. The invited audience, we are told, under the headline "PARISIAN NEWS, . . . just about exhausted their laudatory vocabulary" regarding the performances of the "tired but happy" Italian movie star Raf Vallone and his fellow actors, the author and his "adaptateur," and Brook, who "remained silent under the avalanche of compliments." The public's interest was piqued by a list of some of the *morceaux de bravoure* that the director had used "to particularly fine effect: a police chase, a boxing match, rock and roll, and a knife fight."

Three days later, under the headline "LOVER OF DAMNED PLAYS," *Le Monde* presented its own, considerably more aggressive and chauvinistic advance article, that began:

> Peter Brook is going to present us two accursed plays one on top of the other . . . A View From the Bridge *was banned by the British censor in 1956 . . . a taboo subject across the Channel, much like religion and royalty, homosexuality cannot be mentioned on stage without incurring the wrath of the Queen's Lord Chamberlain.*

In regard to *A View From the Bridge*, Miller's tale of an immigrant Sicilian dock-worker living in Brooklyn, and of his incestuous passion for his adolescent niece that leads to madness, betrayal, and suicide, Brook mentioned that it was a powerful piece by his favorite author, and that he had met with him the previous summer in London, when Miller had accompanied Marilyn Monroe while she was shooting *The Prince and the Showgirl* with Laurence Olivier. It was then that they had set the details for *A View From the Bridge*, which Brook viewed as a response to Kazan's film *On the Waterfront*.

Ever in a tizzy, *Le Figaro's* Jean-Jaques Gautier was divided in his response: "I don't like the play, but I am all for those who played it." The play, he felt, was: "a great, crude, thick, enourmous and authentic melodrama in

the finest tradition of the last century;" he found the language "simplistic
. . . or naive . . . or frankly elementary . . . or a little on the intentionally
impoverished." Having noted that it was a play where "we are never finished explaining things that we have already long understood, because the
American longshoremen, born in Sicily, take hours to clarify even the simplest of questions," he nonetheless acknowledged that "Mr. Peter Brooks
[sic] has invented some handsome lighting and masterfully structured the
arrest scene with long trills of a whistle." The acting fared better, indeed,
Gautier felt that it was largely responsible for the public's enthusiasm on the
opening night; in particular, he felt that Lila Kedrova (doubtless at Brook's
provoking) was:

> *. . . extraordinary. She has passion, she breathes fire, she overflows with ardor and life. She*
> *burns and burns up the boards . . . Her high voltage . . . her vibration of all her being*
> *expresses a sensuality, a kind of primitive savagery.*

Kemp's review in *Le Monde* began with a laconic observation: "I
predict a long success, the play holds its own. It has the size and momentum
of a ram . . . It brutally brings to mind a boxing ring." He too appreciated
the "eyes of fire and the splendid exuberance of Lila Kedrova," but, once
again, it was Brook's work with his *jeune premiere* that clearly aroused the
mesmerized academician, who, with surprising candor, even entering into
the fray in the first person singular at one point, managed effectively to
convey some of the steamy sensuality of the production.

> *Her seventeen years, her provocative breasts, her soft eyes, her smooth shoulders . . . this*
> *Catherine doesn't hold back, she rubs herself on him like a little cat . . . makes a collar with*
> *her fresh young arms around her good doggy-daddy's neck and, cheek-to-cheek, I embrace*
> *you with a feast of kisses . . . Don't plead purity, innocence. I won't say Catherine is a*
> *little bitch, but I would really like to . . . The idyll develops . . . furtive caresses, looks,*
> *bodies magnetized . . . . When Eddie catches Catherine and Rudolpho together in their*
> *underwear he becomes crazed with fury, abusing the young girl by savagely devouring her*
> *lips; then, with a bravado that seems to me to be unprecedented in the theatre, [he does the*
> *same thing to] the lips of the boy, who does nothing to resist . . . Is he then abnormal? Ugh!*
> *[Fr.: Pouah!] 'You see who you love, you slut!' That's at least the sense of it.*

Raf Vallone's Eddie certainly didn't get that response from the critics. It was felt to be so strong that he wound up playing the part in the movie
version, for which he also got good notice.

Brook's set design was made up of ramps, platforms, and doors that
sealed in the family in its eat-in kitchen: Kemp felt the choice was excellent.
He pointed out, though, that the crowning glory of the production was
Brook's melding of the actors, the tempo, and the emphases of the play
at its climax: "Oh what a miracle!" he concluded, " . . . and the show has
tone." Clearly Kemp had his finger on the pulse of the Parisian theatre-going
public, for the play was to run for two years.

A week later, in the Paris edition of the *New York Herald Tribune*, Thomas Quinn Curtiss noted that the Paris production was an elongated version of the second of two short plays on a Broadway double bill of some three years earlier, that it was rewritten for Brook's 1957 London production, and that it was the London version that had been translated for Paris. He then commented:

> A View From the Bridge *has more violence than strength, and, by extending the running time of his orginal text, Miller has robbed it of some of its intensity. His mistake, however, has been cleverly corrected by Peter Brook's sharp direction, and once—after a rather ponderous start—the drama takes its stride and begins to tell its savage story, there is an evening of turbulent and engrossing theater.*

Curtiss felt, as did his colleagues, that the work was closer to melodrama than to tragedy, as it lacked "a genuine tragic sense, the dark and poetic conception of life's mysteries . . . ," but he noted: "In any case, theatrical excitement awaits you at the Antoine, where Peter Brook has staged the Miller script in dynamic fashion and provided some impressive scenery to evoke its changing moods."

47

May 5, 1958

The Visit
(Der Besuch der alten Dame)
by Friedrich Dürrenmatt
Translation/adaptation by Maurice Valency

Lunt-Fontanne Theatre, New York
(190 performances)

Drama Critics' Circle Award
Best Foreign Play 1957–58

Director . . . . Peter Brook
Producer . . . . The Producers' Theatre
Costume/set designer . . . . Teo Otto
Supervision/lighting . . . . Paul Morrison
Music . . . . James Stevens
Miss Fontanne's dresses . . . . Castillo
Assistant to Peter Brook . . . . Mary Lynn

CAST

Hofbauer . . . . *Kenneth Thornett*
Helmesberger . . . . *David Clarke*
Wechsler . . . . *Milton Selzer*
Vogel . . . . *Harrison Dowd*
The Painter . . . . *Clarence Nordstrom*
Station Master . . . . *Joseph Leberman*
Burgomaster . . . . *Eric Porter*
Professor Muller . . . . *Peter Woodthorpe*
Pastor . . . . *William Hanson*
Anton Schill . . . . *Alfred Lunt*
Claire Zachanassian . . . . *Lynn Fontanne*
Conductor . . . . *Jonathan Anderson*
Pedro Cabral . . . . *Myles Eason*
Bobby . . . . *John Wyse*
Police Chief Schultz . . . . *John Randolph*
First grandchild . . . . *Lesley Hunt*
Second grandchild . . . . *Lois McKim*
Mike . . . . *Stanley Erickson*
Max . . . . *William Thourlby*
First Blindman . . . . *Vincent Gardenia*
Second Blindman . . . . *Alfred Hoffman*
Frau Burgomaster . . . . *Frieda Altman*
Frau Block . . . . *Gertrude Kinnell*
Frau Schill . . . . *Daphne Newton*
Ottilie Schill . . . . *Marla Adams*
Karl Schill . . . . *Ken Walken*
Doctor Nusslin . . . . *Howard Fischer*
Athlete . . . . *James MacAaron*
Truck Driver . . . . *John Kane*
Reporter . . . . *Edward Moor*
Townsman . . . . *Robert Donley*
Townsman . . . . *Kent Montroy*

47a

June 23, 1960

Royalty Theatre, London
(148 performances)

Director . . . . Peter Brook
Producer . . . . H. M. Tennent Ltd.
Costume/set design . . . . Teo Otto
Music . . . . James Stevens
Lighting . . . . Joe Davis
Miss Fontanne's dresses . . . . Castillo

CAST

Hofbauer . . . . *Henry McCarthy*
Helmsberger . . . . *Ralph Nosseck*
Wechsler . . . . *Robin Chapman*
Vogel . . . . *David Nettheim*
The Painter . . . . *Ian Wilson*
Burgomaster . . . . *George Rose*
Professor Muller . . . . *Brian Wilde*
Pastor . . . . *Richard Dare*
Antin Schill . . . . *Alfred Lunt*
Station Master . . . . *Howard Douglas*
Claire Zachanassian . . . . *Lynn Fontanne*
Conductor . . . . *Richard Scott*
Pedro Cabral . . . . *Myles Eason*
Bobby . . . . *John Wyse*
First Townsman . . . . *Michael Browning*
Second Townsman . . . . *Richard Huggett*
Police Chief Schultz . . . . *Kenneth Thornett*
First grandchild . . . . *Irene French*
Second grandchild . . . . *Valerie Newbold*
Mike . . . . *Terry Richards*
Max . . . . *Bruce Wells*
First Blindman . . . . *Harry Ross*
Second Blindman . . . . *Alfred Hoffman*
Frau Burgomaster . . . . *Nuna Davey*
Frau Schill . . . . *Daphne Newton*
Ottilie Schill . . . . *Diana Beevers*
Karl Schill . . . . *Philip Lowrie*
Athlete . . . . *Trevor Barnett*
Doctor Nusslin . . . . *Nicholas Grimshaw*
Frau Bloch . . . . *Madge Brindley*
Truck Driver . . . . *Roy Pattison*
Reporter . . . . *Clinton Greyn*
Radio Reporter . . . . *Harry Ross*

In *Der Besuch der alten Dame*, an impoverished town awaits the return of a woman who left the town as a girl and has become fabulously wealthy. The woman, Claire Zachanassian, promises the town a million dollars but with one condition. She requires the death of Anton Schill, a respectable citizen of the town, revealing how he had denied paternity of their child, bribed witnesses in the trial, and thus started her on the road to prostitution. While the town is shocked and outraged at the proposal, Claire insists that she simply wants justice and says that she will wait. The rest of the play chronicles the shifting attitudes of the townspeople, the attempts to talk Zachanassian out of the condition, and, finally, the murder of Schill.

Peter Brook saw the play performed in French and then read Maurice Valency's English translation. He met with Alfred Lunt and Lynn Fontanne who were intrigued by the play but had already turned it down. The Lunts approved of Brook's ideas for the production and agreed to act if Brook could get approval for certain modifications of the text. Brook then met with Dürrenmatt and Valency in Paris, and the three worked on a revised English script. Some of the more grotesque and expressionistic elements were removed. In the English version, Claire is not presented as an ugly, deformed hag, but as an elegant, cool, beautiful woman with an ongoing love for Schill. The protrayal is much more sympathetic, which, in turn, forces the audience to consider the guilt of the townspeople and the relativity of justice.

Rehearsals began in November 1957, at the Lyric Theatre in London. By this time the play was no longer referred to by a literal translation of the title, *The Old Lady's Visit*, but was called *Time and Again*. The Lunts, who frequently worked without a director were impressed by Brook and had confidence in his direction. Jared Brown, in *The Fabulous Lunts*, quotes Lynn Fontanne:

> *Alfred and I have been directing each other for over thirty years. You know, we never really trusted anyone else, but he's the first person we really trust when it comes to taste. He appeals to the actor's imagination—the area where the actor is a specialist—and that's why we're so excited about him.*

Brook was equally impressed with the Lunts. He said:

> *Directing Lunt is a revelation. You can't imagine the countless tiny details that Alfred puts into a performance. This may sound like finicky acting but these painstaking details make up an enormous conception. It is like one of Seurat's pointillist paintings. Each little dot is not art, but the whole is magnificent. Alfred and Lynn start by getting a broad outline of what they're going to do and then they fill in the details. It's absolutely like somebody making a mosaic. They work endlessly from one detail to the next—fine, fine points—one after another. They're deep and flexible people and they have lightening speed and great artistic glory.*

Time and Again opened December 24, 1957 in Brighton, England. The date seems an unfortunate choice as most theatregoers apparently expected some light holiday entertainment with the delightful Lunts. Instead, many in the audience were appalled by the bleak presentation of greed and evil. The production toured the English provinces, Ireland, and Scotland, with the goal of a London opening in the spring of 1958. Reaction to the play was mixed, with very strong feelings for and against it. Probably due to reports of intensely unfavorable audience response, no London theatre was available to the production for its planned opening. An unlikely offer was then made by Roger Stevens of the Producers' Theatre in New York. He had seen the production, by this time renamed *The Visit*, played to a particularly hostile audience in Dublin on February 22, yet he thought the play would be successful in New York. Not only did he offer to bring the production to America, but he also suggested that it reopen the Globe Theatre on 46th street. That theatre, under renovation for conversion back to a theatre after many years as a movie-house, would be renamed the Lunt-Fontanne.

The Lunts and ten other actors from the production travelled with Brook to New York. The other roles were recast and rehearsals were conducted in the roof theatre at the New Amsterdam on 42nd street. Final rehearsals were held in Boston before the out of town opening of *The Visit* on April 9, at the Shubert. The production also played in New Haven before opening the Lunt-Fontanne with a large celebration on May 5, 1958. Because of an earlier booking, the production was forced to leave the theatre after July 5. This gave the Lunts a welcome rest, as Alfred had been hospitalized in June and had missed five performances. The fact that the production carried on with an understudy demonstrated that the play, for once, was as much of a draw as the popular Lunts. *The Visit* reopened August 20 at the Morosco Theatre and had another very successful run until November 29 when again it had to leave the theatre for scheduling reasons.

The production was not seen again until September 19, 1959 when it began a tour sponsored by the Theatre Guild and the American Theatre Society. Alfred Lunt took on directing responsibilities, rehearsing the company with some new members, but it was essentially the same production with all of Brook's blocking maintained. The tour was also successful, despite the difficulty of making money on the road with a serious drama and a large cast. Playing in seventeen cities, including Chicago, Philadelphia, and Los Angeles, the tour lasted six months and concluded with a two-week stand at the City Center in New York. Finally, after its success in America, the production was invited to England, again to open a theatre. *The Visit* opened the Royalty on June 23, 1960. An initial 8-week run was extended to 20 weeks and the production received notices similar to those it received in New York.

Whether people loved or hated *The Visit*, they usually agreed that it was effectively directed. Harsh critics of the play admitted a compelling fascination with the production. Descriptions of the direction featured the words: masterful, impressionistic, magnificent, brilliant, resourceful and eloquent, highly imaginative, and visually spell-binding. Brook was credited with creating a highly charged atmosphere with tension that mounted throughout the play. According to Richard P. Cooke, in the *Wall Street Journal*, the production relied on "much use of shadow and illumination to heighten the emotional effects." Within a somewhat expressionistic framework, Brook focused on realistic details particularly in the relationship between Claire and Anton. The nightmarish aspect of the play was made more haunting because of the convincing detail. Brook's skill in delicately maneuvering a crowd to visually project an emotional atmosphere was often noted. Key moments included Anton's departure by train being blocked by a wall of backs, and the striking of a match to light a cigarette by each person on stage following the strangulation of Anton. "Something of the appalling fascination that seeps through the playhouse is due to director Peter Brook's manipulation of abandoned figures in constantly constricting space," noted Walter Kerr in the May 6 *New York Herald-Tribune*. "The idle, silky, subtly threatening movement of presumably innocent townsfolk as they halt their man's escape by night, the terror of a line of stubborn backs blocking his every turn, the infinitely slow and quiet encircling that ends in a most discreet murder—all are images of insinuating power."

48

July 17, 1958

London: Lyric Theatre

Irma la Douce

Music by Marguerite Monnot
Book and Lyrics by Alexandre Breffort
English book and lyrics by
Julian More, David Heneker and Monty Norman

(1512 performances)

Director . . . . Peter Brook
Settings and costumes . . . . Rolf Gérard
Choreography . . . . John Heawood
Orchestrations . . . . Andre Popp

Vocal arrangements..Bert Waller
Conductor..Sydney Williams
Producers ....Donald Alberry and H. M. Tennent

CAST

Bob-le-Hotu .... *Clive Revill*
Irma-la-Douce .... *Elizabeth Seal*
Man with a Juke Box .... *Howard Short*
Jojo-les-Yeux-Sales .... *David Evans*
Roberto-les-Diams .... *Ronald Barker*
Persil-le-Noir .... *Frank Olegario*
Frangipane .... *Gary Raymond*
Polyte-le-Mou .... *John East*
Nestor-le-Fripe .... *Keith Michell*
Police Inspector .... *Julian Orchard*
M. Bougne .... *William Thorburn*
Counsel for the Prosecution .... *Howard Short*
Council for the Defence .... *Harry Goodier*
Ab Usher .... *Roy Evans*
An Honest Man .... *Roy Desmond*
First Warder .... *Harry Goodier*
Second Warder .... *William Thorburn*
Third Warder .... *Howard Short*
A Priest .... *Roy Evans*
A Tax Inspector .... *Harry Goodier*
A Flic .... *Howard Short*
Another Flic .... *Bill Morgan*

Police, Irma's Admirers, Prisoners

48a

September 29, 1960

New York: Plymouth Theatre
(524 performances)

Director...Peter Brook
Settings and costumes......................................Rolf Gérard
Choreography ....Onna White

Orchestrations..Andre Popp
Vocal arrangements...Bert Waller
Conductor...Sydney Williams
Producer..David Merrick

CAST

Bob-le-Hotu .... *Clive Revill*

Irma-la-Douce .... *Elizabeth Seal*

Man with a Juke Box .... *Eddie Gasper*

Jojo-les-Yeux-Sales .... *Zack Matalon*

Roberto-les-Diams .... *Aric Lavie*

Persil-le-Noir .... *Osborne Smith*

Frangipane .... *Stuart Damon*

Polyte-le-Mou .... *Fred Gwynne*

Nestor-le-Fripe .... *Keith Michell*

Police Inspector .... *George S. Irving*

M. Bougne .... *George Del Monte*

Counsel for the Prosecution .... *Rico Froehlich*

Council for the Defence .... *Rudy Tronto*

An Usher .... *Elliot Gould*

An Honest Man .... *Joe Rocco*

First Warder .... *Elliot Gould*

Second Warder .... *George Del Monte*

Third Warder .... *Rico Froehlich*

A Priest .... *Elliot Gould*

A Tax Inspector .... *Rudy Tronto*

Police, Irma's Admirers, Prisoners

Irma La Douce is almost a fairy-tale, if an adult one. Irma, a prostitute, works in Paris where she meets Nestor, a law student. He soon falls in love with her and becomes jealous of her other clients. In order to "protect" her, he dons a false beard and glasses, pretending to be a rich suitor. When Irma falls in love with Nestor's alter ego, he commits an imaginary crime and kills off the "suitor." He is sentenced to life on Devil's Island, but returns to Montmartre in time to rejoin Irma for Christmas and a happy ending.

Irma La Douce had a very successful Paris run. The London run of *Espresso Bongo*, a play with music set in the seamier side of London's theatre world (Paul Scofield played a cockney talent agent) caused Brook to propose to *Irma's* authors that they naturalize the French musical.

It was a failure in Brighton and a success in Bournemouth before it opened its almost four-year run in London. Those who disliked it found it presented a type of French humor which didn't travel, calling the production "frisky," and Elizabeth Seal "suburban." But most critics praised it and felt that Seal played Irma with "enchanting freshness." *Theatre World Annual* said: "Insofar as the English are ever able to interpret the delicate nuances of French humour and satire, Peter Brook, with an inspired stage presentation, succeeded in his version of *Irma-la-Douce*." Milton Shulman summarized the success of the production, in *The Evening Standard*, saying: "Brook's production is a miracle of shifting colors, blinking lights and animated sets that drip with atmosphere and get more laughs than the lines."

Seal, Clive Revill, and Keith Michell came with Brook to New York, the rest of the cast and the choreographer being American. The show repeated its London success. Critics had a few questions about the basic quality of the material, some finding the songs overly similar and the gags too artificial, but Richard Watts wrote, "*Irma La Douce* is more than a collection of good individual numbers. Its chief virtue as a musical play is that it has taken the materials of cynicism, sentimentality, and sexual preoccupation." All praised the performers and Brook. *Newsday's* George Oppenheimer felt his direction was a triumph over the material, and Whitney Bolton wrote, in *The Morning Telegraph*: "confer the lion's share of the credit on Peter Brook, whose staging is as heady as a fine dry French wine."

1959

49

December 8, 1959

The Fighting Cock
by Jean Anouih
Translated and adapted by Lucienne Hill

New York: ANTA Theatre
(87 performances)

Producer . . . . Kermit Bloomgarden Productions, Inc.
Director . . . . Peter Brook
Sets and Costumes . . . . Rolf Gérard
Lighting . . . . Howard Bay

CAST

The General	*Rex Harrison*
The Doctor	*Geoffrey Lumb*
Toto	*Claude Gersene*
Marie-Christine	*Judy Sanford*
Milkman's Son	*Rhoden Streeter*
Milkman	*Roger De Koven*
Father Gregory	*Michael Gough*
Sophie	*Margo Anders*
Tarquin Edward Mandingales	*Roddy McDowall*
Bise	*Jane Lillig*
Aglae	*Natasha Parry*
Lebelluc	*Arthur Treacher*
Michepain	*Gerald Hiken*
Baron Henri Belazor	*Alan McNaughton*

UNDERSTUDIES:

Aglae, Bise–Elizabeth Hubbard, Milkman–Bill Howe
Sophie, Marie-Christine–Avra Petrides,
Priest, Doctor–Roger De Koven,
Lebelluc, Baron, Michepain–Don Doherty

The Fighting Cock revolves around a retired French general, the youngest to retire after World War II, who became a dubious hero after a series of odd incidents during the war and now, in his restless retreat, plots to get rid of the "maggots" of benefaction, advantage, and opportunism that infest France. For the General, a satirical portrait of Charles De Gaulle, a "maggot" is anyone who would threaten his ideal of restoring the country to its past moral values and glories. He is a fuzzy-minded, bitter eccentric, so involved with his dilemmas as a domestic hero that he is unable to grasp the reality of the changing modern world and to understand the attitudes and actions of his family and friends.

In a short period, he suffers a series of defeats in his personal battle. He learns that the authorities know about his plans but do nothing, considering them harmless. He is brought down by his daughter's fiancé, the son of a plastics millionaire, and by the local milkman, a rude, cruel proletarian. His daughter and friends desert him, and his faithful young wife seems destined to abrade under his inquisitorial attitude. The only two people who remain faithful to him in the end are his small son and his assistant. His only consolation is to chew on the scarce small pieces of red paper which he thinks have the magical power of infusing courage.

Brook's production was fairly well received when it opened on Broadway. There was mixed opinion as to the worth and interpretation of the play itself, but the performances were generally praised, especially that of Rex Harrison as the General; all agreed on the excellence of the sets and costumes, and most saw the staging as a successful, significant achievement of the young British director.

The negative comments objected mostly either to a lack of unity and thematic focus or to the translation. It was argued that the lack of unity, combined with a plot many felt uninteresting in itself, made the production boring, obscure or confusing. Critics John Chapman, of the *Daily News*, Hobe Morrison, of *Variety*, and John McClain, of the *New York Journal-American* blamed the manner in which the play was conceived. Morrison allowed, however, that the comedy could be "fascinating and touching" for a limited audience, and that the production values outshone the play, making the whole worthy of Broadway. For McClain, neither the outstanding cast nor Brook's perceptive direction saved the evening.

Rowland Field, of the *Newark Evening News*, and Thomas Dash, of *Women's Wear Daily*, disliked the translation. Field did call the play "a tedious Gallic fable," but also suggested that its Parisian success was due to the language, considering the "deliberately paced adaptation" reduced pleasure and significance. Dash said that play suffered seasickness crossing the Atlantic and that it "lost whatever spontaneity, fancifulness or irony that intrigued the Parisians."

Other aspects were less bothersome. Morrison thought that Brook's direction gave the production a level of excellence not found in the play, saying:

> Peter Brook's staging is masterful . . . With less than brilliant direction, The Fighting Cock might seem an absurd charade, more in the nature of a high school theatrical than a quality Broadway production. But Brook's staging is inspired, sensitive, and expertly controlled, and the overall performance is a masterpiece of humor and pathos.

In the *New York Times*, Brooks Atkinson, who admired the play, also admired Brook's work with the text. He said that Brook "has woven all its contrasting moods into a pattern of living," and found Harrison's performance a creation superior to his Henry Higgins. McClain thought Brook directed with taste and perception; Robert Coleman, of the *New York Mirror*, said that Brook succeeded in combining "Gallic reason with action; and George Oppenheimer, of *Newsweek*, said that "under the expert direction of Peter Brook, Harrison is comic, touching, and admirable."

Only three critics had negative things to say about Brook. "J. T." of the *Village Voice* thought the play better than the production and called Brook's direction "crisp and uplifting as wet flannel." Both Walter Kerr, then of the *New York Herald-tribune*, and Dash thought that Brook's direction emphasized the flaws of the play. Dash thought Brook had failed in making it "either palpable and comprehensible or sufficiently screwballish," and Kerr said:

> . . . *what the play did not find, at least as Peter Brook has interpreted it, is a center of gravity. Its moods are tangents; its gestures fly through the air without clear aim; there is no solid vantage point from which we can sit and look at the sputtering Roman candles that are always going off just before we have turned our heads in the right direction.*

Still, cogent as this sounds, it must be remembered that it is usually much easier to focus negative criticism into clear phrases, and the majority of critics were pleased. This was not a "director's play," in the sense that the focus was strongly on the actors, but it shows Brook's secure handling of acting and his continuing interest in French theatre.

1960

50

March 19, 1960

Le Balcon
by Jean Genet

Paris: Théâtre de Gymnase
(50 performance limited run)

As a measure of how totally Brook had entered into French cultural consciousness by this time, the day *The Balcony* opened also offered articles on how his film *Moderato Cantabile* was representing France at the Cannes Festival. *The Balcony*, which had previously provoked a cold response from the Lord Chamberlain and which was reportedly particularly close to Brook's heart, was announced in *Le Monde* for presentation at the Théâtre Antoine in the fall of 1958, although it would not be until nearly two years later, in the late spring of 1960, that Genet's *pièce de scandale* would finally resurface for its French premiere. What most astonished *Le Monde's* reporter was that Sir Laurence Olivier, "one of the rare men of theatre, who enjoys a well-established reputation, would fight against winds and tides to impose such a controversial work."

In the 1958 interview, Brook expressed himself "willingly, in impeccable French, with a warmth and dignity worthy of his thirty-three years:"

> *Finally, this time, we've got it. I would never have accepted to put on the Miller [#47, Vu du Pont] if I had to drop the Genet. The two contracts were signed at the same time, and it will take some serious mulling over to produce this dream that's already a year old. God knows people have frequently attempted to dissuade me. "It's not the right time," they said, "to play a work that cannot avoid exciting the very strongest of reactions." Oh well, I expect them, better yet, I look forward to them . . . Scandal doesn't frighten me. If the theatrical caermony is able to unhinge people, to exteriorize their feelings, to see a way to unchain their passions, what more could one wish for?*

When *Le Balcon* finally did open in Paris, it was the scandal of the season. The balcony of the title is a bizarre brothel, a *maison d'illusions*, where one can act out one's wildest fantasies. However, it appears to have been somewhat of a self-conscious scandal, causing the critics to examine not only the work itself, but also the role and value of outrage itself as both a theatrical device and as a means of communication. Ever in a flap, Jean-Jaques Gautier began his *Le Figaro* review: "A frenzied, nightmarish, demented, morbid work," closing this opening string of adjectives with the opinion that it was, in addition, "scandal-seeking." Above all, he wanted to know what it all meant, beyond leaving the audience with "a stunning migraine" and him wondering if all plays were to become cryptograms; Gautier feared "tres serieusement" for the future of the theatre that "sinks into such obscure pretentiousness." Clearly, *Le Balcon* was no *pièce bien fait*, and Gautier, only five months into the 1960s, already foresaw a fragmentation of form, style, and content, and sincerely feared that the theatre of the late twentieth century could become "no more than an abracadabrant monument to the glory of confusion, pathos, false poetry, sexual obsession, a muddying of all its forms and, above all, a total inability of authors to express their thoughts with clarity, whatever they are." In particular, he found the play "just one enormous solemnity, [with] a huge desire to displease, a monotony sufficient to arouse obscenities, a sad indulgence with none of the striking poetic elements of [Genet's] other works."

What troubled B. Poirot-Delpech, in *Le Monde*, was that this long-awaited scandal might forever obscure the real intentions of the author, that due to "a few graphically indecent scenes, the fans of sacrilege and the anti-conformist snobs mechanically calling out 'Genius!'," the entire work might be condemned. He made the shrewd, if quentionable, distinction that "Genet is not looking to shock . . . he is a living scandal;" observing that Brook, who had also designed the play, could not have done better, having yielded to Genet's nightmare and "married his arrogant symbols . . . One senses, in the frenzy that the actors give in return, that they have had the support of a rare intelligence."

A week later, Thomas Quinn Curtiss, commenting on the late arrival of *Le Balcon* in Paris, observed that Brook's "rare intelligence" had, in fact, obscured the thrust of the work. He compared the production to José Quintero's bare, arena-stage version, which had made some cuts, especially in the second half, noting that in New York the work had:

> *. . . an urgency, a directness, a compulsion, a vibrancy, that have alas, disappeared in its Parisian incarnation . . . Genet writes the old Schopenhauerism with an anarchist fury that resembles a display of brilliant fireworks. He captures the imagination at once theatrically and intellectually. He can stimulate the stage and his language compels. It is a shame that Brook has muzzled him in a polite and heavy production . . .* Le Balcon *only occasionally flickers into flame.*

51

May 24, 1960
Cannes Film Festival

Moderato Cantabile

London: October 1960
USA January, 1964

Lena-Documento

Director . . . . Peter Brook
Producer . . . . Raoul J. Levey
Co-Producer . . . . Jacques Companeez
Screenplay . . . . Marguerite Duras
Gerard Jarlot
Peter Brook

(Based on the novel by Ms. Duras)

Photography (Cinemascope) . . . . Armand Thirard
Editor . . . . Albert Jurgenson
Art Director . . . . Jean Andre
Music . . . . Sonata # 4 in B flat, opus 168, Antonio Diabelli

CAST

Ann Desbaredes . . . . *Jeanne Moreau*
Chauvin . . . . *Jean-Paul Belmondo*
Pierre Desbaredes . . . . *Didier Haudepin*
L'Assassin . . . . *Valerie Dobuzinsky*

La Patronne . . . . *Pascale de Boysson*
Mlle. Giraud . . . . *Collete Regis*

Jeanne Moreau plays a wealthy, bored, industrialist's wife. While she is waiting for her son's music lesson to end one day, a woman's scream is heard from a cafe downstairs. Curious about the uproar, she, her son, and the music-teacher run to the window to watch the commotion. As she and her son leave, they see a man, the presumed killer, being taken away from the body of a dead woman. Obsessed by the incident, Mme. Desbarades frequents the cafe, meeting Chauvin, an employee of her husband. They discuss the murder for several days. When he realizes that she has her own death wish, he leaves her.

In some ways, this little-seen film is Brook's most influential, creating or anticipating many of the themes or techniques of the French New Wave—and it should be remembered that it was a French, not British, entry at Cannes. Brook himself said that he was much influenced by Goddard. Because of what he felt was the "documentary" nature of film, he used much improvisation with the actors until he felt they were totally in their characters, and then shot with a deliberately neutral camera, the idea being to find the reality below the incidents.

Whatever the justification, many people had problems with the result, finding it slow and hermetic. *Variety* admired Jeanne Moreau, but felt she could "not quite overcome the literary quality of the dialogue." Brook's neutral camera produced the response of: "Slowness of direction really drags out the story rather than revealing much visually." When it was shown at the London Film Festival that fall, *The Times* found it a "well-meaning failure," a "textbook example of how not to" adapt a novel. The *Guardian* said:

> . . . *It is a film about emotions rather than events—the emotions of people who fell in love, discussed their predicament, and parted unfullfilled.*
>
> *Quite apart from the unsolved mystery—unsolved, that is, except by anyone but the remarkable Bresson—of putting so inward a conflict into moving pictures, there is something very phony about the conflict itself. We do not share the high-pitched misery of Jeanne Moreau and Jean-Paul Belmondo because we reject them as people.*

In the *Observer*, Penelope Gilliatt got much closer to what Brook was trying to do, but she also had to make the same point as the *Guardian's* reviewer:

> *This is a film of great technical fascination, shot and cut with a staring composure, and using a narrative technique that is much closer to TV reportage than to the planted hints and flashbacks of cinema; but since the film is totally concentrated upon the relationship between the two people, it matters disastrously that the relationship is never felt.*

Moreau won the Best Actress award at the 1960 Cannes Film Festival and, because of its unusual aesthetics, the film was considered one of the most controversial that year. That did not help its reception commercially, and it took more than three years to be released in the United States.

When it did finally open, Bosley Crowther, in the *New York Times*, found that Brook had:

> *fashioned a slowly ambulating succession of wistful images that have the emotional content of a haunting sonata or a poem. After that startling scene of frenzy, which is filled with superb expectancy, the picture drifts off into a ramble through an uncertain maze of murky moods.*

In summing up, he wrote: "There is little dramatic resolution in this film, little psychological clarification, little action, little plot. It is just a very visual, very sensitive elaboration on a mood." He found it "baffling." Many continue to do so, but it remains a very interesting experiment.

48a

September 29, 1960

Irma la Douce

New York: Plymouth Theatre
(524 performances)

1961

1962

52

November 6, 1962

King Lear
by William Shakespeare

Stratford-upon-Avon: Memorial Theatre

Transferred to London: Aldwych
December 12, 1962
(72 performances)

Director, Designer...Peter Brook
Costumes in collaboration with ....Kegan Smith
Assistant Designer ....Adele Hankey
Assistant Director.......................................Charles Marowitz
Fight arranged by..John Barton
Wind Band Leader.......................................Alec Whittaker
Music Director...Brian Priestman
London Music Director ....David Taylor

CAST

Earl of Kent	*Tom Fleming*
Earl of Gloucester	*Alan Webb*
Edmund	*James Booth*
Lear	*Paul Scofield*
Goneril	*Irene Worth*
Duke of Albany	*Peter Jeffrey*
Regan	*Patience Collier*
Duke of Cornwall	*Tony Church*
Cordelia	*Diana Rigg*
Duke of Burgundy	*Tony Steedman*
King of France	*Hugh Sullivan*
Edgar	*Brian Murray*
Oswald	*Clive Swift*
Knight attending on Lear	*Michael Murray*
Fool	*Alec McCowan*
Curan	*Philip Brack*
Servant to Cornwall	*Edmond Bennett*
An Old Man	*Michael Burrell*
Doctor	*Gareth Morgan*
Messenger to Cordelia	*Peter Geddis*
Captain to Edmund	*Ian Cullen*
Herald	*John Corvin*
First British Captain	*Ian Hewitson*
Second British Captain	*Gordon Honeycombe*

Knights, Soldiers, Servants
Michael Burrell, John Corvin, Ian Cullan, Peter Geddis,
Paul Greenhalgh, Ian Hewitson, Gordon Honeycombe,
Martin Jenkins, Ian Lindsay

MUSICIANS
Anthony Chidell, Gilbert Cobbett, Derek Oldfield,
David Richards, Norman Wallis

European Tour
Starting May 18, 1963
Paris:Theatre des Nations
Continuing to
West Berlin, Prague, Budapest, Belgrade, Bucharest,
Warsaw, Helsinki, Leningrad, Moscow

52a

May 18, 1964

New York: New York State Theatre, Lincoln Center

CAST Changes for New York

Gloucester	*John Laurie*
Edmund	*Ian Richardson*
Albany	*Clifford Rose*
Regan	*Pauline Jameson*
Burgundy	*Michael Murray*
France	*Barry MacGregor*
Oswald	*Michael Williams*

Peter Brook's visionary production of *King Lear* marked a dramatic turning-point in the interpretation and production of one of Shakespeare's greatest plays. Brook eschewed a traditional approach, with its preponderance of emotion and its characters stereotyped by time and past productions, and relied instead upon intellectual concepts. The result, however, was not symbol or allegory, but living mortals, each with a viable point of view and justification for his actions. This was a performance for our era; a harsh, brutally unsentimental *King Lear*, set in a dismal and industrialized, abstract world, and it was immediately identified with Brecht and Beckett. It was one of Brook's most influential productions, related in its visual simplicity, to his famous *A Midsummer Night's Dream*, and in its concern with madness, both personal and existential, with *Marat/Sade*. It played a big part in making people see *Lear* less as some type of music-less opera, with mad scenes for basso, than as a window into the particular horrors of our times.

Paul Scofield's Lear was not a heaven-annointed monarch, but a ruthless, self-made, warrior-king, a man of flesh and blood, complete with very human failings. His elder daughters were no longer fiends, and were not unjustified in their treatment of a gruff, crass father. Oswald was a loyal servant and Kent a bullying thug. Discussing Brook's novel approach to the characters, Kenneth Tynan wrote: "He has taught the 'unsympathetic' characters to project themselves from their own point of view, not from that of the inevitably jaundiced hero." Even Cordelia changed, becoming an impetuous young maiden full of pride. By creating these changes, Brook was able to evoke a tragedy not solely focused on the title character, one which extended to the other characters, into the audience and mankind itself. Critics felt that Brook, like no other director before him, had realized the universality of pathos inherent in the play.

He supplemented this universality of feeling by using a vague and timeless set, intended to dispel theatrical illusion. The set was dehumanized, flat gray panels adorned by ambiguous slabs of copper sheet-metal. Props were few and deliberately primitive. The storm scenes were played down, as actors stumbled and staggered on the stage to the accompaniment of rumbling sheets of metal. The lighting was a continuous, harsh flat white throughout, hiding nothing. It added up to an austere expressionism, reminiscent of absurdism, designed to bring the human tragedy to the fore.

The critics universally agreed on the scope of Brook's production. And although some felt a four-hour production could have been shortened, the majority proclaimed it a smashing success. Even those who didn't find it to their liking acknowledged the power and importance of the interpretation. Discussing the demythification of Lear, Alan Brien wrote in *Theatre Arts:* "Almost alone among my critical colleagues I regretted Brook's ruthless clipping of the eagle. And Yet I had to agree that the loss of the elemental Lear was more than balanced by the discovery of Lear, the man of flesh and blood."

This was not, however, a production to be liked or disliked. Brook, in bringing his daring vision to the stage, forced his audience to look at their preconceptions about the play and the philosophical questions at its core. As Howard Taubman put it: "But I find Mr. Brook's approach enormously stimulating and provocative. In its very simplicity and baldness it forces one to reexamine the play and rethink one's ideas."

In the *Sunday Times*, Harold Hobson especially noted how Brook's *Lear* seemed to apply to the audience more personally than the play had before. He pointed out that it was traditionaly produced in a very grand manner, and said of that:

> . . . It is so much outside the range of normal experience that it soon becomes a bore. This is what Mr. Brook had avoided. It is essential to his purpose the his Lear shoud be rooted in the ordinary, everyday life of all of us.
>
> Before the first word is spoken he makes this clear by an invention which is as simple as it is felicitous. The stage is empty but for a side table. One by one Kent, Gloucester and Edmund enter, go to the side table, and provide themselves with gloves and other minor accoutremonts. It is just like a house-party . . . The only difference here is that the guests do

not depart, but stay, and Lear enters; and the business at hand . . . proves to be the division of a kingdom.

Mr. Brook makes us realise, as we rarely do in this play, that apocalyptic punishment is not reserved for giants of spiritual iniquity and magnificence . . .

On the one hand it was "realism," but is was realism as seen in the light of Samuel Beckett. Brook made no attempt to hide the influence. Charles Marowitz, who worked as Brook's assistant, wrote an article about the experience for the *Observer*. In it, he related, as if they were a fable, the strange events of the scene in which the blinded Gloucester thinks he throws himself off the cliffs at Dover. He then continues:

This plot from Lear *is like something out of the plays of Samuel Beckett. The scene is a farce that ridicules life, death, sanity and illusion, it has been the key scene in Brook's production of* King Lear, *and its tone and implications have conditioned all the scenes with which it connects.*

In discussing rehearsals, our frame of reference was always Beckettian . . .

It is not so much Shakespeare in the style of Beckett as it is Beckett in the style of Shakespeare, for Brook feels that the clue for Beckett's bleakness was given by the merciless King Lear.

Kenneth Tynan saw this too, tracing it from Jan Kott's well-known essay comparing *Lear* to *Endgame*:

. . . At times the measurements fail to tally; there is nothing remotely Beckettian, for example, in the Edmund-Regan-Goneril triangle or the battle scenes. But where the concept fits, as it mostly does, the production burns itself into your mind.

There are dangers here, of course, pointed out clearly in Pauline Kael's review of Brook's film version of *Lear*, released in 1971, but done on the same principles, in which she said:

. . . If, as Jan Kott suggested, Endgame *came out of* Lear, *what purpose does it then serve to base one's* Lear *on Beckett? Doesn't that merely reduce* Lear *to the elements Beckett transformed and made his own, and thus turn Shakespeare into imitation Beckett?*

Certainly others at the time had similar quibles, but the general feeling was of admiration.

Marowitz explained the ways this was achieved visually:

. . . The world of this Lear, like Beckett's is in a constant state of decomposition. The set-pieces consist of geometrical sheets of metal that are ginger with rust and corrosion. The costumes, dominantly leather, have been textured to suggest long and hard wear. The knight's tabards are peeling with long use; Lear's cape and coat are creased and blackened with time and weather. The furniture is rough wood, once sturdy but now decaying back into its hard, brown grain. Apart from the rust, the leather and the old wood, there is nothing but space— giant white flats opening onto a blank cyclorama.

Even within this austerity, though, there was a luxuriance of allusion and a willingness to borrow from many schools of theatrical thought. Bamber Gascoigne pointed this out in the *Spectator*:

> *. . . The effect so far is Brechtian, and it remains so in several scenes throughout the production. Yet the production is by no means doctrinaire. Other styles come in where they suit. The big court scenes seem nearer to a French classical production of Racine, with stark formal groupings held rigidly during a speech. Or again, the storm scene stems from the East. Peter Brook lowers three rectangular sheets of metal which tremble in the air while the actors on the empty stage beneath mime their battle with the wind and rain. The precise origins of these various styles may be different—but they do not clash. They are linked by their common attitude to drama—stylised, elegant, intellectual.*

Again though, most felt that all this did not eliminate the humanity. Gascoigne later said: "From the very first scenes this is a play about violent people, not just a poetic fable." And Hobson ended by pointing out: "This *Lear* is for everybody. And unless mankind changes its course (which it shows no sign of doing), what happens in it will happen to everybody."

1963

Xd

January 7, 1963

The Hollow Crown
by John Barton

Washington, DC: National Theatre
Boston: Wilbur Theatre
New York: Henry Miller Theatre

ACTORS
Dorothy Tutin, Max Adrian, Paul Hardwick, John Barton

SINGERS
Richard Golding, John Lawrence, Stephen Martin,

James Walker, Harpsichord,
Brian Priestman, Musical Director

The Hollow Crown, John Barton's compilation of material on over a thousand years of English monarchs, was a surprise smash hit of the London 1961 season and has been frequently revived. Avoiding Shakespeare—except for opening with *Richard II's* "For God's sake let us sit upon the ground/And tell sad stories of the death of Kings."—it discovered a surprising range of emotion, humor and music in various letters, chronicles, poems, diaries, journals and formal histories both about and by various Kings and Queens from the Saxons to Victoria.

This first American tour, successful as it was, cannot be numbered with Brook's others in the chronology, as his input seems to have been merely actor-coaching within those ideas framed by others in the original production; in fact, the programs do not even list a director or give Brook's name except as one of the triumvirate then in charge of the RSC. Of all reviews that could be found, only Henry Hewes, in *The Saturday Review*, even mentions him: "Under Peter Brook's direction, the small cast of actors and singers sits around with notebooks successfully pretending to enjoy each other's delivery more than they do their own."

53

January 9, 1963

The Physicists

by Friedrich Dürrenmatt
Translated by James Kirkup

London: Aldwych Theatre
The Royal Shakespeare Company
(68 performances)

Director . . . . Peter Brook
Designed by . . . . John Bury
Assistant Director . . . . Robert David MacDonald
London Music Director . . . . David Taylor

CAST

Inspector Richard Voss . . . . *Clive Swift*
Matron Marta Boll . . . . *Doris Hare*
Blocher . . . . *Edmond Bennett*
Guhl . . . . *John Corvin*
Police Doctor . . . . *Gordon Honeycombe*
Policemen . . . . *Peter Geddis*
Ian McCulloch
Herbert Georg Beutler . . . . *Michael Hordern*
Doktor Mathilde Von Zahnd . . . . *Irene Worth*

Ernst Heinrich Ernesti .... *Alan Webb*

Frau Lina Rose .... *Patience Collier*

Oskar Rose .... *Michael Burrell*

Adolf-Friedrich .... *Paul Greenhalgh*

Wilfried-Kaspar .... *Ian Lindsay*

Jörg-Lukas .... *Pip Rolls*

Johann Wilhelm Möbius .... *Cyril Cusack*

Nurse Monika Stettler .... *Diana Rigg*

Uwe Sievers .... *Tony Steedman*

McArthur .... *Kenneth Gardnier*

Murillo .... *Jonathan Holden*

53a

October 13, 1964

New York: Martin Beck Theatre

CAST

Inspector Richard Voss .... *Roberts Blossom*

Matron Marta Boll .... *Doris Rich*

Blocher .... *Jack Woods*

Guhl .... *Frank Daly*

Police Doctor .... *Alex Reed*

Herbert Georg Beutler .... *Hume Cronyn*

Doktor Mathilde Von Zahnd .... *Jessica Tandy*

Ernst Heinrich Ernesti .... *George Voskovec*

Frau Lina Rose .... *Frances Heflin*

Oskar Rose .... *David Ford*

Adolf-Friedrich .... *Terry Culkin*

Wilfried-Kaspar .... *Leland Mayforth*

Jörg-Lukas .... *Doug Chapin*

Johann Wilhelm Möbius .... *Robert Shaw*

Nurse Monika Stettler .... *Elizabeth Hubbard*

Uwe Sievers .... *Rod Colbin*

McArthur .... *John Perkins*

Murillo .... *Leonard Parker*

Dürrenmatt's fable, on the surface a combination of murder-mystery and spy-story, concerns three madmen in an asylum, one of whom has evidently murdered a nurse. By the middle of the play, we discover first that they are three nuclear scientists and then that they are not really mad. One of them has discovered a secret which promises such complete destruction that he is pretending madness to avoid revealing it to the world. By the end of the play that charade is useless, for the secret has been discovered by the genuinely mad, but powerful, hunchbacked lady psychiatrist in charge of the asylum. It seems nothing is enough to save the world from evil knowledge.

As befitted a new work on such themes by a major writer, most of the space in the reviews was taken up with a discussion of the issues and merits of the writing, but Brook got his share of praise for a production that matched the suspense. Some critics felt that Dürrenmatt was calling up interesting themes more than he was successfully working them to a clear conclusion, but all admired the moment-to-moment tension. As Kenneth Tynan put it in the *Observer*: "Eagerly abetted by Mr. Brook, Dürrenmatt plays on our nerves, and through them our brains, using the techniques of detective fiction to convey an apocalyptic message: the effect is that of a Hitchcock turned political." Harold Hobson, in the *Sunday Times*, noted: ". . . the jokes were so good, the turns of plot so unexpected, the acting so accomplished, and Mr. Brook's direction so stunningly clever that I quickly . . . surrendered myself to unalloyed enjoyment." *Plays and Players* found it: ". . . a theatrical entertainment, no more and no less, lightweight and very cunningly put together as an essay in intellectual *grand guignol*. Peter Brook's production takes it as such—and it is swift, witty and timed with razor sharpness."

Both Tynan and Hobson noted a resemblance to a play done very early in Brook's career. As Tynan said:

> . . . Mr. Brook's direction, icily flawless, will surprise no one who remembers his similar production, 17 years ago, of another play about three guilty people condemned to perpetual imprisonment—Sartre's Huis Clos. Under pressure from the Lunts, he softened Dürrenmatt's The Visit, but the hard edges of The Physicists are intact and unmelted.

The New York response was similar to London; the same enjoyment of the suspense elements and the same admiration of Brook's ability to bring out the entertainment. True, Walter Kerr in the *Herald Tribune* said of the play itself that: "the hard core of the playwright's thought is just about complex enough to occupy twelve minutes of playing time." Watts in the *Post* found it:" . . . flawed in its story-telling. The ideas and the perversity keep getting in the way." Nevertheless, in the *Daily News*, John Chapman called it: "the most stimulating play we have had this season." Kerr opened his review:

> In the second half of The Physicists, three male nurses are asked to stand guard in a lunatic asylum and the first thing they do is to hurl dinner dishes and chairs in high

arcs across the stage, catching them without fail and without finger damge. Dramatist Friedrich Dürrenmatt is no less skillful than they at manipulating grotesque and outside theatrical effects, and in director Peter Brook he is served by a man who knows how to manage gun duels, dead bodies, overturned spotlights and menacing shutters that close without warning.

In the *New York Times*, Howard Taubman noted that moment, but said: "It wins a big hand, but it is extraneous to the playwright's argument." Even Taubman admitted, however, though he felt that early in the play Brook was filling "in the gaps with theatrical externals," that: "When the three mad scientists reveal themselves and their real interests in the second half, *The Physicists* takes on high excitment," and that: "Mr. Brook makes the most of the material."

Xe

April 2, 1963

The Tempest

by William Shakespeare

Stratford-upon-Avon: The Shakespeare Memorial Theatre

Director . . . . Clifford Williams
"Collaborating Director" . . . . Peter Brook
Scenery . . . . Abd'elkader Farrah

CAST

Prospero . . . . *Tom Fleming*
Ariel . . . . *Ian Holm*
Caliban . . . . *Roy Dotrice*
Sebastian . . . . *Donald Sinden*
Stephano . . . . *Derek Smith*
Trinculo . . . . *David Warner*
Ferdinand . . . . *Ian McCulloch*
Miranda . . . . *Philippa Urquhart*
Antonio . . . . *Nicholas Selby*
Alonzo . . . . *John Welsh*
Gonzalo . . . . *Ken Wynne*

It is hard to tell how much of this production was Peter Brook's, since he was only listed as "collaborating director" with the top-billed Clifford Williams. Certainly there were great similarities with the 1957 version, including the use of *musique concrète* and a general, deliberate, plainness, extending here even to the diminution of the masque. Philip Hope-Wallace in the *Guardian* found it: "an astonishingly original piece of work—the enchantments of the island are those of abstract art and musique concrète . . . "

The only moment of visual lavishness seems to have been in the opening. According to the *Times:*

> The production is at its most imaginative in the opening scene, which brings the shipwreck to the margin of Prospero's cell, a translucent structure with a lurid sun peering through Miró-like designs on the walls. When Prospero casts his spell, jagged doorways crack open with a sound like splitting toffee, and the mariners are drawn in on a conveyor belt under the piercing gaze of the magician.

After this opening, John Percival in *Plays and Players* found the island to be: "a bare place, rounded only by Abd 'Elkader Farrah's magical screen which, tranlucent or opaque at will, can be sky or rock, opening up with the entrances to threatening caves or closing with clouds and mysterious suns."

There seems to have been a deliberate avoidance of "poetry." J. W. Lambert, in the *Sunday Times*, felt this went too far:

> The word "Brechtian," like the word "democracy," bears a thousand different meanings. It could be applied, though, to this production in the sense that the didactic and ideological element of each scene is heavily stressed. I shouldn't have been at all surprised to see placards lowered from the flies telling us the moral of each scene.

The Times, too, felt that it "rarely rises above the mundane," but Hope-Wallace appreciated the avoidance of "meaningless romantic gush." And even Lambert had to say: "I must add that unlike many a *Tempest* I have seen, this one is never for an instant dull; and that, for this great play, is no faint praise."

54

June 12, 1963

The Perils of Scobie Prilt

by Julian More and Monty Norman

Oxford: The New Theatre

This is the most obscure of Brook's later British productions—apparently with good reason. Trewin reports:

. . . under the James Bond influence, it opened among chaos at the New Theatre, Oxford, during the second week of June, 1963: the sets were so big and so full of technical compli- cations, that the original date, a Tuesday, had to be abandoned, and the play opened on the following evening for what proved to be a four days' life. It was a medly of science fiction and secret agents: something about a young scientist (the "pop" singer, Michael Sarne) who had discovered a method of turning people into robots. While he was on the way to a Middle-European country with his large black box, a female spy (Nyree Dawn Porter) blew up his train; the musical went on from there. This chaotic business have everything in it between a rocket-launching and a film show; but in spite of Rolf Gérard's designs and Brook's gallantly inventive production—no longer the classical explorer, but for the last time the young man happy among his toys—nothing went right. Miss Porter played on only one night before a spinal accident obliged her to go into hospital in London; an understudy, book in hand, took over the part at three hours' notice. On the second night another leading member of the cast pulled a cartilage in his leg and had to limp through to the end of the play. After the Saturday night Scobie Prilt *was withdrawn.*

55

August 20, 1963

New York

Lord of the Flies

Continental

Director . . . . Peter Brook
Producer . . . . Lewis Allen
Associate Producer . . . . Gerald Feil
Executive Producer . . . . Al Hine
An Allen-Hodgdon Production
From the Novel by . . . . William Golding
Music . . . . Raymond Leppard
Photography . . . . Tom Hollyman
Editing . . . . Peter Brook
Gerald Feil
Jean-Claude Lubtchansky

CAST

Ralph . . . . *James Aubrey*
Jack . . . . *Tom Chapin*
Piggy . . . . *Hugh Edwards*
Roger . . . . *Roger Elwin*

Simon . . . . *Tom Gaman*

Sam and Eric . . . . *The Surtees Twins*

and

Roger Allen, David Brunjes, Peter Davy, Kent Fletcher
Nicholas Hammond, Christopher Harris, Alan Heaps
Jonathan Heaps, Burnes Hollyman, Andrew Horne
Richard Horne, Timothy Horne, Peter Ksiezopolski
Anthony McCall-Hudson, Malcom Rodker, David St. Clair,
Rene Sanfiorenzo, Jr., Jeremy Scuse, John Stableford
Nicholas Valkenburg, Patrick Valenburg, Edward Valencia
John Walsh, David Walsh, Jeremy Willis

Goldings's novel tells the story of privileged British schoolboys who are being evacuated from London to the South Pacific as a war is brewing at home. En route, their plane crashes. None of the adults survive. The surviving children organize, hoping to be rescued.

A society develops, with Ralph as group leader. Piggy's spectacles are used to make a bonfire, which can be used both to cook and make a signal. Jack, the choir leader, leads the more adventurous boys on a boar hunt.

Gradually two groups emerge. The hunters dress like Indians and paint their faces. They dance wildly, chant, and create rituals. Soon, they begin to intimidate the others.

Hearing sounds, they are afraid of a beast on top of the mountain. When Simon discovers the supposed beast is in fact their former pilot who died in an attempt to parachute to safety, they do not believe him and he is killed. Piggy is also murdered. Finally, Ralph is chased across the island, with the intention of slaughtering him as a sacrifice to the "beast" god.

Fortunately, he runs into a group of rescuing adults. The children revert to their former selves.

Lord of the Files dramatically illustrates Golding's book in a film format. Screen versions were originally written for Sam Spiegal—who dropped his option—by Brook and Peter Shaffer. Unable to come up with a screenplay that satisfied him, Brook decided to go ahead without a script, simply by taking cues directly from the novel. He tried to work chronologically as much as possible, so the child actors would realize what they were doing while being prepared emotionally for the next step. A psychodrama developed, even though it soon became evident that the film equipment was too cumbersome to be moved continually.

The forty preteen school boys were primarily chosen from the children of British diplomats and businessmen living in the United States. Hugh Edwards, who played Piggy, was the only one flown in from England; he had sent a picture to apply for the part. The rest were discovered by Brook and his assistants, while standing in front of the United Nations or the British Embassy. Casting was based on disposition and physical characteristics. None of them had ever acted before.

Brook also hired people who had never before professionally done the job for which they were hired. According to Professor Edwin Wilson, then Brook's assistant on the project, this ensured freshness and allowed Brook to remain in control.

For instance, Tom Hollyman had been a still photographer; this was his first movie. Jerry Feil, the second photographer, had previously made documentaries; he continued to work for Brook after the film was completed. Even the business manager was a writer.

In order to create the conditions the boys would have lived under and to encourage their instinct for survival to develop readily, Brook set up camp for the crew in secluded sections of Puerto Rico and the beaches on Vieques, a Naval Training Area. The boys lived in "Fliesville," an old pineapple factory. They tanned naturally and created their own face paint from native materials intended to shield them from the hot sun. Two sets of clothing were used—one new and one torn. All filming was done during their three-month summer vacation.

Editing was done in Paris for three months after shooting. Originally, Brook wanted no music, only the natural sounds, but the producers insisted there was too much confusion after the first cut. A commercial editor was hired to finish the job. Music and a montage of pictures were added at this time, setting a religious tone, and gaps were filled in. Nevertheless, all major artistic decisions went back to Brook. The story's austerity is emphasized by black-and-white photography.

Despite some opinion that *Lord of the Flies* would be a successful cult film, the haunting documentary quality that Brook introduced through the raw power of rough edges was controversial. It certainly did not attract pre-teenagers to the box-office.

Bosley Crowther, in the *New York Times*, praised the novel as an extraordinarily agitating fable, replete "with awsome intimations of the basic ferocity of the human beast as well as some wonderfully gripping and touching dramatic incidents," but felt Brook's treatment was a "curiously flat and fragmentary visualization of the original." In his view, "It is loosely and jerkily constructed, in its first and middle phases, at least, and it has a strangely perfunctory, almost listless flow of narrative in most of its scenes."

He found the acting "woefully uneven." Excepting two or three "fair performances," he said the overall effect was of "spirited amateurs." Others might say Brook achieved his aim: to create a natural, spontaneous, and unrehearsed explosion of pent-up emotions.

"The youngsters are too often perfunctory or unsure," Crowther said, inhibiting spontaneity in the beginning. He did think James Aubrey was a fairly consistent authority figure, and Hugh Edwards maintained "a solemn, insistent, courageous, and droll attitude." He found Tom Chapin's performance inconsistent, with "a temper of manufactured arrogance" in the beginning, "until he bursts loose in his frightening descent to savagery when the aimless pieces of the picture are finally brought together and set afire." In his analysis, Roger Elwin and Tom Gaman, "two lads who should expose tormenting tensions in the ordeal, are nondescript."

Further, Crowther felt the children did not develop sharp anxiety and, as a result, "a sense of symbolic significance in their spiritual degeneration does not jell." He did find "bits and moments of clarification, such as a poignant scene in which Ralph shouts in sickening frustration at a heedless plane overhead," or another in which a lad can't remember his home address. Mainly, he says, "it is only when the drama reaches the melodramatic point of throwing a large group of the youngsters into savage ritualism and ecstasies that the meaning and horror of it come to brief clarity and the terror of their turning on their old friends is momentarily caught.

56

October 10, 1963

La Danse de Sergent Musgrave
(Sergeant Musgrave's Dance)
by John Arden
Translated by Maurice Pons

Paris: Théâtre de l'Athenée

Mise-en-scène . . . . Peter Brook
Assisted by . . . . Florence Malraux
Jean Laroquette
Decors et costumes . . . . Peter Brook
Assisted by . . . . Adele Hankey

CAST

Sparky . . . . *Jean-Baptiste Thiérrée*
Hurst . . . . *Pierre Tabard*

Attercliffe . . . . *Toni Taffin*
Le Marinier . . . . *François Darbon*
Le Sergent Musgrave . . . . *Laurent Terzieff*
Le Pastuer . . . . *Pierre Le Rumeur*
Mrs. Hitchcock . . . . *Yvette Etiévant*
Annie . . . . *Laurence Bourdil*
L'Officier . . . . *Etienne Dirand*
Le Maire . . . . *Jean Michaux*
Premiere Mineur . . . . *Jean-Luc Bideau*
Deuxième Mineur . . . . *Pierre Decazes*
Troisième Mineur–Walsh . . . . *Gérard Lorin*
Autres Mineurs . . . . *Stéphane Ariel*
                                                                      William Wissmer
Un officier de Dragons . . . . *Jean Larroquette*

By 1963, some three-and-a-half years after *Le Balcon*, and seven years after *Le Figaro* first introduced "Peter Brook, one of the greatest English directors, and probably the one in greatest demand at the present time," the British *enfant terrible* and his successive scandals had clearly been embraced by the Parisian theatre-arts cognoscenti; after a total of only three productions, *Le Monde* dryly welcomed Brook back to the fold for the upcoming season, like a much-missed black sheep: "For his return to Paris, Peter Brook has chosen to present us this Thursday a play by John Arden. This *Sergeant Musgrave's Dance* was directed in 1958 by George Devine at the Royal Court without causing much of a sensation." Even *Le Figaro's* oft-apoplectic Gautier managed to review this tale of four deserters from the colonial British army, who prepare a parody of a recruitment drive while stranded in the middle of a minefield, without even one first-person exclamation mark. Nonetheless, he was no more impressed with this work than he had been with any of the previous plays chosen by Brook for Paris:

> *"Living Theatre," they say. Well, too bad. I am resolutely allergic to this form of life and to this kind of theatre. Never will I become accustomed to boredom, to such pacifico-poetico-politico-religious phraseology.*

Gautier went on to suggest that the play seemed to have been written under the influence of drugs, though it might, nevertheless, accurately reflect the taste of its age, a taste that encouraged works that were "distressing, dismal, and dreary."

Gautier's responses to the four diverse works directed by Brook in Paris between 1956 and 1963 indicate to what a degree Brook was at the head of the avant-garde main-stream; they represent one long cry of outrage at a world of theatre that he perceives to be going utterly insane, a catechism of retrenchment in the face of changing world of postwar theatre seemingly gone mad. Brook's *Sergeant Musgrave's Dance* elicited what amounts to the critic's personal theatre credo, ironically, it is one that could equally have been written, word for word, by Brook: "For me, the theatre was, is, and will remain, a celebration, a ceremony, a thing of beauty, a noble enterprise, a means of refreshment, an entertainment, an order and a music, a joy." Gautier continued more specifically with a criticism that would be raised more than once in regard to Brook's work in ensuing years: "I cannot take pleasure or find happiness in a display that does not arouse the least emotion in me." Apparently, the inverse was closer to the truth, that he could not take the emotion in a display that did not arouse the least pleasure or happiness in him. Finally, his particular frustrations with the work seem more pertinent to the increasingly fragmented, desolate, unanchored, postwar existence that the play attempts to reflect, than the play itself:

> *I look for the story. It doesn't hold together. I seek characters. These are just dealt out, puppets, hypotheses. I seek harmony. I find nothing but ugliness and horror. I seek relaxation where there is only contraction. I seek a world, a universe, a place. I find nothing but extremes in which no-one has attempted to make a marriage likely.*

The following day, *Le Monde's* Poirot-Delpech began his astute review with what seems to be a direct response to his colleague's apparent distress. With all the sagacity and patience of a loving older brother, he explained:

> *The word "dance" may be taken as a literary metaphor . . . as an expression of pure movement, some choreographic ellipse of the genre: a square dance in red and black . . . Thus it's a question of sensing insane impulses, not of reasoning with them; the public experiences the show for what it is, after all, a completely new and fascinating attempt at tragedie-ballet instead of searching in vain for a coherent epic . . . [At first,] everything seems arranged to make us expect a standard parable . . . a delirious fairground ambiance on a silent slag-heap background; everything seems ready for the most orthodox of Brechtian parades . . . we wait for the epilogue to shed some light on these gloomy demonstrations, [yet] it's on an elusive counting rhyme that the curtain falls. Despite appearances, this is the very opposite of Brechtian clarity and didacticism . . .*
>
> *The action and the characters remain even more blurred and defy all conclusion . . . an infernal ballet . . . a mad cry against a mad war. How could one resist the bewitching charm of such a muddle and such disorientation? How could one not passionately seek out the signs and sources of so long-awaited a theatrical renewal amidst the dizzying liberty of this universe? How to resist being won over by the illogical beauties of this stage, more frightening, with its nightmarish symbols, than a real evening of battle?*
>
> *How could one avoid dreaming, faced with these puppets, troubled exactly like the unmotivated, indefinable incarnations of our instincts? How could one not be overwhelmed, throughout Maurice Pons' inevitably simplified adaptation, by the way which Peter Brook knew to preserve the ambiguity of the original text, amd to hire intelligent actors, to the point that one sometimes hears an unknown language.*
>
> *. . . by the repulsion itself that it inspires physically and intellectually, this vision of hell comes closer than any translation; as if the theatrical miracle had abolished most profoundly all the barriers of language and atavism.*

What is most astonishing about this text is that it not only reveals how far Peter Brook had forged ahead in his own research and development in a scant seven years, from his praising of the French theatre-going public in 1956 for its acknowledgment of the primacy of the text in theatre, to the "theatrical miracle," identified by Poirot-Delpech in 1963, but that Brook's realization, Arden's writing, and Poirot-Delpech, in his shrewd analytical perception, were some twenty years ahead of their time, for it was not until the early 1980s that French critics began to view performance in deconstructionist terms.

Xf

December 10, 1963

Le Vicaire

(The Deputy)
by Rolf Hochhuth
French translation by Jorge Semprun

Paris: Théâtre Athénée

Co-Directors . . . . Peter Brook
François Darbon

CAST (partial)

Fontanna . . . . *Antione Bourseiller*
Gerstein . . . . *Michel Piccoli*
Pope Pius XII . . . . *Alain Mottet*
and
Jean Michaux, Pierre Tabard, Jean Todart

As with *The Tempest* (production Xe), it is difficult to tell exactly what Brook's contributions were in a co-directed production. What *is* clear is that *Le Vicaire* shows his concern for politically involved Theatre, and that it brought to a climax the various potentials for scandal that Brook's other Paris productions had promised. The play is an attack on Pope Pius XII for being indifferent to the destruction of the Jews during World War II, and, as such, had a troubled history in most cities where it was performed. Here, it provoked audience demonstrations—encouraged by Maurice Cardinal

Peltin, Archbishop of Paris—to the point where *Le Figaro* gave a daily listing of how many audience interruptions happened the night before, and just when they occurred, minute by minute.

It was, of course, a huge hit. The reviews concentrated on the plot and the political/religious implications, but were still impressed with the direction. *Le Monde* found the two had avoided mistakes that were made in Berlin and London, giving the whole: "a uniform tone of neutral, icy, Cartesian demonstration. And *Le Figaro* ended its review by saying: "I can do no more than say a few words on the marvelous work of Peter Brook and François Darbon, who have refined the mise en scene, the scenic elements and the costumes to a magisterially suggestive synthesis."

1964

57

January, 1964

The Theatre of Cruelty

London: LAMDA Theatre Club

In the fall of 1963, The Royal Shakespeare Company agreed to subsidize an experimental program based on the then highly unconventional theories of Antonin Artaud. The program was initiated by Brook and Charles Marowitz. Its purpose was to prepare a small group of actors to perform Genet's play, *The Screens*. Brook and Marowitz were given a small church-hall behind the Royal Court Theatre in Sloane Square for the workshop.

Auditions for the experimental workshop lasted for several weeks. Actors were asked to do various improvisations which demonstrated their abilities to transform character or situation at a moment's notice. According to Charles Marowitz, in the *Tulane Drama Review*, they were looking for a group of actors "who were open, adaptable, and ready to rush in where rigid pros fear to tread." Approximately fifty actors auditioned, but only twelve were chosen. Among them were Glenda Jackson, Robert Langdon Lloyd, Alexis Kanner, Leon Kissek, Jonathan Burn, John Steiner, and Susan Williamson. The average age was 24.

The workshop met for three months. The first eight weeks were spent training the actors—through various improvisational exercises—exploring sound and movement. Throughout, Brook and Marowitz were attempting to explore the limits of performance through the actors rather than the text. Their "Artaudian" experiments, for the most part, denied the actor the spoken word and instead encouraged means of expression and communication through the use of sound, gesture, rhythm, color, and music.

Towards the end of this process, actors began to work these exercises into a series of "pieces," which were then performed for an audience made up of RSC members. The demonstration was called "The Theatre of Cruelty" (as a tribute to Artaud) and ran for five weeks at the LAMDA Theatre Club in January 1964.

The program included two short nonsense sketches by Paul Ableman; Artaud's 3-minute *Spurt of Blood* (first in sounds, then using Artaud's words); a "movement only" dramatization of a short story by Alain Robbe-Grillet; two collages by Brook: *The Public Bath* and *The Guillotine*; three scenes from Genet's *The Screens*; an anti-Marceauvian mime-sketch called *The Analysis*; a short play by John Arden, *Ars Longa, Vita Brevis*; and a "collage *Hamlet*" by Marowitz. Also included in the program were two "free-sections," both of which were unreshearsed and changed from night to night.

In *The Royal Shakespeare Company: The Peter Hall Years*, David Addenbrook summarizes the varied reviews:

> . . . the Times *was unenthusiastic, while applauding the RSC's attempt to nourish the "British avant-grade";* The Yorkshire Post *headed its review "Four Letter Words and Striptease;" and J. L. Styan, reviewing for* Plays and Players, *felt that although the ideas behind the experiment had merit, the actual material shown left much to be desired.*

Although the workshop was judged primarily by conventional standards and thus was met with a great deal of confusion by a majority of reviewers and members of the RSC, there were exceptions. As J. C. Trewin said in his 1974 biography of Brook:

> *Certain things went extremely well, especially the bath scene in which a girl (Glenda Jackson) was stripped, bathed, and dressed in a prison uniform to the words of a report on the recent Christine Keeler case; the same words were then used to transform her into Mrs. Kennedy at the President's funeral.*

Martin Esslin found that sketch by Brook "magically effective" in its "ritualistic cleaning" and "purely erotic element" and compared it to "the total involvement of the participants in some primeval magical rite or Aztec sacrifice."

This "Theatre of Cruelty" demonstration brought an end to the rigorous actor-training program experiments of the workshop, and rehearsals for *The Screens* began. The company was enlarged from 12 to 17 actors, and rehearsals moved to the Donmar Rehearsal Theatre on Earlham Street in Seven Dials. It was decided early on that rather than performing the play in its (considerable) entirety, they would limit the production to the first of twelve scenes.

Because of the epic nature of Genet's play about the Algerian War, Brook and Marowitz found it necessary to incorporate Brechtian techniques along with those of Artaud. Rehearsals began with a series of readings and discussions. A number of exercises from the earlier workshop were incorporated into the rehearsal process, along with Brechtian story-telling. According to Marowitz, it wasn't until the final moments of the rehearsal process that the play took shape, when Sally Jacobs' costumes and set "spread a great wave of color over the entire play."

Although it was Brook's hope that *The Screens* would be performed for a public audience, the circumstances surrounding it were not unlike the "Theatre of Cruelty" program. Esslin summarized: "In the end these efforts culminated in no more than a production of that very long play behind closed doors for invited guests in an improvised theatre".

Because of this, there are very few reviews of *The Screens*. Perhaps Trewin's remarks best summarize the effectiveness of the production, and acknowledge the extensive and cumulative training that went into the final experimental "demonstration":

> *Whatever one thought of the play, one could appreciate the close subtleties of lighting and movement, Brook's use of moving screens, and the general fluency of a performance that showed the growth of a company since its workshop weeks; clearly it had been trained in the languages of sight, sound, and silence. The strongest passage was the burning of the orchard, symbolized by a headlong rush of incendiarists to paint red flames higher and higher upon the canvas screens.*

The "Theatre of Cruelty" season ended in the spring of 1964 with *The Screens*. What followed was the assimilation of Brook's company of trained actors into the RSC's Aldwych Theatre company. As Esslin reports:

> *Now Brook had trained his company of actors, but there was no play for them to act. It was at this moment that Peter Weiss's remarkable "Marat/Sade" play appeared on the horizon . . . It required just this kind of acting and production . . . The label Theatre of Cruelty instantly became attached to his play, which opened on Aug. 20, 1964.*

Brook and Marowitz, through their "Theatre of Cruelty" workshops based on Artaud's theories, discovered that a language does exist beyond the spoken word. They were among the first to introduce this to the general theatrical world through their brilliant work with the RSC.

52c

from February 12

King Lear
world tour, including New York

58

August 20, 1964

The Persecution and Assassination of Marat
as Performed by the Inmates of the Asylum of Charenton
under the Direction of the Marquis de Sade

by Peter Weiss
English version by Geoffrey Skelton
Verse adaptation by Adrian Mitchell

London: Aldwych Theatre
The Royal Shakespeare Company

Director . . . . Peter Brook
Settings and properties . . . . Sally Jacobs
Associate designer . . . . Elizabeth Duffield
Costumes . . . . Gunilla Palmstierna-Weiss
Lighting . . . . David Read
Assistant to the director . . . . Malcolm Goddard
Music . . . . Richard Peaslee

CAST

M. Coulmier . . . . *Clifford Rose*
Mme. Coulmier . . . . *Brenda Kempner*
Mlle. Coulmier . . . . *June Baker*
Herald . . . . *Ian Richardson*
Kokol . . . . *Hugh Sullivan*
Polpoch . . . . *Jonathan Burn*
Cucurucu . . . . *Freddie Jones*
Rossignol . . . . *Elizabeth Spriggs*
Jacques Roux . . . . *Robert Lloyd*
Charlotte Corday . . . . *Glenda Jackson*
Jean-Paul Marat . . . . *Clive Revill*
Simonne Everard . . . . *Susan Williamson*
Marquis de Sade . . . . *Patrick Magee*
Duperret . . . . *John Steiner*
Abbot . . . . *Wyn Jones*
A mad animal . . . . *Morgan Sheppard*
Schoolmaster . . . . *Timothy West*

The Military Representative .... *Brian Osborn*

Mother .... *Wyn Jones*

Father .... *Henry Woolf*

A newly-rich lady .... *Geoffrey Hinsliff*

Voltaire .... *John Harwood*

Lavoisier .... *Leon Lissek*

Patients
Mary Allen, Jennifer Culow, Maroussia Frank,
June Jago, Michael Jenkinson, Mark Jones,
Caroline Maud, Lyn Pinkney, Bryan Stanyon

Nuns .... *Diana Bishop*
Tamara Furst

Guards .... *Edward Clayton*
Richard Williams

MUSICIANS
Patrick Gowers, Richard Callinan, Michael Gould,
Nicholas Moes, Rainer Schulein

58a

December 27, 1965

New York: The Martin Beck Theatre
(145 performances)

Director..Peter Brook

Producer..David Merrick

Settings and Properties.....................................Sally Jacobs

Associate Designer .... Elizabeth Duffield

Costumes .... Gunilla Palmstierna-Weiss

Lighting .... David Read

Assistant to the director .... Malcolm Goddard

Music...Richard Peaslee

CAST

M. Coulmier .... *Clifford Rose*

Mme. Coulmier .... *Brenda Kempner*

Mlle. Coulmier .... *Ruth Baker*

Herald .... *Michael Williams*

Kokol .... *Michael Williams*

Polpoch . . . . *Jonathan Burn*
Cucurucu . . . . *Freddie Jones*
Rossignol . . . . *Jeanette Landis*
Jacques Roux . . . . *Robert Lloyd*
Charlotte Corday . . . . *Glenda Jackson*
Jean Paul Marat . . . . *Ian Richardson*
Simonne Everard . . . . *Susan Williamson*
Marquis de Sade . . . . *Patrick Magee*
Duperret . . . . *John Steiner*
Abbot . . . . *Mark Jones*
A mad animal . . . . *Morgan Sheppard*
Schoolmaster . . . . *James Mellor*
The Military Representative . . . . *Ian Hogg*
Mother . . . . *Mark Jones*
Father . . . . *Henry Woolf*
A newly-rich lady . . . . *John Hussey*
Voltaire . . . . *John Harwood*
Lavoisier . . . . *Leon Lissek*

Patients
Mary Allen, Michael Farnsworth, Maroussia Frank,
Tamara Furst, Guy Gordon, Sheila Grant,
Michael Percival, Lyn Pinkney, Carol Raymont,

Nuns . . . . *Heather Canning*
                                                                                              Jennifer Tudor
Guards . . . . *Timothy Hardy*
                                                                                              Stanford Trowell

MUSICIANS
Patrick Gowers, Richard Callinan, Michael Gould,
Nicholas Moes, Rainer Schulein

Marat/Sade (as it is usually called) is a play within a play. The inmates of the Charenton Asylum perform a play by the Marquis de Sade
about the last days of Marat. Between 1787 and 1811, the director of the asylum, M. Coulmier, established regular theatrical entertainments in his clinic
as part of the therapeutic treatment of the inmates. These performances soon
became fashionable events for the Paris audience to attend. The Marquis de
Sade, himself an inmate for several years, wrote and directed several plays.
Weiss' play is set within the communal bathhouse in the hydropathic de-
partment of the institution. Two time schemes clash: 1793, against the back-
drop of the French Revolution, and 1808, the year of the stage performance.

The play by its nature requires an exceptionally intense relationship
between the actors and the audience, as the audience is also required to

play a role—that of the Paris crowd visiting the asylum in 1808. There is no strong linear action, the plot working on several levels. The backbone of the play is the debate between the paranoiac Marat, prophet of the totalitarian state, and de Sade, apostle of individual liberty. The dramatic action is the gradual build to Marat's murder at the hands of Charlotte Corday. The play's power is in the complexity of theme and the wide variety of dramatic components. The audience is constantly asked to be shocked by the authentically mad behaviour of the inmates. The serious political debates are peppered with songs and mimes. The action of the play, in short, is about subjection, tyranny, and revolution.

In the English-speaking world, *Marat/Sade* is so identified with Brook that one must be reminded that he saw the world premiere in the Schiller Theatre in Berlin on April 29, 1964, under the direction of Konrad Swinarski. When he started work on it, the core of his cast had previously worked together with him in the Theatre of Cruelty workshops; the rest were chosen from the Royal Shakespeare Company. It was a difficult play to direct, due to its seeming lack of organization. Rather than using the text, Brook began the two-month rehearsal by discussing the actors' personal experiences with madness. He encouraged them to explore the madman in themselves through improvisation, as inspiration giving them pictures by Hogarth, Breugel, and Goya to study.

David Richard Jones attributed the production's enormous success to the combination of power and complexity which Brook was able to generate on stage. Many critics observed that he based his approach on the combination of Artaudian sound and movement (expressed by the behaviour of the inmates) and Brechtian Alienation. As one of the alienating effects, the audience entered the theatre with the house lights up and the bathhouse in full view. Throughout the play, Brook did not let the audience forget that the line between them and the stage was very fine, the open stage and house seeming like a single room.

Grey and white were dominant; the only exception being the French Tricolor. According to Alan Brien, one saw "A lowering, windowless set, walled with tiny bricks, and . . . trapped with sunken pits." The costumer dressed the actors in white and grey clothes, which focused the audience on the actors frighteningly distorted faces.

The combination of rhyming verse and the actors' shockingly realistic behaviour was surprising. Adrian Mitchell transformed Geoffrey Skelton's prose translation into poetry, varying heavily accented tetrameter couplets and free verse, thus adding musicality to the elaborately worked-out speeches and monologues. Richard Peaslee's literal music also added intensity to the performance, and was an organic component of the play, the musicians performing on stage in the roles of inmates.

In London, the production became "one of the most unpredictable successes of recent years." It also created a great deal of tension within London's more conservative theatrical circles. The result of the artistic and political row against the RSC's "dirty plays" was the refusal on the part of the British Council to fund the production's visit to Paris.

Marat/Sade provoked mixed reaction among the critics, though all agreed it was a haunting performance. Some were not satisfied with the pace, and also found the disproportion between the acts a problem, Act I running 85 minutes and Act II for only 30. Other critics found the debates too long. John Gross complained that Revill's (Marat) and Magee's (Sade) speeches were "swamped by the general turbulence." Frank Kermode remembered the debates as moments when, "the brilliantly sustained succession of theatrical coups lapsed with awful doctrinare deliberation into the boring conversation of the principals and tedium became almost a novel theatrical event." *The Times* reviewer wrote: "One is far less impressed by the intellectual line of the play than its impact on the visceral level which in Peter Brook's production is enormous." All agreed on the overabundance of ideas within the play to the extent that it was found to be confusing. Alan Brien wrote: "The audience struggles exhausted from whirlpool to whirlpool only to be assured at the end that they will never know what they have learned. And Peter Brook's direction never allows a moment to dry off."

The actors in general received good notices. Glenda Jackson, who was also in the Theatre of Cruelty workshop, became an internationally acclaimed star as the result of her Charlotte Corday. The critics also found Patrick Magee's Sade one of the era's great acting achievements. Clive Revill, as Marat, got more mixed reviews, many finding his acting lighter and brisker than the part required.

The New York version of *Marat/Sade* had a limited engagement on Broadway. There were differences in both the set and cast. In New York the musicians were not on the sides of the stage, as in London, but sat in boxes above both sides. The major cast change was Ian Richardson taking over the role of Marat.

This more mature production received a very different reception. Although Brook had some reservations about playing Broadway, both he and his company found the play more rewarding than in London. The reviewers all agreed that *Marat/Sade* was a play to remember. Brook was generally praised for his direction, but many questioned the quality of the play itself. Detractors included Harold Clurman and John McClain. McClain said: "I found it merely extremely unpleasant and strangely pretentious. If Mr. Weiss has something important to say, surely there is a more palatable way of saying it." Walter Kerr thought he saw "the substitution of theatrical production for dramatic structure" and felt: "unless the stage games are informed, fed, moved forward by a self-sustaining, inherently commanding text, all the lovely tools of total theatre will, in the end, produce little more than the equivalent of sober-sided review sketches." In his review for the *Village Voice*, Michael Smith dismissed the play as showing emphasis on quantity rather than quality of ideas.

Supporters were, however, more numerous. Stanley Kauffmann found *Marat/Sade* an astounding production, a lucky meeting of minds, where Weiss provided the right opportunities for Brook. Kauffmann also offered an approach to the play, explaining that it "must live by the tensions it generates as it goes, not by plot or by character revelation." He also called attention to Brook's ability in isolating and concentrating tension and attention: "The production surges, opens and narrows like the iris of a camera, using its members in mad, stuttering, but carefully composed movements." Howard Taubman said, "Mr. Weiss' play expresses fresh, probing sensibility in original stage terms. Like its title, it will give you pause, stir your imagination and provoke your mind. It is good to encounter a playwright who dares to challenge the theatre and its audience to full participation."

The critics agreed that the quality of the production was due not only to the brilliant staging, but also to the superb cast. "It is the finest ensemble this town has seen since the Moscow Art Theatre's visit," wrote Norman Nadel. Ian Richardson was highly praised for playing Marat with "burning intensity," and the critics stressed Glenda Jackson's ability to make Charlotte Corday lovely, pitiful, and frightening at the same time. Magee also received only positive notices. The setting did not get as much attention, but was generally enjoyed. John Chapman called it "brilliant in its simplicity."

Marat/Sade was voted best play by the New York Drama Critic's Circle, and won four Tonys: Best Costumes, Best Featured Actor (Magee), Best Play—and Best Director.

53a

October 13, 1964

The Physicists

New York: Martin Beck

1965

59

October 19, 1965

The Investigation
by Peter Weiss

London: The Aldwych Theatre

a staged reading
with members of the National Theatre Company

This was part of an international event, the same play being offered in readings simultaneously in London and in thirteen theatres in East and West Germany. It shows Brook's involvement in social activism. Terry Coleman in the *Guardian* quotes Brook as saying he never got over hearing Alan Resnais's film about the concentration camps being described as beautiful. Peter Weiss asked for no particular style in the "oratorio in eleven parts" that he compiled from the records of the Auschwitz trials, except that he wanted the directors not to reconstruct the scene in the actual Frankfurt courtroom, with all its legal protocol.

Brook's version, which started at 11 pm and went on until 2:15 in the morning, was deliberately simple and fitting. In the *Observer*, Penelope Gilliatt felt: "after seeing it read on a bare stage, without music or costumes, by actors using scripts, I can't think that any of the usual theatrical apparatus could have much fitness or point." J. W. Lambert, in *The Sunday Times*, went into a bit more detail:

> *Under Peter Brook's direction no incidental sound was used, though clearly it could have been deployed to whip us up; no tricks were played with the lighting either.*
> *On a bare stage red leather chairs were grouped around the judge's table. Witnesses sat on one side, defendants on the other. The actors moved quietly, as though in some nightmare game of chess, to the front of the stage and back; except in one regrettable case only the slightest, subtlest hint of characterisation was used in voice, face and gesture.*
> *The total effect was moving, but never tear-jerking; thought-provoking, but never clinical.*

1966

60

October 13, 1966

US

by Denis Cannan (original text)
and Micheal Kustow and Michael Scott
(adaptors of documentary material)

London: The Aldwych Theatre

Director . . . . Peter Brook
Designer . . . . Sally Jacobs
Music . . . . Richard Peaslee
Lyrics . . . . Adrian Mitchell
Associate Directors . . . . Geoffrey Reeves
Albert Hunt
Lighting . . . . David Read

ACTORS

Eric Allen, Mary Allen, Jeremy Anthony, Hugh Armstrong,
Roger Brierley, Noel Collins, Ian Hogg, John Hussey,
Glenda Jackson, Mark Jones, Marjie Lawrence,
Joanne Lindsay, Leon Lissek, Robert Lloyd, Ursula Mohan,
Pauline Munro, Patrick O'Connell, Mike Pratt,
Clifford Rose, Morgan Sheppard, Jayne Sofiano,
Barry Stanton, Hugh Sullivan, Michael Williams, Henry Woolf

MUSICIANS

Michael Reeves . . . . *Musical Director*
Freddie Adamson . . . . *Percussion*
Michael Gould . . . . *Trumpet*
Michael Hart . . . . *Double Bass*
Philip Lee . . . . *Guitar*
Martin Nicholls . . . . *Trombone*
Martyn Sheilds . . . . *Trumpet*
Rainer Schulein . . . . *Flute*

Any discussion of *US* must fall into two parts: its politics and its aesthetics, both of which were controversial. As Michael Billington put it in *Plays and Players*:

> *Whatever one's reaction to US, the Royal Shakespeare Company's semi-documentary Vietnam programme, there is no denying it is a major theatrical landmark . . . . As far as I know, this is something without precedent on the English stage. What little documentary drama we have seen has generally been concerned with the reconstruction of a past event: US involves us in a current happening.*

The methods used to involve the audience were those discovered in the Theatre of Cruelty season and refined in *Marat/Sade*; indeed, Clive Irving in the *World Journal Tribune* called it "a Southeast Asian 'Marat-Sade'."

There was also a heavy influence, pointed out in *The New Yorker*, of Joan Littlewood's *Oh What A Lovely War*, her phantsamagoria on World War I. The large cast played multiple roles, and great use was made of both theatrical violence and symbolic action. Note Irvings description:

> *A tall deathly white-fleshed man wearing only a black velvet loincloth stretches up, twists himself slightly to the right and so assumes a contorted image of the Southeastern penninsula of Asia, with the Gulf of Tonkin beyond his left shoulder. The 17th parallel runs just beneath his rib cage. For a few seconds he is motionless. The two rival mobs come on the stage. The weapons they carry are brushes and pots of paint. Both mobs pounce on the human penninsula, one seizing his arms and torso, the other his legs. A bar of paint is daubed across his navel, his trunk is streaked with red and his legs with green until this tortured figure, wracked and stretched in two directions but physically indivisible, crumples onto a sheet of paper, writhes in a last spasm and then dies. The paper is pulled from under the corpse, still wet with running color, green now intermingled with red—on orgasm of necro-art—and held aloft before the audience by exultant assasins from both gangs.*

From this point the over-three-hour production, "often brilliantly effective, verbose, and sometimes irritating," according to *The New Yorker*, ran through the history of Viet Nam in the first two hours before the interval and through reactions to the war in the second part. It was still somewhat a work-in-progress, and critics described some changes, even between the first and second performances; at other times in the run the opening involved an actor miming a self-immolation as the other actors looked on impassively from behind. The phantasamagorical mixture of violence and stylization continued to the finale, which Ronald Blyden described in the *Observer*:

> *Similarly, in the performance's last moments, an actor releases butterflies from a japanned box. Gravely, enigmatically, as they flutter upward, he retains one [actually white paper, but the audience could not tell] between finger and thumb, then with a cigarette lighter sends it up in a puff of flame. Somehow it sums up all that has gone before.*

All agreed on the theatrical effectiveness of the individual moments; the arguments were over the production's politics, and whether or not it was anti-American. Harold Hobson, reporting from London for *The Christian Science Monitor*, found it was not, but that the general intellectual climate had made so many believe that any work on the subject *had* to be anti-American that people were seeing that even though it was not there. Brook, Denis Canaan, and other company members pointed out that nothing was being said in the play that was as severe as what some members of the United States Congress were themselves openly saying and also pointed to the deliberately punning title which implicated Britain and the actors themselves in the situation.

Nevertheless, there does seem to have been a certain selective vision, pounced on by many critics. *The New Yorker* found the evening was "remarkably silent on Hanoi," and Billington said, "It is also a culpable sin of omission to ignore the Vietcong atrocities. Factually *US* is incomplete; and its value as 'balanced comment' (which is how it is recommended to us in the programme) is thereby weakened." In a *New York Times* article titled "Are We to Blame for US," Martin Esslin disapproved of almost everything in the production, but centered criticism on its one-sided thought, saying, "Only the Americans kill and maim children in this version: there is no mention that the Vietcong also throw bombs into crowded streets."

Esslin even disliked a long passage in the second act which many other critics found a high point. In it, Glenda Jackson portrayed a intellectual girl in a scornful argument with a man planning to immolate himself; she tells him his protest is futile—that the world does not care, that England, comfortable England, in particular, does not care.

US, along with *Marat/Sade* and *Orghast*, marked a high point in Brook's use of free-form and orgiastic techniques. Its more specifically political topic kept it from travelling and made contemporary comment on it center more on content than form, which kept it from having as great an influence on world theatre as the other works.

1967

61

February 22, 1967

London & New York

United Artists

The Persecution and Assassination of Marat as Performed by the Inmates of the Asylum of Charenton under the Direction of the Marquis de Sade

Director . . . . Peter Brook
Producer . . . . Michael Birkett
Screenplay . . . . Peter Weiss
Translation by . . . . Geoffrey Skelton & Adrian Mitchell
Music by . . . . Richard Peaselee
Costumes . . . . Gunilla Palmstierna-Weiss
Choreography . . . . Malcolm Goddard
Production Director . . . . Sally Jacobs

Art Director . . . . Ted Marshall
Makeup . . . . Bunty Phillips
Photography (DeLuxe Color) . . . . David Watkin
Editor . . . . Tom Priestly

"Presented and Performed
by the Royal Shakespeare Company of England"

CAST

M. Coulmier . . . . *Clifford Rose*
Mme. Coulmier . . . . *Brenda Kempner*
Mlle. Coulmier . . . . *June Baker*
Herald . . . . *Michael Williams*
Cucurucu . . . . *Freddie Jones*
Kokol . . . . *Hugh Sullivan*
Polpoch . . . . *Jonathan Burn*
Rossignol . . . . *Jeanette Landis*
Jacques Roux . . . . *Robert Lloyd*
Charlotte Corday . . . . *Glenda Jackson*
Jean Paul Marat . . . . *Ian Richardson*
Simonne Everard . . . . *Susan Williamson*
Marquis de Sade . . . . *Patrick Magee*
Duperret . . . . *John Steiner*
Abbot . . . . *Mark Jones*
A mad animal . . . . *Morgan Sheppard*
Schoolmaster . . . . *James Mellor*
Military Representative . . . . *Ian Hogg*
Mother . . . . *Mark Jones*
Father . . . . *Henry Woolf*
Newly-rich lady . . . . *John Hussey*
Voltaire . . . . *John Harwood*
Lavoissier . . . . *Leon Lissek*
Nuns . . . . *Heather Canning*
                                                                                  Jennifer Tudor
Guards . . . . *Timothy Hardy*
                                                                                  Stanford Trowell

MUSICIANS
Patrick Gowers, Richard Callinan, Michael Gould,
Nicholas Moes, Rainer Schulein, Paul Hiley,

PATIENTS
Mary Allen, Michael Farnsworth, Maroussia Frank,

Tamara Fuerst, Guy Gordon, Sheila Grant,
Michael Percival, Lyn Pinkney, Bryan Stanyon

Most would have said that Brecht and Artaud were incompatible. Weiss disagreed, and Brook put them together by making alienation and menace Brechtian tools. Here, spectators watch inmates interact through bars. The filming was done with three cameras: two stationary cameras outside, to remind viewers that people are watching from a safe distance; and a hand-held camera inside, to get odd angles and close-ups. This last, creative for its time, effectively immerses the viewer in the action by combining film and theatrical media. At the end, the actors playing patients vent their frustrations by destroying the set—something, naturally, possible only for the filming.

Bosley Crowther of the *New York Times* reviewed the film at its February 23, 1967 opening, praising it and comparing it to the theatrical production the previous winter. With the film, he said:

> *We are ushered in with the inmates in their hideously rough and shapeless garb, with their fearfully gray misshapen faces. We bump against them. They bump against us . . . . He (Brook) makes us feel that we, too, are captured inside a giant and teeming cage.*

He describes the feeling "of being momentarily blinded by a whitewash of light, caught by a splash of bright color of a guard's blouse against the deadly gray, seeing the sweaty stubble of beard on de Sade's solemn face, smelling almost the sickly vapors that rise from Marat's hot towels." The image of being in the room is so strong that he acknowledged an "uncomfortable proximity that makes us squirm a little more in our chairs than we ever did while watching the fascinating play on the stage."

1968

62

February 12, 1968

Tell Me Lies

New York

Continental
(A Ronorus Film)

Producer-Director . . . . Peter Brook
Executive Producer . . . . Peter Sykes
Original Text . . . . Dennis Cannan
Adaptation . . . . Michael Kustow, Michael Scott

Based on "US," as presented by the Royal Shakespeare Co.

Photography (Eastmancolor) . . . . Ian Wilson
Music . . . . Richard Peaslee
Lyrics . . . . Adrian Mitchell
Music Director . . . . Michael Reeves
Production Director . . . . Sally Jacobs
Associate Directors . . . . Albert Hunt, Geoffrey Reeves
Editing . . . . Ralph Sheldon

CAST

Mark . . . . *Mark Jones*
Pauline . . . . *Pauline Munro*
Bob . . . . *Robert Lloyd*

and

Eric Allan, Mary Allen, Kingsley Amis, Jeremy Anthony
Hugh Armstrong, Peggy Ashcroft, James Cameron
Stokely Carmichael, Noel Collins, Tom Driberg, Ian Hogg
John Hussey, Glenda Jackson, Marjie Lawrence
Joanne Lindsay, Leon Lissek, Ursula Mohan
Reginald Paget, Jacqueline Porcher, Ivor Richards
Clifford Rose, Hilary Rose, Steven Rose, Paul Scofield
Morgan Sheppard, Barry Stanton, Hugh Sullivan
Michael Williams, Henry Woolf, Peregrine Worsthorne
Patrick Wymark

US, the play upon which *Tell Me Lies* was loosely based, was particularly important to Brook. Performed during his Theatre of Cruelty period, it attempted to disrupt traditional separations between the audience and the actor. In the introduction to *Tell Me Lies: Text and Photographs from the Royal Shakespeare Company's Production of US*, Brook summarizes the company's thinking while developing the piece. He writes of the appalling artificiality of Theatre, comparing it to "more powerful, more acute, more instant" current events. By confronting the public, they hoped to make a significant contribution to society. Their intention was to clarify issues by probing problems associated with the issues.

"We wanted actors to explore every aspect of this contradiction, so that instead of accusing or condoling an audience, they could be what an actor is always supposed to be, the audience's representative, who is trained and prepared to go farther than the spectator, down a path the spectator knows to be his own."

Tell Me Lies presents the diversity of British opinion about domestic and American involvement in the Vietnam war. At the same time, it makes a statement about the tragedy and immorality of war altogether. Actors represent their own characters; key political figures are interviewed.

Mark, Pauline, and Bob are obsessed by a photo of a wounded Vietnamese child swathed in bandages. They are determined to come to some sort of understanding about the Vietnamese conflict, but find it impossible, even after attending a series of discussions and putting on a sequence of skits reenacting various events of the war. They also attend demonstrations, parties and movies; visit Buddhist shrines; and see psychiatrists to discuss their personal problems with the war. Antiwar songs are sung.

The characters/actors seem overwhelmed by the "really frightening amount of individual responsibility" one bears. At one point, one asks, "How long can you look at this before you lose interest?"

In the *New York Times*, Renata Adler saw the film as "a movie straight out of the psychodrama left," and "an extremely trivial enterprise." She explains: "There is no question of acting . . . . And there is no question of directing or camerawork, since Brook allows the camera to rove meaninglessly from fresh, sincere faces speaking directly into it, through documentary material clipped from newreels, into little discussion groups posed for set pieces."

She singles out a "sad interview with Stokley Carmichael, who seems to have become—since his days as an intelligent young man of courage—as clearly an actor as any member of the cast."

As a rule, Adler found "the direction as unintelligent as the dialogue," pointing out that "Heads are cropped near the top of the screen, the camera lingers aimlessly on faces for long, idle, inarticulate sequences," and that "The whole movie reflects the banal assumption that feeling is incompatible with reason."

She did have some positive comments, liking the color, and a scene near the end, when an actor's stomach is used as a television screen for the war. The rest she found to be "abysmal and boring—as though slapdash work had a special authenticity, and the Angry Arts had an obligation to make even less sense than anybody else."

A rambling film, full of horrifying visual imagry, *Tell me Lies* is a disappointment. It exhibits the shocking elements of war early on. Futility soon follows, as we find ourselves embroiled in debates that go nowhere.

Both liberals and conservatives find fault, thinking that their political orientation is criticized. Still, no clear answers or suggestions emerge. People look for clarity, and it does not exist. The same points could have been made in much less time.

63

March 19, 1968

Oedipus

by Seneca
Translated by Ted Hughes

London: The Old Vic Theatre
The National Theatre Company

Director, Designer	Peter Brook
Associate Producer	Geoffrey Reeves
Music and Sound	Richard Peaslee
Special Costumes	Jean Monod
Lighting	Robert Ornbo
Assistant Designer	Sue Plummer
Stage Manager	John Rothenberg

CAST

Oedipus	*John Gielgud*
Jocasta	*Irene Worth*
Creon	*Colin Blakely*
Tiresias	*Frank Wylie*
Manto	*Louise Purnell*
Messenger	*Ronald Pickup*
Phorbas	*Harry Lomax*

and
Alan Adams, Bernard Gallagher, John Nightingale,
Gillian Barge, Jonathan Hardy, Jeremy Rowe,
David Belcher, Luke Hardy, George Selway, Helen Bourne,
Roderick Horn, Terence Taplin, Patrick Carter,
Gerald James, Robert Tayman, Anna Carteret, Lewis Jones,
Gary Walhorn, Kenneth Colley, Richard Kay,

Benjamin Whitrow, Oliver Cotton, Jane Lapotaire,
Judy Wilson, Neil Fitzpatrick, Philip Locke,
Peter Winter, Roger Forges, Kenneth Mackintosh

Seneca's *Oedipus* follows the plot of Sophocles' version with few changes (Jocasta stabs herself in her womb) but with an emphasis on violent and gory rhetoric. Until Peter Brook's production, it was considered untheatrical and unstageable because of its long speeches and onstage violence. Brook turned these "liabilities" into the production's strengths. In his introduction to the published text, he called Seneca's play "a theatre liberated from scenery, liberated from costume, liberated from stage moves, gestures, and business." He spoke of how this rather "motionless actor . . . must set his voice in motion." Not since *Marat/Sade* had Brook worked with a text in which he could further explore, not only the theories of Artaud, Brecht, and Grotowski, but his own ideas about language, actor/audience relationships, and ritual. Furthermore, it gave Brook yet another opportunity to take on a work considered minor or unperformable and transform it into daring theatre.

The production, designed by Brook, was done in contemporary dress: brown sweaters and trousers for chorus, a simple, long black dress for Jocasta, and black trousers and turtleneck for Oedipus. Dominating the stage was a giant golden cube that revolved as the audience entered. This cube could be opened to reveal a raised playing area, and when closed it could hide characters during certain scenes. There were smaller cubes on stage that the actors sometimes sat on or drummed. The great achievement of the production was Brook's ambitious use of the chorus to create a strange, primitive, alienated world. As the audience entered, Brook had chorus members leaning against the pillars of the auditorium droning, hissing, and wailing. The audience became, in Martin Esslin's words, "literally encircled . . . , trapped by the meshes of the tragedy, deeply involved in what is essentially a strange and frightening ceremonial of human sacrifice and shamanistic obsession."

Ritual was at the core of the production; moreover, ritual that the audience could not relate to any familiar experience. The translation by poet Ted Hughes fit perfectly into this Brook scheme. His use of language, with blunt, broken phrases, full of images of blood, pollution and decay, lent itself to the atmosphere and action of a brutish and savage world. There was no intermission; Brook wanted a primitive rite without relief. That he could sustain dramatic tension in a script that had been considered unplayable was his major success. As Joyce Doolittle put it, writing for *Drama at Calgary*, "the electricity which held sophisticated London theatre-goers for an hour-and-forty minutes without interval was both psychic and physical."

All the major actors were praised for their stylized and disciplined performances. The *New York Times* thought that "Gielgud's Oedipus, agonized and baffled," was perfect, as were "Irene Worth's deep-voiced, dark-toned Jocasta and the impassioned messenger of Ronald Pickup." Both Gielgud and Worth in interviews have described Brook's strenuous rehearsals to produce strange, unnatural sounds with their voices.

However, it was Brook's ritualized handling of Senecan violence that created some of the most memorable stage images of the period. For Oedipus' blinding, Brook found the one simple gesture to give form to its lengthy and gruesome description as, after the account was over, Tiresias gravely handed Gielgud his dark glasses. A more disturbing effect was Jocasta's suicide. Brook remained true to the Senecan text and made the audience witness as she slowly and grotesquely impaled herself through the womb by lowering herself onto one of several long thin obelisks that earlier in the play had seemed mere stage decoration. Esslin called it the "ultimate in ritualistic symbolism" and "on the whole, brilliantly done."

The most controversial element of all was the wild, satryc finale, Brook's attempt to cleanse the area ritualistically. As the tragedy closed with Jocasta's suicide and Oedipus' exit, a fifteen-foot gold phallus was wheeled onto center stage. Then the chorus, dressed in gold paper costumes, danced up and down the aisles while a Dixieland band played "Yes We Have No Bananas!"

Critical and public response to this was negative. A number of critics noted both embarrassment and giggles when the phallus appeared. Doolittle found the transition from suicide to phallus to revelers unsatisfying: "I had been engrossed; the jazz jarred." Other responses ranged from confusion to annoyance to clear anger. Irving Wardle, of *The London Times*' Saturday Review wrote: "Even without the sight of that golden fertility symbol ready and waiting on an empty stage, one can identify these violent imaginings as no closer to living experience than masturbation fantasies."

It was felt that the ending marred what had been a shattering and unforgettable production. Clearly it was important to Brook to look back to the roots of tragedy in ritual, and he felt any such examination should include and re-interperet the satyr play after the original tragic trilogies. Considering the experimental nature of the whole production, the attempt is understandable, though it is hard to tell if it was only an apparent failure due to an unready public or if it was a genuine miscalculation.

64

July 18, 1968

The Tempest
by William Shakespeare

London: The Round House

Director	Peter Brook
with the assistance of	Joe Chaikin
	Victor Garcia
	Geoffrey Reeves
Literary Collaborators	Claude Roy
	Michael Scott
Designers	Nestor de Arzadun
	Jean Monod

ACTORS
Philippe Avaron, Paul Boesing, Sylvain Corthay,
Ronnie Gilbert, Ian Hogg, Glenda Jackson, Mark Jones,
Jean-Pierre Jorris, Tem Kempinsky, Marcia Jean Kurtz,
Robert Lloyd, Roy London, Michel Lonsdale, Bill Macy,
Pauline Munro, Katsuhiro Oida, Bernadette Onfroy,
Natasha Parry, Barry Stanton, Henry Woolf

MUSICIANS
Edgardo Canton, Terry Leahy, Eddie Thompson
Paul Mosby, Daryl Waters, John White

     This version of *The Tempest*—not so much a production of the play as an elaborate experiment loosely based upon it—was originally indended for Paris. In April, Jean-Louis Barrault had invited Brook to organize a "theatrical laboratory" under the auspices of the Théâtre des Nations, with the idea of making a radical investigation into the audience-spectator relationship. Brook hoped that a mixture of artists from various cultures could produce a synthesis of styles relevant to the contemporary world and decided on *The Tempest* as the focus of the experiment with the hope that they might thereby uncover the power of that play which he said—despite his having been involved with it twice before (productions # 44 and Xd)—appeared sentimental and pallid on stage. He was given a large gallery in the Gobelins tapesty factory, but that summer's unrest in France led the French government to close the Théâtre des Nations. A number of corporations and individuals donated funds which made it possible to move to England under the auspices of the RSC.

     Brook was given the use of The Round House, a Victorian station house created to be used as a turning area for locomotives, and later used by Arnold Wesker's working-class theatre company. The building itself was one large dome with no stage, but very high ceilings. Several commentators compared it to a gymnasium, and Brook's settings did nothing to dispel that feeling. The center, covered by a white canvas tent, had nothing but low platforms; some spectators sat on large scaffoldings of pipes and planks which could be rolled into the main area and others were seated on various items—boxes, benches, stools and folding chairs—in "safe" areas on three sides.

This meant that audience "participation" was optional. Brook's previous attempt at that was at the end of the first act in *US*, where the actors had originally blindly walked into the audience, bags over their heads. It didn't work and was soon dropped. Now he said:

> *The audience as a whole could feel that it was being respected either as a forthright or as a timid creature, and that seems fundamental to me. Personally, I find it meaningless when a provocation to an audience takes the form of assaulting everyone in the house. The psyche, the kick-state of each member of an audience is so subtly different that no one can really treat the audience as a whole . . . . Real audience participation demands a climate of enormous confidence and security, spreading into the audience the very thing one tries to achieve in a working group of actors where one knows that things only flow when there is great security through hard work on the part of all the members. More than anything else, participation depends on making an audience feel in a totally natural relationship to the performer.*

The event the audience watched lasted only a bit over an hour, and was much more an exercise than an actual performance of Shakespeare. The text was shuffled, mixed with further material from Calderon, and delivered ametrically in an attempt, which foreshadows *Orghast*, to abstract the driving force behind the words rather than the words themselves. Action was non-linear, scenes would appear and fade out. There was much use of mirror exercises, and it was made clear that many characters mirrored each other—Prospero was at times the monster and Caliban the monster-master. There was a great deal of violence and sexual imagery and many mimed sexual acts, leading to a central orgy in which, according to Margaret Croyden, "the 'Garden of Delights' has been transformed into the 'Garden of Hell'." Prospero was captured and raped/consumed as he, according to Ronald Bryden in the *Observer*, "wrestled with the master-beast within himself, forcing himself to own it." After a "post-coital" silence, Ariel brought in ribbons and bright costumes and "the scene dissolves into Miranda's and Ferdinand's marriage ceremony, performed in Hebrew-Hippie-Japanese rites." The end varied from night to night; sometimes it included the Hokey-Pokey.

The production was not covered as fully as a more formal production intended to be opened to the general public over a long span would have been, and some critics who did see it made little attempt to judge it for what it was. Brook later said: "I was disappointed with the critics . . . They reviewed what we were doing as if it were a finished production, whereas it was only a work in progress, a reaching out toward such a production." Certainly not all critics did this. Bryden wrote:

> . . . *Their four displays of work-in-progress last week were given not as an entertainment, but because, as the handouts said, "even laboratory work does not exist until it happens before a spectator."*
>
> *What we saw was not* The Tempest, *but a series of actor's exercises aimed at generating emotions required for that play and gestures to express them.*
>
> . . . *Here was how a play looks to an actor: the private emotional scoring which he contributes to the orchestration of a dramatic text. One would give much to see the final production of a* Tempest *arrived at via such a rehearsal. It could be immensely powerful.*

He did have some reservations, mainly that it was too close to what some lesser members of the avant-garde were offering as finished experiences, and that it indicated that words were somehow separate from emotion. In the *Sunday Telegraph*, R. B. Marriott was even more favorable. He also pointed out it was concerned with *The Tempest* "used as a means of the players finding themselves, trying to realise their potentialities . . . " and as an asking of the questions: "What is a theatre? What is a play? What is an actor? What is a spectator? What is the relation between them all? What conditions serve this relationship best?" and, despite the freedom of it all he found Brook's stamp over it.

> *Indeed the evening was altogether an exhilarating and fascinating experience. One hopes there will be many more Open Presentations. In a year, in two years, yet another question might actually be answered: To what important things can this experimental group lead the changing theatre of the Western world?*

1969

1970

65

August 27, 1970

A Midsummer Night's Dream
by William Shakespeare

Stratford-upon-Avon: Memorial Theatre
The Royal Shakespeare Company

Director...Peter Brook
Settings and Costumes.......................................Sally Jacobs
Music.......................Richard Peaslee, The Actors, Mendelssohn

CAST

Theseus/Oberon .... *Alan Howard*
Hyppolyta/Titania .... *Sara Kestelman*
Philostrate/Puck .... *John Kane*
Egeus/Quince .... *Philip Locke*
Bottom .... *David Waller*
Flute .... *Glynne Lewis*
Starveling .... *Terrence Hardiman*
Snout .... *Norman Rodway*
Snug .... *Barry Stanton*
Hermia .... *Mary Rutherford*
Lysander .... *Christopher Gable*
Helena .... *Frances de la Tour*
Demetrius .... *Ben Kingsley*
Fairies .... *Hugh Keays Byrne*
Ralph Cotterill
Celia Quicke
John York

MUSICIANS

Percussion .... *Tony McVey*
Robin Weatherall
Guitar .... *Martin Best*

65a

Tour

December 4, 1970
London: The Roundhouse/Studio Performance

January 20, 1971
New York: The Billy Rose Theatre

March 16, 1971
Brooklyn: The Brooklyn Academy of Music

March 29, 1971
Chicago: The Auditorium Theatre

April 5, 1971
Boston: The Shubert Theatre

April 12, 1971
Toronto: The O'Keefe Centre

April 19, 1971
Philadelphia: The Shubert Theatre

CAST changes for Tour

Starveling . . . . *Phillip Manikum*
Snout . . . . *Patrick Stewart*
Lysander . . . . *Terence Taplin*

65b

June 10, 1971
London: The Aldwych Theatre

REVIVAL AND WORLD TOUR

August 8, 1972
London: The Aldwych Theatre

August 28, 1972–August 3, 1973
World Tour:
Bristol, Southampton, Berlin, Munich, Paris, Venice
Belgrade, Milan, Hamburg, Budapest, Bucharest, Sofia
Zagreb, Cologne, Helsinki, Warsaw, Cardiff, Liverpool,
London, Stratford-upon-Avon, Los Angeles, San Francisco
Washington DC, Tokyo, Osaka, Kobe, Nagoya,
Adelaide, Melbourne, Sydney

World Tour Company

Theseus/Oberon . . . . *Alan Howard*
Hyppolyta/Titania . . . . *Gemma Jones*

Philostrate/Puck .... *Robert Lloyd*
Egeus/Quince .... *Philip Locke/Denis Carey*
Bottom .... *Barry Stanton*
Flute .... *George Sweeney*
Starveling .... *Richard Moore/Phillip Manikum*
Snout .... *Malcolm Rennie*
Snug .... *Hugh Keays Byrne*
Hermia .... *Zhivila Roche*
Lysander .... *Philip Sayer/Terence Taplin/Brace Myers*
Helena .... *Jennie Stoller*
Demetrius .... *Glynne Lewis/Davis Meyer/Philip Sayer*
Fairies (from) .... *Doyne Byrd*
                                                        Ralph Cotterill
                                                        Patricia Doyle
                                                        Gillian Joyce
                                                        David Meyer
                                                        Tony Meyer
                                                        Pauline Munro
                                                        Roshan Seth
Musicians .... *Tony McVey*
                                                        Robin Weatherall
                                                        John Zaradin

Tour and Stage Manager .... Hal Rogers
Deputy Stage Managers .... Stanley MacKenzie/Barbara Penney
Lighting Designer .... Michael Murray
Chief Technician .... Earl Kay
Technicians .... Charles Kenton, John O'Mahoney
Sound Technician .... Keith Clarke
Wardrobe Mistress.. Lynn Hope
Assistant to Tour Manager .... Jean Moore

This innovative production proved to be one of the most memorable and successful—especially in terms of its tours—in the history of the RSC. In its first brief tour to the United States more than 200,000 people saw it, and it earned the RSC more than £1,000,000 at a time when such income was sorely needed. Performances were frequently sold out, and even over-sold on the tours.

Considering the critical outrage which had greeted some of Brook's prior RSC adventures, and the extremely unusual nature of the physical production, it is interesting that only a few minor reviewers complained. The *Evening Standard*'s Anthony Hern objected that Brook had cast the "biggest little people you ever saw . . . great galumphing humanoids . . . ." and a Sheffield reviewer sulked about "players who rarely exceeded run-of-the-mill adequacy." John Barber's notice in the *Daily Telegraph* was more typical, glowing: "He has found new ways of giving form to its latent poetry and power . . . . it was Mr. Brook's triumph to generate an atmosphere in which only the poetry mattered." Specifics Barber admired included: "For setting he offers a dazzling white box. The actors, too, wear white—or else plain colors as vivid as a conjuror's silks. The only furniture is four cushions, also white." Lest this sound too spartan, he noted: "The naked harshness of this environment is used by Mr. Brook as a means of exposing the actors' words and emotions. Its coldness suits the palace scenes admirably, and we are at once seized by the pathetic vehemence of the lovers' protests."

The *Times'* magisterial Irving Wardle thought it "the apex towards which the RSC has been moving for the past two years . . . .it brings Brook himself to a new point of rest. You could not have predicted what he would do with the play; but after seeing the production you feel you ought to have known, and it is a simple and inevitable crystallization of what has gone before." Wardle saw this as the greatest extension of the ensemble's "efforts to develop bodies as well as voices," noting its relation to Meyer-hold and his theories of Biomechanics, giving the play "a continually animated physical line, occupying the whole cubic space of the stage as they shinny up and down vertical ladders and stamp about on enormous stilts." Among the "breathtaking" effects, Wardle admired a stage deluged in confetti for the sham nuptials of Titania and Bottom, and Oberon in a purple gown swinging "across on a trapeze to the roar of Mendelssohn's Wedding March." He also liked the idea of Puck's magic flower "as a spinning juggler's plate, which he and Oberon nonchalantly toss from wand to wand." Wardle saluted Brook's use of music to ward off "false stage rhetoric," with "a running musical accompaniement (by Richard Peaslee) mainly scored exotically for percussion, autoharps, tubular bells, bongos. He also uses a guitar. The effect these have on the text is to make it natural for characters, at moments of high emotion, to pass over into song . . . " Arching over all, he suggested, was Brook's concept of the parallels among the three social groups, rather than their differences: "Brook shows them all as members of the same world." And it ends "on a note of calm social harmony."

In the *Birmingham Post*, J. C. Trewin also mentioned modern theatrical theories, if only to show how Brook wasn't tied to any of them. He saw it as "Brooke's joke at the expense of the pundits. Many people had expected him to direct the *Dream* as a variation of the complicated theories of Professor Jan Kott." But Brook, of course, "never does anything he is expected to do. Here he has sought, as it were, to conjure this play from the air." After detailing some of the more unusual bits, he conceded: "This sort of thing may start a royal rage in some quarters. For me it was so gay and young and amusing that I cannot find it in my heart to object."

Among the other raves, it is interesting to note Ronald Bryden in the *Observer* observing its similarity of effect to other important works of the period: "It was poetry, ritual, ballet and circus rolled into one; as hieratic as an investiture, as spontaneous as *Hair* . . . . they ranged effortlessly between the kind of avant-garde improvisation one associates with the Living Theatre and its progeny, and the most traditional, formalized speech and playing you look for in the great classical ensembles like the Comedie Francaise."

Clive Barnes, then critic for the *New York Times*, also reported from Stratford-upon-Avon, perhaps sensing that the production would come to the United States. Five months later, that came to pass, with the *Dream* on Broadway half a year before it was seen in the West End. (The reason for that was the RSC's policy of moving successful Stratford productions to its London venue, the Aldwych Theatre, the season following the debut.) Reprinted in the Paris *Herald-Tribune*, the review was rapturous: "Once in a while, once in a very rare while, a theatrical production arrives that is going to be talked about as long as there is a theatre, a production which, for good or ill, is going to exert a major influence on the contemporary stage." And Brook's *Dream* was that production: "It is a magnificent production, the most important work yet of the world's most imaginative and inventive director. If Peter Brook had done nothing else but this *Dream*, he would have deserved a place in theatre history." After it opened in New York, he continued his praise, saying: "This is without any equivocation whatsoever the greatest production of Shakespeare I have ever seen in my life—and for my joys and sins, I have seen literally hundreds."

The reviews, in fact, are so uniformly good that it can be more revealing to quote the negative comments, some of which are negated even within the review. In *Life*, for instance, Tom Prideaux spoke of the intense physicality and then asked "Do his circusy didoes really serve the play?" He answered: "These age-old aspects of entertainment—juggling, tumbling, acrobatics—have a valid, though limited, place in serious theatre, and I am glad to see them restored." But he added, "We should hope, naturally, that circus tricks don't take over all of civilized drama." *Cue*'s Marilyn Stasio felt Brooks ideas were "not radically different from the play's current academic interpretation: that 'fairyland' is the collective psyche of the court and its menace the terror of the subconscious." She hoped for something deeper, without mentioning Brook's extreme success at the level he had chosen. More influential were those who felt the play had been coarsened, among them Walter Kerr and John Simon. The latter, accusing Brook of "depoeticizing everything," felt the treatment had two purposes: one "to rejuvenate an old warhorse," and the second: to force audiences to admire Brook's cleverness.

Despite that, David Merrick, as the New York producer, ran a full-page ad in the *New York Times* on January 26, 1971, proclaiming "UNANIMOUS RAVES FOR A MIDSUMMER NIGHT'S DREAM." Granted, he omitted Simon and Kerr, but the *Post*, the *News, Time*, the *Wall Street Journal, Variety, Newsday, Newsweek*, and the Associated Press—among others—were enough to be impressive.

66

November 22, 1970

King Lear
adapted from Shakespeare

Produced by Michael Birkett
Presented by Filmways, Inc.
in association with the Royal Shakespeare Company
distributed by Altura Film International

Director . . . . Peter Brook
Screenplay adaptation . . . . Peter Brook
Director of Photography . . . . Henny Kristiansen
Editor . . . . Kasper Schyberg
Production Designer . . . . Georges Wakhevitch

CAST

King Lear . . . . *Paul Scofield*
Goneril . . . . *Irene Worth*
Fool . . . . *Jack MacGowran*
Duke of Gloucester . . . . *Alan Webb*
Duke of Albany . . . . *Cyril Cusack*
Duke of Cornwall . . . . *Patrick Magee*
Edgar . . . . *Robert Lloyd*
Earl of Kent . . . . *Tom Fleming*
Regan . . . . *Susan Engel*
Cordelia . . . . *Annelise Gabold*
Edmund . . . . *Ian Gogg*

Oswald . . . . *Barry Stanton*
Duke of Burgundy . . . . *Soren Elung Jensen*

Peter Brook filmed *King Lear* during the winter and early spring of 1969, in the frozen terrain of North Jutland, Denmark. It was shot entirely in black-and-white with no musical score. It is a *Lear* stripped of all sentiment and romanticism. This stylized distillation of the play was, in a sense, a continuation of Brook's successful stage version of 1962, but Scofield, Worth and Webb are the only principals repeating their stage roles. What sets the film apart from that stage production is that Brook actually created a world of darkness, waste, and deathly cold light. On film, *Lear* became even crueler and colder, a truly existential universe. Unlike his film of *Marat/Sade*, where he attempted to fuse theatre with film, *Lear* is a purely cinematic creation. Thus, in cinematic terms Brook could further develop this new interpretation of *Lear* first brought to light in Jan Kott's famous essay, "King Lear or Endgame." Kott felt that only the new theatre of the absurd and grotesque could interpret the true cruelty of *Lear* that was an Elizabethan reality. He saw Shakespeare's tragedy more as tragicomedy, comparing it to Samuel Beckett's *Endgame, Waiting for Godot* and other absurdist plays.

In this film Brook presents a pre-Christian, primitive and savage world. The characters are dressed in the skins and furs of animals. Brook sets this up from the opening shot, as the camera slowly pans across a room of immobile faces waiting for the King's decision. The first shot of Lear is from behind his massive, phallic throne, underlining his masculine authority. When Lear finally speaks to his daughters (the first sound in the film), one sees no love in the face of the father, and only fear in the eyes of the children. The absence of music—for this is an age devoid of song and dominated by silence—gives the sound of words a vivid presence. In Vincent Canby's highly favorable reviews, he said that "Brook's performers discover the language," and that Paul Scofield "speaks the lines as if they'd just been created—with intelligence and surprise."

There are other elements that made this *Lear* startling and new. Brook cut some scenes, reversed and split others. Edward Trostle Jones pointed out that this "fragmentariousness," especially of the Gloucester sub-plot, "strengthened the cruel, insistently absurdist interpretation of the principal action." In fact, this splintered, at times de-constructed form is often the film's style. To perhaps heighten the characters' (and audiences') sense of alienation, Brook quick-cut shifts of perspective, angle, and light. During Lear's mad scenes Brook used more hallucinatory collage effects. He was probably his most imaginative in his use of light, which becomes as important as one of the characters. Indoors there is always the primeval light from a fire where the characters gather and huddle about for warmth. Outdoors there is the overpowering light from the sun and endless snow that seems literally to swallow up the characters.

Some mention must be made of Brook's cinematic handling of violence. It is swift, terrible, at times grisly, but shot to give visual impact a ritualistic effect. For example, Gloucester's gruesome blinding is shot in such dark close-up that the act becomes a dizzying abstraction. The climactic battle between the brothers Edgar and Edmund is shockingly quick, brutally won, with no mercy, without poetry. There then immediately follows in rapid succession the deaths of Regan, Goneril, and Cordelia. The series of death shots hits the audience like the blows of an ax, leaving a sense of life's fragility in a blind, unmerciful Nature. The final death is Lear's. We see his grizzled head, lifeless as a statue's, slowly swing out of the picture in a background of overwhelming light that finally leaves us with nothing.

The critical response was mixed. It should have been expected that many reviewers would miss the tragic highs of the more traditional *Lear*. Pauline Kael would certainly speak for this group. "Brook's *King Lear* is gray and cold, and the actors have dead eyes. I didn't just dislike this production—I hated it." John Simon, in his review for *New York*, yearned for the entire text. He also called Brook's directing "facile and flashy." T. E. Kalem of *Time* complained that "It is unthinkable that at some moment the destiny of Lear would not move one to tears. That moment never came in this film."

While American reviews were generally more positive than those in Britain, few understood why this greatest of tragedies directed by England's most famous directors didn't, "move one to tears." Perhaps it is not surprising then that the film was a box office failure. Brook did provide a typically Brookian answer for all those unmoved critics. It came in an interview about his staged *Lear* that is equally applicable to the film. He said "We set out not to move you. I don't feel that being moved in *King Lear* is as exciting as what is really happening to the people and what this means ... We [lost] romantic illusion but gained something much more considerable, modern and Elizabethan." To be both modern and Elizabethan may sound like a paradox, but it is the key to Brook's remarkable career. And there may be no work that presents this duality better than *King Lear*.

67

August 28, 1971

Orghast at Persepolis

Persepolis

The International Centre for Theatre Research

ACTORS

Nozar Azadi (Persia), Malik Bagayogo (Mali), Farkhundeh Baver (Persia), Michèle Collison (USA), Claude Confortès (France), Sylvain Corthay (France), Dariush Farhang (Persia), Mohamad-Bagher Ghaffari (Persia), Hushang Ghovanlou (Persia), Daniel Kamwa (Cameroon), Andreas Katsulas (USA), Robert Lloyd (Britain), Paloma Matta (Spain), João Mota (Portugal), Pauline Munro (Britain), Bruce Meyers (Britain), Katsuhiro Oida (Japan), Said Oveysi (Persia), Natasha Parry (Britain), Parviz Porhosseni (Persia), Fahime Rastkar (Persia), Syavash Tahmoures (Persia), Irene Worth (Britain), Sadreddin Zahed (Persia), Lou Zeldis (USA)

WRITER
Ted Hughes (Britain)

DIRECTORS
Peter Brook (Britain)
and
Arby Ovanessian (Persia)
Geoffrey Reeves (Britain)
Andrei Serban (Romania)

DESIGNERS
Eugene Lee (USA)
Frannie Lee (USA)
Jean Monod (Switzerland)

COMPOSER
Richard Peaslee (USA)

Research On Avesta
Mahin Tadjadod (Persia)

DRUMMERS
Lloyd Miller (USA)
Bahman Rajabi (Persia)
Phil Schutzman (USA)

ADMINISTRATIVE DIRECTOR
Micheline Rozan (France)

COMPANY MANAGER
Mary G. Evans

LIASON
Behruz Nikzat

TECHNICAL & ADMINISTRATION
Robert Applegarth (USA)
Isabelle Cardin (France)
André Collet (France)
Faez Shabrokh (Persia)

Orghast at Persepolis was the culmination of Peter Brook's first re-search with his International Center for Theatre Research Group in Paris. The "big investigation was language," Brook said—an attempt to rediscover its essential nature by taking "the conceptual level away," and through what was discovered "to be able to return to [conceptual] language . . . more properly."

The work began with his feeling that "the further back you went . . . the less words" there were. He felt that, "this wasn't a poverty:" but that language was then even richer.

By working with different languages, with ancient Greek, and then with ancient sounds in a new language created by the poet Ted Hughes, Brook said his company was able to "understand something about the taste of the tragic experience." They found that sound carried "hundreds of over-tones depending on how it was spoken."

The name "Orghast" given to the language created by Hughes came from the root *org* meaning "sun," and *ghast*, meaning "spirit." It evolved, Brook said, through Hughes's "going into a curious state . . . in between the ordinary fluid state . . . .and the subconscious . . . twilight zone," so that the "unconscious was proposing elements to the conscious mind." Hughes said that the "new sound" in which the consonants were fixed, but with the vowels free, led the actors to "reach for the most living feeling in them at the moment."

Brook had long been interested in the Prometheus myth, and so it was used as the central image in the piece that evolved. As Geoffrey Reeves, one of the three directors who worked with Brook on the project, describes it, Orghast was the expression of Promethian mythology. The original myth "led to many varied texts." Aeschylus' version, for a start, but also to material from Goethe, Gide, Calderón's *Life is a Dream*, Seneca's *Hercules Furens*, and *Thyestes*, and an Armenian play, *The Chained One*.

> We did not intend "precise meaning" that comes with attempting to tell a tale. It was the
> basis for something much looser, much freer. What the actors were playing was a series

of scenes based around key images, or relationships, improvising on the very tight sound
structure of Hughes' Orghast.

An invitation from the then Shah of Iran and his Empress to create a summer project and perform it at the Shiraz-Persepolis Festival of the Arts—1971 being the 2,500th Anniversary of the Persian Empire gave the project its final direction and form.

Brook's acceptance upset some in the theatrical community. Eric Bentley, for instance, felt that Brook had missed an opportunity for "political warfare" that would have endangered no one. Reeves answered by saying that: "though we were exploited by the Persians for publicity, we did manage to . . . extract from Persepolis some of the artistic answers we were seeking: in that sense, the screwing was mutual." And Brook went further, answering that "It would be complete humbug for us to work in France as though we naively believed that there was no repression or police brutality there, and suddenly discover it in Iran." He also claimed that the hour-and-a-half "direct confrontation" he was granted with the Empress "balanced the account" in itself.

Brook insisted that *Orghast at Persepolis* was a work in progress, and that the experience of the Persian world was as much of a part of the experiment as the language and myth—that it was necessary. "In Persepolis," he said, "there is still life." "We know the story is almost impossible to tell. The tomb did something for us: we used its atmosphere and presence." And in his program notes, he defined the work as "the product of work done in Iran and of the effect of Iran on the work."

Rehearsals began, in essence, with the opening of the International Center for Theatre Research in Paris on November 1, 1970, with the language experiments and improvisations around the Prometheus myth. In June 1971, Brook took the company to Tehran to join the Persian actors he had hired in the spring for the Shiraz project. All worked together for three months.

The first performance of *Orghast: Part One* began just after sunset on Saturday, August 28, and was the first time the Center had played to paying spectators. It was repeated under the half-moon, just before sunrise, and again the next day at dusk. Brook said he was interested in seeing "what happens in the two conditions: twilight and darkness." The second pre-sunrise performance of Part One was cancelled and rescheduled for the following Saturday when Part Two was performed twice. Each performance had an audience of two hundred.

In Shiraz, Brook explained to reporters that the Promethian myth was "completely central" to *Orghast*, but that "then, the withering away of the forms themselves, of the details, of the narratives, of the anecdotal side of these myths, led just as naturally to the attempt to look at what lay beneath." Ossia Trilling, in *Theatre Quarterly*, explained the imagery as: "Prometheus' theft of the gift of fire and the cruel penalty of self-destruction imposed on man ever since this act of hubris."

The sites Brook chose for the two parts of *Orghast* were two spectacular tomb sites of Persia's great ancient kings. Part One was performed in front of the tomb of one of the Artaxerxes (there is confusion as to whether it is I, II, or III) which overlooks the ruins of Persepolis, a city built by Darius in 500 BC. Many who saw it have remarked on the stunning opening, as a huge ball of fire was lowered slowly from the top of the hill down to the audience below. Fire images were naturally to play a significant part in the Promethian-based work. Four actors were crouched on the sides of the massive raised tomb and Prometheus was chained on a ledge just below the top.

Part Two played at a site six miles from Persepolis at Naqsh-i-Rustam, another royal burial site, on an open piece of ground. The audience moved from place to place, following the story of the destruction of the Persian army by the Greeks. (A strange choice, perhaps, for an event done for this celebration)

The cast, an international group of whom the best known was Irene Worth, became not so much human characters as images, sounds, places, and times of the distant past. There was choral work, guided by Andrei Serban. All of this was in the invented language of Orghast.

Brook said much later that the analytical confusion expressed by many was "exactly the same as *The Mahabharata*," and he blamed a "certain kind of critical mind . . . that worries [itself] into a state of non-understanding" instead of "receiving directly" the experience at hand.

If Brook's *Orghast* asked, as he says it did, whether "certain forms of truth and emotional involvement [can] be communicated without going through the normal channels," the answer seems to be a guarded "yes."

"What we saw, and above all, heard, was riveting, beautiful and disturbing, but what it meant, precisely, was elusive, and still is," wrote Richard Findlater in *The London Times*. This frustration was in many of the critical responses: an insecapable yearning for meaning.

Henry Popkin, of the *Guardian*: "To the unaided observer it does offer some striking moments of theatre, but these . . . .seem not at all unified by any intelligible plan." The key word here was "unaided." Popkin was not alone in feeling that *Orghast* was an insiders' piece—for the initiated members of Brook's privileged world—and that little effort was made to allow others inside.

In an article in *Theatre Quarterly*, Ossia Trilling spoke out for those who struggled to find meaning in Brook's world:

> *If in the long run, one forms the impression that what one is hearing is really pretentious gibberish, one may, I think, be forgiven . . . . If I had not been warned in advance, I should altogether have failed to get the literary references . . . I have been careful not to treat* Orghast *as anything but a tentative search . . . impressive, but entirely unconvincing.*

But even for Trilling, the reenactment in Part Two of the destruction of the Persian army was brilliant theatrically:

> *Here, for the first time in my experience, Brook fully achieved his ambition . . . to get his audience fully involved in the action, despite themselves . . . it was breathtaking, spectacularly impressive and on the whole spell-binding.*

Margaret Croyden, one of Brook's most ardent supporters among journalists, seemed best to understand his attempt. In an article in the *New York Times*, she spoke of *Orghast* as a "religious experience," rather than a "linear plot with discernable characters." She accepted the experience Brook offered and asked no more from it. She was very much correct when she forsaw that it would be the beginning of a new theatrical form:

> *The work in Iran has linked Brook's theatrical genius to the Middle Eastern and Oriental art and philosophy, resulting in a synthesis that seriously challenges conventional western theatrical patterns . . . which might very well restore to the theatre its original transcendant power.* Orghast *may be a beginning.*

In an interview at Shiraz with Erica Munk, perhaps speaking out of irritation with the analytical criticism and "hype" surrounding the project, Brook summed up the meaning of his attempt by saying: "I don't give a fuck about ritual, about myth, about universal language or universal brotherhood. This is a stage of work—this sharp emphasis—the defining quality of research work—on one thing." He told reporters: "We shall certainly never play this material in this form again anywhere else, because the unity we have attempted here will already have been broken."

For Brook, then, *Orghast* was the answer to a research problem, and opportunity to explore the origins of langauge and Theatre in an environment as ancient as the first tragedies. *Pace* Margaret Croyden, it does not stand alone in its innovations: there are great similarities with what such groups as The Living Theatre were also doing from the period of the mid-60's on—but it was by far the most elaborate and thoroughly worked-out of such experiments, and it prepared for much of what Brook would later do.

Interviews
Oxford to Orghast to India

MYTH AND MUSIC: RESONANCES ACROSS CONTINENTS AND CENTURIES AS EXPLORED BY PETER BROOK AND HIS ENSEMBLE
Glenn Loney

Judging from some of the critical complaints about Peter Brook's production of *The Mahabharata* at the Brooklyn Academy of Music, it might as well have been performed in Orghast as in English. That's an exaggeration, of course, but so were some of the objections raised about the nine-hour tripartite marathon mythic reduction which Brook, his adaptor Jean-Claude Carrière, and his ensemble had developed, based on this ancient and essential Hindu narrative.

Writing in the *New York Times*, drama critic Frank Rich objected first to the production's milieu, calling it "chic, post-modern asceticism" and contrived. For Rich, it suggested: "an environment for a Beverly Hills ashram rather than for a genuine rendition of a Hindu epic." More "problematic" for Rich, however, was the delivery of the Carrière-Brook text. In Paris, at Brook's *Bouffes du Nord* theatre center, it was performed in Carrière's original French, to general critical acclaim, even though some members of the international ensemble were not so fluent in French.

For the projected performances in Los Angeles, New York, and Australia, Brook himself devised the English text. His aim, he said, was to be as faithful as possible to Carrière's "gigantic achievement." Although *The Mahabharata* took a definitive narrative form as long as 2,000 years ago, both Carrière and Brook realized that "archaic or old-fashioned languages" should not be text-models. Seeking to recreate the effect of an ancient, venerable Sanskrit poem by inflecting it into the rhythms of a medieval Mystery play or a lost masterpiece by Shakespeare would not work; such solutions would further distance already strange and unfamiliar codes, characters, and customs. Nor would intensely modern, even "street-smart" English be appropriate, since that might suggest a particularity and relevance at odds with the ideas and events presented. The sterile, elegant purity of Neo-Classic French—the diction of Racine and Corneille—was also clearly wrong. Instead, as Carrière noted in his introduction to the published English text, the collaborators "settled on a simple, precise, restrained language which gave us the means to oppose or juxtapose words which are ordinarily never used together."

So much for their goals. The achievement, according to Frank Rich, was dubious and it undercut their aims: "Mr. Brook has translated the script into mostly prosaic, sometimes unidiomatic English, which is then spoken by an international company for whom English is, in too many cases, an awkward second language." It's clear from the context of his review that he found the prosaic and unidiomatic text inadequate to communicate the multi-layered mixture of the theological, philosophical, mythical, and historical in *The Mahabharata*. (In fact, Brook does slip into the idiomatic at one point, when the image of "mind-blowing" oddly emerges.) In effect, the difficulty Rich experienced in trying to understand the spoken text created for him a distancing: "as if we were listening to a dubbed foreign film."

In the next paragraph of his critique, Rich noted "a number of glorious sequences for the eyes," going so far as to praise each scene as "handsomely set forth," following this endorsement with the observation that there was "also an avalanche of tedious talk."

Other reviewers also complained about the diction of some of the international company. John Simon, of *New York* magazine, asserted that they had been recruited from the "first, second, and third worlds, and some of them from out of this world." Describing them as "fanatical cultists or unemployable anywhere else," which Simon attributed to the players' long hours and years spent acquiring "the Brookian style," he went on to complain of "accents ranging from the opaque to the inscrutable and, even when scrutable, often cacaphonous." In fact, although some spectators also fretted about difficulty in understanding some of the performers, others—from random samplings at various performances—insisted that they were able to understand most of the text by listening carefully. Brook himself professed surprise and puzzlement at the critical objections to the text and the diction. Presented in French in a quarry in Avignon, in a Zurich playhouse, and at the *Bouffes du Nord, The Mahabharata* had not been attacked as unintelligible. If anything, critics from major British and European papers and journals were ecstatic, as were Los Angeles reviewers when the English version had its American premiere.

One thing is certainly clear: Brook had no intention of repeating the *Orghast* experiment with Sanskrit tales and texts. Presenting *Hamlet* for a Moscow audience-admittedly with simultaneous translation-back in 1955, and later touring his celebrated Royal Shakespeare stagings of *King Lear* and *A Midsummer Night's Dream* successfully to a variety of lands where few understood English, Brook had become interested in the late 1960s in the possibilities of dramatic communication between performers and spectators, without the customary vehicle of a shared language. At the same time, he was fascinated by the wide, possibly universal, relevance of some major myths and tales, such as the legend of Prometheus, the Fire-Bringer, and the imprisoned wild prince in Calderon's *La Vida Es Sueño*, as well as some resonant ancient traditions in Persian texts.

Having begun his post-RSC work with the founding of a new Paris International Center for Theatre Research (C.I.R.T.), he decided that an area of exploration might well be the presentation of a mingling of such fundamental myths about the dawn of civilization from varied cultures, in fragments of actual ancient texts, delivered in languages now dead to virtually all listeners, aside from scholars and priests. Accordingly, the classic Greek of Aeschylus—from the *Agamemnon* and *The Persians*—and the elegant Latin of Seneca were blended with the almost forgotten ritual language of the Zoroasterian religion, Avesta. Central to the entire two-part work, called *Orghast*, was a new, constructed, artificial language, also called Orghast by its creator, now Britain's poet-laureate, Ted Hughes.

This production was staged at Persepolis, under the patronage of the late Shah of Iran's Queen, in August 1971, as part of the Shiraz Festival, to which other avant-garde theatre ensembles were also invited. The impressive and forbidding rock-tombs of great Persian rulers such as Darius and Xerxes provided unforgettable performance venues. To those critics who wondered why the enlightened and very liberal Brook agreed to accept the subsidy of what many perceived as a tyrannous, repressive regime, Brook and his coworkers responded that they had been invited, and that the financial and material support—such as it was—flowed not from the Shah's bounty, but from the Queen, who professed an interest in the arts and a desire to enrich the cultural experience of her rather benighted people. Iranian television was the direct source of subsidy. Finally, the often frustrating experiment was judged by Brook to have been rewarding in various ways, but that *Orghast* was not a work on which he and the Center would want to continue. And, as A. C. Smith notes in his account of this adventure in theatre-research, *Orghast at Persepolis*, those involved felt that if the Iranians had used them for their own image-building purposes, then Brook and company had also used the Iranians, to be able to conduct this major and—to those who witnessed it, at least—unforgettable experiment.

Interestingly enough, although some critics who were able to travel to Persepolis for the event professed bafflement when exposed to incomprehensible speech sounds of Orghast, most of them intuited meanings from the sounds themselves—the intonations, inflections, pitches, tempos, and rhythms, inextricably linked with the physical performances of the actor-speakers, providing a powerful sense of the newly invented legend, compounded out of existing ancient myths. In fact, it was a music critic, Andrew Porter, then of London's *Financial Times* and later *The New Yorker's* resident music-historian, who most effectively perceived and described what Brook had attempted and achieved with Ted Hughes and his co-workers in *Orghast*. (Porter is an admired translator of operas for English-language performance: his version of Richard Wagner's *Ring* had been used in Seattle,

San Francisco, and elsewhere.) As a translator, he emphasized his own parallel concern with "matching sound and sense, with finding the words which fitted, were dictated by, [and] embodied a theatrical, musical, and emotional movement."

Also very perceptive was Irving Wardle, of the *London Times*, who saw *Orghast* as: "something without parallel in theatre history: the creation of a form of drama comprehensible to anyone on earth." Dismissing the admittedly elitist circumstances of the Festival itself and of the dramatic event—few Iranian commoners were among the distinguished international audiences—Wardle saw Brook and Hughes' achievement as: "an attempt to melt corresponding national myths down to universal archetype," with the constructed language as a possible means of putting an international company with many native tongues on an equal performance footing. Wardle suggested that negative judgements were in fact effectual "intellectual barricades against a work intended to awaken the prelogical faculties and conjure buried music out of the earth."

That is an amazing perception—and a brilliant formulation of Brook's essential intention, and it is also importantly operative in Brook's *Mahabharata* production, although, in a variety of public utterances and written commentaries, Brook had steadfastly urged that the work be, initially at least, accepted and viewed as an exercise in story-telling. Several influential New York reviewers rejected this approach, either as being simplistic and ingenuous—something they could hardly believe of a talent as sophisticated as Peter Brook—or as an unacceptable and unworthy reduction of a great work of Hindu literature, philosophy, and religion. But, as Brook had noted, in the preface to his translation of Carrière's text: "In the performance, whether in English or in French, we are not attempting a reconstruction of Dravidian or Aryan India of three-thousand year ago. We are not presuming to present the symbolism of Hindu philosophy. In the music, in the costumes, in the movements, we have tried to present the flavor of India, without pretending to be what we are not."

Curiously though, Brook and his ensemble were blamed by some critics for not being faithful enough to Hindu essences. Among them, the *Times'* Frank Rich, who wrote: "The spiritual import of this *Mahabharata* remains elusive, crowded out rather than expressed by the plot. Much of the work's moral substance is reduced to easily digestible sermons and homilies that only superficially explore the enigmatic Hindu concept of self-fulfillment ('dharma')." Perhaps to mitigate his condemnations, Rich observed: "For all the Eastern exotica, the staging and the script still end up accentuating the common ground shared by *The Mahabharata* and the West." For Peter Brook, this was an interesting comment, primarily because— although it suggested a slight, rather than praise—Rich had perceived what Brook had hoped would be essentially intuited.

Only a few days after the BAM premiere, Brook discussed his own reactions with members of New York's Drama Desk, a society of drama critics, editors, and journalists. He noted that, had *The Mahabharata* opened on Broadway, as had his memorable RSC production of *A Midsummer Night's Dream* in 1971, which won ecstatic reviews, he and his C.I.R.T. ensemble would at that moment be back home in Paris, unpacking the props and costumes. Although calm and thoughtful, Brook was clearly disturbed and baffled by the initial New York reviews, notably those of Rich and the *Village Voice's* Michael Feingold, whom he did not mention by name at the Drama Desk. But he did profess profound perplexity over the import of Feingold's *Voice* essay about the true nature of the epic as a form.

As Brook said then: "I read a long and, I felt, irrelevant article about 'is this epical; is this drama?' This is a meaningless quibble because it's *not* epic; it's *not* drama. We are *telling a story*. And to tell a story through the theatre form, one has to use many different devices. Sometimes the story is told through music, sometimes through movement, sometimes through people, and, in the Eastern way, often stopping one story to tell another story, which leads to another story, which leads to an action. And this changing of style is all to support a vast story."

Brook went on to note that those who accepted the *Mahabharata* production as a story being told would find that it is: "one of the richest stories that one can experience." In fact, for Brook, the only way to approach the production was by the route of "direct experience." All forms of intellectual, textual, semiotic, deconstructive analysis, Brook suggested, were self-defeating. Instead of aiding understanding of the work in performance, they erected intellecutal barriers, preventing or perverting understanding. He did not cite the actual biblical text, but his appeal for a direct, even childlike openness to his *Mahabharata* echoed that venerable piece of advice about being as little children, in order to enter the Kingdom of Heaven.

Without raising his voice, Brook made it abundantly clear that he was disappointed and disturbed by the potentially influential reviews of both Rich and Feingold. Nonetheless, he took comfort from the fact that the BAM engagement was protected—by subsidy and virtually sold-out houses—from the customary rapid Broadway closures of shows not smiled upon by whoever may be reviewing for the *Times* at the moment. He noted the difference in London, where no one critic can kill or close a show with a negative review. In fact, carping critiques often intrigue otherwise indifferent readers to make a point of seeing such productions.

Having himself been briefly an eloquent critic of ballet for the *Observer* of London, under J. C. Trewin, who later became his biographer, Brook outlined some of the problems he discovered about writing "notices" with some regularity. He also observed that among his critical confrères were some worn-out journalists who had no background whatsoever in theatre or the other performing arts. Editors had given them the drama beat as a kind of pre-retirement post or as a reward for all those hard years on the police beat. He didn't suggest that such was the case with Rich or Feingold, but it was clear that his regard for newspaper drama critics, as a whole, was not high.

Perhaps New York critics were still remembering the Deconstructive discoveries of Brook's RSC *Dream*, or the devastating demonics of his *Marat/Sade*. The inspiration he derived at that time from his studies of the writings of Antonin Artaud, such as *The Theatre and Its Double*, and his initial RSC explorations in the Theatre of Cruelty, as well as the co-eval resonances he recognized in the theatre criticism of Poland's Jan Kott and the theories and productions of the innovative director/teacher Jerzy Grotowski, were later assimilated, absorbed, and adapted in the Paris work. During the London Theatre of Cruelty explorations, Brook was personally attacked, both as a stage-director and as one of the managing triumvirate of the Royal Shakespeare Company—with Sir Peter Hall and the late Michel St. Denis— for the series of "dirt plays" presented at the Aldwych Theatre. This angry complaint was made in the press in an open letter by Emile Littler, a leading London commercial producer and a member of the RSC's board.

At that time, Brook responded—again in apparent surprise and disbelief at Littler's outburst—by noting that he had already staged, as Littler and the mass of informed theatre-goers knew only too well, virtually every kind of theatre-work, from *Hamlet* and *King Lear* to *The Little Hut, House of Flowers*, and *Irma La Douce*. Brook had resoundingly demonstrated his brilliance as a director in farce, musical comedy, opera, comedy of manners, the range of Shakespeare, including such "problem" plays as *Titus Andronicus* and *Love's Labour's Lost*, and interesting modern works like T. S. Eliot's *Family Reunion*, Arthur Miller's *A View from the Bridge*, and, in Paris, Tennessee Williams' *Chat sur une Toite Brûlante*. It seemed there was no dramatic challenge Brook could not meet, including designing sets, costumes, and composing *musique concrète*.

Putting all these successes behind him, Brook said at that time that he was certainly satisfied with what he had accomplished, not ashamed of it, but that the theatre of attractive visual effects, of impressive surfaces, of calculated and conventional entertainments no longer offered any challenges or interest to him. He answered Emile Littler by observing that he, like Shakespeare, was now going through his "dark period." And he wasn't sure when—or if—he would emerge from it, but his agenda had now become a much more serious exploration of the powers and essences of drama and the theatre-experience.

Those New York critics who saw Brook's Paris production of *The Conference of the Birds*, based on an ancient Sufi manuscript—and shown also in different seasons at BAM and at Ellen Stewart's La Mama E.T.C—certainly had already had some exposure to a simple, almost childlike presentation of an allegorical search for God, made by a group of birds, whose few survivors discover that the god-essence is actually within themselves. For Brook, it was difficult to reconcile the admiration and acceptance shown that work and the objections or indifference registered for *The Mahabharata*. He told the Drama Desk, in fact, that *favorable* reviews are not so important for those involved in a production as the other kind. When the report is positive, either the critics have rightly understood what was intended, or they haven't, but their praise won't discourage possible spectators, who can then discover the work for themselves if they wish. Indifference, however, means something—text, performance, passion—failed to connect with the reviewer, and such failures may offer food for thought. Negative reactions from intelligent, experienced critics, of course, can give directors and performers even more pause. What is the reason for the disparity between what the creators thought they were doing and what the critics perceive them to have done—or not to have done?

Discussing *The Mahabharata* at Barnard College, Brook explained his and Jean-Claude Carrière's longtime interest in this Sanskrit epic, culminating in repeated trips of exploration to India. Although Brook had been accused by some militant champions of Third World customs and culture of effectively "ripping off" the Hindus by appropriating and adapting their major epic, he, of course, did not view his *Mahabharata* production in this light at all. And some critics accused him of creating an "elitist" event, especially in Brooklyn. But if there was anything even elusively elitist about BAM audiences or their reactions to the production, that was hardly Brook's intent or concern. The media, if anything, conspired to make *The Mahabharata* the "event" of the cultural season.

In any case, versions or portions of the great Hindu epic had already been seen in New York, sometimes at the American Museum of Natural History or at Asia House, performed by Kathakali dancers, by native players, and even by Asian puppets. So the proprietors of the original legends had also been able to offer their own visions of the myriad of tales which comprise the work.

Peter Brook told Barnard students that *The Mahabharata*, as a major work of Asian literature, religion, philosophy, and cultural tradition, should be as well known in the West as the Bible and other major Western works are known in Asia. Without seeking to explicate the complexities of its mythic riches, Brook and his company, he observed, had simply tried to make it available, accessible, to Western audiences on the level of an extended and fascinating story. If the images retained after seeing it provoked thought and discussion, with an attendant desire to read the work and explore it in greater depth, so much the better. When possible, Brook said, his company liked to discuss productions with the audience after the show.

In further explaining his fascination with *The Mahabharata*, Brook made the interesting comparison: "Myths are like music." Some resonance in the listener responds to the tale of the teller, he suggested. "Why is it that some stories are told over and over—and others are not?" he asked. He noted that some legends and fables have enjoyed currency over the centuries, and not solely in one culture. "We recognize something in them and we respond to that," Brook said. And, he added, it is the same with music, even music from an alien culture or a past period.

Several weeks later, enlarging on this in a special interview, Brook restated the parallel between myth and music as a kind of fundamental resonance across cultures. To explain the way in which myths may arouse or awake such resonances, Brook used the analogy of viewing Abstract paintings: "Anybody going to a great collection of Abstract painters, like Joan Miró, experiences a succession of images as the eye travels across the canvas. It goes through a journey of shapes and colors. And the net result of that eye-traveling is receiving something that can move one very deeply. Now a myth, in that way, is also like a moving-picture. It's a series of images which are very rich. They move; they talk; they are inter-related. And, if one follows it in *that* way—in the traditional way that a story is listened to, or, in other words, as music is listened to, or as the eye travels across an Abstract painting—as one receives it, as a series, as a sequence, a *living* sequence, something has been deeply stirred in one."

Despite the often simplistic presentation of myths and fairy tales, lacking the dimension and detail of specific human stories, it is just possible that *they* are more true than observed recorded realities. "They embody our deepest hopes and fears," I suggested to Brook in our interview. "That's absolutely true," Brook agreed. "And I would say that this is an example of something very deep within us, a deep fear perhaps, which has no shape but a reality all the same, which has to find its form. And the form it takes is this particular language of story-telling and myth, which is beyond analytical language, beyond a discursive language."

Nonetheless, the fact that Brook has been drawn to Persian, Indian, and African cultures and sources, for materials and texts for his theatre researches-in-performance in recent years in Paris and in the Third World, suggests to some that his ultimate aim may well be a kind of universal or international theatre, performed by a multi-national company, which he already has had, in effect. Actually, it's hardly that simple. Although Brook has drawn on talents from diverse nations and cultures, he has no fixed ensemble, creating specific companies for each project. He does, however, often employ certain artists with whom he can work most productively. But his goal, even in a single production such as *The Mahabharata*, is not to create theatre-works which are amalgams of materials and styles from various national or tribal traditions. It is true in *The Mahabharata*, however, that specific techniques from several Asian/Oriental performance forms were used. Japanese drums, Peking Opera military costumes, Asian puppets: these are some of the special effects which enhance those which are specifically suggestive of the Indian experience.

The ultimate purpose, for Brook, is to find the form—the right, the effective form—for the myth to manifest itself. Some years ago, during UNESCO's "Year of the Child," Ellen Stewart brought thirty performing artists from as many Third World nations to La Mama E. T. C. in New York so that they could inter-stimulate each other with specific mythic or historical materials and performance techniques from each culture. The culmination was a group-created work embodying something from each of the traditions represented. Instead of being greater than the sum of its parts, it was still only an anthology of often disparate ideas and production elements. That is not what Peter Brook is seeking. In effect, the La Mama venture was, like Brook's adventure with *Orghast* at Persepolis, a piece of theatre-research which was useful in that it vividly demonstrated the limits of the possibilities of such inter-cultural co-operation.

Confronted with critiques which complained of Brook's apparent failure to present *The Mahabharata* with more regard for its epic nature and its Indian performance traditions, Brook insisted that that was never a goal. He noted that actors who have not grown up in a specific cultural performance tradition—and who have not trained in it—cannot master or even effectively copy such styles as Kathakali or Balinese dance. Not that this hasn't been explored in Paris by Brook and his ensembles. Once he asked an expert in Balinese dance, a company member, to teach others these delicate skills. It didn't work. "Half-way looks embarrassing," Brook commented. The fundamental problem in trying to assimilate alien ethnic styles, Brook believes, is that—unless one trains in them for months or years—performers will never be able to fully "inhabit" the movements or techiques. They cannot make them their own. And yet, Brook observed, it's just possible that, with tremendous motivation and *belief*, a performer can suggest the effect or quality. He offered as an example an awkward actor, unable to recreate the graceful manners and movements of an 18th century gentleman, who managed nonetheless to *suggest* such grace because of the intensity of his belief. But Brook is not interested in having his performers build up an anthology—or an arsenal—of ethnic styles.

To explain what he is seeking, Brook outlined some relevant analogies: "One of the most boring clichés that one hears, year after year working with actors, is: 'I work from the *inside* out,' or, 'I work from the *outside* in.' That's an ancient cliché that has got into the actors' vocabulary. But, like all clichés, the actual thought does have a grain of truth in it. And I think that today, when we talk about theatre in general, almost all the time we are talking about 'from the outside in.'

"So that, when one talks about 'putting cultures together,' this is the trap. One is talking about 'from the outside in,' as if, when we get a nice bit of the results of one culture and fit it together, like a jigsaw puzzle-piece, with a nice bit of the results of another culture, somehow something deeper will be born inside.

"Now I think this is a very, very dangerous trap! Because, in most cases, what happens when you put a jigsaw puzzle together is that you start with a surface fragment and then you fill in that surface until there are no gaps in it. But there's really *nothing* underneath."

Possibly a card-table? Brook grinned: "Well, yes, a card-table." To contrast that kind of outside-in work with its opposite, Brook used another arts analogy: "What one means by the inside-to-outside way of working is the process which was better described, I think, than anywhere else in the famous film Jacques Clouzot made about Picasso, *The Picasso Mystery*.

"If you remember that film, the camera was placed on the far side of a translucent piece of thin canvas. So you never saw Picasso. You never actually saw the artist. Instead, you saw what was happening. You saw, suddenly, a stroke. And then you saw that stroke produced the need to search for another stroke. And when the two strokes were there, you saw how the process—the need for expression, the need for finding the form that related to it—suddenly made a line between the two strokes. And, once the line was made, you could sense Picasso looking at it and feeling: 'No, that isn't the right line.' And you could see him scrubbing it out and starting again, until, by an enormous process of searching, trial-and-error, using one part of the palette and another part of the palette, eventually the jigsaw puzzle was completed.

"But here—and that's where we come to what we're talking about— the process *in* the painter, *in* the writer, is first of all that inner need for finding the appropriate *form*. The one-and-only form that exactly matches something inside that hasn't yet found a form. Then there's the experimenting in different forms—blue, green, orange, yellow; sharp, narrow, broad, thick, heavy—until that moment, which is a creative moment, when the need of the formless to be born into form suddenly becomes a form. What hasn't a form—that energy needing to make itself concrete—that is what one really calls creation. And that's where I feel, absolutely, radically, fundamentally, that the effects of a culture are just that: only effects, not *causes*. They grow out of . . .

Trying to be helpful, I suggested: "Needs? Traditions? History?"

"No," Brook said. "They grow out of something more fundamental still, which has neither name nor shape. Otherwise . . . well, if it had a name or a shape, it wouldn't be fundamental. What is fundamental is the *need* to make a shape. And *that*, as it is pre-shape, cannot have a shape. As it is pre-form, it cannot have a form. As it is pre-name, it cannot have a name. On that fundamental level, every human-being can meet!

"The making of form is, in itself, a making of divisions. In the act of making a form, something becomes individualized and, consequently, separated from the next. So that, on the fundamental level, there is the point where understanding between people begins. Because understanding is not through codes. Oh, I think a superficial understanding is: you produce a series of codes; I learn your codes; therefore, I understand you.

"But that is not *deep* understanding. You could call it 'intellectual understanding,' and it can go to a very high level of intellectual understanding. But, of course, it is not total *human* understanding. Total human understanding one recognizes, one knows, one feels, and one sees that it is on this level that people of totally different races and cultures can understand one another in the most rich way as human beings.

"What I've always stressed, however, is that each race and each culture develops more intensely one part of the human possibility than another. So then when a group of people from different cultures works together, provided they don't fall in love with codes or get stuck on codes—"

I thought of an example: "'Look! I can mimic your gestures! I can do your dances!' But it must go deeper than that?"

Brook nodded: "A code is a code, neither to be despised or exalted. What matters is what's *behind* the code. Then the mere fact of working together enables each person to have a new stimulus brought to that part of him which is least developed. It helps him to grow, as a person, as a performer.

"I've said this also on other occasions: each man is an incomplete man. So when one has a big group of people, with many different natures and backgrounds, genuinely reaching the point of being able to work together, then that group becomes like a picture of a more normal, more complete individual. A nobler individual, of which there are very few in the world: a man or woman who would have inside him an African, an Asian, and an American!"

"In other words, it's not our glory, but our limitation, that we cannot reach that. And, as theatre—the aim of theatre—is in all forms a temporary opening-up of everyone concerned, our projects are among the temporary openings-up."

Such an ensemble, sharing so many elements of human possibility, Brook observed, can itself then become complete, an organic whole. But there isn't a single, fixed Paris ensemble for Brook's work. "It depends on what the project is," he explained. "If we're doing a project like *The*

Mahabharata or *The Cherry Orchard*, the first basis of company formation is that of all theatre castings: that you don't give the oldest part to the youngest actor. You don't begin by putting a woman in the men's parts, because there is a simple level of story-telling in which, like casting a film, you want people, broadly speaking, to correspond to the parts.

"In *The Mahabharata*, with only five women, we obviously needed more tough guys than women. In another project, it could be the other way around. But that's the first common-sense thing, as in the theatre. Unless we're doing, as we have done in the past, purely improvisational work over a long period of time, where, of course, you're not looking for an actor for a special role. In the present group, however, with those who've been with us for a long time, we've tried to develop to the maximum their ability to go against type. To the limit, knowing that everybody has a limit.

"The second level in casting is that each person should be as unlike the next as possible. That's a principle of a theatre company, as opposed to a dance company, where uniformity is often sought. Whereas here, the principle of contrast will run all the way through. And then, of course, there's the need for actors to be open and interested. Interested not in their egos, but in the work. Otherwise, they're disappointed—and then I'am disappointed, and it's a bad basis for work.

"Most important of all—because they not only have to be talented— each must bring his own 'baggage.' I don't think the director makes possibilities. I don't see myself as a music-teacher who takes raw talent and then shapes it. I never have felt that, particularly if you want to do difficult work. If people come to me and say: 'I am putty in your hands,' well, that's bad for them and bad for me."

I interjected: "But putty's inert. It can't move of itself!"

"Exactly!" Brook responded: "You want someone who has, well, more than one can just call experience. Experience in every way of life: real baggage! All the best collaborations I've had have been with people who have had very strong convictions, and ideas which were not 'bloody-minded.' I've also got strong convictions and ideas, but that doesn't stop me from listening—and yielding immediately to someone else's ideas.

"But with someone who's bloody-minded, it's not worth even attempting to work with him. With someone who hasn't strong convictions, you can ask him to search. And out of searching, in his own way, loyally and passionately for the same thing, there comes a point when what he proposes back to you is in the same direction in which you're working, but infinitely better than what you proposed," Brook insisted.

And just what did he mean by "bloody-minded," which is not a familiar idiom to Americans?

"You don't say that? How very interesting! It means someone who is obstructionist," he explained,

Critical complaints in New York about alleged unintelligibility of some *Mahabharata* cast members continued to puzzle Peter Brook. He related it to previous New York responses to his *La Tragédie de Carmen*, which was widely admired by drama critics—who had few preconceptions about the work, either as *novella* or opera—and was generally dismissed or condemned by music critics, who had rather definite ideas about what could or could not be done with *Carmen* on stage.

Brook noted what many American tourists have also discovered in Paris: no matter how good you think your French is, natives will affect to misunderstand you. Yet, at the *Bouffes du Nord*, neither critics nor public made a fuss about not being able to understand actors who were not native French-speakers.

"These objections are a very interesting new phenomenon, but I don't think they are deeply true. Because we've played in many different countries in both French and English, and the normal person *listens*. Sometimes, you have to listen even more intently, just as you have to in the street when you meet a foreigner who wants directions.

"In France, if anyone has a strong accent, they may shout at him. They get uptight and annoyed with foreigners. And they are not really listening. But in the theatre, we've never had this problem before. Here's what is interesting: in New York, there's a certain form of specifically East Coast intellectual who is, as the French say, *plus royaliste que le roi*. This is also related to the response to *Carmen*.

"In Paris, there wasn't a single academic, or classical musician, or critic who raised a single objection to the fact that *La Tragédie de Carmen* was a new view of a traditional French monument. We had to come to New York to encounter, for the first time, that form of conservatism: jealously protecting values here—*European* values—which in Europe are much freer. It's exactly the same thing with the language: the uptightness of a man who prides himself on a certain level of education and who is, therefore, defending a theory of linguistic purity." Brook laughed wryly: was he imagining the presumed uptightness of Frank Rich?

Brook was clearly still disturbed by some of the New York critics' objections to *The Mahabharata*: "They are defending cultural values which do not at all correspond to the experience everyone else had," he insisted. But it's also possible that the production had been oversold in advance, in a kind of media blitz which had implied that *The Mahabharata* would be *the* theatre event of the fall, if not of the entire New York season.

Consider this BAM press-release: "*The Mahabharata* is a nine-hour epic presentation with an international cast of 30, representing over 18 nations world-wide. The Sanskrit poem of the same name, written over 2,000 years ago, is ten times the length of the Bible, and is the basis by which all Hindu culture guides its existence. From the highest class of society, to the common man in the street, this spiritual text permeates every facet of daily life."

And there was more: "*The Mahabharata* has no equivalent in Western culture. It is a combination of religious text, epic poem, myth, historical tableau, and a series of short stories about the early history of India's ruling houses . . . It unfolds in a swirl of color—saris, gowns, and garments of saffron, crimson, and gold; umbrellas of rippling blue silk; red banners and snow-white robes. Heroes lose kingdoms; virgin princesses elope with gods . . . ." This is partly true and partly hype, since it in part refers to the Hindu masterpiece as written, and in part to the Peter Brook production, which is not quite the same thing.

So it may well be that critics not only came with certain preconceptions which were unfair or irrelevant to what Brook and his ensemble were trying to achieve, but that they also arrived with heightened, but unreal, expectations, encouraged by advance reports of remarkable theatrical wonders and glowing reviews from critics in Paris, London, and Los Angeles.

US REHEARSAL BREAK:
COMMENTS BY PETER BROOK
Glenn Loney

[London: July 8, 1966]

We are searching for a union of ritualistic and popular theatre. The Elizabethans found such a form, but we cannot copy Shakespeare today. We have to experiment—to find our *own* way of expressing these qualities: the reality that cuts right through to the ordinary man in the audience, and the heightened, condensed formalized expression that gives *meaning* to idea and emotion.

Peter Weiss has largely done this with *Marat/Sade*. There, as in a film, the experience is a totality: language, action, emotion, spectacle.

Our season of Theatre of Cruelty was not like the present season. There we went "far out." At present, with *Tango* and *Days in the Trees*, we are searching for the formal/popular equation. *Tango* is really a boulevard theatre formula: too facile, too shallow.

[Michael Kirby's *Happenings* lies on Brook's table: noticed in the context of this discussion of *US* by Loney.]

Vietnam [as *US* was then called], with a series of writers, developed from the current situation and a sharp awareness of the problem.

For the RSC, the idea of contemporary plays at the Aldwych is designed to contribute to Shakespeare: to give leaven, balance, and insights.

The text is *not* the play, only a small part. Words change, or say different things in another time. The director has to go beneath them and find the author's true indent.

[With Peter Weiss, Brook could ask him directly?]

That was good to have, but one could do *Marat/Sade* without Weiss. That's the way we have to do Shakespeare! A play is really a mass of material: thoughts, feelings, ideas, actions—of which the actual printed words are only a very small part. Printed Shakespeare is *not* what Shakespeare did on stage, but that *man* [Here, a churning-together of Brook's hands and fingers.] is still there! We have to find him.

Brecht's Epic Theatre is not the ritual answer. At the end of his life, Brecht was beginning to realize its real limitations. Within the bounds of his theories, Brecht could never have written *Hamlet*. In *Mother Courage*, he shows us the *outside*. He cannot show what goes on inside. Of course, he oversimplifies. His theories cause him to have a biased view of humanity.

In the RSC, I don't always approve of what is done. But, if I am overruled, well, that is our freedom to do what we want to do.

[Some critics had complained that Peter Weiss's intellectual argument between Sade and Marat got lost, perhaps purposely, in the tumult of the RSC production.]

Those critics went to the theatre prepared to see "something." When they didn't find what they were looking for, they took that defense.

[Wasn't the author's use of the Charenton madhouse as a dramatic milieu tremendously important to the effect of the debate?]

Yes, it was!

[The baths sunk into the floor of the set were inspired by similar ones at St. Bartholomew's Hospital, used in the 19th century for syphilis patients. Did that have any resonance in regard to the patients in *Marat/Sade*?]

I really don't know. It *sounds* interesting.

A MIDSUMMER NIGHT'S DREAM AT THE DRAMA DESK: PETER BROOK AND MAJOR PLAYERS DISCUSS THE PRODUCTION IN NEW YORK

[On January 25, 1971, shortly after the Broadway opening at the Billy Rose Theatre, Peter Brook and *Midsummer Night's Dream* cast-members were guests of the Drama Desk for a session of questions and answers about production concepts and practices. Among the performers were Alan Howard (Theseus/Oberon), John Kane (Philostrate/Puck), and David Waller (Bottom). The Drama Desk is a professional association of New York writers on theatre. One of the members, Margaret Croyden, chaired the meeting, with the group's president, Henry Hewes, acting as co-host. Ms. Croyden saluted the production for its excitement and innovation and introduced the guests. Hewes began the discussion by asking Brook why the "Dream" was chosen—and not some other Shakespearean play.]

BROOK: It's almost impossible to answer. One really doesn't know. Amongst the plays of Shakespeare, there are some that one has an affection for—a particular feeling for. For an actor or a director, this means that sometime we want to come into closer contact with that play; to have a living acquaintance with that material. That stays in the back of one's mind for years. In my own experience, I find that one never finds anything taking form at all, as long as it's theoretical; I've been saying the *Midsummer Night's Dream* is amongst the plays I'd like to do at Stratford. Why, at a certain moment, all the elements come together, has quite a lot behind it. It could have happened five years ago; it could have happened two years from now. An event does become *right*. It does happen at a time when I think there is a possibility of the play making more sense. I think the work we're doing with the play does correspond rightly with the moment in which we're doing it. Everything has seemed to come together, and the right people have been selected for the cast—because there was a degree of selection.

But there is that *moment*. This is why I think, for a director, the first rehearsal of a play is the most frightening. Because you know that either this mysterious conjunction is right—in which case the total event is the combination of all the people assembled on that first day, and of all their work— or someone, somewhere, has made a very bad decision. And we are then gathered together for a false event, and no matter how hard anyone tries or works—and usually one works much harder under those circumstances—nothing good ever comes out of it.

So I don't think one can fairly say that there is a day when one can say: "This *must* be done. Now, how does one put it together?" The thorn is not so much to be found in saying: "How are we going to do it?" For instance, in the case of "The Dream," this is a play by Shakespeare—not writing a play for children—but an adult writing very clearly and consciously for adults a play about fairies. It's quite clear, however, that this line which runs throughout the play cannot be presented convincingly through dead or second-hand imagery.

How one captures this moment in the 20th century—a life that could be meaningful to an audience in a play about magic—is such a difficult and strong and clear starting point that one can say that everything else—all the forms of the production—stem from having to face that question.

[Brook was asked why he decided to give the production a circus format.]

BROOK: I don't think we ever thought of it as a circus. What we thought about is that the play is a *celebration*. It's a celebration of the theme of theatre: the play-within-the-play-within-the-play-within-the-play. One of its themes is theatre, at least. And to celebrate the arts of acting, you have to celebrate as wide a range as possible. Isn't there something very joyful for actors to play, for actors to perform? There's something very joyful for actors to do technically and physically difficult actions with ease. For instance, to us, juggling seemed *part* of the actor's arts—rather than something we were going toward the circus for, to pull it back into the theatre. The complete actor juggles all the time, in one way or another.

[Brook was queried: How was the white "empty space" setting arrived at?]

BROOK: Sally Jacobs, who designed the show and who is so close to the work of the actors, could not be here today. But I think she would affirm, as much as anyone else, that the only reason we have white walls is because we're in a theatre-building. When, for instance, we've played the same production outside a normally constructed theatre—as we have done in England—we've done it without any scenery or any costumes.

And the cast has managed to produce exactly the same meanings, without color, without costumes, without background—and without swings! These things are important to us within the sort of buildings we've been working in. And yet, what is most important is that all we wanted was to make *nothingness* around the work. So the white walls are not there to state something, but to *eliminate* something. On a nothingness, moment by moment, something can be conjured up—and then made to disappear. The bare stage is a form of nothingness, but it's a joyless form. Playing on a bare stage where you see the ropes and the back wall has been done before in the theatre. It is a sort of neutral nothingness, but it is not a very happy solution. The nearest thing we could find to something completely neutral which said nothing—and yet had an element of joy and excitement which correspond to a celebration—was a brilliant white. It was a solution to that problem.

[The players were asked how they and Brook had interacted in rehearsals. Alan Howard, the Thesus/Oberon, answered first, followed by John Kane, the Philostrate/Puck.]

HOWARD: I think one of the most remarkable things Peter made available from the word "go" was the situation whereby anything is possible. And anything is available to anyone's imagination, inclination, and instinct. This was incredibly exciting. In the early stages, we just very simply read the play very quietly several times through. All the time searching for things which are unexplainable: they become more explainable, the more you investigate them. But you investigate them not entirely on your own; rather, in conjunction with the other people who are reading the play.

Feeling the incredible reverberations of this play. . . it was especially exciting for those of us who were playing more than one part. It seemed a terrific idea, but one wondered exactly how one was going to do heavy, complicated characterizations and transformations. To be able to *feel* this text in an atmosphere of serenity: that was, first of all, the most exciting thing from all our points of view.

[Had Howard deliberately avoided such ideas of the play as that it is a *dream* of Theseus's?]

HOWARD: Yes, as far as we could. It obviously came up in conversations, after we had read a bit, then everybody was very much encouraged to say what they thought about it, what they felt. It could be anything. Gradually, over a period of time, millions of ideas were disseminated. Sort of a blueprint.

What Peter wanted us to do was—somehow, in our own ways—get further and further into this play. It's a play of so many levels—extraordinary! Sometimes, just by suggestions offered by Peter, or other actors, or people involved in the production, hatches were opened up; you might not have seen them that particular day, but three days later! It was just incredible.

KANE: I think one of the strangest things about working for Peter for the first time is the realization that—and this is very true of the way we work at Stratford—we *do something* with the play. What was novel in working with Peter was that he wanted the play to *do things* with us. It was very difficult for us to break down our desire to immediately seize on scenes and characters and start doing things with them. Making them fit a rational concept.

Certainly, for people who like to plan everything out for their work—and I'm one of those people—I found it very, very difficult not to start bending the play *my* way. It was hard to clear my mind—it was a purification—to allow the play almost to drip through your mind and color you, without you coloring the play. This was quite revolutionary to me.

In demanding this incredible mental discipline, he also demanded a physical discipline. We would start the day—for the first half-hour, we would practice with the plates and stilts and balls and everything else, so that we were physically geared to approach whatever we would be doing that day: There is no contrast of the extrovert-introvert in the play; they are parts of the same whole, part of the unity which is our approach to the play.

BROOK: I'd like to add something to that. It's quite obvious that the role of the director, in relation to a group of actors, has to be to hold certain things very firmly, very intensely. Something, from the first day of rehearsal, has to be maintained. And, in this case, one of the things that had to be maintained very, very strongly was an elimination of the barriers to the play that can come from the sort of rationalizing, of intellectualizing working-habits that has just been described.

The reason the director here has to take a very positive role in holding the company to this is the *purpose* behind it: to get rid of useless interventions by the actors so that one can reach the level where the actors' own truest, most individual creativity really comes into play. When that happens, a group begins thinking and working in one direction. At that moment, all the ideas, suggestions, thoughts, and pieces of action that begin to get found all relate to the play.

The end of this process is that what you see on stage from one end to the other, unit by unit, physical image, idea, thought, is a collective creation. But collective creation doesn't happen by a lot of people sitting down in a room and saying: "We are a collective. Let's create!" It just doesn't happen that way.

It doesn't happen either by one person coming and working out methods and giving them instructions or giving them ideas—in which the actor is a divinely intuitive but ultimately passive agent.

Eventually, the more the work develops, the more each person's role becomes clear and indispensable. The result becomes more and more complete, where you cannot separate one person's contributions from another's. For instance, in reworking the play between Stratford and New

York—and we've done a great deal of work—the group had reached sufficient confidence in itself that suddenly someone would hear *seventeen* different versions of what he was doing wrong. That takes a lot of security, and it's only just beginning to be possible. It's a very perilous thing, but the result is that the solution that comes at the end of all these interventions influences the whole group. Eventually, it becomes a complete piece of collective work.

[David Waller, the Bottom for Stratford and New York, was asked about the novel transformation he experienced, being magically turned into an ass.]

WALLER: I'm not particularly articulate when talking about plays or acting. And I'm only occasionally good at actually doing it but that is, in fact, how the particular aspect of the transformation of Bottom into an ass came about. Because we did an enormous member of quite extraordinary improvisations on the theme of transformed nightmares in magic woods, without any props, or actions, or words, or songs. Anything that we could think of at the moment.

At the end of Act I, the whole transformation into an ass and the transformation of the rest of the rehearsing Mechanicals into terrified fugitives is a distillation of the games we played and the fun we had. Trying to think of what would actually happen—or what could *not* conceivably happen next.

If you make a beautiful ass's head out of donkey-hide, if you like, with ears and moveable eyes, and put it on your head—somehow the whole thing disappears immediately. Obviously you cannot turn an actor into an ass, so you might just as well not pretend you can. All you're left with is the *idea* of turning into an ass, and this is what we tried to demonstrate.

KANE: There was one particular rehearsal, the first run-through we had of the first act: at the end of ten days, we had a run-through. We had no moves planned. We could move wherever we liked. The four Fairies—we called them Audio-Visuals, because they made sounds and moved things around—they could be benches, chairs, anything. And sometimes they moved actors around the stage like chess pieces: they still have a tendency to do that!

The run-through was incredible. We all had books in our hands. We really didn't know what we were doing. *We* were a rival gang of bricklayers. The problem that Quince, Bully Bottom, and the Mechanicals had was to find a quiet enough place to rehearse, because we were intent on sawing our wood or tearing down walls. We did everything in our power to end this rehearsal by a group of faggot workers, and things really got heated up.

From that moment on, once people were actually concerned with *doing* something—they were determined to rehearse, and we were determined to stop them—well, the thing took off and went at incredible speed right through to the end, the wedding. We tore everything up: newspapers; we threw cushions about.

At the end, when everything quieted down and the last newspaper flicked to the floor, we stood and looked around at the incredible chaos—the debris we had created during the course of the rehearsal. We had *wrecked* the entire studio. Hardly a chair was left with a leg on it. It was the first glimmer we had had of how a play—without thinking about it, by just going along with it—of how a play can drive you with it. How it can change you; how it can transport you. I think the majority of us were transported. We had little recollection of what had happened.

I suppose it would have been appalling to watch. You wouldn't have understood what the play was about: Peter had talked about a parallel of savagery in the play. Yes, we *understood* what he was saying, but we couldn't quite see it. Then, suddenly, we had *felt* it, because the savagery had moved us. We had become incredibly primitive and we had created all that destruction. We had got a hint of that "secret play" that Peter still talks about: the play that will never be found by us, but "we keep working at it."

[Clive Barnes, *New York Times* drama critic at that time, was at this point asked to share his reactions to the production.]

BARNES: Really, it's much more interesting to listen to them than to listen to me. Out of the conversations so far, two things strike me. The first is *elimination*. It does seem to me that this is a play from which more has been taken away than given to. It's the cleanest Shakespeare I've ever encountered. It's the newest and the freshest. The other thing is—and what I think has changed from Stratford to New York, to some extent—the sense of *fun*. The actors have mentioned fun. They were obviously enjoying themselves. I think this sense of fun has become more accentuated in New York than it was originally. Another thing that has changed is a sense of sensuality. That has gone down. There was a much more sexual feeling to it originally. Now, it's much lighter. Hearing about "The Dream" rehearsals, I can only wonder what happened at Joe Papp's *Two Gentleman of Verona* rehearsals.

[Brook was then asked which themes he thought he had uncovered or discovered in stripping away traditional trappings of "The Dream."]

BROOK: One can only answer that by going off at a tangent. Any of the great plays of Shakespeare contain an infinite number of themes, and you can even say an infinite number of *main* themes. This is what is unique about Shakespeare. This is the way in which Shakespeare is like life. By life, I mean both something complete that you can cover with one word. And then, if you say, "The life in a city," you mean a million different things. When you talk about life in the United States, you're talking about a million different themes, and yet about one thing, aren't you?

The plays of Shakespeare give you this sense of life because they are condensations—the life of a country which lasts over centuries. In his plays, this life is crammed by an extraordinary series of devices into two or three hours. If your job is to try to bring these plays off the page into living form, you must always prevent yourself, as far as possible, from imposing anything that is going to cut down those areas to your own chosen ones.

Unfortunately, the history of Shakespeare production, of Shakespeare design, of Shakespeare acting is a history of someone saying: "For me, this play is about greed, sex, money, love, man's inhumanity to man, failure of communication!"—anything you like—and then the whole production is geared to that. And you get the most *horrible* thing—which has been turned into a term of praise—which is: "Oh, look! What great *style*! The scenery is all conceived in the style of a Venetian painter!" And then everyone moves and holds their bodies in the style of that painter's subjects. And the music—and everything else—is in that style. One asks, "What *style* was it?" As though this were important.

To approach Shakespeare and produce either "style" or clarity of certain ideas is only a *reduction* of the play. It's not possible for any of us, no matter how hard we try, to reveal the *complete* play. What we do will always be a restriction: it will be our own limited view of a play that is much more complete.

But the direction we can take at each point can try to capture in our net the richest amount of the contradictory, clashing, opposed, discordant elements that criss-cross these plays. In fact, a number of things that Theseus says in the play are directly on this theme. The talk of Theseus and Hippolyta about how the sound of trumpets and hounds barking can make a conjunction of two images-it's a concord-discord. In "The Dream," in all Shakespeare, it's there: that co-existence. There is vulgar sex. There is metaphysical love, and the two exist side by side. You do not say: "If there's one, we can't have the other." In all our work, we try to replace "either/or" with a greedy "both."

[What does Brook expect of his audiences? Does he consider that they may make comparisons with other productions?]

BROOK: One can't prevent them from doing that. What we do want to make clear is that it isn't the tradition as such that is a dirty word. But there is tradition and *tradition*. Perhaps the most hateful and destructive thing there is the oppression of *bad* tradition.

Had we a tradition anywhere in the world that stemmed *directly* from Shakespeare, then we would be deeply respectful of it. But there isn't a tradition to do with the performing of Shakespeare that is worth a farthing, because it all comes from 19th century sources—all quite arbitrary—when there was nothing in theatrical memory or in society that had any relation to Shakespeare and his conditions or his theatre. It's not for nothing that the whole of the Baconian controversy didn't spring up around Elizabethan London when Shakespeare was living, but in Boston in the 19th century, when a lady called Miss Bacon suddenly thought: "I know who wrote Shakespeare's plays! A man called Bacon!"

It was round about the same time that people living in different parts of the world were evolving theories about the plays, based on their own ideas, on the lives *they* were leading, on what made this whole superstructure of Victoriana. Which is a tradition of no use and no value, and totally alien to the plays.

If our spectators can come to the play with *no* traditional notions of that sort, that would be our ideal. But there are very few people who haven't absorbed these images from children's editions, so the most one can hope for is that, if they make comparisons, they will find our production more alive than the alternative tradition, which has been with us for only a hundred years or so.

[Brook was asked if certain plays should not be avoided because "they embarrass us by having a point of view which we no longer encourage?" Had there been any objections to the class-structure evident in "The Dream"?]

BROOK: The 19th century tradition assumes that because people are workmen they are comic and empty-headed and they're to be laughed at. There is a nauseating superiority toward workmen trying to do a play, in the 19th century tradition. It seems to us that there is nothing in the text that suggests they are stage-yokels from the country. The play itself seems to suggest an accurate observation of class differences, with a completely non-snobbish attitude on the part of the author. The play shows different social levels, and when a character so clearly says to an audience: "Lord, what fools these mortals be," surely that means that each one of these levels is shown in its full range of being both absurd, ridiculous, and, from another point of view, understandable. Shakespeare doesn't spare anybody! Each layer of the play has shown a moral ridiculous at some point or other.

[Was Jan Kott, author of *Shakespeare, Our Contemporary*, an influence on "The Dream" production?]

BROOK: I can really only go back to the same thing—a view of the play and the time in which someone writes about it. Lots of scholars write lots of pieces, and sometimes in the course of that, they eliminate one particular thing.

I think Kott has very valuably drawn everybody's attention to the fact that this so-called play for children has got dark and powerful currents of sensuality running through it. His essay, however, if you follow it literally, would give you a play without any joy, any gaiety, and any sparkle. But I think he has thrown light on one side of the play; without question he has.

[Alan Howard was queried about the courtliness and thoughtfulness he, as Theseus, accorded the Mechanicals as they presented their play, since they are so often, in other productions, mocked by Theseus and his court.]

HOWARD: Theseus is such a wise, experienced, *full* person—full of understanding—that it's very difficult not to make him condescending and curt. His problem is to see how people, all people, can go through a process. In the last sequence, he knows—in his strange relationship with Puck, who is also his Master of Revels, and in his relationship with Hippolyta-Titania— he knows that this play to be performed offers a valuable lesson. A lesson to be learned, as far as the lovers are concerned. They are feeling giddy and flip. Theseus has to make them go through this process. At the end, all parties on that stage, whatever their differences, are at one—as much as it is possible at any moment to be at one.

[One member of the Drama Desk asked what had become of the fog and mist Oberon is supposed to create during the magic night of "The Dream."]

BROOK: The first thing the play has running through it is Darkness. And from that everything else stems. An audience is willing to join in any games and play by any rules, if they're clearly announced. If you once fade down the lights and suggest to the audience: "We'll take care of you," and you help their imagination with effects of night and fog, then you have set out on a path which must be followed all the way. Then fog must be suggested, and so forth.

Having committed ourselves to the opposite direction, there's nothing we can do about it. Which is to say that this is why we're making a white opening into which the imagination of the audience can pour. We're holding up a white screen, and the imagination of the audience can paint on that screen what it wants.

The most extraordinary power comes from the words once the audience knows you're alone with those words and their image. I think, on the whole, we find that an audience is actually more completely involved with the play and gets more for itself, if instead of plastics and technology making it, they do it for themselves. I think that all of us wouldn't be here if we weren't overjoyed with our work and the opportunity of having the material of Shakespeare to work on. So, in a way, the task of bringing the text of *A Midsummer Night's Dream* alive in the theatre couldn't be more rewarding or complete.

At the same time, it doesn't resolve the fact that there is a need for a theatre of our own today—one that is not always bent on going back to that perhaps one-and-only great source of material in the past. But we can't allow the theatre to take care of itself, while we stay locked away in the classics. The first great change in Shakespeare at Stratford was introduced by Peter Hall, when he announced this vital principle that it was actors, in touch with contemporary life—through contemporary works—who had to be the people to interpret Shakespeare. The notion of a Shakespeare company as something cut off from the world could no longer be tolerated. Everything that is good—and bad—eventually *all* that has grown from the Royal Shakespeare Company, has come from this policy, and all the attendant problems it has brought along with it.

PETER BROOK'S *BIRDS* TAKE WING:
WITH SALLY JACOBS BEFORE
THE AMERICAN TOUR
Glenn Loney

[Paris: Summer 1973]

One takes the Paris Metro to Gobelins. There, in a block behind and down-hill from the noble Gobelin edifice, is the much more modern, but no less imposing, *Mobiliér National*. It's not exactly dark at the top of the *Mobiliér's* central stairway, but the vast long hall is dimly lit. Over at one side, an alert young woman is rapidly brushing bright swirls of color on a long white scroll.

She is Sally Jacobs and she has, she explains, just five minutes to complete this handsome symbolization of a head of wheat. Downstairs, a half-lettered sign had advised that a *SPECTACLE* would take place from 2:30 to 4:30. It is already 2 p.m., and this is to be the final dress-rehearsal/performance of Peter Brook's new theatre-piece, *The Conference of the Birds*, before he and his Paris-based group leave for an American tour.

Surely she has more than five minutes in which to finish? Sally Jacobs laughs and shakes her head: "You'll see why when the performance begins. Here, can you help me?" She is taking a hanger off a long white scroll covered with oriental dragons in black outline. The hanger is then firmly attached to the newly painted scroll. "This is typical," she says, obviously not minding at all. "We've been using this other scroll for *weeks*, and only now, at the last performance, have we realized it's not right. You like it? Well, I rather like it myself, but it won't do. Oh, here's Peter!"

Peter Brook has come to inspect the scroll. He is pleased. He is also pleased with the text of a production record and acting version of his Royal Shakespeare *A Midsummer Night's Dream* which I have assembled for publication. Only one thing is missing: an interview with Sally Jacobs on how she and Brook have so successfully collaborated on such ventures as the RSC Theatre of Cruelty, Jean Genet's *The Screens*, Peter Weiss's *Marat/Sade*, Brook's *US*, and Shakespeare's *Dream*.

Guests are already arriving for the performance. Brook hastens to greet them. "Look," says Sally, "when I wrote you that today would be OK for an interview, I didn't know we'd be playing. So why don't you find a cushion in there, and we'll talk after?"

One section of the *Mobiliér* has been curtained off into a square arena. Three sides are lined with cushions on the floor and two rows of elevated platforms. A very tall double-ladder stands in a corner. A few cardboard boxes and an assortment of musical instruments are lying around the playing area. In rehearsal and continued performance, Brook's productions tend to become more and more simplified, reduced to only what is essential. Apparently, *The Conference of the Birds*, which has been worked on during the troupe's West African tour in the spring and in special school performances in Paris, is already elemental.

Spectators, about evenly divided between intense young people and more conservative older ones—some of whom look very much like patrons of Brook's Paris experiments—find cushions or chairs and concentrate on the curtain backing the arena on its fourth side. Through this curtain come the players, all of them in simple white costumes, some the worse for wear. Two performers, a man and a woman, the Two Charlatans, have blue smocks over the white. They proceed to urge both actors and audience to: "Listen!" "Watch!" "Listen!" "Watch!" After this prelude, they announce: "An astonishing thing!" "An astonishing thing!"

A large cardboard carton is shoved forward. One of the white-garbed players, a bird—all the performers in white are birds, one soon realizes by listening and watching—is challenged by the Charlatans. Intrigued, he starts opening the box, only to find a smaller one inside, and so on and on until he reaches a very tiny box. Inside this is a wooden egg. Inside that—surprise!—is *not* a series of wooden eggs, but a key.

The Charlatans bring in two more large cartons. Inside one, it is suggested, are Mysteries of Light; in the other, Mysteries of Darkness. Using the key, the bird finally finds the treasure in one of the boxes. It is wrapped in layer after layer of crepe paper. The bird impatiently tears away the gaudy covers and finds the scroll with the colorful stalk of wheat Sally had painted! No wonder she had only five minutes to finish the scroll! It must have taken the remaining twenty-five minutes till curtain-time to wrap it up. But it, like so much else, was discarded or replaced on the American tour.

The thread which holds the various episodes of *The Conference of the Birds* together is an old mythic device. It is a perilous search, through the joys and terrors of life, for attainment of ultimate wisdom and oneness, a unity with a kind of all-wise God-force. The birds are fearful of undertaking the journey. Many will fall by the wayside. The end cannot be known, but they are told they will never again be what they were—nor will they want to be. The Charlatans urge, tease, taunt, and challenge them at every turn. And, during the journey, parables and fables are acted out which illustrate certain principles and peculiarities of conduct. Of *human* conduct, for it is apparent that the birds represent generic Man.

Some of the tales have biblical counterparts. Others recall Aesop, La Fontaine, the Brothers Grimm, and Hans Christian Andersen. Actually, these beloved children's tales are all contained in a 12th century Persian Sufi manuscript and they embody essentials of Sufi thought. Among them are: The Moth and the Flame and the fable of the king whose face was so magnificent no subject could look upon it and live. He had a mirror made so his people could look upon his *image* instead. One tale is a very instructive: a great king asks his devoted slave if he loves him. The slave swears he does. The king then asks him to prove it by suffering instant death—or eternal exile. Of course, if one really loved with passion and dedication, death would be preferable to life without the beloved. The slave, however, chooses exile. And his reward is death. But, had he chosen otherwise, he would have been made king and the king would have become his willing slave. Food for thought: If you can believe that, you could believe anything.

This is all performed with minimal means. Costumes are a few robes made of narrow hand-woven bands, the white blouses, skirts, and pants, and a few props. The stories are performed with great concentration and intensity. So much so, that the players really do seem to become birds, even when they are acting out human stories. No need for elaborate feathered costumes at all. Such triumphs of the designer's art would seem intrusions. Obviously *The Conference of the Birds* has not offered Sally Jacobs much opportunity to show off her own talents. (Nonetheless, in a later incarnation of this production, seen in New York, the birds had masks mounted on sticks, to assist audiences' imagination, no doubt.)

During the performance, everyone watches with close attention, no one more so than Peter Brook, even though he has been watching it for weeks and weeks. At one point, he is obviously delighted at some group interaction. At another, a player's work seems to be bothering him. Has it not found its proper expression yet?

When a tiny white mouse is let out of its box, no one is more fascinated by its unscripted, unrehearsed movements than Brook. His capacity for attention, for integration, for imagination is clearly very great. And yet *The Conference of the Birds*, compared with *Marat/Sade* or the *Dream*, is really a very simple, unassuming production. The secret, perhaps, lies in its material. It offers a series of life-problems which invite thought. Splashy production techniques would only interfere with thinking, even discourage it.

That may be why the American tour of *The Conference of the Birds* was not booked into the Billy Rose in New York—where *Dream* had played. Actually it began in and around San Luís Obíspo, in California, where Brook's troupe were working with Luis Valdez and his *Teatro Campesino*. Performances were given here and there for audiences who were receptive. Aspen, Colorado, was another tour stop. The troupe also visited a

Sioux Reservation in the Mid-West. And finished off with scheduled performances at the Brooklyn Academy of Music, where Brook's *Dream* played after its Broadway engagement.

When Brook was attacked at the Royal Shakespeare for his Theatre of Cruelty season, he made it clear that he was finished with bright, attractive, commercial entertainments. He suggested that he, Peter Brook, was going through a "Dark Period." The *Dream* indicated his emergence: its commercial success was really incidental to its basic values for Brook as performance and expression of a vision. *The Conference of the Birds* is composed of essential paradoxes and truths; it, too, is obviously beyond Darkness.

The performance is over. Brook is listening to comments from admirers and critics. Sally Jacobs is doing last-minute fittings of costumes. Soon the troupe of birds will take wing for California. Later, after dinner in an elegant old Art Deco restaurant near the *Mobiliér*, S. C. Nott, the English translator of *The Conference of the Birds*, joins Sally and me to find out what we think about the production, which is only now falling into place, after weeks of improvisation and experimentation. Only now is Brook actually writing out a script for those Charlatans to speak. (And in America, the sequence of performance elements and the quality of their realization will continue to change.)

Nott produces a copy of his translation, taken from an 1887 French version by Garcin de Tassy. *Mantic Ut-tair*, he says, is the Persian title. And Farid Ud-Din Attar is the author, a 12th century Persian perfumer and Sufi thinker. According to Nott, a Dervish spoke to Farid and died immediately afterward. Not unnaturally, this sequence of events made quite an impression, and Farid Ud-Din Attar gave up his craft to travel and write. Nott talks about the values of repetition in Sufi teaching, about the relations between the tales in the old Persian manuscript and similar fables in other cultures. In a sense, the end of the birds' journey is achieving union with God, and living in the City of God, but, in discussion, neither Nott nor Sally Jacobs want to assign any specific meanings to the work.

Nott goes even further: the work—excellent as he finds it in Brook's troupe's performance—is not what is important. Brook's theatre experiments are what are important. Nott compares Brook to Stanislavsky and Diaghilev. He approves the group's openness to new ideas and their stern regime of practical body and mind exercises: "A reaction against disciplines which suppress is quite right. But a reaction against *creative* disciplines is not right. You cannot emote all over the place."

And where can one get Nott's translation, if a British edition is not to be found in America? "Shambala, in Berkeley, California," Nott says. "He has printed it."

Dinner costs as much as three days in a hotel, but it is a good dinner, and the company is excellent. Sally and I say good-bye to S. C. Nott and his son, returning to talk in the *Mobiliér*, now plunged in darkness. Beginning as a production secretary and continuity-girl for various British films, Sally says her career began when she decided that she really wanted to be a designer. From 1957–60, she studied at London's Central School of Arts and Crafts. She started work as a scene-painter for the Colchester Repertory Theatre, soon moving to London, where she helped design Arnold Wesker's *The Kitchen*, at the Royal Court Theatre, for director John Dexter. Between 1961 and 1964, she designed for a number of noted British directors—both plays and films: Anthony Page, David Jones, Clive Donner, Trevor Nunn, John Barton, and, of course, Peter Brook.

"I began to work with Peter Brook when he did his first program based on Antonin Artaud's ideas: The Theatre of Cruelty. I read about that and decided that was the kind of theatre I wanted to be involved in. I was at a very frustrated stage in my own work. I'd had a few good experiences, but I hadn't yet found my form. I went to see Peter and showed him some of my work—and that's how we started working together. We did all sorts of things, in all different directions. I went through projections, films, painting—all sorts of experimental things. Everything was made from nothing because we had very little money. A lot of it I did all by myself. It was a marvelous experience, but I worked myself to the bone." She laughs, thinking back. "Just about every idea we wanted to try out, we did! That was my first encounter with Peter Brook. It was very hard. I wasn't used to working that way—where you work through an idea to see if it's actually going to work or not. Even, up to a point, building something to see if it can be used.

"There were a number of pieces in the Artaud program. As a designer, I had to see how I could deal with those Surrealist images. What kind of visual language could be used to express those ideas? Through trial and error, we finished up with an interesting project. In a funny sort of way, I was blind—I didn't quite know what I was doing. I was missing things, without realizing what the broader context was. I just responded and reacted to what was demanded of me. But I knew at last this was a theatre in which I could work. It wasn't a matter of keeping busy as a designer. I feel I'm in the theatre because I'm interested in *theatre*, not because it's a place where I can apply my craft."

After the first collaboration came another experiment: the first half of Genet's *The Screens*. Brook was continuing to work with the nucleus of actors from the Theatre of Cruelty experiments, building on discoveries made in those rehearsals. Genet, says Sally, proved too literary, too disciplined to be opened up by Brook and his group. They were seeking to make a play more than it is on a printed page, and, in Peter Weiss's *Marat/Sade*, they found a work which would profit from such treatment.

Although Sally Jacobs usually does both sets and costumes for Brook, the costumes designed by Weiss's wife, Gunilla Palmstierna-Weiss, for the first production in West Berlin's Schiller Theatre seemed right to Brook and were recreated for the RSC version, with sets by Sally.

"I don't do every Peter Brook production, unfortunately, because we live all over the world now. But we do seem to have a nice kind of continuous need of each other. We don't seem to use up what we give each other. It gets better and better. We're getting simpler, and, as we go on, it's easier to work with each other," Sally says.

"After the *Marat*, we did the Vietnam thing, *US*. Then I stopped work for a while. I'd had a long stint of working non-stop. I wanted to step back for a while. And I wanted to have a baby!" She laughs. "So I got all that together in one bundle and went to live in Los Angeles with my husband, Alex. Peter and I kept in touch, of course, while I was doing my domestic thing. But it wasn't until the *Dream* came along that I felt the project was important enough to go along where he was and work for him again. So there was a gap of three years when we didn't work together." For the production record of Brook's *Midsummer Night's Dream*, Sally describes the evolutionary process of creating sets and costumes in detail.

When Brook invited her to work on *The Conference of the Birds*, the troupe was already touring Africa, picking up indigenous dances and rites and trying out segments of the Sufi work. When it was played in Nigeria, it had no written script or dialogue, Sally comments, but audiences showed great interest in and understanding of the basic movements and outlines. In the performance version, movements occur suggestive of a Yoruba *Gelede* Dance, in which a spirit takes possession of a dancer's body. But, as Sally points out, only someone who is familiar with Gelede Dances would notice that. In any case, Brook's *Birds* is not a sampler of international folklore and ritual, even though the troupe's members came from many cultures and they have traveled widely. The work is about a journey anyway, says Sally: "Anything that is a function of the group's activity becomes part of the piece. It's like their *language* now."

The boxes-within-boxes, for instance: boxes have been used in improvisations for some time in the Paris studios. The bamboo sticks, which are used to mark off the seven valleys the birds have to cross, before achieving union with the god-king, the Simurgh, are regularly used in group exercises. They were even used by the cast of the *Dream*, when they were preparing in Paris for the world tour!

And why make a new scroll, with a different design, at the very last minute of the final Paris performance?

"It's like the real key used to open the boxes. Only today does the key suddenly look wrong. It's—as you have just suggested—too real. We should find something else. Often you don't see something like the key until you've solved a lot of other problems. When other things suddenly start coming right, then a thing like the key looks wrong. One thing shows up another, until they finally all catch up with each other. And you're able, quite simply, to cut out all the wrong things. And find all the right ones, but only at a very late stage. That almost never happens, rehearsing for Broadway. There isn't time to experiment, and no audiences to try things out on.

"If you work in the more conventional way, the most difficult thing is how to keep a production *open* and *alive* in the last week of rehearsal, when producers want everything 'frozen.' When a lot of money and time have been committed to doing a thing in a certain way, and only then, at the last minute, does it become clear that has to be changed. Three weeks before, you couldn't have known that! That's what's difficult: having to compromise over what's right, absolutely *right* artistically."

Working with Peter Brook, Sally Jacobs is a very fortunate designer. She no longer has to make such compromises. And she can serve the production, the piece, the performers, without feeling she has to show off her talents. That is why Brook's birds will not be covered with colorful feathers or hidden behind bird masks. [At least that was so at this point in the production's evolution!] Their bodies, their faces, their voices all create the vision of a flock of oddly assorted birds on a mythic quest. Sally Jacobs has merely provided them with clean white outfits, suggesting no particular time, place, or culture. Instead, her costumes subtlety imply the universality of *The Conference of the Birds*.

PETER BROOK ON *LA TRAGÉDIE DE CARMEN*
Glenn Loney

[New York: May 9, 1983]

[On his induction into **The Theatre Hall of Fame**, after walking down the Gershwin Theatre staircase:

I suddenly realized that I've never been an actor—but I've had all the actor's dreams. In the middle of the night, I've found myself preparing to go on stage, but realizing that I don't know my lines. I've been in the middle of a performance and realized we haven't had a single rehearsal. And just now, I realized I never dreamt another actor's dream—of walking down a great staircase with music playing! (laughter) But everything can happen in New York. I'm always greatly at home in New York, so that's why I'm so touched today, not only to be at home, but to be made to feel, with you, part of the city.]

Later, in conversation with Glenn Loney:

LONEY: In taking a new look at Bizet's *Carmen*, why have you gone all the way back to its original source, the novella by Prosper Mérimée?

BROOK: It's something special to *Carmen*. In almost every opera, you can say the original literary source is central—in *Carmen*, this really is true. It's quite clear that Bizet was unusually inspired, literally by something that struck him really hard. And how did he meet the Carmen story? He met it through Mérimée's story. If you look at it, you see that the Mérimée story is behind all that Bizet's expressing. Bizet really is expressing that story, but, at the same time, on the way it gathered a whole lot of additional material. If one looks very carefully, one sees that some of that additional material actually obscures qualities and values that are there in the Mérimée story. So going back to the Mérimée story is a very, very useful way of analyzing and expressing Bizet's opera. When you use the Mérimée story as a reference, a sort of reference and background, you then see how much Bizet was forced to change it, not because he wanted to, but because of the taste of the time. That's what's interesting, to see this great comparison.

Deeply inspired, Bizet was working at a time when the public taste prevented him from going as far as the original did. What was *just* possible in literature was not yet possible on the stage. The stage has always been in that way more vulnerable. In England, when there was heavy censorship of the theatre—up to 20 years ago—what you could write in a novel, and which no one would dream of censoring, would cause howls of protest if it was played on the stage. Everywhere you can see this—the stage is much more immediate and touches people more. Mérimée's book was considered scandalous. It was too strong for its time. It *just* got by. He was nearly arrested. He was nearly in trouble. One knows he wrote an introduction to the book. You know the Mérimée story, don't you?—how it starts with a whole long spiel about the gypsy language, which was all a way of concealing his story and passing it off as anthropology, because otherwise it was too hot to handle.

LONEY: Present it as a sociological study then?

BROOK: Yes. If it had been put on the stage in the way that we could today—it's really the difference between movies today and movies in the 1930's. The double-bed, the Catholic, cleaned-up language.

Did Bizet change Mérimée, with the help of Mielhac and Halévy, because they really wanted it—that they had a conviction that this was a better way of telling the story? Or were they softening it, taking a lot of the punch out of it to suit the taste the times? It's absolutely clear about Bizet that one side of him was the composer with deep instincts; the other side was the practical man of the theatre, knowing that if you do something for matinées at the Opéra Comique, there's a limit. And he did sail too close to the wind even so.

It's for this reason that we reinvestigated *Carmen*. We went right back to Mérimée. In doing so, one can see in fact what is strong and what is weak—and what Mielhac and Halévy brought to it.

LONEY: You retain their Micaela, who isn't in Mérimée's original?

BROOK: These men were real experts, these two libretto writers. Very practical men of the theatre, who really knew their public: what was required. They were professionals. On the one hand, they softened the story a bit. They softened Carmen: they took out a lot of her immorality—amorality, let's say—that's in the novel. She goes from man to man, and then she's living in total married bliss with Don José, and suddenly it turns out she's got a gypsy husband, Zuñega. All this was pruned and pruned out.

LONEY: The heroine can't be odious to the audiences?

BROOK: Right. But, in cleaning her up, in softening the hard edges, the humanity was taken out as well. So she became a play-figure whore, without the usual heart of gold, so that she's far from a fully-rounded character, fully described. That was the first loss in the transposition to the opera stage. The second loss is stylistically. Mérimée was an extremely economical writer, whose faith, literally, was in minimal writing.

LONEY: The spareness you find in *Matteo Falcone*?

BROOK: Not wasting a word and getting right to the point. Bizet's best music is exquisitely to the point, in human terms. And what Mielhac and Halévy brought into the opera was a superstructure that was anti-Mérimée, in the sense that it was totally decorative. Mérimée was a man who wouldn't use one showy phrase for the sake of it, but this story, turned into opera, has this whole structure of what was expected in the times: the choruses, the children's choruses—a whole big icing on the wedding-cake, to make it palatable. But in making it palatable, it also took some of the balls out of it.

LONEY: It becomes a Spanish *show*?

BROOK: You're absolutely right! The book is Spanish in a different way; there's no local-color for its own sake. But it feels Spanish. There's a barrenness about it—hot rocks, burning sun. It's like Graham Greene's Mexico. Again, there's a writer who takes you right *into* Mexico, and there's not a word wasted on local flora or landscape description. You're in the essence of it. So these were the negative aspects. On the other hand, one must give them their due. As skillful professionals of the theatre, they made two masterstrokes. Because a novel has a flowing structure, it's very different from what you need when you're trying to do something in four acts.

LONEY: Narrative versus dramatic?

BROOK: To condense the action into four different acts and settings, they said, Don José has a background. His mother's in a village. It's very important to feel he has a settled background: on one side, the traditional life, and on the other, the gypsy life beckons him. How do you dramatize this simply? Without having to have flashbacks, or start in the village? A simple human solution: you turn all that background into a character. You invent a girl, his girl-friend Micaela, and the girl-friend comes from the village to see him. So the whole background is there—at the moment when he meets Carmen, the girl has come from the village.

LONEY: But you have made her Carmen's rival?

BROOK: In the original book, there's a very strong pull on Don José. As it turns out in the opera, having invented Micaela, tradition has turned her into a soppy, milky, whimpering sort. But we felt, here in Micaela, they've done a brilliant stroke to concentrate all this background into a human being, and this human being is as strong as Carmen, in her way. Here is the country-girl, there to fight for him, and to be the other side of his life. That was a masterstroke of Mielhac and Halévy: turning Don José's background into a human being in Micaela. In the opera world, Micaela's never taken seriously. People only like her because she's got one big wonderful aria. We felt this was a real person to be developed. That was where we were faithful to the development that Mielhac and Halévy brought the story. In the book, part of Don José's suffering is that he has, with Carmen, an endless series of rivals. She sleeps with every man that she comes across.

LONEY: Which makes his love seem even more doomed and grotesque?

BROOK: Yes. The librettists said: We can't bring all this on stage. It will weaken our form to have a succession of lovers. We'll combine them into one great lover, the picador Escamillo. The last lover in the book is a bull-fighter. That was an inspiration, so they said: Look! We'll turn this one into the character! Again, I think Escamillo is falsely treated by operatic tradition. Because of the opera's general superstructure, his role has been forgotten. You never feel in the opera that he is an intrinsic part of the drama. He's usually a man who comes on, creates a love diversion, and sings a big song—which has nothing to do with Carmen.

I always talk about finding a manuscript in the middle of the desert. You know nothing else about it. Look at it, as for the first time. You listen to that music: extraordinarily sensual, erotic music—beautiful music. One shouldn't think of it as a sort or rollicking drinking-song. It's the complete expression of self-confidence of a man for whom success, sex, and death are strangely mixed together. That's a very powerful, very virile piece of music.

There again, we've paid another homage to Mielhac and Halévy, for creating this great figure. Our version, I must stress, is not *Carmen*, but *The Tragedy of Carmen*. We make it absolutey clear that we're not rivaling Bizet's opera. It's *there*! We're doing a new investigation—thus the new title—and what we're investigating, what we are drawing out of it—like fishbones out of the filet—is the central core, which is the tragedy. In the sense that it's just an intense relationship between four people, everything's trimmed away to focus on the interaction of four people.

There are four Carmens and Don Josés in New York, three Micaelas and Escamillos. There are speaking roles which are very important. In Hamburg, the reviews only spoke of them, not the singers. Two actors, who were part of our old International Theatre Centre group, were involved in all the rehearsals when we were evolving this, between them, to bring into the opera the rest of the world. These four characters, whose destiny we follow, live in a world: that world which, in the big Bizet opera, is suggested with chorus and supers and subsidiary characters. One actor plays Lilas

Pastia. The other plays Zuñega and various other parts. So it's a six-handed
show. And the actors and the singers have worked together for so long that
they are all part of the same way of working.

LONEY: Could you talk about your previous work in opera?

BROOK: I had a theory—when I first started working, when I was about
21 or 22, when I worked for two years as a director at Covent Garden—
and I started with *Boris Godunov*: first, with an Italian singer, Silveri, and
then with Boris Christoph. His English debut. We had legendary quarrels.
That was, in fact, the first time anyone had done the original Moussorgsky
score. I was amazed two years ago here when I saw big publicity about
the first performance of the Moussorgsky. Twenty-five years before, we'd
done the original, which was marvelous. With the different ending, with the
Revolution scene. I'd always studied music at school. Then I did a *Bohéme*.
Ljuba Weltisch singing Musetta. Then I did a *Figaro* with Schwartzkopf as
Suzanna (long before her Countess). And a new opera by Arthur Bliss and
J. B. Priestley, called *The Olympians*. And then I did a *Salomé* with Weltisch
at Covent Garden.

LONEY: It was a scandal of sorts?

BROOK: It made such a scandal, that I was turned out of the opera, and
never let in again. But I was already working in the theatre—I'd done two
productions at Stratford. Then I came to the Met, when Bing was here. I
did a production of *Onegin* and a production of *Faust*, with Monteux. The
Onegin, with Mitropolous.

LONEY: But why did you decide to do a new *Carmen* in Paris, when the
Opéra was already doing a gigantic one?

BROOK: Because I'm in the theatre, I'm most interested in what can speak
most directly to the most widely assorted people. That is why I'm not interested in any difficult or intellectual opera. *Carmen*, perhaps of all the
operas, has the greatest marriage between being musically marvelous and
absolutely true human content. Those two go hand in hand. It's totally accessible. The music can appeal to absolutely anyone, without any difficulty,
any effort. There are no cultural barriers. You don't need to belong to any
cultural formation to appreciate Bizet's music. And yet, at the same time,
it's not easy music.

 After we'd taken a completely fresh look at it, we were casting for a
long, long time for young, unknown singers. We auditioned a tremendous
number from musicals—rather than operas—with that sort of background.

In fact, somebody who hasn't got a very strict classical training or formation just can't sing the notes of *Carmen*. It's just too difficult, as you know.

LONEY: After *Carmen*, are there other operas you want to explore?

BROOK: Oh yes!

LONEY: And strip away the operatic conventions?

BROOK: Many, in different ways, *Pélleas*, for one. *The Magic Flute*, for another. But not doing the same thing as in *Carmen*. You have to look at the problems of each work afresh, each time. For some, there might be a point—or no point–to making radical changes in the story-line.

LONEY: In *Flute*, strip away some of Schickaneder's shenanigans?

BROOK: Yes, that's possible. The funny thing about the *Bouffes du Nord*, where we play, is that it's a remarkable space—that's why I'am so attached to it. It's a space that lends itself to the most different things. Whenever we do something there, people say: "Ah, the theatre was *made* for this production." We did *Carmen*: it was right. Now, we're doing *The Cherry Orchard*, and it seems to be made for *The Cherry Orchard*.

We tend to vary it little: we change the floor, for instance. For *Conference of the Birds*, the whole area is covered with great, enormous Persian carpets. For *Carmen*, it seemed the most important thing—to really sense her whole environment when you enter the theatre—was putting all this red earth down, which is the open-air, the country, the mountains, the arena. It's all there. This opera is something that takes place on the ground. *Carmen* couldn't take place on a carpet. One day, someone came up to me after the performance and said: "I'm so glad you have taken all the dust off *Carmen*." Without thinking seriously, I said: "That's what we're using for our playing-space." For one marvelous moment, I looked at the ground and saw it was all the dust off *Carmen*. [laughs] It's the dust that came out of shaking off the work.

LONEY:What about the musicians?

BROOK: I think it's 14, plus the piano. Without the piano, you'd have an even number. So it must be 15. What happened was, with Marius Constant, the conductor—it was the director of the Paris Opera who brought us together. He was the matchmaker. Marius is the perfect person for this. We understood each other perfectly in the first day, and as we started working, we agreed on a number of basic things, like the necessity to liberate the singers from this dependence on the conductor's baton. And he, as conductor—he conducts very well—didn't have the ego-necessity to feel that he's dominating the singer. On the contrary, he wanted to liberate them. Because he's a great lover of chamber music—he has a chamber-music orchestra–he made for *Carmen* a chamber ensemble.

All the time, his principle was that he was doing this like *Lieder*. The whole opera! He found that Bizet's music is not bombastic. But the more intimately you take it, the more you get the true quality of this French music, which isn't brash, noisy, loud music for the *Palais de Sports*, where the monster version was sung. Yes, there's a strong rhythmic quality, but it's not music for blasting and shouting. It's like a Debussy or Duparc song. Bizet, in that fine tradition, created very sensitive music. So the line always was that we were doing *Lieder*: a chamber-opera, telling a very intimate story with chamber-opera resources. So that his aim was, with the orchestra, to get a little group of soloists playing as an ensemble. And the singers should be like part of the ensemble. And then the orchestra, by studying the score, was perfectly capable of playing it without a conductor.

LONEY: But what if the singers miss a cue?

BROOK: This doesn't come from necessity, but from insecurity. It's not the same thing. I'm very struck by the fact that when I first came to Paris, the French theatre still had prompters. Years after the English theatre had given them up. A little lady sat there in her box, prompting. As long as you have a system like that, it can go on for 100 years. It's laziness. If you know there's going to be a prompter there, you may never learn your lines properly. You can hear two versions, and the prompter's is sometimes louder. I once saw a deaf old Italian actor, and the prompter was much louder. It's the same in Italian opera. It all comes down to money. It's always commercial, so that the singer can get away with less rehearsal than anyone in the legit theatre would believe possible. And so that they can rush round the world doing more work than they need to do, on the false premise that their careers are so short, they've got to rake it in now. When you look at how long careers are, you don't have to feel sorry for these "butterflies." It isn't really true. Some careers go on for 50 years.

LONEY: What about doing a Bayreuth-conceived Isolde around the world in productions which have nothing to do with Bayreuth?

BROOK:That's why I gave up doing opera. I realized that it was not possible, in the current conditions of world opera, to do good work. So I gave up. Until I could be in a situation, as in Paris, where we could change the conditions. One of the conditions was having adequate rehearsals. So we rehearsed for 12 weeks. That was the first condition. The second condition was to work with people who were young singers, who were really eager and enthusiastic to work for 12 weeks.

The next thing was to ask: is it true that a singer who's a good musician cannot work like a member of a chamber orchestra? Does he have to be glued to the conductor? No, he just has to know the score. And Marius Constant did a sensational work with the singers, by making—not making, but encouraging—them to do an excercise in which they sang the score. So they sang the *orchestral* parts. So then, like the conductor, they really knew it all—their parts and the instrumental parts. The result is that gradually, by working in the same space—another part of the principle was to have lots of performances, because I've observed that singers in good circumstances may rehearse for six week, even longer, but they only get to do three performances—five, maybe—and it's over. In the normal laws of theatre, or of chamber-music, you're only just beginning in your fifth performance to settle into something.

Each of our singers, in our first season, played over fifty performances in identical circumstances. There were over 150 performances in the first season, so there was a growth that nothing else could have given them. That's the way it happens with string quartets. That's what makes an ensemble—working together over a long a period of time with the same conductor. We could experiment in rehearsal, put the orchestra in different positions—side, back, middle, in the balconies. In the end, we found the best position was the orchestra split in two parts. Percussion/piano on one side and the rest on the other, near the back, so they're half in view, sharing the same space with the actors and audience. The music is very present: it envelops the singer, but it is not between you and the singer. It's extraordinary the difference it makes.

LONEY: Opera orchestras may drown out singers?

BROOK: Right. The orchestra is here treated as though they are part of the stage action. Not because they get up and do things, but because the whole piece is one thing. In an opera, the music is dramatic; it's telling a story. Nine out of ten times, it's part of the subtext of the character. The singer and the orchestra need to be very, very closely related. Music isn't an in-between; it's an extension or a preparation of what the singer sings. The singer has to feel the orchestra is part of his story. He and the orchestra have to be in such a position that they can sense, feel each other. That's why the orchestra-pit tradition is very destructive. In the 18th century, the small orchestra was on the same level, conducted from harpsichords. Very democratic. Everyone was making music. The proper democracy of music—as you have in Indian music and jazz—people making music together.

If you're telling a story, you make Music-Drama together. The story comes through. The sinking of the orchestra into the pit certainly made this terrible division, which makes the musicians into paid "hired hacks."

One side of the orchestra not knowing what the other is doing has a grain of truth. That's why they're such difficult people. You have no chance to shine. As a result, the conductor has developed as an artificial representative of the orchestra. For a man, a dictator, to go up, others must go down, be crushed. The boss and the worker relationship should be very harmonious. But if the boss is an autocrat, it's at the expense of the individual artist. Even in Communist countries it's a cliché, but in music, everyone still respects the autocracy of the conductor. That's very old fashioned. We pay a very high price for that in opera. Not only in human terms is the orchestra crushed, but because the conductor is there in the pit, bang in the center, all the time the action has to be turned out front, not only acoustically, but to watch him.

The basis of all theatrical truth is to find your reality by looking other characters in the eyes, intimately connected with someone. It's destroyed in traditional opera. Real life begins for singers or actors when you can look at each other, not when you have an eye straying toward the pit and the baton. This breeds a destructive fear in singers, particularly those who are underehearsed. They have to hang onto a conductor with a fear that you see in performance.

Could I share a story with you? It's something very amusing, very surprising. There is a small group of old-fashioned monsters in opera. I've worked with them. They really are monsters. When I was at Covent Garden, the great and famous people I worked with were shits; they were monsters. They were congenital idiots. They were dinosaurs. They belonged to a pre-historic age, but they happened to have had big voices. And there was nothing you could do with them. I could tell you stories, for instance, about Christoph, when he arrived in London. A great voice, but what a struggle it was. But today, there's a whole generation of young singers who are dying to work in a way that they feel is honest and honorable.

There is a possibility for a singer to act better than an actor. This is very surprising, but it's for the simple reason that an actor has nothing but acting. He's not got any real craft. Only a very old actor has that much experience, craft. A young actor acts with the training he's got, but he has only himself to fall back on. Because of his insecurity, every actor hides himself to a degree. Otherwise, it's too frightening. He just can't go out there without finding some ways of "tricking his way through." Some way, he hides.

LONEY: Grotowski's concept of "armoring" yourself?

BROOK: Yes. Exactly. But a young singer is like an actor, except that he has the craft. He has learned the hard way something very demanding. He has learned music. He has learned breathing. He's learned vocal technique: some actual craft, which gives him something very firm. If he has also had only the corniest of stage experiences, it's very easy to take that away.

He doesn't believe in it anyway. He does it because no one's shown him anything better. He's been asked to throw his arms out wide—or he's seen other people do it. When that is gone, he doesn't need to conceal himself in any way, because he's got his real professional craft—unlike a young actor—to sustain him.

I find that potentially a singer with intuition, sensibility, and a wish to do truthful work, can actually be simpler and truer than a professional actor, because he doesn't need to do so much. He can actually open up his nature. I would say that the greatest challenge now, at this point in the 20th century, is to replace in the minds of performers and audiences the idea, that, well, opera's artificial, with the idea that opera is Natural. That's really the most important thing—and I think it's possible!

LONEY: Music tells singers how to "read" the lines, with effective inflection, emphasis, emotion? It provides clues to emotional reactions?

BROOK: Yes, as in Shakespeare as well. But what I think has been ignored in opera is that what the music contains is not the full information on what's going on inside the character. There is, beyond that music, a subtext. Exactly in the way there is for an actor, for instance, playing in a movie. What he is supposed to be doing is described in the scenario very simply: "He goes to the window and looks out, sadly." The adjective is *sadly.* But with a great movie-actor you can see that at that moment, 900 things pass through him. And you can read the descriptions of Sarah Bernhardt's acting, and you can find that in a split-second, one could write a page on all the conflicting emotions. Joy that's not quite joy, because it's sadness, but not sadness, because there's a moment of hope, but that hope is tinged with a bit of fear. You know that goes on and on.

Now, if a singer only expresses what's in the music, it seems very wooden, because in fact his mind is asleep. But if a singer understands the real inner life of the character, he's going at a rate even faster than the music. With the music living on one level, it's like going to the window and looking out sadly, The music has that sadness, but music is not subtle enough for many conflicting emotions. But behind it are all these other little details. And the acting starts to become convincing when the singer is filling in what is even quicker felt than the music.

When you've seen all the great singing actors, somebody like Callas, or like Stratas in Zeffirelli's *Bohéme*, if you stopped the movie, you'd find that in between any two notes, Startas is filling in with 20 more things. Just the subtleties of human life are played. And that's what gives you the impression of real life.

LONEY: Even if you have to die in four measures? The music is not a restriction, but a kind of freedom?

BROOK: Yes! Absolutely!

LONEY: You have moved from the old furniture factory?

BROOK: The *Bouffes du Nord* is our theatre. When we don't use it, we let it out. We were turned out of the factory at the Gobelins after three years. President Pompidou had bought the furniture of one of the great Rothschilds who had died, and the state had no place to put it. So, from one day to the next, they said President Pompidou needed this space, so we were out. And the furniture moved in! It was after three years, and we'd begun to feel that we couldn't do public performances, only some invited people in, because it was too small—not licensed for anything. It wasn't set up to be a theatre. So we started looking around and in the end found the *Bouffes*. A forgotten theatre—it had been empty for 20 years. The International Theatre group I stopped about two years ago, so that everybody had been together for ten years. We wrapped it up. Everybody needed to have some new experiences. We're starting again next year, when we have a new project.

MARAT/SADE AS PLAY AND FILM:
STANLEY KAUFFMANN COMPARES!

[New York: October 6, 1987: Kauffmann, a longtime film critic for *The New Republic* and a highly regarded drama critic, at this time was Visiting Professor in the CUNY Graduate Center Theatre PhD Program.]

KAUFFMANN: I *had* to see the film of *Marat/Sade* again. And I'm glad I did. It's astonishing what you don't remember about a film that you thought you remembered. This film is very good—and very interesting. Those two things don't always occur together. Off-hand—well, more than off-hand—I cannot remember any film made—not just from a play, but from a theatrical production—as good as this one is. it is, in my view, the best film of Peter Brook, but it's also, therefore, the best from any of his productions. He's made films of *King Lear, US*, and *Tell Me Lies*.

The only time I ever met him was in 1967. I was doing a series for PBS on television about film. He came on to tell us how the film was made. It was shot in fifteen days. Now fifteen days, compared with the two-and-a-half hours of a theatre performance, is gargantuan. But compared to the usual time required to shoot a film, it is minuscule. The whole doing of this film was couched in the context and the ambition of the theatrical production. He used the set—or a reasonable facsimile of the theatre-set in the studios at Pinewood. And he and his cinematographer—one of the best living English cinematographers, named David Watkin—worked out a system of lighting. This may be apocryphal, but this is what he told me: a system which allowed him to do a day's work almost continuously. That is, he didn't have to stop to reset lights. He had different areas pre-fixed with different kinds of lighting. So he could say to his actors: "Now, go to spot #23, and we'll do the next scene." And he shot the film, he said, sequentially. That's also a rarity in film-making. He wanted, within the limitations—and, I would say, the powers—of the film-form, to preserve, as far as possible, the impetus, the impulse, the continuum of the theatrical performance.

There's something else that's true of this film that is *not* unique. It's not the only time it's happened, not even the only time in Brook's career, but very important to remember. Absolutely crystal-clear and obvious once you say it—but the custom of film-going is so ingrained, you might forget it—these people had been playing these roles together for well over a year!

And after weeks of rehearsal. He didn't call up William Morris and say: "Send me one fat man and one thin man, and we'll start on Tuesday." These people were already so well acquainted that they both hated and loved one another. This is notorious by now, but they were working out—through the film and through the original performances—all kinds of states, reactions, secrets, animosities, and loves that were in them. About themselves, about the others in the cast, about life and death—about everything possible!

You're seeing, therefore, the crystallization, for permanency's sake, of something that's usually lost: the quintessence of months and months of *theatrical* work. And the triumph is that it doesn't damage film as film: it uses, it employs, it *empowers* film! It's really an extraordinary piece of work!

I have a bee in my bonnet about something that I call theatre-film. Not because I invented it, but because I have seen it. I believe that there exists a *locus*, a blended medium of theatre and film. I'm not talking about using films in plays: that's something else. That's quite different. I'm talking about using theatre on film. *Marat/Sade*, for me, is a prime example. The filmmaker I can think of who was has attempted it most frequently and most successfully is the German, Hans-Juergen Syberberg. His *Parsifal* is also a prime example again of what I'm talking about. The idea is to let all the things happen that irritate us in the theatre, because theatre can't do them and film can, and let all the things that irritate us with film happen, because theatre can do them and film can't. Of course, this is an ideal. What's wrong with that? But it is more than an ideal; it is an adventure.

This man, Peter Brook, at this moment in his career, was ready. He had the right instruments at hand to proceed on that adventure. In his new book, *The Shifting Point*, he includes essays which have appeared before. One of them, "Filming a Play," was used as the preface for the text of *Marat/Sade*. Let me read from this: "When I directed the play, *Marat/Sade*, for the stage, I had not attempted to impose my own point of view on the work. On the contrary, I tried to make it as many-sided as I could. As a result, the spectators were continually free to choose, in each scene, and at every moment, the points which interested them most." Parenthetically, I think that's baloney.

No director in the theatre wants the audience to be free to look anywhere it chooses. In film, the camera decides where we look, but, in the theatre, no director wants you to be free either. If there's a scene on stage, and Fred is talking to Harry—while Jane and Mary are overhearing—if your attention is logically on the men, but it wanders to Jane and Mary, then something's wrong.

But this is a valid point, I think. He says: "In the theatre, a thousand spectators see the same thing with a thousand pairs of eyes, but also, at the same time, they enter a composite collective vision. The opposite is true of film, and that's what makes the two experiences so different." He talks of having only two cameras. There were two fixed cameras, but you could see shots from a hand-held camera as well. What he did—shooting a hundred-thousand-feet, which is as much as twelve times what he actually used—was to create for himself a "basket of tiles" that he could then assemble into the mosaic that he wanted. But in order to have the tiles that he did want, he had to have a minimum of "stoppage."

These people were not used to being stopped in these performances. They understood there would have to be cuts. But he wanted to preserve all the generated well-springs of *texture* that they could possibly provide. With the lights pre-fixed and two cameras mostly pre-fixed, he could enable the actors really to act, largely without interruptions. That's what makes this film so extraordinary. When you talk about a film, you may say: "It's very well edited, very well photographed," or, "It might be better edited, better photographed." But it would not exist, if it weren't for the *acting*. And that was what Brook knew he had to get.

Another thing that's been overlooked—and I was struck with it again when I saw the film today: this may sound like a silly, school-teacherish thing to say—but when you see the film itself, the *diction* of the actors is what makes this film click! Those words come at you like perfectly formed jewels, every one of them. And it's not a question of school-room elocution. It's a matter of understanding that, when you say *Death*, the *D* and the *th* are important to the *idea* of the film! And so on and on, over and over again! Every actor in this film speaks well. I don't mean they speak beautifully, like a TV evangelist. They speak well, like actors. They understand their responsibility to the word.

Phenomenal, the beauty this film gets out of just the way the actors speak. Of course, that was true of the stage-performance as well. That's my point: that this film is *nourished* by the performances which preceded it.

Some years ago, they were about to make a film of Athol Fugard's *Boesman and Lena*, one of the best new plays I've seen. They asked me for advice, but I said: "Don't ask me, go see *Marat/Sade*! Get those three wonderful actors from the play and *do* it! Then shoot five times as much film as you need and put it together!" Not that they disregarded me; they disregarded *Marat/Sade*.

This film of *Marat/Sade* is really a *locus classicus* for the idea of making a play into a film. Not imitating a play, but making a play into a film. Alfred Hitchcock's *Rope* had the same idea, the same procedure. And I think it's valid to say that much of the time Ingmar Bergman works that way. Much of the quality of Bergman's best films comes from the fact that—not that these actors have done the text that much before—but that these actors have worked together so much before.

Two elements, two sources, nourish Peter Weiss's script, as far as I'm concerned: Brecht and Artaud. They are said to be incompatible. Weiss disbelieved that, and Brook was the man to realize it in *Marat/Sade*. I once interviewed Weiss; he was a very gentle man. The show was then running in New York at the Martin Beck. I asked him a few questions, and he very circumspectly intimated that this was not his play; it was Brook's production of it. He preferred Konrad Swinarski's production of it at the Schiller Theatre in Berlin. He soft-pedaled his answer, but it's that whole 20th century-long question of Stanislavski versus Meyerhold. In this case, Brook was the Meyerhold.

LONEY: Weiss has said that the argument between the Marquis de Sade and Jean-Paul Marat got completely submerged in Brook's theatrics. That most Americans who saw it had no notion that an argument was going on. Doesn't the film focus our attention much more on the argument?

KAUFFMANN: Oh, yes! Because of the film's power of *isolation*. It's able to isolate factors. To return to Brook's point about actors talking in the foreground, you can still be conscious of what's happening in the background on stage—in some relationship, if not equally. But in film, that background can be very well controlled. It happens all the time in this film, with what they call "rack-pulling," focus-changes in the middle of shots, from the front to the back. Most scenes are focused in the front.

I brought up the Brecht-Artaud matter as a property of the play, because Brook responded to it with marvelous kinds of energy. This is highly personal, but it's not only a question of finding these impulses in the script, but in also sensing—in a certain way—a defect in the play. The main defect in the play is that it has no dramatic continuum. It doesn't exist as a drama. It exists as a series of more or less dramatic scenes. And the only way you can keep the audience interested, Brook obviously felt, was to invest each one of those scenes with such texture that you are deluded into thinking it's a drama.

Take that little bit with Patrick Magee as De Sade, and Glenda Jackson as Corday with the knife, as she's singing that song. That business with the knife is not in the play. There's no stage-direction that says: "Teases her with the knife." That was all—I don't say imposed—but evoked by Brook, to make that scene more interesting. He does that moment-by-moment in the play and in the film. I can't begin to cite all the instances. Sade is sitting on one end of a bench, with the so-called "Mad Animal" on the other. That is all composed so that you'll think something is happening. But it's really a reflective scene. This happens moment after moment after moment in the film.

Another thing that struck me very forcibly when I saw the film again was the importance of the music. This is a play-with-music, if there ever was one. In its accents—as well as a chorus telling you what's going to happen—it's as Brechtian as could be. Peaslee's music is wonderful, I think. It's used the way Kurt Weill wrote music for Brecht, but, for me, it kept suggesting Arthur Sullivan, another great *theatre* composer, who's overlooked as such.

LONEY: Didn't Weiss conceive this play as a Brechtian Epic, with the songs as an Alienation Effect, spaced between the segments of the developing argument between De Sade and Marat? But Brook has, instead, made the hostility and wildness of the mad people in the asylum the alienating element?

KAUFFMANN: I think that's true.

LONEY: Doesn't this go back to Brook's Theatre of Cruelty and Artaud: the Alienation Effect there was the menace the actors offered the audiences? That the audiences were actually terrified that the actors might break out of the boundary of the stage? Another *kind* of Alienation?

KAUFFMANN: Come over and kill them? Yes. That's a sound observation about this work, as well. Weiss meant this play to be Brechtian, but Brook—consciously or unconsciously; it doesn't matter—divined that it needed some theatrical sustenance, some theatrical menace, and used these mad people legitimately to provide that menace. And used them over a period of some 14 months before we got to meet them in the film.

There's a danger in this, in using the mad people that way. I don't think it's in the play, but it is in Brook's production. It is what I call the "Cuckoo's Nest" fallacy. Which is the implication that the mad people are really the sane ones. I think that's a cheap, sentimental bit of nonsense. And there are times when this work comes close to that. Now we're talking about Brook's work, not Weiss's. What saves it: first of all, the mad people are acting, as they are not in the film, *One Flew Over the Cuckoo's Nest*. In that, they are just mad. But here, in *Marat/Sade*, they are mad people who are acting sane people in a play-within-a-play. And the words they are given to speak—supposedly written by De Sade—have this twin-strata of one person's utterance conveyed through the mouths and distortions of insane people. So that takes a little of the edge off the facile idea that the real lunatics are the people out in the street. The idea is dangerous: ideologically, intellectually.

Plays on film generally—I'm not talking about this film—that is, more conventional plays than this, successful plays, often look bad, specious, hollow, even if they're filmed fairly well in conventional terms. This is because a play depends on a symbolic language that is, in some ways, foreign to that of film. An example of this—which is almost an insult to mention in reference to *Marat/Sade*—is a film made from a play called *Orphans*. Not a very good play. But there are three very good actors, especially Albert Finney, in the film. The film seems fake because it's still relying on theatre abstractions, while it's happening in a medium of potentially the highest realism. Near the end of the play, the character played by Finney comes back, wounded, dying. We've been shown in the film that the house is in a lonely place, but, in the film, he just comes in. In the theatre, this entrance was taken by the audience as a symbolic act. In the film, when he staggers in, bleeding, the first thing I thought was: I didn't hear any car! With a fatal wound, how did he get to that lonely house, twenty miles from anywhere? This is a small question, but it's not trivial, because it says something about the limitations and powers of the two mediums, film and theatre.

LONEY: But *Orphans*, as a play, was Theatre of the Absurd. Nothing really made any sense. Ferocious energy in the playing took the place of dramatic logic. Shouldn't they have made the film in this way also?

KAUFFMANN: Exactly! And Peter Brook—this is another very simple thing that he did, which ensured that the theatre-audience would understand the style. This is obviously not realistic; it is a highly abstract piece of work. Yes, there is realism in the details, but it is not a realistic work. He made it a point that we see the audience on stage. Sometimes, we see the play from behind the audience. You see bars, a wall of bars, separating the madmen and the play from the audience. That is not a trick. It is a very clever action in art, to make sure that you understand that you are not seeing a film: you are seeing a theatre-film! Just think what it would be, if that audience weren't there in the film! You'd say: "What the hell is going on here? Who are these people? They're crazy!" [He laughs.]

LONEY: So the asylum director, his family, and the invited guests accept the insult and the menace that's really meant for us in the film audience?

KAUFFMANN: They are our shock-absorbers! But they are also our "certifiers," that what is happening here is happening in a "third" world. Not the world we live in, not the world of the theatre, but a world someplace else. Walter Benjamin once said that translations are in a third language: they aren't in the language of the original and they are not in our language; they are somewhere in space. That's also true of a work like this.

    A note on the debate between these two men, Marat and Sade. It's a serious one and an important one. A debate between the man who believes that actions are necessary to bring about the ideas you have in your head. Marat believes that: for the betterment of all you see around you, and for the fulfillment of the best in yourself. You get that only by action, and killing people is only one necessary form of action. Sade is a liberal and thinks that the only perfection that can exist is in your head. The minute you take steps to try in implement it, to crystallize it, you're bound to do something towards coercing other people.

Somewhere at the back of every idealistic political program is the policeman! Kafka said: "Every revolution evaporates, leaving a sludge of bureaucracy behind." A liberal idealist like De Sade doesn't want that kind of thing. The play lives—and it ends—without making any attempt to resolve the debate. Weiss was a Marxist, but he was very careful not to make this a Marxist work. He wanted to *impale* us on the dilemma of the rightness of both views. This remains a dilemma for all liberals, and I'm one of them.

At my urging, a friend went to see the play. He came back and said: "This doesn't say: 'Change the world!' It says: 'Change the theatre!'" That was a very perceptive remark. Brook's production of the play—and his film—have done a great deal more toward changing the theatre and film than they have about political programs!

RICHARD PEASLEE: CREATING MUSIC
FOR PETER BROOK

LONEY: Was *The Theatre of Cruelty* the first time you worked for Brook?

PEASLEE: Right. *The Theatre of Cruelty, The Screens* and then *Marat/Sade*.

LONEY: How did you meet Brook?

PEASLEE: I was in London, working with a jazz ensemble called the London Jazz Orchestra. The guy who ran the orchestra, Bill Russo, had orchestrated a show for Brook. It was a musical written by the same people who had created *Irma La Douce*, which Brook directed. This was going to be a big smash-hit sequel. But it never even got to the West End. Fortunately, Brook asked him if he knew anybody who might want to work in experimental theatre for £12 a week. Obviously Bill was not intersted, so he mentioned my name. At that point Brook was doing *King Lear*, with Paul Scofield as Lear. I had just seen that, but otherwise I didn't know anything about Brook. He said "Come over to the rehearsals. We are working on this thing called *The Theatre of Cruelty.*"

LONEY: Had you heard about Antonin Artaud or his theories about this form of theatre before?

PEASLEE: No. I was interested in big-band composing. I had no interest at all in theatre. But Brook didn't take the usual approach; it was only incidental music at first. I always thought that incidental music should be *very* incidental. Pretty watery stuff! But we started fooling around with some John Cage ideas and some tricks with percussion instruments that I had picked up. When you submerge a gong in a huge pot of hot water while you are playing and the pitch changes, you get a real glissando! One part of an evening was filled entirely with just the gong glissandi.

There was this Artaud piece, *The Spurt of Blood*, that was pretty wild! First of all, however, Brook took a theatre in London—not the Aldwych Theatre. It was a small theatre, the Lamda, and the first thing he did was to turn things around. The playing area was where the seats had been, and he put the audience where the stage was. This caused a bit of chaos with the lighting guy, because the lights and the controls were now facing the wrong way! But Peter never worried very much about the lighting anyway. He started out with a nucleus of actors, which has partly carried through. Bob [Robert Langdon] Lloyd, who is in the *Mahabharata* was in that original Theatre of Cruelty nucleus, and Glenda Jackson, who is now the best known of that group. We did *The Theatre of Cruelty* and then we did *The Screens* of Genet. And then, with the same nucleus, we did the *Marat/Sade*.

LONEY: Most of these people were unknown in that time: Glenda Jackson was certainly unknown when Brook started working on *The Theatre of Cruelty*. It had no major Royal Shakespeare actors in its beginnings. Patrick Magee appeared as the Marquis de Sade in *Marat/Sade*, but he was not part of the original experimental work. Nor was Ian Richardson, who played Marat.

PEASLEE: No. I don't think they would have worked for £12 a week!

LONEY: Paul Scofield, who was in *King Lear*, never worked for Peter again after that, because he said the special performance exercises were a waste of time. Can you tell us about *The Spurt of Blood*?

PEASLEE: As I remember, there was a lot of screaming and very little language. And it only took five or ten minutes. I think I liked that best of all the pieces that evening. Except maybe for Charles Marowitz's *Hamlet*, which took only twenty minutes.

LONEY: Were you involved in creating music for *The Spurt of Blood*?

PEASLEE: I can't remember. I think it was mainly sounds. Probably a lot of percussion.

LONEY: Did Brook speak specifically about working with *music concrète* then? Was that a term that you used at that time? He had been very interested in it in some earlier work.

PEASLEE: When we first got together, I didn't know who he was. And he certainly didn't know who I was, so we were kind of talking around, trying to figure out what common ground there was. When we first realized that we were interested in the same areas of music, I think that's when we talked about *music concrète* and John Cage.

LONEY: Considering Cage's fondness for spontaneity and "chance" in performance, does that mean that some of the music you composed then was not really scored? That every night it turned out a little different—that it was aleatory in nature?

PEASLEE: During the performances, we tried to keep things pretty consistent. Otherwise, some actors, and especially dancers, would really be thrown if things change from one night to the next. A little story: In the *Marat/Sade*, we had a drummer who was a bit psychotic, and the on-stage atmosphere of the insane asylum didn't help him any. When we were doing the show in New York, one night in the middle of the show—I forgot who was speaking—he took his wig off and threw it down on the stage and yelled: "Three cheers for Dixie!" He'd periodically do things like that. We couldn't predict what was going to happen. I wanted to get rid of him, but Peter said: "Oh, that's great!" He wasn't interested in predictable slick performances all the time.

LONEY: But if you're on the light controls, you need stage-cues you can depend upon!

PEASLEE: Well, yes. But that's an example of how Peter works. He loves to have things "happen." Accidentally—and then work off of them.

AUDIENCE QUESTION: You mentioned you wanted to do big-band jazz. What was your background?

PEASLEE: I studied at Juilliard, after Yale. So I had formal training. We had a composer's group which was doing performances periodically to smaller and smaller audiences. Finally, some of us got fed up: was *this* what we spent all those years studying for? One of those guys was Peter Schickele, of P. D. Q. Bach fame. We decided there were other ways to communicate, so people went off in different directions. I happened to be working with Bill Russo in New York—he was a big influence on my work—but he went over to London to start this jazz orchestra. He said: "Come over and write for the band. That's how I wound up with Peter Brook.

LONEY: For the *Marat/Sade*, we found a kind of classroom introductory film which shows you at the rear of a piano, its sounding-board removed, massaging the strings with the backs of spoons. How did you happen to develop that kind of sound?

PEASLEE: Of course a lot of that stuff was going on with John Cage and others: "prepared" piano, playing *inside* the piano.

LONEY: Inside? What do you mean by that?

PEASLEE: Playing the strings. You can hit them with all kinds of things. You can pluck them—play them like a harp. The hard thing is figuring out which string is which note. When you're doing work with a "prepared piano," you usually put pieces of tape on the strings so you can tell which note is which.

QUERY: Did you ever have artistic differences with Peter Brook?

PEASLEE: It's hard to say. No. But I didn't like *The Screens* as a play. As for working with Peter, at that time, I think, he represented an approach to theatre that I really liked. I didn't know what "my" approach would have been, but I liked this top-to-bottom versatility. Like Shakespeare himself: from low comedy to the most elevated ideas. I also like very much anything political, like the *Marat/Sade*.

Q: Did you write a complete score for *Marat/Sade* and then make changes when you were in production?

PEASLEE: The Royal Shakespeare Company usually insisted on an eight-week rehearsal period, but we ended up with something like seven. We went into rehearsal with quite a bit of the score. Of course it had changes, and a lot more was written during the rehearsals.

Q.: With song lyrics by playwright Peter Weiss already in the text, did you have to re-write any of the songs you'd already composed?

PEASLEE: In most of Peter's productions, the music got written during rehearsals. This was a little different in that we wrote some of it before; we didn't go in completely cold. Adrian Mitchell had done the English adaptation—from the German text—so there were a lot of lyrics.

But things would happen in rehearsal. For instance, at one point there was no song for Charlotte Corday. So Brook said: "It would be nice to have a little waltz here." Adrian wrote a lyric, which he said was based on *The Blue Danube*. Well, I wanted to have something ready for rehearsal next morning. So I did something just for blocking purposes in the scene. And I wrote a really banal little tune. Well, those things tend to stay in a show! Whereas the things you really like get thrown out.

LONEY: Didn't Noel Coward say something about the potency of cheap music? An "in" joke in *Private Lives*, when one of his own songs is being played? In fact, Corday's song is memorable: simple, not banal. Did you do anything—other than that piano—with bizarre instruments in *Marat/Sade*, or were they largely conventional?

PEASLEE: The basic on-stage band was called for in the script. Five players: trumpet, drums, guitar. That's what Peter Weiss asked for. We didn't use any taped music or hidden sources. Peter Brook likes live music; you hear what you see. But he did fool around with electronic music early in his career.

I think we used more of a sound-score in *Midsummer Night's Dream*. Things like the Free-Kas, which whistled when you waved them about.

People have asked if that was an electronic score. They even wanted to know if the guy on the lighting-board was playing a synthesizer. There were only three musicians in *Dream*. It took place in a white box, with two percussionists up on the top wall of the set.

Peter told me he was working on *Midsummer Night's Dream* in 1968 or 1969. It was the summer of Kent State, the Black Panthers, and all that. I was being really "relevant" then, so I didn't think the *Dream* had anything to do with what was happening. So I really did not want to work on this production. At first he said they were doing fine with improvisation; Ben Kingsley, who was to play Demetrius, could play the guitar. But after about three weeks of rehearsal, Peter called up and asked: "Are you sure you don't want to come over?"

I figured it would be a nice family vacation to go over to Stratford-Upon-Avon. But I knew I should arrive with something: some ideas at least. I'd been wandering around Greenwich Village, where there was this place called Music Inn, with a lot of exotic music instruments. You know, it kind of scares me now, that I almost missed out working on this production. Anyhow, the Music Inn had these strange plastic things—the Free-Kas—which I'd never seen before. The guy showed me how they worked.

LONEY: Ribbed plastic tubes in fluorescent colors, with holes in them, so when you whirl them in the air, they give off a humming noise which can rise to shriek when you rotate them very fast. They were even sold to the audience so they could help the cast along! Like getting audiences at Brook's Old Vic production of Seneca's *Oedipus* to join in at the close with a Dixieland band parading down the aisles and an immense orgiastic golden phallus on stage.

Q: Do you think that any of Peter Brook's work is irrelevant?

PEASLEE: Well, in that it may not be designed to carry a message, sure.

LONEY: But is that a fault?

PEASLEE: No! "If you want to send messages, go to Western Union." Who said that? As for communicating, at the end of *Midsummer Night's Dream*, the audience seemed genuinely delighted to make contact with the cast. Then we did another show, *US*, which was about Vietnam.

LONEY: We are going to see the film version, *Tell Me Lies*.

PEASLEE: That has nothing much to do with the stage production. They used my music, but the film is totally different from the stage version. I think the stage production was much better. There is a film record of the stage production which is more interesting.

LONEY: Brook has said that the stage version was really more about English people dealing with this era in terms of their own problems and reactions. But he wanted to make the film more universal.

PEASLEE: Well, it was hard to come to grips with that whole situation. In *US*, there was this kind of hostile moment, where Bob Lloyd took two butterflies out of a box. And he let them go; then he burned a third one. Then the cast, which was sitting on stage, just continued to sit there in silence. Not exactly glaring at the audience, but Peter didn't want any applause. Well, Kenneth Tynan, the critic, heard about this. He'd said he was fed up with this kind of thing in the theatre. So he just said: "Are we waiting for you, or are you waiting for us?" And he got up and walked out of the theatre.

LONEY: What happened to the Free-Kas in *Dream*?

PEASLEE: Oh, when I brought them to Peter, he said: "Great! Let's take them into the rehearsal and not tell them what they are." It took a few moments before the actors discovered what they could do with them. At first they tried to sing through them, or put them up to their ears.

Brook worked on the *Dream* script differently than most people have. There's this whole section at the end which is usually musicalized.

LONEY: Mendelssohn made it memorable!

PEASLEE: Right! But even in the script, it's supposed to be a kind of pageant. So Peter cut all the music. Actually, we never even wrote any. He said: "This would be much better in silence." But then we'de go through the script, and he'd finds bits and pieces of dialogue and say: "Hey! That would make a nice song!" So we'd make a song out of it.

LONEY: Were there times, in your various collaborations with Brook, that he didn't tell you what his concept of the production was? Or that he was himself waiting to see what would evolve during rehearsals?

PEASLEE: Yes. Very true, because he likes to work off of what happens in rehearsals. Sometimes, you feel he arrives at rehearsal without an idea in his head. And he'll just say: "Start." But obviously he's been thinking about it. But he wouldn't tell me what to write; he wouldn't tell me exactly what he wanted. He would tell me what he'd like to have set to music, but he wouldn't tell me how to set it.

LONEY: How did he react to your work? Did he ever say he hated it? That he wanted you to go home and think about it some more? That it would have to be done differently?

PEASLEE: It did happen, but not too often. Which is why we worked so well together. Generally, we agreed. But there were some songs—well, he'd always be very diplomatic: "Could we make it a little *more*?" Or else he'd try out a lot of different things before choosing one. In *Marat/Sade*, I did several versions of a Marat song before we went back to the original.

LONEY: You worked on specific musical moments in the plays, but beforehand, did you talk about the entire play with him? Did he talk about the play musically, or use musical metaphors?

PEASLEE: That's an interesting question. If he saw the plays *musically*, I don't recall it. But really, we weren't all that intellectual in our discussions.

LONEY: In *Dream*, there's another specific place for music, when the fairies sing Bottom to sleep. What did you do about that?

PEASLEE: Well, let's look at the book. [laughter as he pretends to consult the production book] Oh, that's a case where he was specific. He said he wanted something very Eastern, Oriental. The little princeling Titania has comes from India.

LONEY: We've heard so many opinions in this seminar about Peter Brook, most of them laudatory. Can you give us one or two impressions of your own?

PEASLEE: The thing that impressed me most about working with Peter is the way he can collaborate with people and use the fund of ideas that was out there. It never bothered him that he didn't have the idea first. Some directors have to feel it is *all* their ideas, nothing borrowed. He'd listen to anybody who wanted to suggest something: his secretary, an actor, anybody. He'd be very open and say: "Oh, that's a good idea! Let's try it!" He was constantly open to all the new ideas: what was happening in the avant-garde. In New York, we'd go down to what's now TriBeCa to hear new talent. Peter was always exploring—and using this stuff. Putting all this into his mental computer. Which sometimes exposed him to the accusation that he was borrowing other people's ideas. But he always filtered them through his own discipline.

It was really great: I learned a lot just by listening to him. One day when I was with him on *Marat/Sade*, when I came into rehearsal, he said: "Listen to this!" And he took out a funnel and dragged it along a grating in the floor. It sounded like a rachet on the guillotine! So we used it! And some chains. At first, I was kind of angry, because I hadn't thought of it. [laughter] But there was never any jealousy with him. If it was a good idea, no matter who'd thought of it, he'd use it. Anything that would make for a better production . . .

LONEY: Having worked with Brook, how has that experience influenced your later creations, such as the musical *Boccaccio*?

PEASLEE: Well, there was one scene in Purgatory . . . But that show was kind of a "learning experience," as we say when things don't work out on Broadway. Character-building. [laughter] We had a lot of fun when we did it in the Kreeger Theatre at the Arena in Washington, D. C. Why'd you mention that one?

LONEY: I wondered if there wasn't a specific production in which some signs of Brook's influence might be seen. Of course, with other collaborators, the chemistry is different, probably not Brookian.

PEASLEE: Well, with a guy like Andrei Serban—there's a lot of Peter Brook in his thinking. We were all out there in Iran, at Persepolis with *Orghast*. Working with Serban is something like working with Brook.

LONEY: Persepolis! How could the music be heard in those vast spaces?

PEASLEE: First of all, there were two spaces. One was an enclosed area—a cut in a cliff, a tomb cut into a cliff. The acoustics there were excellent, so these was no problem. The other spot has a long cliff-face with three or four tombs cut into it, high up. Tombs of the Persian kings. The cliff-face was used for the second half of *Orghast*. That was more of a spectacle in front of the cliff. We put speakers in some of the tombs, spread them around. All outdoors, with a lot of dust. It took place in the middle of the night, so that the end came at dawn, when the sun came up.

One night we were spread out and didn't have walkie-talkies. The idea was the whole production would begin when the music started. They could all hear that. Well, that night, I was testing the tape decks, just testing, and they heard it and the whole show began. Too soon. [laughter] There was no way to stop it.

LONEY: As the text contains passages of Latin, Greek, and Avesta—a sacred language—as well as the invented, constructed language of Orghast, a creation of the poet/playwright Ted Hughes, how did you manage to compose music for such a cockamamie collage? [laughter] Well, maybe not cockamamie, but "challenging"?

PEASLEE: Well, I wrote cockamamie music! [laughter] For sure. There were those songs. Mainly we put it on tape. But I worked a lot with the language, with the actors' voices speaking in it. I found myself teaching Persians—in the chorus—ancient Greek! I didn't know anything about either Persian or Greek.

Orghast was really more of a Life Experience, than a great theatrical one. Oh, it had its moments, no question! In the first part, in the confined space, that was very effective.

LONEY: It's reported that Irene Worth—after Peter Brook had spent a day with her clambering all over the tombs, to see how her voice would sound— said: "No living actress has done for Peter Brook what I have done today!"

PEASLEE: It's amazing what she had to go through. That summer everyone was completely exhausted. I think it even broke up a marriage or two.

LORD OF THE FLIES IN PRODUCTION
Edwin Wilson

[New York: September 2, 1987: Wilson is Emeritus Professor in the CUNY Graduate Center Theatre PhD Program and a former drama critic for the *Wall Street Journal*.]

WILSON: I let it slip that I worked on *Lord of the Flies*. If you look very closely on the credits, you'll see that I was really a producer's assistant. This was Lewis Allen's second feature. Lew was working for Robert Whitehead, the producer. And I went to work for Bob, with the idea of working with Lew when he formed his own production company, which he did shortly thereafter. The first thing he did was make a film of Jack Gelber's *The Connection*. This was directed by a woman called Shirley Clarke. They really just filmed the play. They created a set, but it was very much like the one used in the theatre by The Living Theatre.

Our second film was *Lord of the Flies*. I have to tell you that I have very mixed feelings about the production. I was working in Lew's office, doing a lot of odd jobs, but I followed the development of this project very closely. I was very interested. I admired Peter Brook as a director. I'd seen his production of *The Visit*; I'd seen *Irma la Douce*. The commercial theatre lost a great asset when Peter Brook decided to devote his life to theatre experiments.

I should explain what I mean by "mixed feelings" in regard to *Lord of the Flies*. Peter Brook is a *presence*, a tremendously talented person. I'm enormously fond of his book, *The Empty Space*. He's a marvelous raconteur, with a wonderful twinkle in his eye. But he's also very enigmatic: he plays his cards very close to his vest. In terms of *Lord of the Flies*, the thing I think that Peter did that was admirable: he was aiming for a kind of purity and simplicity. There was a pre-existent script; there had been several, because it was a very successful and highly acclaimed novel. Widely read, especially by young people and students in English courses. Sam Spiegel, who went by the name of S. P. Eagle, had a version with girls in it. Peter and Lew wanted to do this with a certain purity and honesty, so they rejected all those scripts. They had trouble getting the rights, but they finally obtained them—and I'm sure Peter had something to do with that.

I admire the fact that they stuck to the story, to the novel; doing it in black-and-white—again, a kind of austerity, a kind of purity. Not trying to romanticize it; not trying to soften the edges; not trying to enlarge on it; not trying to enhance it: all of that I find admirable. In many ways, it's an interesting film because it's such a powerful, incredible story. That's the good news.

I had very strong reactions to the way Peter undertook this project. Lew wanted to do whatever Peter wanted. This was after all Peter's film. If you hire Peter Brook, you don't then say: "Peter, I don't like the way Puck comes on in the fourth scene." But there are two ways to look at the way he went about hiring people for this production. First, let me say that in most every case, he hired people for a job they'd never done before. Now you can look at that as purity and innocence, or you can look at it as intentional, to make sure you control every element in the film, since you are working with people who have never done this before.

Tom Hollyman, who was the chief cinematographer, had made a reputation for still photographs in Puerto Rico. He had done some memorable photos of Puerto Rico, absolutley stunning: the harbor, walking on the beach with a black umbrella! But these were stills, and he'd never made a movie before. The first thing he did was to go out into Central Park with an 8 mm camera. That was his first experience of working with a film-camera.

The business-manager was a very engaging guy named Harold Heinz, who had written a book called *Lord Love a Duck*. And even when we went over budget, it was not that bad. In fact, there were a lot of talented people involved. The second cinematographer had done some filming, some excellent documentaries. And he continued to work with Peter after this production.

Of course the boys had never acted before. We recruited them everywhere. We had a fellow named Mike Macdonald, the son of the critic, Dwight Macdonald. He was a very interesting young man. He'd meet the *Queen Elizabeth* and try to snare young boys as they were coming off for roles in the film. He almost got arrested. He also went to the UN, and we even sent him once to Bermuda, trying to find English schoolboys.

The only boy we couldn't find this way was Piggy. We just couldn't find one who was right. And then, I think it was on top of the Empire State Building, we found him; he'd just arrived in New York. All the other boys had already gone to Bermuda. We also had three or four mothers who went down there as chaperones. We found an abandoned factory where the boys lived.

We shot it on an island called Vieques—an absolutely gorgeous island with three beautiful beaches. There was a wonderful sort of French planter's house near the beach, which was where Peter, Lew, Tom, and the others stayed—and where I got to stay when I went down. I was the one left in New York when they all went down to the island. Then I went down later. There was also a girl named Ellie Jones: she and I were assistants to the producer.

There were a few mishaps. It was a naval training-area. The first day of filming, somebody had failed to check this out. They started filming, and a whole fleet of helicopters flew over! So they had to arrange what hours the copters would fly and what hours they could shoot. Peter didn't use a script; he just used the novella. It was all improvised, but that was very much in vogue at that time. But little boys are not necessarily the best improvisers when they are facing a camera. It was all shot from the novel. The original idea was to shoot it all in sequence. All of this was—Purity—authentic and pure.

Well, as you know, nobody ever shoots movie-scenes in sequence. For one thing, it costs too much to move from set to set. But this was what Peter was determined to do. After the second or third day, I got this call from Vieques to go to Brooks Brothers and buy 25 blazers. They had blazers already, but when they realized that they were not going to be able to shoot the film in sequence, they had to have two sets: one of them new, the other torn. I also had to buy I don't know how many gallons of body make-up: the little boys had to look sunburned after being stranded on the island.

Peter's idea, of course, was that, in shooting in sequence, gradually the boys would get sunburned; gradually their blazers would get torn. But a number of things crossed that ideal. It couldn't be done that way. Fortunately, as one would suspect with Peter Brook, there were also a lot of fortuitous things. The boy playing Ralph really turned out to be a natural actor. He really got into the experience and developed in the role.

Some wonderful things did happen in the film, often because the boys were really living like this, almost as in the novel. There was a certain authenticity about it. The boy playing Piggy: that part about his home-town and family was his own story. Peter talked to him one day and asked him to talk about his town. They just put the camera on him, and he told the story. So a lot of the improvising did work out fortuitously.

Peter deserves a lot of credit for this. He held the whole thing together, creating the atmosphere which made it possible. The assistant director was Toby Robertson, who's done a lot of work in provincial theatre and once was at the Old Vic. For a time, he was one of Peter's protégés, but he had some reservations about the filming. He told me later he thought the fire was dangerous, that the boys were too close to it. Some of the boys got very scared. A very sensitive situation! But again, when you are seeking authenticity, how far should you go? If you are running a real risk? But I wasn't there, so this is only Toby's report. I was there only the second and third week of the filming.

They finally finished, but there were some scenes that had to be redone. And it was hard to keep track of all this. There was a script-girl, but when you're really "winging" it like this, not working from an actual script, you can have a lot of problems when it's time to edit the film. After they finished shooting, Peter—and the second cameraman and a woman editor—rented an apartment in Paris—Peter loves Paris, of course. And they worked four or five months—I'm not sure how long—on the editing. They brought the first cut back to New York. Lew Allen and his wife, the playwright Jay Presson Allen—who's a very sharp, tough lady, who doesn't mince words—along with me and several others, sat in a screening-room to watch this rough-cut.

And it was rough! There were a lot of things that did not work. Some things just didn't make sense. The continuity was hard to follow. Jay couldn't understand how the boys had got from there to here. *Why* were these boys fighting here? And, again, Peter's curious "purity": he wanted no music. Just the natural sounds the mikes picked up of the boys on the island: their sticks, the fire crackling, their voices.

In the film, in the stunning first scene on the island, as I recall, the boys march along the beach in their choir-robes. And there's this *Kyrie Eleison* in the background. They were boys in choir-school. Originally, that *Kyrie* was not there at all. Peter didn't want it. He didn't want *any* artifice. But obviously, it makes a big difference. It's haunting, and it also sets up the religious thing, against the later descent into savagery.

By this time, I'd moved on, but I came back for the screening. They hired someone—I don't know how this came about—but they hired a very commercial editor to redo part of the cutting. Obviously, Peter made the final cut; it couldn't have been released without his approval. But Lew and Jay were very insistent that the continuity had to be clear. By that time, he had other commitments and had already spent a long time on it. I suppose they said to him: "We'll never be able to release this if we don't make some minimal changes here."

This has become a very popular film, even a cult film. And it has some wonderful things in it. Some wonderful performances, and a very austere, haunting quality. It does remain true to the spirit of the novel, to the uncompromising message of the novel. And it's very much in the vein of *Cinema Vérité,* which was very popular at that time: a rough, raw, documentary quality. All of that comes through powerfully!

But it would have been interesting to see what might have happened if *Lord of the Flies* had been shot from a real script, with some experienced cameramen. As it is, every decision in the film was Peter's. He had to take total responsibility for all the artistic decisions. Toby Robertson would work with the kids on a scene before it was shot, it's true, but the final shooting was directed by Peter. And Toby, Tom Hollyman, and the rest were all Peter's choices. No question about it. As it was Peter's choice in the way it would be shot and edited. If he'd had real professionals with him on the film, he surely would not have had the same kind of control over it. And slick professionalism would have taken away the primitive, natural quality of the finished film.

PETER BROOK'S QUEST:
MARGARET CROYDEN TRACES IT

[New York: November 10, 1987: Croyden, who contributes frequently to the *New York Times* and the *Village Voice*, is also the author of *Lunatics, Lovers, and Poets*—which features the work of Peter Brook—and of *In the Shadow of the Flame*. Long a Professor of English, she has recently retired.]

LONEY: Margaret Croyden may not yet be Peter Brook's Boswell, but she has surely done more than any other American critic to bring his innovative work to national attention, notably in the *New York Times*. This has been important because some of Brook's most challenging productions have not been shown in the United States. She was with the cast of Brook's *Midsummer Night's Dream* backstage on Broadway when I first met her. Now she has come to share her impressions of the man and his work. When did you first come into close contact with Peter Brook?

CROYDEN: When I met Brook in 1968, he was doing an experimental production of *The Tempest*. Actually, I'd like to start from *The Mahabharata* and go backwards, because there is a link among his works which most people don't recognize. When I asked Brook about *The Mahabharata* and why he chose to do such an esoteric work, he said: "Well, I liked the story." That's what he said! He said he remembered years ago, when he was doing *US*, that somebody came to him with a one-page script about a man who was engaged in a war, and then stopped: he wouldn't fight. This was the story of the great warrior, Arjuna, from *The Mahabharata*. Brook had never heard of this great Hindu epic at that point, but the image stayed with him.

Later, he met a Sanskrit scholar, and they spent the whole night with stories from *The Mahabharata*, and Brook and his collaborator, Jean-Claude Carrière, became very intrigued with the material. That's how it all started, Brook claims. But I think it began differently. I think Peter Brook's whole career has been based on his own *quest*—a search for something that is not so obvious, something that is beyond what you see. Searching not only for new forms, but also for new sensibilities. He began his career that way. When he came out of Oxford, he directed a production of *Salomé* for Covent Garden that provoked a scandal. But you may already know about this?

LONEY: Anything you can share with us is of interest!

CROYDEN: Then I'll review his beginnings very quickly, because the through-line to *The Mahabharata* seems clear to me. That *Salomé* got him fired from the Opera House. He was really put down by the critics for that.

LONEY: His instincts were right, but traditionalists weren't ready for his innovative ideas about opera staging. They never are!

CROYDEN: Then he became heavily involved in the commerical theatre. He did everything from Arthur Miller to Shakespeare. But he was always changing, always doing something different, always "off-balance," never settling for past successes or wanting to repeat them. He's always going on to other things. One year he'd do a musical; the next year, a drama. Then he went over to Paris and did *A View from the Bridge*. He went through the whole canon of important playwrights: Beckett, Dürrenmatt, Anouilh, and others.

But, as he went along, there was a turning point, when he linked up with the Royal Shakespeare Company. With the RSC, he began to do experimental work seriously. In fact, he told Peter Hall that he would only join the RSC if he could have an experimental workshop at the same time. Which he did create!

One of the things that he was responsible for at the Royal Shakespeare was the revolution in Shakespeare. It was Brook who took a new look at Shakespeare, closely followed by Peter Hall. Up to that time, most Shakespeare in England was done in a rather romantic fashion, rather traditional. Ermine capes and all that kind of thing.

LONEY: Historicism?

CROYDEN: Yes, all kinds of historical flourishes! With the inaguration of the RSC, the principal was to get away from all that. Brook really made a powerful impression with *King Lear*. He designed the sets himself and collaborated on the costumes: he can design also. Are many people aware of that?

LONEY: Sometimes he even composes the music!

CROYDEN: *King Lear*, I think, influenced most Shakespeare productions afterward. After that, people didn't dare to do romantic Shakespeare anymore. Critics have said this was based on the theories of Jan Kott. So, what's wrong with that?

LONEY: Brook insists that Kott was not really an influence. Rather, that they were thinking along the same lines at that time.

CROYDEN: I believe that, because these ideas were in the air. America and Britain were just being introduced to Beckett, Brecht. We knew very little about them. The RSC introduced their work in England, but we never saw the Berliner Ensemble here in New York. The company never came here.

LONEY: All those years when Brecht was living in Santa Monica, most Americans didn't even know who he was!

CROYDEN: When Brook had set up his experimental workshop, he tried out some ideas of Brecht and Artaud as part of the Theatre of Cruelty work. Two important things followed: *US* and the *Marat/Sade*. *US* was very important to Brook. He refers to that production of *US* often when you talk to him. It was the time of the Vietnam War, and he became interested in the element of violence. He'd already dealt with it in *Titus Andronicus* and *King Lear*. He was concerned with what violence did to people, ordinary people who were obsessed with violence, why there was so much violence. That question stayed with him, and it ended up with *The Mahabharata*.

You can see a direct link if you know what *US* was about. *Marat/Sade* has the same idea, though it's a political play. It also deals with violence and madness. *Marat/Sade, Lear, US,* and even the *Midsummer Night's Dream* have this same element. In the *Dream* there was also the idea of *hidden thoughts*. Things that you couldn't say: somewhere in the sub-conscious, things that are invisible. Brook always talks about the visible and the invisible—aspects of things people have in themselves but are not aware of, the things you cannot say. Brook constantly looks for ways to get the actors and the audience to examine themselves.

He challenges them in many different ways. At the end of *Marat/Sade*, for example, he directed everything toward the audience. The mad ones came forward, advancing on the audience. The audience applauded them, and the actors applauded the audience—but menacingly, as if to say: "You are as just as crazy as we are." This was talked about a lot: that Brook was aggressive towards the audience. He was also accused of that in *The Mahabharata*.

There was even an objection to his *King Lear*. He was criticized for leaving out an essential part. When Gloucester is blinded, a servant comes to help him compassionately. Brook left that out, to make his point: to show how awful people are. That there are really not very many good people left in this world. Leaving out this scene was really a breach, but he did it to make his point.

LONEY: In the *Marat/Sade*, was Brook intending to be aggressive against the audience only to annoy or to scare them? Just a little theatre-game? Or was this also to make an important point? To make it impossible to forget the production after they'd left the theatre? He has written about asking actors to hold pauses as long as they could, until the audience seemed ready to break. Is this merely aggressiveness—as it has seemed to some, such as the critic Kenneth Tynan—or simply a device to achieve dramatic effect? And, perhaps in the process, to discover how long you really *can* hold an audience's attention?:

CROYDEN: Anyway, in *Lear*, he did take out those lines of Shakespeare!

LONEY: Yes, but he has said there in nothing wrong with re-working Shakespeare as long as you remain true to the essence.

CROYDEN: That's debatable, isn't it?

LONEY: In an essay in *The Shifting Point*, he suggests that if Shakespeare is to be more meaningful or impressive for us today, it may be advisable to rearrange some scenes. In *Lear*—both in the stage production and in the later, and rather different, film—he seemed intent on stressing the images of sight and blindness again and again. Not just in physical terms: those who can see and those who cannot, but also those who see but who do not *understand* what they see. Gloucester sees the truth about himself and others only after he's lost his physical sight. Maybe that's why Brook cut those lines? To make this constrast stronger for the audience?

CROYDEN: Being *true* to Shakespeare? Look, Peter Sellers thinks *he's* being true to the essences of the operas he revises. This is of matter of opinion. When Brook took out those lines in *Lear*, he showed us a world that was very bleak. Shakespeare already shows us enough of that, but he also shows us that there were compassionate people, too. But you may be right—he may have done it for the impact it makes. It was quite an impressive moment in the theatre!

Brook directed against the *Lear* text. If you saw Paul Scofield on stage as Lear, doing his big scene on the heath: "Blow, ye winds," it was quite underplayed but very powerful. The production was almost an Abstraction visually. Scofield looked like a man of stone: gray, crew-cut, out of the Stone Age. The film is totally different.

LONEY: In its very spareness, the stage production looked Japanese. Abstract, and very simple. There was a great round table that was overturned: this looked like a Noguchi sculpture.

CROYDEN: But the leather costumes seemed inspired by Brecht's use of leather.

LONEY: Some of them even looked like Samurai warrior garb. But maybe I was seeing it all as Japanese-influenced?

CROYDEN: You certainly see some of that in *The Mahabharata*.

LONEY: The drums and the way they are played—like Kodo drums—seem another Japanese influence.

CROYDEN: And the way that they sit in the final act.

Q: When was *King Lear* done by the RSC? What was the date of this production?

LONEY: Check your chronologies! It officially opened the then new New York State Theatre—along with a wildly amusing RSC production of *The Comedy of Errors*. These were cultural treats for the 1964 New York World's Fair, which gave the state the excuse to build a theatre in Lincoln Center for the New York City Ballet. I was there! The RSC did it earlier in England: at Stratford in November 1962, and in London in December of that year. It was revived in February 1964 for the world tour.

Q: I asked because there was a lot of trouble then in England with Skinheads and violence. Maybe that was the reason for the crew-cuts and brutality.

CROYDEN: I don't think it had anything to do with that. There weren't any Skin-heads in the play. Everything he did was abstracted, in a certain way. Many people thought it was cold, but I thought it was brilliant! Because he did not play into the text but against it. And that holding-back of emotion: it was terrifying! Parenthetically, the same year, I saw Morris Carnovsky play Lear at Stratford, in Connecticut. It was such a difference! Although I liked Carnovsky, it was entirely traditional. If you had seen those two Lears, you could see the birth of a new way to do Shakespeare—and the death of the old. Unforgettable!

Now, another turning-point for Peter Brook was the last commercial thing he did under the auspices of the RSC. This was the RSC's *Midsummer Night's Dream*. Oh, it's true he did an *Antony and Cleopatra* for the RSC after that, but it was not a big success. The *Dream*, however, was especially interesting. The Living Theatre had already appeared. The whole Counter-culture was at its height. But Brook did something that was really unusual. Have you seen photographs? That was also a revolution in stage-craft. That white-box of a set, in a way, imitated Shakespeare's theatre, with galleries from which the actors could watch the action below. This was not the first time scaffolding had been used, of course. The Living Theatre had used scaffolding, and the Russians also, long before, in the 1920s. But I think this was the first time in West that they used it successfully. This was also the time of the "Mods," the Mod fashions. So he used that in the costumes. They were satin; they had no shape, just flowing flashes of white and color. Just extraordinary!

This production is famous now, with its swings and trapezes and all the tricks in the air. If anybody puts the actors on swings now, they say: "Yes, that's *à la* Peter Brook!"

Anyhow: just before the *Dream*, Brook was invited by Jean-Louis Barrault to set up a workshop in Paris with a group of international actors. He did that, but then the great student revolution broke out there. They closed everything down, so Brook had to go back to England. I was there at that time, and he did a production of *The Tempest* in a workshop. It was really not meant for the public; it was a fragmentation of the play: he took only some ideas from *The Tempest*, and the company dramatized them. It was ahead of its time, a kind of a deconstruction of the drama. It was not recognizable as the play, but the themes were recognizable.

One of the themes, again, was violence. The violence in *us*. He worked with scaffolds, movable scaffolds this time. By this time, he'd work-ed with a lot of international people: Joe Chaikin; Yoshi Oida had come from Japan; people from the RSC; all kinds of people came. It was quite interest-ing.

At first, I didn't understand it, never having seen Shakespeare done that way. They wearing jeans; there were no costumes. And they worked only with these huge movable scaffolds on wheels. That was the turning-point for Brook's leaving England. He became imbued with the idea of setting up an international theatre workshop and went to Paris. He orga-nized his *Centre* for "research," as he claims, with Micheline Rozan. They started to work with a small company—only a few of whom are left—just doing odd things. I went to observe the workshop for a couple of weeks.

LONEY: Did you do the exercises with the bamboo poles—for a whole morning?

CROYDEN: I was just *observing*. So you know about the bamboo poles?

LONEY: I've been there, too. What do you think about the usefulness of such work?

CROYDEN: Well, I found it boring to look at, but that's not the point. It's not a performance for spectators.

LONEY: When you throw a bamboo pole at someone who may not be expecting it, it's true that it forces him to react. But how does this help in making a play? Does this free an actor's fantasy and imagination? Or does it have some other purpose?

CROYDEN: It has to do with the *rhythm*. These actors pick up a certain rhythm; they develop a certain sensitivity to each other.

LONEY: So, when an actor throws someone a pole, it's metaphorically like throwing him a line of dialogue? Or vice versa?

CROYDEN: No! It is simply an exercise for developing sensibility. When you work with a company like that, you must *feel* the other members in some way. You sense an actor's presence and you feel his rhythm, and you have your own rhythm, if you have been doing the exercises. This is the theory. I can't guarantee that it works on the stage, but it certainly did in *The Ik*. I'm not so sure about *The Mahabharata*, because there were problems with it: recasting, length of the performances, and so on. They were able to work so well because of the exercises. But the poles was only one of the exercises The work with bamboo poles really comes from Japan. They throw them, stamp with them, catch them, all kinds of things. It's almost like catching balls in the air: you don't know where the bamboo pole is going to come from. It seems obvious to me that it creates a certain kind of alertness, a certain kind of energy, an awareness of your partner. And that is essential to acting. It helps form an ensemble: you have to be totally engaged in it, like a baseball team.

Q: Doesn't Brook also have his actors throw a ball to each other? And each time it's caught, the actor has to say a word: anything that comes into his head? Free-association?

CROYDEN: There are many exercises they've done. I was in Paris last year, when they did an open workshop. If you are not participating, it's not all that interesting. It's like a secret only the players share. As an onlooker, I don't know what they are feeling or experiencing. The group is clearly experiencing *something*, and this goes on and on. But if you're just watching, you really become an outsider. Actually, when Brook does these workshops, he takes young people from the audience and brings them up on stage and they have a great time.

LONEY: The explanations are sometimes more inspiring than the exercises, for observers, at least. When he brought *The Conference of the Birds* to BAM, he held an open workshop also. John Simon and Walter Kerr were among the audience, but the volunteers were often novice actors—with a few professionals. All too often, they seemed either to be auditioning for Brook, or showing off for their peers. Brook had forewarned them not to do this. He asked them just to explore the possibilities of the various exercises openly, without thinking about self or "giving a performance." Even when they failed to do what he had requested, his explanations of why and how they failed were as interesting and instructive as the exercises which clearly worked. I think Peter Brook could make reading a menu interesting!

CROYDEN: Exercises aren't for show. You really can't do them for an audience; that's hopeless. But Peter is trying to show those who really are interested what the training is like. Of course the exercises are not boring for those who are doing them. I think it may have been a mistake to show them to an audience. In his defense, when he does open workshops, he really does try to get the audience involved in actual *doing*. They do the drums, various things. After all these years, they still do the poles. And story-telling—he's very big on that now! But open workshops are as far as he will go. You cannot observe a rehearsal. He doesn't allow that now.

Back to my story: the Center was set up—not in any commercial way—simply as it is now, a center where people from all over the world gathered. Arthur Miller came; a lot of people came to watch. So did I, to see what he was doing. At that point, he didn't seem to care where it might go: he was just searching for things. It was rather vague. He would work all day. Don't ask me what they got out of it, but they must have got something. You always get something in a relationship with Brook.

You have to know Brook, to realize what he can do. The energy that he gives off to the actors is fantastic. He is an amazing personality. He never raises his voice, but the energy comes through to the actor. They won't talk about it. You could call it charisma, but I think it is more than that because he is totally concentrated on what he is doing. He practically *zaps* you with his eyes, if you've looked into them. Isn't that true?

LONEY: You can't look away. And you don't want to—you might miss something!

CROYDEN: The way in which he handles people is really quite extraordinary: the care, the patience, the stamina, and the attention that he gives! As an actor, you can get a tremendous amount from him. As a journalist, too, taking notes, you can also see things, but you don't experience what the actors do. But once you know Brook, when you are in his presence—he has Presence! It's there. Of course all great Masters are that way, and I do believe he is a Master in the theatre.

LONEY: I was amazed how long his quest has been going on, perhaps from his very beginnings in the West End theatre. Although he may seem to be repeating himself in *The Empty Space or The Shifting Point*—which is, after all, a collection of essays—he only repeats what is *fundamental*. In a way, they are not repetitions at all, but variations on a theme, or developments, enlargements, of it!

The other day, we were talking about a problem in the commercial theatre. With some urgency, he made his point about the matter, and it was almost word-for-word what he wrote in *The Empty Space*. I'm sure he hasn't memorized the text of that wonderful, seminal book. It's just that this is the best formulation of this particular idea. It's an articulated principle, not a spontaneous reply.

CROYDEN: You see, he has a basic philosophy that stays the same. The techniques of a particular production may change, but the basics remain. And his search, his quest, is always the same: it's for illumination, for consciousness, for awareness. It's for what he calls the "invisible." It's for transformation of himself and the ones he works with. And the audience is a very essential part of that. He feels that he can give audiences an insight into something that they have not actually experienced for themselves.

As he said about *The Cherry Orchard*: "We are not doing to do it better than any other *Cherry Orchard*; we aren't trying to compete." He's trying to give us an idea beyond the moment, beyond the banal. He is really interested in *transcendence*, I would say. It sounds very grandiose to say that, but that's my feeling about it: his own transcendence and that of the people he works with. Nevertheless, he is not the kind of a man to go around talking about such things. He might be furious that I've said this, but I think that's what is underneath.

LONEY: Don't mistake me: it's a *reinforcement*! Even his simplest comments inspire some deep pondering. And I think you are right about transcendence. Why else is he so interested in the mystic, Gurdjieff—and the lives of remarkable men? You know, even in an ordinary conversation—if a chat with Peter Brook can ever be said to be "ordinary"—his formulations are always so precise. Unlike most of us, he clearly thinks before—and as—he speaks!

CROYDEN: Because he is terribly sure of what he is looking for in life! He told me this in a piece I wrote for the *New York Times*: he's seeking a greater existence, greater consciousness, greater perception—very many different levels of conception. Finer emotions, finer perceptions, no end to it! And I think he relates his private life to his artistic life in that way: it's an interaction. As he's said in print, there is no break between what he's looking for in art and in life. The Center was organized that way. He deliberately took people from many lands and different cultures, because he was looking for these things.

There's another important thing: the harder the task, the more Brook likes it! The quest to conquer something, and to go on from that to a new challenge. The obstacle—the opposing force in any situation—is really his meat. To overcome it and move on, building on the experience. It's actually a dialectical approach to his life.

LONEY: Challenges like the Carpet Plays in Africa? Native audiences, with no language in common with the actors? A carpet with some shoes on it?

What to do with the shoes? How to make a show on the spot? Didn't he put his actors on the spot, to see what they were going to do with the shoes?

CROYDEN: I don't think he was putting anyone on the spot. Everything he does is simply to see what is going to happen; he really doesn't know beforehand. He likes to get into situations that are surprises: What is going to happen? I think that's what keeps him so young. As some of the actors say: "Peter Brook will never grow old." Why? Because he is always in this condition: "What's going to happen now?" He is always traveling. He finds life interesting. Very few people do, when you come down to it. Most people are bored.

Brook does not have this attitude towards life, and I think that is part of his own quest, this continual energy going on and on. But it's not a frenetic energy; it's more like a steady path.

LONEY: In my limited experience, talking with Brook is like a conversation with no one else! He talks *to* and *with* you. When Brook talks to you, you get his entire attention: it's focused and it's intense, but, at the same time, he is pleasant and relaxed. He treats you like an equal, even an old friend. In the moments you have with him, he can be marvelously amusing and deeply serious—sometimes simultaneously—but you have his absolute, total concentration on the questions at hand. And you go away feeling full of excitement, energy, and ideas. It's like having been plugged-in for a quick mental and physical re-charge!

CROYDEN: If you spend time with Brook, you do come away with that. Some of his energy comes right into you, even if you're working as a journalist. It's amazing to watch him go through a day. I think the Elizabethan theatre must have been something like that. In fact, he talks about that, but, never in reference to himself. Being around him like this, the actors get on fire. I'm not saying you can actually see this in the productions, but it does show up in their spirit, in rehearsals, how they behave, how they live. He always seems to be energized.

Q: Doesn't he need this energy for his projects? To carry them through?

LONEY: Even if he's not sure at the outset what the outcome will be. You need a lot of energy for that kind of work. Also a lot of inner security and confidence!

CROYDEN: Well, he does often speak about having *hunches*.

LONEY: Obviously, he wouldn't decide to take a new look at *Carmen* or *Cherry Orchard*, unless he thought there was something new to be discovered in them.

CROYDEN: Yes, he has his hunches. Otherwise, it would be hopeless. Of course he does have some idea of what may happen, but he doesn't plot that out. It's more like a vague dream, I think.

LONEY: As with *Titus Andronicus*? It had been a Shakespearean curiosity. Most critics said it not only couldn't be done, but that it shouldn't! "Unactable," said some. "Enter Lavinia ravished": *what* can you do with that? But Brook saw something impressive in it—violence not being the least of its powers. He has said, however, that people who saw that production only seem to remember its "theatrics." As though he had imposed something exciting, but alien, on the drama. But he couldn't have done what he did with any other play.

CROYDEN: With all of this energy, he also has a wonderful quality of serenity. I don't know what happened in his life to give him this sense of serenity, but that is his main quality. This combination of energy and serenity is one of his secrets, because the combination is extremely attractive. You often can get a director who is very excitable, screaming at his actors. Harold Clurman used to scream to the heavens, just giving a lecture. Brook, on the other hand, is quite calm, serene, quite sure.

At the Paris Center, when he began to work on *The Mahabharata*, the inner idea was always on his mind. His *Timon of Athens* had the same idea: how human society operates. And his *Ubu* also dealt with violence, grief, and politics. *The Ik* certainly had the same idea: the terrible hunger and violence in the tribe and in the families themselves. *The Conference of the Birds* was of course closer to Brook's theory of life, I think. The birds go out to look for something; they want to find a god; they go on this long journey, and, as they do, each one becomes discouraged. One wants to turn back another says: "This is all baloney!" And so on. Finally, there are practically no birds left, or only a handful of birds. And what did they discover? The answer was like a sermon: that God is within, of course. It is kind of simplistic.

LONEY: Kind of! Thank you, Mary Baker Eddy! But this "discovery" was also the secret of a popular American sermon by H. Russell Conwell: *Acres of Diamonds*. You may travel to the ends of the earth, seeking riches, but, in the end, you will find they were at home all the time, in your very own backyard! But it's an interesting contrast that, in the American version, we are seeking riches, but in the ancient Sufi tale, we are seeking God! Times change; values change, but the quest goes on.

CROYDEN: Then Brook took a new departure. He made the film on Gurdjieff, *Meetings with Remarkable Men*. But this was also the same idea: searching. Gurdjieff was a spiritual master; the fact that Brook was interested in that shows something about him.

LONEY: It's been said that *The Mahabharata* was seven years in gestation!

CROYDEN: All the time he was doing this film, he was also working on *The Mahabharata*. They were meeting and reading, Brook and Jean-Claude Carrière, making the script. They had to shape the scenes, to make schedules and preparations. I find that rather fascinating. Even when he did *Carmen*. He was running to India right after *Carmen* opened in New York. He was on to *The Mahabharata* form the time he went to Africa: I remember that.

Incidentally, he went to Africa with his company on another search: for affinities with the Third World. It sounds like British colonialism, but I don't think he is like that; he really wanted to see what response natural people—people who aren't used to it—would have to theatre. He wanted to see what he could learn from those audiences: what was the common denominator in performances between the First World and the Third? A rather fascinating project: he came back with a lot of experiences.

Now, with *The Mahabharata*, the search goes on. The same idea: Man's Condition. That's what Brook has always been interested in. He is one of the few theatre people who has been really consistent in the investigation of man's condition, man's existence. He's also one of the few in theatre who has tracked mankind's obsessional qualities. You get that everywhere, in almost all of his work. Certainly you get that in *Carmen*: It's the essential quality: an obsession—madness, almost—in the central characters, which leads directly to their destruction. They are so obsessive that they cannot be conscious of what they are doing. And it's the same in *The Mahabharata*: the obsession with war, the obsessive drive for power, despite the fact that these will lead everyone to his death. Certain death.

It's interesting in this work that some of the main characters are told: "You will lose this war. You are not on the winning side; you and your clan will die!" They go on anyhow. They are told to give back the land they have taken to Arjuna and his brothers. They refuse: "Not even a fraction of it!" And Krishna says: "Then you must die!" This is fantastic, even if this is a myth. Wars are still fought to the death over pieces of land. This investigation of why people are like that—why they do those destructive things—that's in all Brook's works. Unfortunately, the New York critics never see beyond their noses. They never discussed the *themes* of the work. Not one! The pageantry, the movement, yes. But not the ideas.

LONEY: There's also the idea of *honor* in this. Knowing you're on the losing side, but being bound by honor to remain loyal to your leader and fight on to the death. For centuries, this was also a Western idea, but soon it may be replaced by: "He who fights and runs away, lives to fight another day!"

CROYDEN: I can't argue with that. There's no time. The question in this work is: *why* did they make the choices they made? What is it: greed, rivalry, obsession? All of those are in *The Mahabharata*. And, of course, the philosophical idea of *Dharma*, which is just Determinism. I'm making it very simple, but it has to do with honor: your place in society, your role. What are you destined to do? Obviously, all this would interest Brook, who has said that the theatre cannot be a place for repetition.

But people said: "Why didn't he stick to Shakespeare? He was so good at that!" From the very time he was a young man, he was traveling, reading, questioning, learning. He went to India, Africa, Iran, into other cultures, and then used it on the stage. I don't think there is another director in the western world who is trying to do that. Or who actually has done it! The fact that Brook got all this together: this nine-hour epic; raised the money to do it, and spent ten years of his life on it, and put it on stage for the world to see: I find that rather remarkable!

The Mahabharata is a combination of the comic, the tragic, and the metaphysical. This is what Brook is always looking for in a work: this combination. It's also in his model, Shakespeare—in almost all of the plays. So Brook is always looking for this kind of material. But it's very difficult in modern world to find a playwright who can give you that. *The Mahabharata*: it's really a history of the theatre on stage, in terms of techniques. I think every technique is there!

LONEY: But, in general, do you think the New York critics didn't understand—or appreciate—what they were seeing?

CROYDEN: This was a shock. I saw it in Europe, and several times in Paris. This kind of criticism did not appear in Europe. I saw if first in Avignon. Of course, it was a different production from that in Paris, at the *Bouffes du Nord*, because it was open to the sky, in a quarry with giant rocks all around, a massive stage. And you had the moon and the stars, which added to the production. The seats *were* far more uncomfortable, and apparently some critics were more concerned with their behinds than anything else. To me, it was rather interesting, although irritating, that they would emphasize *that*: to write about their own comfort or discomfort.

Some American critics here have seemed to want to give their readers lessons about Hindu myths and the difference between dramas and epics. Or how *The Mahabharata* should have been done: should we do the whole thing, or half of it, or what? That took up a lot of space, but the issues, the ideas, weren't discussed. But the British critics—and the French—were very perceptive about the production. It was a huge success. You couldn't get a seat, either in Avignon or Paris. They were also able to listen for a long period of time. No one there complained about the length. Europeans are used to longer evenings in the theatre than we are.

But the low level of criticism in New York was astonishing. One said that Brook was not really interested in *The Mahabharata* at all, but in nuclear war instead! Another wrote that he had grafted onto *The Mahabharata* sensibility full of Western concerns. One of them even said outside the theatre: "I've always hated myths, and now I'm convinced that I hate them even more." And opened his review that way. How can you review this work with such an attitude? There was no dignity in much of this writing. They don't really care to analyze. They just react! And they write as if they were in competition with the artists. As if their work was on the same level.

WORKING WITH BROOK: BRUCE MYERS AND ROBERT LANGDON LLOYD DISCUSS *THE MAHABHARATA* AND OTHER ADVENTURES

[New York: December 15, 1987]

LONEY: At the Brooklyn Academy of Music, Bruce Myers is interpreting Krishna, and Robert Langdon Lloyd, who was so impressive in the play and film of *Marat/Sade* is Vyasa, who helps provide a narrative thread for the epic. Despite their demanding performance schedule, they have come to discuss their work in *The Mahabharata*—as well as other experiences in working with Peter Brook.

MYERS: When we were working on *The Beggar's Opera*, on one occasion Peter asked us to do *The Marriage of Figaro*! He told us the story of Figaro. And with this same company of innocent whores and general vagabonds, we played this more sophisticated story. The beggars playing on a higher level, telling a different story, but the important thing in all of this was the *real energy* generated in telling a story to the audience. That was where all the energy was; it wasn't in creating a character. Kinetic energy—speed and quickness and improvisation.

LONEY: So you were aiming for a direct contact with the audience? Aren't you doing the same thing in *The Mahabharata*?

LLOYD: I can't say what Bob [referring to himself] as a performer is thinking, walking out on that stage with a lamp and a blanket at the beginning. That certainly isn't Bob as I am. [laughs] Even on that first walk down toward the audience, I'm already doing something. So it isn't Bob or Bruce you're seeing. There isn't an element of that. But Bruce may come on to change something, to infuse some spontaneity. You can't nail these things down. That stroke is a moving, flexible living stroke.

LONEY: Stroke? Suddenly doing something different? Speaking of that, I understand that Peter Brook and some of you were at Barnard College to talk about this production. When Peter was to speak, he walked out on the stage, but in fact it wasn't Peter! Was this another "stroke"? Actually, it was somebody wearing his jacket.

MYERS: [laughs] I wonder who that could have been?

LONEY: Yes, indeed! Then this person gave a very good account of Peter Brook and his philosophy of theatre. Only then was the real Peter Brook introduced!

MYERS: He rigged that. Peter said: "Look, I don't want to go out there. I'm always being asked to make a speech about what I believe. When the chairman of theatre introduces me, without saying anything, you go out for me." Well, I was dressed in my Indian story-teller garb. He said: "Here, quickly! Put on my coat!" So I put on his coat and his red scarf. Then there was this speech about what a great artist of European theatre we are going to hear from, and I came out. Of course the chairman [Dr. Elizabeth Swain] instantly knew what had happened, but the audience didn't. [laughter] So I said: "So you're in university here! That remainds me when I was at Oxford in 1940. For my first production"—this is one of Peter's anecdotes— "I planned it all out. I even cut out cardboard figures for the characters and made them move around in the set. Then in rehearsal, I did the same thing with my real actors."

LONEY: And he found out it didn't work? That the actors turned into cardboard themselves?

MYERS: It didn't work. So I told them that story, and then I told them about a time I was in Bombay. Of course, they knew straight away I wasn't Peter Brook. Then Peter came out: "Who are *you*? You're wearing my coat!" And we had a kind of Abbott-and-Costello exchange. Peter's a great improviser, a great performer.

LONEY: Working with this vast manuscript of *The Mahabharata*—even in Jean-Claude Carrière's reduction of it, it's still a very long play—how did Brook help you draw out the ideas in it? Recently, someone asked him what *new* ideas he was going to bring to his production of *The Cherry Orchard* at the Brooklyn Academy of Music. And, predictably, he said he was, instead, going to look for the ideas already *in* it. Some of which we might not have noticed or understood before.

Now *The Mahabharata* is considerably more complex, even though the playing-text—in English or in French—is deceptively simple. How did he help you draw out the ideas which shape this production? How did you work? Can you cite a particular passage or moment you worked on? Some afternoon when you had a major breakthrough? How did it happen?

MYERS: In the end, you can't really understand Krishna. But you have to play the part as honestly as possible. You try to be as true as you can to the script, but when you don't understand something, you've got to ask questions. Make references to other sources, ask other people, ask Peter, to try to find out where all this is coming from. Read *The Mahabharata*; read *The Bhagavad-Gita*.

I've been playing it now for quite a while, and there was a moment, that had a kind of inner force and a strength and an energy. So the image of somebody manipulating, provoking, suggesting—which Krishna does—a kind of driving-force, was existing. But Peter said—and, in fact, he says very little—he said: "Yes, but there's a certain *compassion* lacking." Now that's an extraordinary thing to notice. I thought I was playing compassion, but then I realized one can think one is: look like one is playing compassion, but not be *feeling* it. What was going on in the imagination? Did Krishna feel guilty about this war? What did he feel about the people involved? This was a provocation from Peter. A very interesting one: and it demanded that I think more carefully about acting than ever before. That's only one example, but very often there's a remark made by Peter . . .

LONEY: A hint? Or a spontaneous remark?

MYRES: That's all. Then it's up to you to figure out what that possibly means.

LONEY: In *The Mahabharata*—at least as I understand it from a cursory reading and from the production—in this great war, in a sense, Krishna undercuts all of the human moral values; he urges them to violate an agreed-upon rule about not shooting the knees; he seems to deal in deceptions. He is, after all, a god, not a man, but this doesn't seem very compassionate. In the end, however, it turns out that none of the suffering really mattered—except as it tested people, since all life on eath seems to be a kind of illusion.

But, as a man, as an actor ready to play Krishna, how do you deal with all these complexities and contradictions? What was all this struggle about, if the outcome of the war had been determined since the beginning of time? If all this was predestined? Or are we only dealing in probabilities? Possibilities? How do you deal with that? Are there resonances in the Western Judeo-Christian beliefs, or is the Hindu vision totally alien to us?

MYERS: Is that a question or a comment? I wonder if any of you who have seen the production would like to answer that? What do *you* think? This is interesting: obviously, it's the essential question.

LONEY: It's a great—perhaps cosmic—puzzle.

MYERS: Yes, it is a puzzle.

Q: I'd like to hear *you* answer it! Personally, I think Krishna has to fulfill his own destiny, just as do the other characters. He also cannot escape it. He cannot escape his identity: who he is.

MYERS: Yes. He is a god, but he comes down to earth in a human form. He has come down before, of course, in other forms.

LONEY: Similar to Zeus in Greek mythology, but *he* did it mainly to take advantage of nubile young ladies. Krishna has a higher ethos perhaps? [laughter]

MYERS: Well, there was that matter of a thousand wives, but he explains it as teaching them to discover their own secret emotions. He must have had a *great* time, and I'am sure they were grateful. [laughter] Very practical lessons! But in this war, Arjuna's forces have to win. They are the forces of Light and they must overcome the forces of Darkness. He says very clearly at the beginning that it is an inner battle and an outer battle, and there's no real difference between the two. That's very clearly put at the outset. And he also says that where the real battle is, there are no arrows and no warriors. He is clearly talking on two levels at the same time. But there's real, terrifying action in a war. Imagine a war in which the people you hold most precious—not necessarily one's own family—people of great courage, of great wisdom, can be destroyed. Krishna says, of course, there are laws; it's good to have them; they must be respected. But this war must be fought and won: otherwise, the world will be destroyed.

Interestingly enough, it's only Indians who have seen the show who understand this immediately. It's very odd. For us, that's been the most rewarding thing. Krishna comes from a Source of Infinite Wisdom. He does what must be done; it's not a suggestion that one should, as a rule, lie and cheat. But the war *must* be won, and his advice to Arjuna is extremely practical, in spite of everything. For me, that's been an interesting source of reflection: how people need to be reminded of certain essential things.

LONEY: In the West, we might say it means: "Winning at all costs." How about: "Krishna appeared to me in a dream and said that I shouldn't pay the rent anymore"?

MYERS: [laughs] Well, you could *say* that, but try convincing the judge!

Q: Wouldn't this have been made more clear if *The Bhagavad-Gita*—"The Blessed Lord's Song"—had been included in this production?

LONEY: Well, Krishna did whisper it in Arjuna's ear, before the battle, but we didn't get to hear that. It is actually a part of *The Mahabharata*.

MYERS: There was no way we could open the production up more. It is already very long. Even if you do read *The Bhagavad-Gita*, it's very difficult. Krishna does seem to skip direct answers to the questions raised by the war. And very difficult things like: "You are already dead, so don't worry about dying in the war. Do not worry about death." Philosophically, I haven't the slightest idea about the solutions to questions raised in this epic. But practically, I have to act something. This thing—fate or destiny—is going to happen anyway. There have always been wars, and they are likey to go on.

Oh, you could take a counter-action, and people do: "Stop Wars!" And some spend their lives at it. But I think Krishna's probably saying: "That's a waste of time." Instead, we need to find out how we can exist and protect what is fragile and most serious, the most profound thing within us. How can we protect that, given the appalling and terrifying conditions of human life? I find this particularly refreshing and useful in playing certain things—and with a necessary kind of energy—without being too ambiguous.

LONEY: Are there also problems for Vyasa in dealing with the moral orientation of this epic? As a person of the West—and as an actor?

LLOYD: To begin with, I do have great problems, which have as much to do with my own psyche as with the material obviously. More, probably. I found it to be relentlessy *male*. I have recently been more interested in the Goddess religions. So I found it all men, men, men: hearts of men, what men will do, what men will think. I found that difficult, and I tried to change some of that. I managed to change one, which was that this war coming up will be an outrage to intelligent men. I changed that to: "an outrage to intelligence." But most of them I wasn't allowed to change. [laughter]

I happened to feel that—probably because I am alive *now*, with what I've been reading and certain influences in the air—that was outrageous when I arrived at rehearsals. So I tried to change it. Other things almost took me back to, you know, Latin schooling, the classical schooling that I had in England. This is a personal thing—not about *The Mahabharata*, really—but I find the Kings, all standing there, and the warrior arriving and wanting to fight, fighting for honor—Ohhh! Is *this* all you can come up with? How to behave? Is this the only solution? Fighting? So I had to change my psyche about that. It was disappointing to me to go all the way to India, the home of this great epic, and come back with all these Roman and English ideas of honor. [laughs] Well, those are my associations, and they are probably wrong. But this idea of Determinism we've just been talking about: it's very difficult, but the meaning I've got is that, yes, it seems to be a predetermined world, but we've got to live as if it's indeterminate!

LONEY: We couldn't go on if we *knew* we didn't really have choice? That it had all been determined before, but we have to live through the Divine Scenario for the *experience* of it?

Q: It's fascinating that you are doing new and challenging work, work that isn't following traditional patterns in theatre. But I'd like some background. Mr. Lloyd, did you come out of an academy? Could you bring us up to the point where you met Peter Brook? Is it: "I love this man!" "I hate this man!"; "I'm going to give it all up and follow that Master!?" There's so much *mystique* about Brook's work and ensembles. How do you survive the intensity of the work? In Ariane Mnouchkine's *Théâtre du Soleil*, it's acting, living, working, sleeping as an ensemble. Some of them have told me they were dying to get away and just do a commercial production!

LONEY: You make it sound like a prison-sentence!

MYERS: An explanation: there is a difference between Brook's ensembles and Mnouchkine's. The *Théâtre du Soleil*—the company and Mnouchkine—are very, very, very committed, passionately committed, to the idea of living together as a company. As in the 1960s, with Julian Beck's Living Theatre. Very much committed to that possibility. And she takes it as High Treason if you go somewhere else. That would not happen with Peter. He's more likely to say: "Go!" There are important differences. Both Bob and I have been away from Peter's work for long time. And there's never been the slightest suggestion that we had defected in doing other work.

LONEY: In fact, it's never been a fixed company, has it? Members are often changing: going away, returning for a new project? Doesn't Brook say he has to cast the right people for each venture? He's not using the major members of the *Mahabharata* cast for *The Cherry Orchard*, which follows it immediately, is he? No matter how much he respects the talents some of his male actors, he cannot use them if he's planning to do *The House of Bernarda Alba*—unless he wants to experiment with cross-dressing, or cross-gender-casting—can he? Or you could play a stallion—offstage, in the unseen stable.

LLOYD: I'll take it! Of course there have been gaps in working with Peter. I have said no to him. In fact, once, when I said no to him, it led to a nine-year gap. [laughter] But, over the years, I've come back and forth.

Q: Forgive me, but I still don't know your career background. These gaps—what were they? Were you in Rep? In the movies? What?

LLOYD: Other theatre. Briefly: I trained at the Central School of Speech and Drama in London. Just three years: the school after that was quite different. Then into the Royal Shakespeare Comapany and then working with Peter Brook, which was about 1964: *Theatre of Cruelty*, *The Screens*, and then the *Marat/Sade*, and the film of *Marat/Sade*. Then other theatre-work; then *US* with Peter for the RSC. You never knew which it was supposed to be: *US* or *U.S.*

LONEY: When I visited a rehearsal, I gave Peter—an ironic gift—a lapel-button featuring an American flag, with the motto: "God Bless America." He promptly put it on, with equal irony, considering the work at hand.

LLOYD: Then I went into the *Lear* film. Then I went into the first experimental company in Paris in1968. The first international company, but not the real beginnings of CIRT [*Centre International des Recherches Théâtrales*]. Then, a couple of years later, *Orghast*, at Persepolis, in Iran. Then *A Midsummer Night's Dream*, followed by a big gap. I worked at Stratford for the RSC; I lived in America for a while. Then *Conference of the Birds*, then *Carmen*, and now, *Mahabharata*. In America, among other things, I did two operas, one in San Franscisco, one in Houston, with a wonderful director, Jean-Pierre Ponnelle. I did a bus-and-truck tour all over America. I think I was the only one who enjoyed it! I had the front seat! Nothing to do with the part, but I loved it. I was playing not a big, but a very rewarding part that I could do drunk, exhausted, in any kind of state. Just go on and get wonderful laughs. How the lead could do it I don't know.

Q: What was the show?

LLOYD: *Amadeus*. A grueling thing, a tour like that, but for me: I saw America! Parts of America I never would have seen, jetting from New York to San Francisco. So I've done lots of other stuff, but no television. No commercials, and apart from the two with Peter, no films. Frankly, I think I'd learn so much from working in television, especially a series. I learned a tremendous amount about film, working on *Lear*. If I'd had charge of my career then, I'd have wanted to make three more films in a row. It's hard as an actor to keep your development going—it just doesn't work like that.

MYERS: My experience is similar. Most of us who have been with Peter for a long time are, in one way or another, working professional actors. In a certain sense, we take what comes; otherwise we couldn't be together. I feel this very strongly. What's behind all this—apart from the fine ideas and the high-quality work and all the rest of it—is that we all work, and in the normal way. I went back to the Royal Shakespeare. I was at the Public Theatre in New York. I wrote my own play. I've done TV and films. I was even in a film with Charlton Heston. I think it was called *The Mummy's Revenge*.

LONEY: The sequel to *The Ten Commandments*?

MYERS: I was the first person to get killed by the mummy's curse. [laughter] I was run over by a Cairo bus! They made it backwards: the most amazing thing! It began with me being hit; then they drove the bus backwards, and I walked backward and into the car I was getting out of when I was hit!

LONEY: Krishna would love such an illusion!

Q: How much time was spent in India, and what kind of preparation did you do?

MYERS: I'd gone to India and went round to various cultural centers to interest them in my play. I got a feel of the country. I even taught in university, and I got the best reviews I've ever received—in New Delhi! I was there for four or five months.

Q: Mr. Lloyd, did the overall image of *The Mahabharata*, or other Brook productions, bother you?

LLOYD: Not the "overall image," no. I don't think so, but there were things which seriously worried me. Yes. But I'am not quite sure what you're after? One I do remember was with the production of *US*, for which we had several writers. Basically, a team of about five writers, writing from the North Vietnamese point of view, and five writing from the American point of view. Both teams very much wanted their viewpoints to be in the play. At the time, I thought Peter should have got rid of *all* his advisors, all his writers, a week before we opened. Instead of which, the wrangling among them went on right up until the last moment.

In those days, there were no previews, only First Nights. We'd done a dress-rehearsal the night before for an audience of five people. On the afternoon of the opening—with critics and a full house in front of us—we re-wrote the whole order of the show! Very calmly: "Yes. Oh, I see. Yes. And then what? Oh, yes, I do see. Oh, then I do that, yes?" It was amazing. We went out that night and played it. But I wish he'd been much stronger much earlier—and told them all to get out! But he didn't. Maybe we—the actors—could have made a few decisions without all the advisors. This is probably a *false* memory, but I remember the *Marat/Sade* as being filled with improvisations and tryings-out, all the rest of it. But I also remember Peter Brook actually directing it in three days. He was sitting there in the audience, putting it all together. Very crafty, with a lost voice, so someone else had to do all the talking: "You move over there!" And in three days, he had a perfect production! Now that is a false memory. Obviously, we were rehearsing all the time, but my *memory* of it is that it was all all-over-the-place until the last three days. And then, this calm knitting-together till it was good.

LONEY: What about these fabled post-performance discussions among Peter and the cast? Say, you're sitting on a carpet in a Nigerian village?

LLOYD: It is not an everyday thing. Even when it's not work at the *Centre*, even in a proper theatre—where it could also happen on a carpet! Peter will come back and back. We were here in New York six months with *Marat/Sade*. On and off, we saw him all the time. He'd see the show and give notes, give notes, give notes. And hear what we had to say, as well! It was very much done for us! He was very much interested in how we were experiencing it.

MYERS: Very much so!

LONEY: When I was preparing the RSC Production Book of Brook's *Midsummer Night's Dream*, the Deputy Stage Manager showed me, in the promptbook, how movements and business had changed over the two years it had been presented. On tour, some innovations crept in, which Brook removed when he discovered them. Others he kept.

LLOYD: It happens: something that has been absolutely wonderful begins to go a little dead. It is a living thing, after all. A production is made by living people. Every time you do it, certain parts begin to die. So you have to rethink, find something else fresh. On Broadway, there's this aim of getting a play to run like clockwork. "It works!" they all cry. What this really means is that you can put anyone into it, in any kind of part, following this kind of choreography, and it will please the Broadway audience. It doesn't matter about the actual quality of the interaction of the performers; the audience doesn't expect that anyway. Well, that's not Peter Brook's way. He doesn't want clockwork and dead. He'd much prefer something that's risky, alive, spontaneous, touching.

LONEY: You were both in *Conference of the Birds*?

LLOYD: I was in it in Paris, New York, and Australia. But Bruce, you did it all over the place.

LONEY: Peter Brook has told us about the reactions—as have other observers and critics—of audiences with no prior experience of theatre, virtually no expectations. What were *your* reactions to these audiences?

MYERS: Only at the beginning of the tour in Africa, did we have a vaguely fixed idea. There were boxes, and someone would be in a box and come out and put a mask on. And be transformed into a bird. And someone would collect a pair of boots and put them in a box, and they'd disappear. And we'd appeal to the audience: "Where are they?" But the moment we had anything remotely prepared, it never worked. So, in the end, we threw the boxes away.

LONEY: Why didn't it work?

MYERS: It wasn't "ready." There was no such thing as a prepared play that one could take to an African village. No one knows how that audience will behave. They don't know anything about theatre. They don't know about sitting down. They don't know about shutting-up. They don't know about the "Velvet Curtain" opening up. They don't know about the three raps before a performance begins. [laughter]

LONEY: But that's a French tradition. We don't know about that here in New York either.

LLOYD: Bruce, do you think you could have played the finished *Conference of the Birds*, which we did in New York at BAM, in Africa?

MYERS: No. The nearest thing would be the opening moments of *The Mahabharata*—the story-telling. But there was always the problem of language in Africa. There is no common language.

LONEY: It's said that Nigeria has some 270 different tribal languages and dialects! But they also have age-old religious ceremonies and rituals. Not to overlook the lively and traditional Yoruba traveling-theatres, with simple plays geared to village-life. I spent some time in West Africa a year before you went there, and I saw, among other exciting theatre-events, a dance-music-drama about a Devil-boy who seduces a pure, innocent village girl. She is saved in the final moments by the ghost of her grandmother. This was followed by a ritual cleansing of the village. The whole performance was accompanied by the "Talking-Drums," which had summoned the audience—seemingly out of nowhere—in the desolation of a ruined French airbase in Thiés, a remote spot in Senegal. So I wondered just how naive your audiences would be, when I heard that Brook planned to take *The Conference of the Birds* on tour there.

MYERS: Our experience was marvelous! The excitement, the expectation of those audiences! That has never left me. And that's why I take every opportunity now to talk to schools, to anyone who will listen, about this kind of theatre. Even if it's just a moment when something is made spontaneously and then is sustained through practice: the relationship is made with the audience, and the story is told. And then you may panic, and someone else has to come in and take over, because he senses your panic. That's marvelous. There is no perfect work. What we're doing is no Broadway show!

PETER BROOK AT THE CUNY GRADUATE CENTER

[The culmination of the Fall 1987 semester seminar on the work of Peter Brook held at the Graduate Center of the City University of New York—in conjunction with the presentation of *The Mahabharata* at the Brooklyn Academy of Music—was a two-hour session with Brook himself. Before a large audience of students, faculty, and theatre experts, he discussed aspects of his theories and experiments, with seminar-leader Professor Glenn Loney as interlocutor. This transcript has, of necessity, been edited and abridged but it preserves the most interesting and important observations.]

LONEY: I won't say: "Without further ado, this is Peter Brook." As I told Peter, we've been having a semester seminar surveying his work, and a number of our students have been looking at older productions. There are questions that they'd like to ask about some of these. But we'd also like to know more about your International Center for Theatre Research in Paris—and what exactly you mean by theatre research? You don't do empirical research to see how audiences respond to a particular scene—or do you?

BROOK: When we began the Center in Paris, I had been working for a long time in many, many different sorts of theatre and the moment came when I thought it was interesting—and necessary—to take on the challenge of being responsible for an entire organization, because, in a way, I'd been spoilt up until then. When you do guest productions, it's marvelous because there are always other people who have to take care of all the problems; somebody has to find the money; somebody has to make it possible, and you come on and you go with your actors into a little sealed world and you just work on the practical, artistic problem. That's difficult enough, but eventually there comes a time when one feels one must take on a bigger responsibility, and I felt that the time had come to take on the responsibility for a whole organization and, therefore, do it in a different way.

Having, in that way, found a partner, in Paris, and a place where we could work, I thought about the name of what we were going to do. I thought: Well, if we give this a name like a theatre company, if we called it "The Starlight Theatre," or "The Modern Dynamic Group," or "The End-of-the-World Players," or anything like that [laughter], we'd already be locked into something that would prevent us going freely into doing what we wanted, when we wanted, in the way we wanted.

And it was quite clear that one of the first advantages of having our own theatre and our own organization was to break away from all the usual structures, including the responsibility to deliver work, whether you like it or not, within a certain time, within a certain deadline. Also, I wanted the beginning of this work to have peace and quiet. So I thought: Well, what *could* we call it? If I could only find a name that is dull and academic [laughter] with which we could buy several years of peace! Well now, to call this, already, an "International Center," that's boring enough, but an "International Center of Theatre Research"? The word "research," we knew, would keep all the impresarios, journalists, ambitious actors, and theatre writers really at bay for a long time. That would give an edge to this dull name: we saw the advantage, which was, as we needed support, we could then go to governments and foundations with something much more attractive to them than a theatre company, because a theatre company is something that's here today, gone tomorrow. But a "center of research" has got a good sound. So, that's how it got the name, and immediately, in our very first public pronouncement—because we had to make some to get going and justify our existence—we at once tried to make it clear that theatre research cannot mean working in theoretical conditions.

It can't mean sitting round a table discussing, writing, doing what you're doing at this moment, making notes. Theatre research has to be done in the field; it has to be practical field work, so that meant that the first step of theatre research was making a group. So this immediately became a group, mainly of actors, a working group, and, having got this working group, we then set out to put ourselves in conditions that one wouldn't find oneself in any normal theatre company. So the research was research through doing work that enabled all of us to understand better what we were about.

LONEY: You've said that you learn more from failure than you do from success? Could you give a particular example of that?

BROOK: I don't think I've ever said that. [laughter] No, I think that you learn by meeting obstacles. The point is, if you know that doing something in a certain way works, and it does work, then you haven't learned anything at all. So the *unexpected* thing is—I know that if I do something in a certain way, it is bound to work, and, suddenly it doesn't work. Well, questions and answers: why doesn't it work? Now, in our first year, we touched on a great number of different areas.

One area—and they were very separate—one area was a big program based on language, and here the work was to think of unknown—to us, unknown—languages, and to see how far, and to what degree, one could communicate with words that had all their conceptual level taken away. Now, this to me, is something very obvious as a starting point: that words are like icebergs. And there's a bit up there which is what we call sense, in the ordinary, intellectual, conceptual sense, and then the word carries on with an enormous, below-the-surface entity that is part of the juice, part of the life of that word, but which carries meaning, but not conceptual meaning. Now this to me was, and to all of us was, very obvious. But I was really interested, at the time, to meet professors of this whole great school of linguistics that's swept across the world from Chomsky and Wittgenstein onwards, who looked at me with total bafflement, as though this was to them a total linguistic absurdity: "How can a word be other than its concept?"

And at once one saw something that went out of existence, perhaps, with the beginning of the printed word, which was that before printing, when every use of the word was from voice through space to ear, it was quite clear that any word was carrying hundreds of overtones, depending on the way it was spoken. And that words in theatre, and words in great ceremonies, moved people, and moved them profoundly, through all this mysterious area of sound; that was really what the word was about. So that led us to a big investigation of ancient languages, and we found something very, very clear, and very simple: the farther back one went in history, the more the languages were concentrated.

In other words, there were fewer words in the languages, but this wasn't a poverty of a language. A language that had less words was not, as somebody could foolishly say to be: "Oh, primitive, therefore poor," but, on the contrary: primitive, therefore richer, Because each single word carried within it infinitely more substance, and so, when that word was spoken by somebody conducting a ceremony, or by an actor, he had to bring the whole of himself—which meant the whole of his body, his heart, his feelings, as well as his mind, into making the word come to life, which in fact is what an actor's job is, And this led us straight into *tasting* and, I think, understanding Greek tragedy in a new way, because we made experiments. We took passages of Greek tragedy and learnt them and played them amongst ourselves, deliberately refusing to let ourselves know what they were about; just acting with the word-structure, ignorant of its meaning, and we were thrilled to discover that in speaking it, one knew—knew in a far different way—one knew what it meant, and the other person knew what it meant and could respond to it, and the third person, listening, felt what it meant. One understood then something about the nature of the tragic experience, which is not a mental experience, but something much more visceral. We were confronting there something that seemed to be very strange: that all over the world people study and play Greek tragedy without having ever tasted, *on their tongues*, this particular raw material.

learnt that sometimes out of nothing something begins to be—to come into existence—that takes the form of theatre. In the sense that it passes through actors, through actors using their normal implements, which is their bodies, their voices, their capacity to move, to make sounds, to sing, to make rhythms, and to enter into characters and situations. How that evolved; where that got stuck; where you saw on the faces of the people that instant response, either of a smile or a laugh, an interest or a yawn, somebody in the third row getting up, putting on his coat and leaving: this is where you begin to learn.

LONEY: When you did *The Conference of the Birds*, and you were traveling in Africa, one of the points you made was that sometimes you would have your carpet and your boxes, and nothing prepared, but you were thinking about local expectations and customs. That women were not supposed to perform in an Islamic community, and so the women of the group just stayed on a carpet. Afterward, the audience wondered why the women hadn't performed, because it didn't occur to them that people coming from somewhere else might not. So sometimes you set up expectations that were wrong because you just hadn't left yourself open?

BROOK: Yes, that's certainly true, but one of the things that we went to Africa to do was to put ourselves in a situation as remote as possible from our conditioning. Certainly the audience didn't know anything about us, but we, in turn, didn't know anything about them. The audience in Africa is imaginative and generous; so that, on the whole, they were quite simply attentive and interested in a group of foreigners, and, on that level, it was very rare that there was any cultural misunderstanding of that sort. There was one great occasion, when we were using Ted Hughes' text of *Orghast*, which we'd originally prepared to be used in a highly cultural situation in Persepolis. We weren't using that sort of material at all then, but we were in the middle of Africa, in Nigeria, in Kano. It's a big, throbbing city, with a very sophisticated audience, and we were asked to play in a sort of ruined fortress.

A big audience—an enormous audience of several hundred people—swarmed into this place, and we thought we'd have to do something very vibrant. That just a little, a sort of small situation—what we called our carpet show—wouldn't be enough. So we said: "We'll do a piece of *Orghast*." We'll be very interested to see here, for an audience totally unprepared, how these strange and very powerful words and sounds that Ted Hughes had invented—a whole great chain of sounds, words to be spoken—how much they could indicate to an audience that hadn't even been told: "This is a play written by a poet in a language of his own making." They knew nothing about that; for all they knew, this might be our native language. So, we started doing this section of *Orghast*.

Ted Hughes wrote these words by going into a curious state—which he recognized as being the state in which he wrote all his poetry—where he was in-between the ordinary, fluent use of words and his subconscious. He said there was a sort of twilight zone where he could actually see the mind, the subconscious mind, proposing different words and sounds for the conscious mind to select. And he knew, as a poet, that unconscious, proposing elements to the conscious mind, was often doing this in forms of words only half-formed, just as a word that is like a shape and a sound that hasn't yet completely formed itself into a word he knew, and so he'd work on that level. And after that, he found many, many strange words which had—after the event, we discovered—resonances in other languages.

On this occasion, the passage we were doing built up to somebody calling out a word that for him was the word for the most terrible darkness, which was *Bulorgha*. It was a splendid word for an actor: it had great resonance. "Org" was "fun;" it had all the association of "organic," "organ," a vibrant source of light, and "ghast" was like "ghost" and "geist" in his associations. It was the spirit of the organic, and "Bul" for him was an antithesis: it was the powerful anti-form of this vibrant, organic life. So when the actors called out *Bulorgha*, there was the most enormous laugh from this whole African audience. But they roared with laughter; they fell about—a very unexpected reaction. So I took one of the Hausa Africans aside and asked: "Why are they laughing?" He said: "But that's the word for the female sex-organ!" [laughter]

LONEY: The Hausa people are Muslims. They're not even supposed to like theatre in Kano.

BROOK: Well, that's the word for it, and Kano will never forget our ode directed to its adults.

LONEY: When you did *Orghast* at Persepolis—we've been looking at some of the reviews. A. C. Smith, who wrote the book about it, suggests that Andrew Porter—who is a music critic—perhaps understood or intuited what was going on better than many of the drama critics, except for Irving Wardle, of the *London Times*, who seemed to get a lot from it. But a number of them said that, although they didn't really understand what was going on, it was terribly impressive. How do you feel about the way in which the critics responded to *Orghast*, or were they not the right audience for that production?

BROOK: No. I've always said about critics, that the men change, but the functions remain, so it's as though it's the same man going all through history. [laughter] Because what you are saying is exactly the same experience we've had with *The Mahabharata*.

LONEY: Could we talk about that?

BROOK: Exactly that same reaction: a certain type of critical mind looks at something, wanting to understand in a certain way, and naturally doesn't. It's no surprise. He worries himself into a state of non-understanding, but sitting next to him is somebody who understands perfectly.

I learnt this, actually, here in New York, where, years and years ago, I did a production of *King Lear* on television with Orson Welles. The condition was—I was approached by a special program on CBS: could we do *King Lear* in fifty minutes? [laughter] Why not? These two extremes: either the very long or the very short, so, why not? I did a drastically, ruthlessly cut version, and I remember the next day the man who ran the entire program for CBS told me that he had been sitting at home watching it with all his invited guests, all his most sophisticated, grown-up friends, to watch it. All through it, he said, they were saying: "I can't understand it." People who knew the play backwards, but because they knew the play backwards, they were saying: "It doesn't make sense, and I can't understand it." His twelve-year-old son, who'd never heard or read the play, understood every word, every situation, every character. And, in a way, it's exactly the same thing: because you know and you have all that information, your mental computer is blocked by the non-information. If that isn't there, you can receive differently.

LONEY: It was the same with *La Tragédie de Carmen* here, wasn't it? The music critics, most of them, professed to find it not satisfactory in certain areas, but the drama critics, many of whom had no preconceptions about productions of *Carmen*, seemed to be tremendously moved by it.

BROOK: That is a very, very interesting example. I mean it's not that in that case that the drama critics were brighter or nicer men than the music critics [laughter], because you can easily find the reverse of that situation.

LONEY: You are always the enemy!

BROOK: You know, we could invite music critics to *The Mahabharata*, and they could provide their completely different response. The difference, where *Carmen* was concerned, is that none of the drama critics had any particular stock of ideas or information about what *Carmen* should or should not be—what it was, how it's been done in the past, or anything—so they received it directly, as one should in the theatre, as direct experience. But the music critic saw and heard it through an enormous set of constantly flashing lights in his head: warning lights, red lights, all relating to this whole structure of ideas he'd already brought to it. In that way, it was a very interesting case.

LONEY: Essentially then, *The Mahabharata*, as you said, is telling a story, and, if we approach it on that level, and let it work for us, we shouldn't have any difficulty?

BROOK: What's interesting is that "Indians" here have a great difference of response from Indians in India who, almost universally, recognize with great pleasure their major work and feel very happy that it is not only being brought out of India with, I think, a lot of work and deep respect, but also that it's been brought with a lot of imitation of their forms. But on the other side, one has the amateur Indianologist who says: "How could you do this? You've changed *The Mahabharata*! You have brought it up-to-date. You have Westernized it!" None of which is true for an Indian, but very, very clear for somebody who has set himself up as an expert on India without leaving Brooklyn.

LONEY: There were several critics who were very cross that Vyasa and Ganesha, the narrators, seemed to be having a terribly good time: that they seemed to be cheerful and amusing. They were annoyed that the production began on this non-serious level, which was *quite* inappropriate to a great epic!

BROOK: There are people as stupid as *that*? I can't believe it. [laughter] Well, if there is one thing that we know from all the Center experiments we're talking about, that is that if you want to bring an audience—a mixed audience, which is what any good audience must be—to a real point of intense interest, involvement, and concentration, the only way to do it is to start through something simple, relaxed, and pleasurable.

It's like somebody coming in here and beginning to speak immediately on the level of a higher course on some abstract subject at Princeton. I mean, if one starts immediately on that level, no relationship can be established. This is something that, curiously enough, the Sanskrit drama knew perhaps before anyone else: all the manuscripts that exist of fourth century Sanskrit plays start with a stage-manager and a poet coming in and talking to the audience, making jokes, talking about the plot that's about to come in the most easily and often debunking terms, until everyone is sufficiently together for it to be possible to begin to take the play into a more serious climate. That, for us, was absolutely fundamental.

The original couple who played Vyasa and Ganesha were actors who'd been with me for a long time and we'd been together in India. So when we started rehearsals, for weeks we improvised around the situation of these two actors just as story-tellers within an Indian village, leading into all *The Mahabharata* stories, as in a village, with all the rest of the cast just their audience. Originally, in fact, we were going to open it with everybody sitting round in a circle and then talking to the actors. Then we got beyond that, but the first step was to say to an audience: "In coming to see something called *The Mahabharata*, you may have that dread feeling that you're coming to a solemn, philosophical, classical event, so let's first of all wipe that away by saying: "No, this is something natural and simple that can speak to anybody anywhere, in their own language, which is how it is in India.

LONEY: If anyone has questions about *The Mahabharata* or any of Peter Brook's earlier work, who'd like to pose one?

BROOK: There's a golden rule about questions: they always must be loud!

Q: Okay! *Venice Preserv'd!* Remember? [laughter] I was wondering, did you come to direct that with the play already cast? Do you remember?

BROOK: How do you mean, the play already cast?

Q: Because it's here in our chronology as "John Gielgud's Season." He had a company of actors, right?

BROOK: Yes.

Q: So were you called in with a cast already in place?

BROOK: I see your question, but I don't think that it happens in that way. Because there's always, or very, very often, something quite different. Things arise with people one knows very naturally through friendship that—well, John Gielgud wanted to do a season. We'd already worked together; we had a very close relationship, as I had with Paul Scofield. They thought that it would be very interesting to do something together. I— John had—I—which of us thought of *Venice Preserved* I can't remember any longer, but whether he, sitting over a table, had said: "What about *Venice*?"—you know, going through twenty plays—" How about our doing *Venice Preserv'd*?" or if I'd made the suggestion, or if a third person. . . I know we came to the same idea at the same moment. What else did he do? I think he did *The Way of the World* or something like that. At that time, I would have said I wasn't interested. If he'd proposed doing *Timon of Athens*, well. . . If *I'd* proposed doing *Timon of Athens* at that time, I know he'd have said: "Oh, very stupid play. I don't want to do it—it's no good for me." [laughter] It's that sort of exchange that you have. The three things came together: a small theatre, a very good group of actors wanting to work together, and a play that suited them.

Q: I want to ask about you about your conception of *The Cherry Orchard*. What ideas are you going to bring to this play?

BROOK: I try not to *bring* ideas to a play. [laughter] Let a play produce the ideas! When we first did the play in French in Paris, the strong core of our work was, first of all, to *discover* the play, by taking it away from the two big clichés was: this is basically sad, romantic, and nostalgic. That was the cliché that had come from Russia through Europe. All the early productions that I saw in England of Chekhov, all were productions that were not only slow—I mean that was considered the beauty of the play, that beautiful, languid slowness—but they even had what became known as the "Chekhov voice," which was [he slows his pace and whines] at— once— slow—gray. [laughter] This was considered incredibly romantic and beautiful: to see people just walking, walking in sets where there were windows that you could slowly open, [laughter] and you'd stand there, and then, in the distance, somebody'd be playing a guitar. And someone then would say: "Aaah." [laughter]

That was Chekhov, and so, through that, you read a play like *The Cherry Orchard*. Everything confirms that view, which then fits into a certain social pattern: that theatre is an upper-class English occupation, for people who went to the West End theatre, who paid the prices. I mean, the theatre-going community was either upper-class or a gathering public that longed to be part of that dream upper-class world. So, for them, the meaning of the play was very simple: it is about how sad that, since the First World War, these beautiful values of old Europe are crumbling away. So it was a play of regret, and there was even a man called N. C. Hunter who wrote two plays in that vein which were done—I think directed by John Gielgud—in the West End.

LONEY: *Waters of the Moon* is one of them.

BROOK: *Waters of the Moon* and something else, which were great successes and have now passed into oblivion.

LONEY: It was revived at the Chichester Festival not so long ago—with Wendy Hiller.

BROOK: Those plays were considered "Chekhovian." Chekhovian, because they were about English country houses and people sadly —

LONEY: Stanislavsky started this, didn't he?

BROOK: Yes, Stanislavsky started it, and Chekhov wrote him letter after letter saying: "Please, these plays are comedies; the plays are farces." And Stanislavsky said: "You've got it wrong. [laughter] We play it as human tragedy, human drama."

The New Wave looked at them and said: "But here are real comedies!" Chekhov himself, who wrote one-act farces, said: "All my plays are funny." So now we play them as comedy, a second cliché. I have seen

Chekhov plays where all the mysterious, magical overtones of the play suddenly vanished, because there was nothing but tough, hard-hitting comedy. All the characters as funny as possible, played as a lot of absurd people.

Then I saw other productions where that side—that you're looking at a totally absurd world—pushed it in the other direction. Returning to looking at the plays not only for what is there, but also trying to understand the play not only from what you see in front of you, but, in this case, in relation to Chekhov himself, and Chekhov's own life. Something very different emerges: if you look at Chekhov's life, you see, in a very short life, the amount of activity that that man managed to put in his life is extraordinary.

Chekhov—who was dying of tuberculosis from a very young age—managed within any given day to get up early, to write, to then see—although it drove him up the wall—all the people who came to see him with manuscripts, asking for advice. Women who came: "You are the greatest of authors; you must read my short-story." And he was so kind-hearted that he would give time to all these people, and before he'd finished, there would be a line of peasants at the door, waiting to see him as a doctor.

So that he would then spend another part of his day as a doctor, not only being there, but going on every sort of house-call, going through the snow to visit people who naturally he'd never take any money from, and then be so outraged at the conditions that he saw that he would get involved in enormous schemes for building new schools. He then found time, when he was already sick, to go all the way across Russia to inspect—the only writer at the time to do it—the vast prison penal settlement. He traveled to Europe; he got involved in endless different relationships with different women; he wrote diaries; he wrote hundreds of short-stories and hundreds of letters.

And one saw that, from all of this, on one hand he never lost a sense of distance that enabled him to see all of life as a comedy but that he also never lost that *profound* compassion—that poetic sense or sensibility and compassion—that made him suffer directly and intensely with everyone, every situation he met. If one reads his short-stories, one sees some things that throw great light on the plays, because they give all the subtext that isn't in the plays; the short-stories are visions of human beings in all their complexities that are dramatic, tragic, infinitely comic, and never judged. And behind that, if you look at his short-stories, one sees something further and that is that—although Chekhov refused to be part of any organization, any religious sect, any political party, seeing all the comic and tragic blockages that all of those produce—he still had an infinite idealism, which he spoke about, and—which he also spoke about, but which is very rarely quoted—a profound, very Russian, mystical sense.

So all of that means that if you look at his plays, if you look at *The Cherry Orchard*, you can see that *The Cherry Orchard* is not a slice of life. It's a cunningly constructed mosaic that puts human beings in situations where they're absurd, comic, deeply moving, infinitely tragic, and infinitely absurd. And yet the totality of their circumstances reflects not only their own particular involvements, but also involves the whole social-political scene, and a metaphysical sense. I mean, *The Cherry Orchard* is, beyond all this, about life and death. All of this is contained within the same work, but which is brought down to something very concrete, because it is, first and foremost, about the interrelations of people, and where, in working on it, before and now again—and relating it to Chekhov himself—one sees something essential, which is that each one of these characters is trying to live.

What led to the languid school, the languorous school of Chekhov, came out of a false, outside judgement that boring people, living boring lives, are without vitality. The fact is just the other way round, and that's there in all his plays, and, they say, in the man himself. We, as superior judges, can look at these people and say: "How boring your life was," and some can say: "How boring it is to live in a provincial town in Russia!" and so on, but they themselves have such passion to live—which is part of the overall tragedy—such a wish to squeeze the utmost out of their lives that they live even the tiny possibilities: the fact that someone's come to dinner, the fact that somebody's dropped a flower, the fact that somebody has looked at someone else and gone away. They lived those with a tremendous intensity. So that the starting point for work on the production is to look for the true vitality that the characters are expressing in their wish, each one, to find his way of living, which, of course, leads to all the strong conflicts out of which come all the situations of the play.

Q: I'd like to know about your continuing relation with the Royal Shakespeare Company, after setting up your own Center.

BROOK: Precious little—friendly. And we're close in spirit; I mean close enough. The fact that, when we've been in England with our work, the RSC—as an organization of which I'm still an official board member—has presented our work. When *The Mahabharata* came out on tour, it was the RSC that said they would take on the management, the touring management. It was presented by our Center, but we haven't the means, the organization, to do such a big tour, and so it is a joint production with the RSC. As I say, it's an old association, but I haven't got, at this moment, any real, direct relation with the work that's being done there.

Q: Michael Billington wrote that it was a scandal that *The Mahabharata* was not to be seen in England. What was the reason for that?

BROOK: That is really a very simple thing: that the English, ever since the Thatcher Government, began a policy of cutting down, cutting down on support for the arts, which was a big historical change because the English tradition, rather like here in America, had originally been never to give a cent to the arts. Gradually, since the end of the war, that support grew and grew and became a recognized part—and a very healthy and fruitful part—of English life. Then suddenly a new Government, with a completely different conception—I mean with the sort of pragmatic, right-wing view that more and more exists all over the western world—its first casualty was the arts, as being something that you must economize on. Culture: that not only isn't necessary but—with this terribly dangerous thought—that private sponsorship is just as good. A government proves that that's right because they make a void, and no theatre's going to allow itself to go out of existence, so it goes with its begging-bowl and will find a sponsor. Having found a sponsor, the Government then says: "You see, you don't need us," and they retrench a bit, so today there isn't any longer in London the money there used to be. In the old days, the Aldwych Theatre ran a World Theatre Season every year!

LONEY: Under Peter Daubeny's supervision.

BROOK: Peter Daubeny ran it, and there was money to bring international companies to London that has disappeared. So, although there've been organizations looking for funds for us, they really haven't found them. So we're going to Glasgow, and not to London.

They have an annual May Festival and a mutual interest in this. They are going to be, next year, something that's called "The Cultural Capital of Europe." That's something like the Olympic Games that rotates, and so, for Glasgow, it's worth making a great effort for their own audiences—for the town itself, as against Edinburgh—to develop something out of Glasgow, not only locally, but also on a broader scale. So their Festival is something that they're going to put a lot into. They have the interest and the determination and the means, to produce this. It's a big show, and because we need an official space and all that, it costs a lot of money.

LONEY: I found buried in the program for *The Mahabharata*, in very fine print, the news that, in remodeling of The Majestic Theatre, BAM's Director, Harvey Lichtenstein, has intended to make a home for you here, in Brooklyn, and America. I wonder if you might speak to that point? May we look forward to see you in New York a part of every season? And will you create some works here at The Majestic to take back to Paris?

BROOK: The most I can say is that *Carmen* was a case in point. Until now, there was no compatible space that we could come to, and so Harvey very much had that in mind.

LONEY: What if one of our City University students wanted to be in the company for a forthcoming production? What's the basis on which you take people on for these projects? If somebody comes to you and says: "I'm putty in your hands," what do you say? [laughter]

BROOK: I would say: "I don't want putty." [laughter] No, that's quite true. The thing is, if one talks about theatre in practical terms, one has to recognize the practical and, from one point of view, unfair nature of all theatre, and that is that whatever the theatre is, wherever it exists in the world, a group that does a play is smaller than the number of people who wish to join it. If you have a play with two characters? The most one could do in *Carmen*—because opera singers can't sing every night of the week—we had a performance with six characters. Two of them were actors, so they played every night of the week; four of them were singers, so we had three casts, which still brought it, in all, up to sixteen people, but beyond that there's a limit.

How do actors get in the company? There are no two cases the same. There have been cases of somebody who has just turned up on the doorstep just at the moment when you need someone. It does happen that somebody just by design or accident is there at the right moment. It does happen that you suddenly need somebody and you think of somebody that you know well. All I can say is that, because of the nature of work we do, there are masses of people—and it's very touching and heart-breaking—who write in or come, feeling that the fact that they want passionately to be part of that group, is in itself a credential. There are only so many places in the cockpit that, for the aeroplane to fly, those particular places have to be filled by people who can bring what's needed to those functions.

So that, in a small, international group, trying to do a form of what we call "advanced work," the people who come have to be different from whoever is already there. In other words, they have to bring something of their own, so "putty," already, is no use. To be different from someone who's already there, it's not enough to be pure, open, and idealistic; that person has to be marked by something that already has patterned them, has made their own contribution substantial, and *then* they have to be open.

Now what is very difficult is that we always have to take experienced but marginal people, because the really good, experienced actor, ninety-nine cases out of a hundred, is not looking for anything other than the mainline, career production, where he gets his biggest satisfaction, emotionally, artistically, and financially; so that he's not going to give that up.

The people who give up everything to come and join in our sort of activity very often are people who can't join us because they haven't got those capacities, and, in between the two, there is a narrow margin of people who have strong capacities, individual color of their own, something to bring, and are anxious to take part in work that can open them, disturb them, call on what they can bring and yet challenge it. So the answer to how to get in is crossing a tightrope of qualification and luck and chance.

Q: Earlier you said you consider your trips to other places around the world, and to unusual performance configurations, as sort of your fieldwork; that it was somewhat like social science in its orientation. But it seems to me that the other half of that equation is the presentation of what was learned in your fieldwork: how do you personally disseminate this information, or do you do that at all? Do you feel that this is part of what you do?

BROOK: It's a big question, a very interesting one that can be gone into in many different ways. In the last resort, the only real way of disseminating it is through the performance, and that's, in other words, the fruit. We defined our work in this way: because of the original group, it led to work in the way that you make real yogurt, which is that you have a bowl of milk and you put a concentrated substance in it which ferments it, and in this way it is possible for a nucleus group to work with a wider group of actors, and the wider group of actors, working on a project with me, gradually acquired the ferment; so that then something from a small group comes to a wider group. That wider group has helped, to a degree—things we've written; things that have been written about our work; there are some films; there are some videos, and they've, in a way, marginally helped certain specialists.

I'm doing my best at this moment, in answering your questions, to disseminate something by non-theatrical means, but basically, the only real expression is through the experience itself within a performance. So that anyone who sees the work and experiences something that touches them in a particular way and makes them feel different from something they've seen in other conditions and therefore makes them question how and why that is, is in the situation of receiving whatever it is we have learned ourselves. Because all our discoveries, if you like, are non-intellectual.

Q: You talk about Chekhov being the contemporary reality in his life and society: how far does the work of your artists confront their contemporary realities, and how far does it affect them in their work, in the political sense, rather than as a spiritual experience of theatre?

BROOK: I've spent many years exploring what one calls political theatre. I think that how you relate to this question—the basis is obvious: the world is in a disastrous state; nobody can question that—what can one bring oneself, of one's own efforts, to be useful? That's really what political theatre is all about: using one's efforts, within the form that one makes one's own, to be useful to others, taking into account that one can't, anywhere in the world, do work—like a national anthem— to say that society is really magnificent, so let's all lift the flag and glorify it in a great theatrical act, like pageants. Pageants are made to do that.

So, how does one relate to it? Then one thinks that the answer becomes very personal, not only for each person, but for each group, depending on things that are changing, depending on where you are in the world. In other words, who your audience genuinely is, or is likely to be: that's the first question, and the other question has to do with changing conditions: that an issue of ten years ago is no longer an issue today. I mean, things are all changing, and I think that there I have to just see the trap: that it is very easy for a lot of people who are genuinely concerned and well-meaning, for instance, to put on a play by Brecht, because it's by Brecht, in front of an audience which can no longer directly relate to those questions in that way. One very often sees young, dedicated groups—in France one sees this all the time—playing Brecht very passionately and even angrily in front of empty houses in small towns, saying: "It's disgusting! These people are so indifferent. They'll go to see any idiotic play, and here is a play that means something to their lives, and they don't come."

Now you can also take that equation differently, as in my own work within our own group, and that is to realize that one has an influence, that if you do anything in public you have an influence, but one must be exceptionally modest and realistic. To think that you can directly influence any form of social structure is unreal, is a dream. You actually cannot, except in certain very precise conditions. These conditions existed for the *Teatro Campesino* in California at the very beginning of their work, when they grew out of the need within a strike to do fifteen-minute sketches to get a certain number of people to come over to the other side of the will-we-strike-will-we-not-strike barrier. That's how the company came into existence. Ten years later, they recognized that was no longer relevant, but there was a local situation.

Now for us, for instance, in an international group, for us to pretend that we can come here to New York, be in Paris, or go anywhere else and topple a government, sweep a dictatorship out of Chile by opposing it, change what's happening in South Africa by showing this, I don't believe it. I believe those are pure dreams and often self-indulgent dreams, because it gives one good conscience and a sense that one's really working for something.

On the other hand, one can see action, positive social action in a quite different way. That is to say that one has a few in society that one can genuinely influence, the people who are in the audience at that particular moment, not more and not less. You are responsible for the people who are with you in the room; you're responsible for perhaps five-hundred people. Now, in what way are you responsible? To change their ideas? I think that's pretentious, and also self-defeating. I don't think you can; it's like an argument. You know, you get into a political argument, and how often can you actually do more than get the pleasure of asserting your own ideas? But how often has one ever known one of those late-night discussions to end in transforming someone else to your point of view?

What you can do with five-hundred people—and I think this is socially, politically, and humanly of the greatest importance—you can bring that group of people, because I think you're doing the same in yourself, to point of confrontation and opening. In other words, you can burst open what ever fixed ideas, prejudices, and points of view that they bring with them. You can open that up in a way so challenging and so vital that that that person, that group of persons, will leave the theatre less dogmatic and less negative, less belligerent, and more concerned than they were when they came in. Now that's an enormous aim, and, there again, one must be modest. I always say to our actors: "If we can touch as many people as we are, that if there are twelve of us, that we can actually produce a deep effect on twelve people, that's fantastic. So one has again to see that an audience as a whole can be touched—and one knows this. Five years later, somebody comes who says: "That evening in the theatre actually gave me the force to go through a serious operation." "Somebody gave me the force to change my career." In that way, in political terms, I must have the fundamental optimism to believe that, if people are nourished in this way, that will make them more ready and more open and more alert to make their own decisions, which eventually people have to take, in a more grown-up and a more lucid way. For myself, I wouldn't presume to go beyond that.

Q: What about your work with actors? Can it be observed?

BROOK: Continually I'm asked if people can come and observe rehearsals. There's an absolute, constant demand, and I hate saying no. I hate saying no repeatedly on anything, but here, for years I've said no by experience, and the experience is that the first thing that you need to do good work with actors is to create conditions of confidence. So that how you start rehearsals, whatever techniques you use, the first aim must be for there to be the creation of a circle. In other words, for the actors to trust one another, to trust you, to trust the general climate, so that they can slowly, and reluctantly, allow themselves to open up and take risks; this is one of the reasons why you need a lot of time, where you need a lot of different methods, you need a lot of different exercises, to make that climate.

Now, one of the things that's essential is that there should be no judgement, or that the judgement comes from the group and not from outside. So there mustn't be somebody watching who you feel at any moment might break this confidence...Imagine that you're doing an exercise and you try something; you really make a complete fool of yourself, and everybody else laughs, but they're friends, so you don't mind them laughing. But the next day, you read something about this in the *New York Times*. In fact, one of our actors in *The Cherry Orchard* was approached the other day by *New York Times*: "Would you keep a diary for us to print, about what goes on during the rehearsal process?" He at once said no, for these reasons.

Q: What do you see as the difference in the use of the imagination in theatre and the use of the imagination in film?

BROOK: Oooh! [laughter] A very interesting question, but I'd say really chalk and cheese. I mean they're really different forms: a film, a good film, is the work of one person's imagination. I've tried experiments in film—they interest me very much—of letting things happen, of not putting my own stamp on things, shooting in an improvised way and then putting it together in the cutting. Even then, when you come to do the editing, it's one person putting it together. In a way, it's like a journalist: he goes off with his tape-recorder, but, in the end, he shapes his story. Film-making is one person's imagination.

In theatre, the more the better: the fruit of a collective imagination. And the better the rehearsal process, the more confidence there is, the more there is of this continual exchange between director and actor and designer and author, so that what comes out—however strongly the director is guiding in a certain direction—is a collective product, a product of many, many understandings coming together. So that in the theatre, you have the phenomenon that when rehearsals are good, you suddenly do reach a point of real super-imagination: when the collective imagination is not only different imaginations, but a super- imagination—everybody is really conceiving the same thing, but they couldn't do it singly.

We saw that once—after many years of improvisation—with nothing prepared, we did one improvisation only, which we all have never forgotten, in a girls' school somewhere in France. It took off and for about two hours, just one person starting something that everyone present thought could only have been a highly developed play: complex structure, characters—never stopped—in their situation, people coming on like something that was written and rehearsed, which was a phenomenon of the super-imagination of the whole group, functioning and binding everyone together.

BROOK: If somebody could tell mankind how to remove his conditioning... [laughter] For each person this is a genuine problem, but, in the whole of his life, every minute, he is in this conflict, knowing that life is receiving, at every moment, a fresh experience in innocence. How else can one be genuinely open to life? And yet, one knows that, as one grows up, every thing, every impression, every experience that one receives constructs a whole chain of responses that more and more take one away from innocence. Anybody in relation to children knows what innocence one has lost; so how you face that problem is very personal and absolutely essential.

I do think, though, that in every real problem, the first step—and it's a major step—is recognizing the existence of the problem. I think that if you don't put the question—you said that this was a terrifying question—if you don't feel it as a terrible question, then it's quite clear that every academic who goes to a play, without even questioning the nature of the experience, or why he's going there—really, at Stratford you see people at a Shakespeare production with the book out, and you can see that they haven't asked themselves that question. It's sufficient to face the fact that there is no shame and no liability in having a highly developed and sophisticated understanding and knowledge of something, but, at the same time, the need is *not* to encourage that, but to do what one can to find one's way through it, and already the door begins to open.

Q: A last question: I wondered if you thought there was *anybody* writing today, or in the last fifty years —

BROOK: Fifty? Perfect timing! One always knows when one's forum should come to an end. [laughter]

Q: A writer who will deserve the kind of exploration in fifty to a hundred years that you have given to Shakespeare and Chekhov?

BROOK: I don't know who that will be; that doesn't mean that much. I don't follow that in great detail because our own projects, one by one, take a great deal of time. So we're not running the sort of theatre where one's receiving manuscripts and looking at them. But there's no real reason for history to stop; there shouldn't be. I think that you can look at it the other way round: what I've always felt quite strongly about, that playwriting is so difficult that it doesn't happen automatically that every generation should produce its great master; it's too difficult for that, because it demands something quite exceptional. A playwright not only has to have a particular talent, a born talent, great imagination, etcetera. He also has to have that particular, deep, human sympathy that enables him to enter equally into all the different characters. To be a great playwright, he has to go beyond his own point of view.

In fact, what is the nature of drama? The nature of drama is that there are two protagonists, each of them defending a totally different, passionate conviction of life, and what makes the drama is that they're opposed. Now, what makes the satisfaction and the excitement and the challenge for the audience is that the audience, as individuals, will side, normally, either with one or with the other. In normal life they would be taking the side of the husband or the wife and, if they were involved in it themselves, they would be taking their own side. The husband would believe that he is in the right, and the wife would believe that she was in the right. When you have a theatrical situation, you have that triangle, so that the person who is watching—which is where being a spectator is not a dull and passive role—the spectator is in that tremendous position of being opened to being himself drawn totally into something that normally in his life is impossible: totally living opposing viewpoints. And if that's strong enough, really something explodes inside him.

Now for a playwright to be able to do that with a whole range of characters, a range of characters within different social conditions, within different philosophical, metaphysical, and religious circumstances; for him to enter into that world, means that he has to have a generosity and a vision that, obviously, the world doesn't dispense. I would say that the social conditions we live in, all over the world, are less than ever conducive to that sort of vision. You have only to look at the condition of anybody sitting in a subway train, to see how hard it is for any writer to be deeply nourished by a real sense of living exchange between different people, when you see a phenomenon that has never, I'm sure, in history got to such an extreme as this absolute isolation, based on fear and a number of other causes that makes people so separate. So I'm afraid that we are in a very difficult moment for that to appear. It may perhaps, by sheer friction, produce, in a certain moment, the super-Shakespeare, but it may not.

LONEY: Thank you very much, Peter! May I point out that Peter and the company will be at the Majestic Theatre on Friday. From twelve o'clock to six o'clock, there will be workshops, discussions, and demonstrations on what the work on *The Mahabharata* has involved.

BROOK Originally, we did this in Paris, finding how it's possible to reply to the people who say: "We want to observe," and not just say no. I thought the only way is to create a sort of open day in which it's possible, not just to talk, but to show in practice how we work on certain things. So that the person is like an observer, but it's much less boring because it's all crammed together in a shorter space of time.

BIBLIOGRAPHY

Note: *The Times* and *The Sunday Times* refer to the London papers.

ACOCELLA, J. *The Mahabharata* [review] *Art In America*, March, 1988, p. 29.

ADAIR, G. "A Meeting with Peter Brook." [interview] *Sight and Sound*, Winter, 1979/80, pp. 11–3.

ADDENBROOKE, David. *The Royal Shakespeare Company: The Peter Hall Years*. London: William Kimber & Co., 1974.

ADLER, Renata. "Tell Me Lies Tells You How to Go Mindless." *New York Times*, Feb. 18, 1968.

AGATE, James. "The Brothers Karamazov." *Sunday Times*, June 9, 1946.

ALBERA, Philippe. "Attentat a l'Opéra." [interview] *Révolution*, #136, 1982.

ALBERT, Hollis. "Boys Will Be Boys." *Saturday Review*, August 17, 1963, p. 14.

––––––––. "Race and Outrage." *Saturday Review*, Feb. 3, 1968, p. 46.

ALVAREZ, A. "Peter Weiss: The Truths That Are Uttered in a Madhouse." *New York Times*, Dec. 26, 1965.

AMBROSE, Jules. "The Players Can Go Dotty." *New York Times*, July 17, 1966.

ANDERSON, Michael., et al. *Crowell's Handbook of Contemporary Drama*. New York: Thomas Y. Crowell Co., 1971.

ANSORGE, Peter. "Peter Brook: Director in Interview." *Plays and Players*, Oct. 1968, pp. 18–9.

––––––––. "Director in Interview: Geoffrey Reeves." *Plays and Players*, Nov. 1968, pp. 69–71.

––––––––. [interview] *Plays and Players*, Oct. 1970.

ARTAUD, Antonin. *The Theatre and its Double*. New York: Grove Press, 1958.

––––––––. *Selected Writings*. New York: Farrar, Straus & Giroux, 1976.

ARTFORUM. [review of *Carmen*] Sep. 1982, pp. 76–7.

ASLAN, Odette. "'Les Paravents' de Jean Genet." in *Les Voies de la Création Théâtrale*, Vol. III, Paris: CNRS, 1972.

––––––––. *Le Masque: Du rite au theatre*, ed. and introduction by Odette Aslan. Paris: CNRS, 1985.

ATKINSON, Brooks. "Theatre: Rex Harrison." *The New York Times*, Dec. 9, 1959.

————. "Rex Harrison at Top of His Form." *New York Times*, Dec. 20, 1959.

ATTAR, Farid Ud-din. *The Conference of the Birds*. London: Routledge, 1978.

————. *The Conference of the Birds*. adapted by Jean-Claude Carriére and Peter Brook, Connecticut: The Dramatic Publishing Co., 1982.

AUSLANDER, Philip. "'Holy Theater' and Catharsis." *Theatre Research International*, Spring 1984, pp. 16–29.

AVIGAL, Shoshana and RIMMON-KENAN, Shlomith. "What do Brook's Bricks Mean? Toward a Theory of the 'Mobility' of Objects in Theatrical Discourse." *Poetics Today*, Spring 1981, pp. 11–34.

BABLET, Denis. "Rencontre avec Peter Brook." *Travail Théâtral* #10, Oct/Jan. 1973.

BAKER, Peter. "Moderato Cantabile." *Films and Filming*, Aug. 1961, p. 24.

BAKER, Rob. "Playing With One Foot in Each Camp." *Parabola*, Aug. 1980, pp. 89–91.

————. "Reaching for the Trapeze: An Interview with Peter Brook." *Parabola*, Spring, 1990, p. 104.

BANU, Georges. "Peter Brook, ou l'écume du théatre." *Travail Théâtral*, #18–19, Jan/June, 1975.

————. "Le cercle et le fleuve: notes sur Peter Brook et Jerzy Growtowski." *Le Scarabée International* #2, 1982.

————. *Brook: Les Voies de la Création Théâtral*. Vol. XIII Paris: CNRS, 1985.

————. *Le Mahabharata*. in *Alternatives Théâtrales* #24, July, 1985.

BANU, Georges and MARIENSTRAS, Richard. "Timon d'Athénes' de Shakespeare, et sa mise en scene par Peter Brook," in *Les Voies de la Création Théâtrale*, Vol. V, Paris: CNRS, 1977.

BARBER, John. "For Curious Piano and Guzzler." *Daily Telegraph*, Aug. 11, 1957. [on *"music concrète"*]

————. "Magic Touch of Fairyland." [Review of *MND*] *Daily Telegraph*, Aug. 28, 1970.

————. "Interview with Peter Brook." *Daily Telegraph*, Sep. 14, 1970.

————. "Brook in Full Flood." *Daily Telegraph*, Nov. 15, 1971.

————. "Real food for thought." *Daily Telegraph*, Jan. 20, 1975. [*ik*]

————. "Down to the bare boards." *Daily Telegraph*, Dec. 10, 1977. [interview]

————. "All a question of experience." *Daily Telegraph*, Nov. 24, 1980. [*birds*]

————. "'Dream' come true." *Daily Telegraph*, Aug. 30, 1982. [brought on by on *Dream* book]

BARKER, Ronald. "Enfant Terrible" *Plays and Players*, April, 1954, p. 6.

————. "The Dark is Light Enough." *Plays and Players*, June, 1954, p. 13.

————. "Peter Brook Talks." *Plays and Players*, Oct. 1955, p. 7.

BARNES, Clive. "The Faces of Scofield." *Plays and Players*, Jan. 1963, pp. 15–7+.

_____. "Seneca's Oedipus is Presented in London." *New York Times*, July 31, 1968.

_____. "Historic Staging of The Dream." *New York Times*, Aug. 28, 1970.

_____. "Magical Midsummer Night's Dream." *New York Times*, Jan. 21, 1971.

BARTER, Christie. Video Review: "The Arts." *Video Review*, June, 1988, p. 76. [*Carmen*]

BARUCHA, Rostom. "Peter Brook's Mahabharata: A View from India." *Theatre*, Spring, 1988, pp. 6–20.

BEATON, Cecil and TYNAN, Kenneth. *Persona Grata*. London: Wingate, 1953.

BEAUMAN, Sally. *The Royal Shakespeare Company: A History of Ten Decades*. Oxford: Oxford University Press, 1982.

BECKLEY, Paul. "The Beggars Opera." *New York Herald Tribune*, Aug. 25, 1953.

BEHR, E. [*mahab.* review] *Newsweek*, Aug. 19, 1985, p. 65.

BENTLEY, Eric. [on *Orghast*] *Theatre Quarterly*, pp. 93–4.

BERMEL, Albert. *Artaud's Theatre of Cruelty*, Taplinger, 1977.

BERNARD, Kenneth. "Some observations on the theatre of Peter Brook." *Theatre*, Fall/Winter, 1980.

BERRY, Cicely. *The Voice and the Actor*, London: Harrap, 1973. [Brook Preface]

BIESINGER, Kathy. *Style and Signification in Shakespeare Film: A Study of the Narrative Realism of Franco Zeffirelli and the Symbolism of Peter Brook*, Unpublished PhD dissertation, Brigham Young University, 1991.

BILLINGTON, Michael. "RSC in US." *Plays and Players*, Dec. 1966, pp. 12–3.

_____. "From Artaud to Brook and Back Again." *The Guardian*, Jan. 6, 1976.

_____. "Brook takes Paris on the Shakespeare Express." *The Guardian*, Nov. 20, 1978.

_____. and Brook, Peter "Written on the Wind: The Dramatic Art of Peter Brook." *The Listener*, Dec. 21 & 28, 1978, pp. 848–9.

_____. "A Sandwich Course by the Signpost Man." *The Guardian*, Jan. 22, 1982.

_____. "A Fire Snake in the Sand." *Théâtre en Europe*, #8, Oct. 1985.

BIRMINGHAM GAZETTE: "'The Olympians': is it too new for us?" Feb. 12, 1950. [actually more on *Measure for Measure*]

BOLSOVER, Philip. "Stratford-on-Shakespeare." *Daily Worker* (London) April 11, 1947.

BOOTHROYD, J. B. "Titus Andronicus." *Punch*, Aug. 24, 1955, p. 226.

BRAHMS, Caryl. "Pace Without Poetry." *Plays and Players*, Jan. 1956, p. 23.

_____. "Titus Andronicus." *Plays and Players*, Aug. 1957, p. 11.

_____. "The Lovable Ones." *Plays and Players*, Aug. 1960, p. 11.

_____. "Toddling on to Triumph." *Guardian*, Sep. 19, 1970.

BRECHT, Bertold. *Brecht on Theater*. ed by John Willett, New York: Hill and Wang, 1964.

BRIEN, Alan. "Metaphysician Heal Thyself." *Sunday Telegraph*, Jan. 13, 1963.

_____. "Openings." *Theatre Arts*, Jan. 1963, pp. 57–9.

BRITTON, David. "Theatre, Popular and Special, and the Perils of Cultural Piracy." *Westerly: A Quarterly Revue*, Dec. 1987, pp. 66–73.

BROOK, Peter. "Letter on *King John*." *The Sunday Times*, Jan. 13, 1946.

_____. "Richard Strauss's Salome." *Theatre Newsletter*, Nov. 5, 1949, p. 3.

_____. "The Vitality of the English Stage."*The Listener*, May 4, 1950. p. 781+.

_____. "From A Memo To A Movie." *New York Times*, Aug. 23, 1953.

_____. "Ways of Telling An Immoral Tale." *New York Herald Tribune*, Oct. 4, 1953.

_____. "From Marlowe to Gounod." *Opera News*, Nov. 30, 1953, p. 12.

_____. "Style in Shakespeare Production." *Directors on Directing*. ed. by Toby Cole and Helen Krich Chinoy, Indianapolis and New York: Bobbs-Merrill, 1953.

_____. "Hamlet Fat and Hamlet Lean." *The Sunday Times*, Dec. 18, 1955.

_____. "To Moscow to Put on Hamlet." *Vogue*, April 15, 1956, p. 74+.

_____. "Quarter-Ear Music." *The Sunday Times*, Sep. 22, 1957. [on *music concréte*]

_____. "A Realistic Approach to Eugene Onegin." *New York Times*, Oct. 27, 1957.

_____. "Oh for empty seats." *Encore*, Jan. 1959.

_____. "From Zero To The Infinite." *Encore*, Nov./Dec. 1960, pp. 6–10.

_____. "The Cuban Enterprise." *Sight and Sound*, Spring, 1961.

_____. "Search For a Hunger." *Encore*, July/Aug. 1961, pp. 8–21.

_____. "Happy days and Marienbad." *Encore*, Jan. 1962. [reprinted in *The Encore Reader*]

_____. "Peter Brook on The Secret of King Lear." *The Stage*, Jan. 10, 1963. [interview]

_____. "Review of 'Marguerite and Armand'." *Observer*, March, 1963.

_____. "Filming A Masterpiece." *The Observer*, July 26, 1964.

_____. "An Interview: On 'Marat/Sade'." *Daily Mail*, Aug. 24, 1964.

_____. "The Road To Marat/Sade." *New York Herald Tribune*, Dec. 26, 1965.

_____. "False Gods." *Flourish*, Winter, 1965.

_____. Introduction to Weiss' *Marat/Sade*, London: John Calder, 1965.

_____. "Interview." *The New York Times*, Jan. 9, 1966.

_____. "Peter Brook Talks About Theatre." *Harper's Bazaar*, March, 1966, pp. 84, 224.

_____. "Finding Shakespeare on Film." *TDR*, Fall, 1966.

_____. "Putting Marat/Sade on The Screen." *New York World Journal Tribune*, Feb. 17, 1967.

_____. "Is 'McBird' pro-American?" *New York Times*, March 19, 1967.

_____. "Vietnam Film Rouses American Anger—and Fantasy." *The Times*, Feb. 17, 1968.

_____. "Immediate Theatre." [excerpt from *The Empty Space*] *Atlantic*, Nov. 1968, pp. 82–4+.

_____. "The Need For Ritual." Theatre Program *Oedipus*, National Theatre of Great Britain, 1968.

_____. "The Chorus For The Senecan Oedipus." *Drama At Calgary*, Vol. III, No. 1 (1968) p. 41.

_____. *The Empty Space*. Penguin, 1968.

_____. Preface to Grotowski's *Towards a Poor Theatre*, Teatrets Vorlag, 1968.

_____. "Interview by Sydney Edwards." *Evening Standard*, March 7, 1969.

_____. *US: The Book of the* Oakes." *Sunday Times*, July 5, 1970.

_____. "Interview." *Guardian*, Oct. 2, 1970.

_____. "Les Lieus du Spectacle." *Architecture d' Aujourd'hui* #152, Oct./Nov., 1970.

_____. "A Talk With Peter Brook." *The American Theatre* 1969–1970. ed. Martha Wadsworth Coigney, et al., New York: Charles Scribner's Sons, 1970, pp. 17–23.

_____. Preface to *The Voice and the Actor* by Cicely Berry, London: Harrap, 1973.

_____. "The Complete Truth is Global." *New York Times*, Jan. 20, 1974.

_____. "The Theater of Life." *New Society*, Nov. 7, 1974, pp. 385–6.

_____. "Lettre á une Etudiante Anglaise." in *Timon d Athénes*, Paris: C.I.C.T., 1974.

_____. "The Three Cultures of Modern Man." *Cultures*, The UNESCO Press, Vol. 3, #4, 1976.

_____. "Théâtre Populaire, Théâtre Immédiat." *Le Monde*, Nov. 24, 1977.

_____. "On the Rocky Road to Afghanistan." *The Observer*, Sep. 9, 1979.

_____. "The Living Theatre of the Outback." *Sunday Times*, Aug. 17, 1980.

_____. *The Shifting Point*. New York: Harper and Row, 1987.

_____. , et al. "Artaud for Artaud's Sake." *Encore*. May/June, 1964, pp. 20–31.

_____. , et al. "The Marat/Sade Forum." *TDR*, Summer, 1966, pp. 214–7.

BROOK, Peter and MAROWITZ, Charles. "A Theatre of Nerve-ends." *Sunday Times*, Jan. 12, 1964.

BROOK, Peter, and MORE, Shiela. "The Lessons of Lear." *The Observer*, April 5, 1964.

BROOK, Peter and REEVES, Geoffrey. "Shakespeare on Three Screens." *Sight and Sound*, Spring, 1965.

BROOK, Peter, and TRILLING, Ossia. "The Prospect Before Us." *Theatre Newsletter*, Dec. 13, 1947, pp. 4–5.

BROOK, Peter and TONKIN, Boyd. "The Reluctant Hero Comes Home." *New Statesman*, April 22, 1988, pp. 22–4.

BROWN, E. Martin. "A Look Around The English Theatre." *Drama Survey*, Winter, 1968–69, pp. 143–145.

BROWN, Georg. "Blood and Sanskrit." *Village Voice*, May 1, 1990, p. 78. [film of *Mahab*]

BROWN, Ivor. "On the Avon Again." *Observer*, April 13, 1947.

————. (ed.) *Theatre* (issued yearly).

————. *The Shakespeare Memorial Theatre* (1954–56). London, Reinhardt, 1956.

BRUBACH, H. "Music." [on Carmen] *Atlantic*, Nov. 1983, pp. 130–1.

————. "Carmen—The Vamp Revisited." *Vogue*, Nov. 1983, p. 436+.

BRUSTEIN, Robert. "Review of 'King Lear'." *New Republic*, May, 1964.

————. *Seasons of Discontent*. New York: Simon and Schuster, 1966.

————. *The Third Theatre*. New York: Simon and Schuster, 1969.

————. "Whose Stage Is It Anyway?" *New York Times* (Book Review Section) July 27, 1986.

BRYDEN, Ronald. "Into war, everyone." *Observer*, Oct. 16, 1966.

————. "Interview with Peter Brook." *Observer*, March 24, 1968.

————. "Stripping Down the Dream." *Observer*, Dec. 13, 1970.

————. "Dream in a Persian Market." *Observer*, June 20, 1971.

BURGESS, Jackson. "Lord of The Flies." *Film Quarterly*, Winter, 1962–63, pp. 31–2.

BURROUGHS, Catherine B. "The Immediate Classroom: Feminist Pedagogy and Peter Brook's 'The Empty Space'." *Feminist Teacher*, Fall 1990, pp. 10–4.

CAANAN, Denis and HIGGINS, Colin. *The Ik.* Connecticut: Dramatist Publishing Co., 1982.

CALLENBACH, Ernest. "Marat/Sade." *Film Quarterly*, Summer, 1967, pp. 54–7.

CAMPBELL, Ken. "Peter Brook Schedules U. S. Tour." *ATA Theatre News*, Aug. 1976, pp. 1–3. [*Ik*]

CANBY, Vincent. "Screen: Peter Brook's 'King Lear'." *The New York Times*, Nov. 23, 1971.

————. "A 'Lear' Full of Exquisite Terror." *The New York Times*, Dec. 5, 1971.

CAPELL, Richard. "Review of 'Salome'." *Daily Mail*, Nov. 12, 1949.

CHAPIN, Louis. "Moderato Cantabile." *Christian Science Monitor*, Jan. 10, 1964.

————. "Weiss: 'I Can Only Yell . . . !'" *Christian Science Monitor*, Jan. 8, 1966.

————. "Shakespeare and the Commune." *Christianity and Crisis*, March 8, 1971, pp. 33–4.

CHAPMAN, John. "Harrison in a Pointless Comedy." *The Daily News*, Dec. 9, 1959.

————. "'Marat/Sade' Horrifying Drama Brilliantly Staged and Played." *Daily News*, Dec. 28, 1965.

CHRISTIANSEN, Rupert. "Opera: Impassioned Smooch." *Spectator*, Dec. 1992. [*Pelleas*]

CLURMAN, Harold. "Theatre." *The Nation*, May 16, 1959, pp. 462–3.

————. *Lies Like Truth*. New York: Grove Press, 1960.

————. *The Naked Image*. New York: Macmillian, 1966.

————. "Theatre: Production of Mind." *The Nation*, Feb. 8, 1971, pp. 188–9.

————. *The Divine Pastime*. New York: Macmillian, 1974.

CODY, Gabrielle. "Art for Awe's Sake." *Theatre*, Spring, 1988, pp. 32–4.

COHEN, H. U. [review of *Carmen*] *Theatre Journal*, Dec. 1982, pp. 530–1.

COHEN, Paul B. "Peter Brook and the 'Two Worlds' of the Theatre." *New Theatre Quarterly*, May 1991, pp. 147–59.

COLE, Toby and CHINOY, Helen Krich. *Directors on Directing*. New York: Bobbs-Merrill, 1953, new edition 1963.

COLEMAN, Robert. "'Fighting Cock' is Season's Best Play." *New York Mirror*, Dec. 9, 1959.

COLLINS, David G. "Beyond Reason in A Midsummer Night's Dream: Stratford, 1981." *Iowa State Journal of Research*, Nov. 1982, pp. 131–42.

CONSTANT, Marius; BROOK, Peter; and CARRIERE, Jean-Claude. *La Tragédie de Carmen*. Paris: CICT, 1981.

COOK, Judith. *Director's Theatre*. London: Harrap, 1974.

COOKE, Richard P. "Venality and The Avenger." *Wall Street Journal*, May 7, 1958.

COOKMAN, Anthony. "At The Theatre." *Tatler and Bystander*, March 23, 1949.

COURSEN, H. R. "The Peter Brook/Orson Wells King Lear." *Shakespeare on Film Quarterly*, April 1991, p. 8.

COVENEY, Michael. "Mesure pour Mesure." *Financial Times*, Nov. 20, 1978.

COWIE, Peter. "Lord of The Flies." *Films and Filming*, Aug. 1964, pp. 21–2.

COX, Frank. [Interview] *Plays and Players*, April 1968.

CRIST, Judith. "Lord of The Flies." *New York Herald Tribune*, Aug. 20, 1963.

————. "Madhouse World of Marat/Sade." *The World Journal Tribune*, Feb. 23, 1967.

CROWTHER, Bosley. "Screen: Woman of Morbid Disposition." *New York Times*, Jan. 7, 1964.

———. "Marat/Sade." *New York Times*, Feb. 23, 1967.

———. "'Marat/Sade' — or Who's Looney Now?" *New York Times*, March 5, 1967.

CROYDEN, Margaret. "Exploration of the Ugly; Brook's Work on Oedipus." *TDR*, Spring, 1969, pp. 120–4.

———. "Peter Brook's Tempest." *TDR*, Spring, 1969, pp. 125–8.

———. "A Hidden 'Dream' of Sex and Love." *New York Times*, Jan. 17, 1971.

———. "Peter Brook Learns to Speak Orghast." *New York Times*, Oct. 3, 1971.

———. "Peter Brook's 'Birds' fly to Africa." *New York Times*, Jan. 21, 1973.

———. *Lunatics, Lovers and Poets*. New York: McGraw, Hill, 1974.

———. "Filming the Saga of a Sage with Peter Brook." *New York Times*, Feb. 26, 1978.

———. "Getting in Touch with Gurdjieff." *New York Times*, July 29, 1979.

———. Peter Brook's Search for Essentials." *New York Times*, May 4, 1980.

———. "Comedy, Tragedy and Mystical Fantasy: Peter Brook's New Trilogy." *New York Times*, May 25, 1980.

———. *The Centre: A Narrative*. Paris: CICT, 1980.

———. "Brook Explores Opera as Theater." *New York Times*, Nov. 13, 1983.

———. "Peter Brook transforms an Indian Epic." *New York Times*, Aug. 25, 1985.

———. "Peter Brook Creates a Nine-Hour Epic." *New York Times Magazine*, Oct. 4, 1987, pp. 36–8+.

———. "Brook and the Band." *Village Voice*, Feb. 12, 1991, p. 94+.

CUE. "On Directing." Nov. 7, 1970, p. 42.

CURTISS, Thomas Quinn. "Theatre in Paris." *New York Herald Tribune*, May 17, 1957.

———. "Paris Finally Sees Genet's Balcony." *New York Herald Tribune*, May 29, 1960.

———. "Peter Brook Opens His Dream Theatre in Paris." *International Herald Tribune*, June 19, 1970.

CUSHMAN, Robert. "Swinging back to words." *Observer*, Jan. 8, 1978. [*Ubu* & others]

DALLAS, Ian. "An English Lesson." *Films and Filming*, Feb. 1962, pp. 38–9.

DANIELS, Barry. ed. "Letters on Peter Brook's 'US'." *Theatre*, Spring 1988, pp. 41–5.

DARLINGTON, W. A. "Masque Great Scene in 'The Tempest'." *Daily Telegraph*, Aug. 14, 1957.

DASGUPTA, G. "'The Mahabharata': Peter Brook's 'Orientalism'." *Performing Arts Journal*, 1987, pp. 9–16.

DASH, Thomas. "'The Fighting Cock' Proves To Be a Tame Rooster." *New York Journal American*, Dec. 9, 1959.

DAVID, Richard. "Dreams of Eale." *Shakespeare Survey*, London: Cambridge University Press, 1957, pp. 169–73.

DAVIS, Peter G. and Simon, John. "'Carmen'à la Mode." *New York*, Nov. 28, 1983, pp. 76–8.

DAWSON, Helen. "Brook Goes Backwards." *The Observer*, Nov. 31, 1968.

DENBY, David. "La Tragedie de Carmen." *Atlantic*, Jan. 1985, p. 38.

DEVEREAUX, Kent. "Peter Brook's Production of The Mahabrahata at the Brooklyn Academy of Music." *Asian Theatre Journal*. Fall 1988, pp. 225–32.

DOCKER, John. "In Defence of Melodrama: Towards a Libertarian Aesthetic." *Australasian Drama Studies*, Oct. 1986, p. 6381.

DOOLITTLE, Joyce. "Oedipus-Sophocles-Seneca-Brook." *Drama at Calgary*, Vol. III, No. 1, pp. 37–40.

DRAMA REVIEW. "The Mahabharata." Spring, 1986, pp. 52–99.

_____. "Grotowski, Art as a Vehicle." Spring, 1991, pp. 92–4.

DRIVER, Tom. "Masterpiece." *The Christian Century*, June 4, 1968, pp. 668–9.

_____. "As Flies To Wanton Boys." *Reporter*, March 14, 1963, pp. 44–6.

DRUTMAN, Irving. "Was Peter Brook Its Brain?" *New York Times*, Jan. 9, 1966.

DUPONT, Joan. "Cameos: Peter Brook." *Premiere*, June 1990, pp. 60–3. [on influence of film]

EARL, Laurence. "Backstage prodigy who steals the show." *John Bull*, Aug. 13, 1949, pp. 15–6.

THE ECONOMIST. "Getting Past Shakespeare." April 23, 1988, pp. 99–100.

EDER, Richard. "Peter Brook Stages an Austere 'Carmen' in Paris." *New York Times*, Nov. 30, 1981.

EDWARDS, Christopher. "Epic Grandeur." *Spectator*, April 23, 1988, pp. 52–3. [*Mahab.* in Glasgow]

_____. "Theatre: The Thrill of Simplicity." *Spectator*, April 22, 1989, pp. 49–51. [*Carmen* in Glasgow]

ELSNER, John. "The Poetic History of Mankind: Peter Brook's Production of the 'Mahabharata' in Glasgow." *Month*, June 1988, pp. 725–7.

ESSLIN, Martin. "The Public Bath (LAMDA Experiment)." *New York Times Magazine*, Oct. 4, 1964.

_____. "The Theatre of Cruelty." *New York Times Magazine*, March 6, 1966, pp. 22–3.

_____. "Are We To Blame for US?" *New York Times*, Nov. 6, 1966.

_____. "Oedipus Wanted Power Not His Mother." *New York Times*, March 31, 1968.

_____. "Oedipus Complex." *Plays and Players*, May 1968, pp. 22, 24.

_____. *The Theatre of the Absurd*. Pelican, 1969.

EYRE, Richard. "My Hero: Richard Eyre on Peter Brook." *Independent Magazine*, April 1, 1989, p. 62.

FAGG, Martin. "Paperbacks." *New York Times Educational Suppliment*, May 12, 1989, p. B7.

FARRELL, Joe. "La Tragédie de Carmen." *Plays and Players*, June, 1989. pp. 30, 31.

FAY, Stephen. "A Stage for Three Carmens." *Sunday Time Magazine*, Dec. 14, 1983, pp. 74–7.

FIELD, Rowland. "'The Fighting Cock:' Play Starring Rex Harrison Disappoints." *Newark Evening News*, Dec. 9, 1959.

FINDLATTER, Richard. "Shakespearean Atrocities." *Twentieth Century*, Oct. 1955, pp. 364–72.

_____. "Myth and Magic among the Persians." *Observer*, Sep. 12, 1971.

FREEDMAN, Samuel G. "'Carmen' Brightens Beaumont." *New York Times*, Dec. 1, 1983.

FREEMAN, Ira Henry. "Comprenez-vous Irma?" *New York Times*, Sep. 25, 1960.

FRENCH NEWS. "Theatre Research Center." No. 46, p. 9.

FREUND, Andreas. "Peter Brook is Setting Up a Theatre Center in Paris." *New York Times*, June 5, 1970.

GANELIN, Charles. "Peter Brook: Performance Theory and the Comedia." *Bulletin of the Comediantes*, Summer 1991, pp. 101–8.

GARDNER, R. H. "'Marat/Sade' Theatrical Success." *The Baltimore Sun*, Feb. 4, 1966.

GARNER, Ken. "Wall-to-Wall Theatre." [*Mahab* in Glasgow] *Listener*, April 7, 1988, pp. 33–4.

GASCOIGNE, Bamber. "A Lear of The Head." *The Spectator*, Nov. 15, 1962.

_____. "The LAMDA Experiment." *Observer*, Jan. 1964.

GASSNER, John. *Dramatic Soundings*. New York: Crown Publishers, Inc., 1968.

GELLERT, Roger. "The Plays on Impression." *SC: The Crucial Years* (pamphlet), London, 1963.

GIBSON, Michael, "Brook's Africa." [interview] *TDR*, Sep. 1973.

GIELGUD, John "Interview" in *Great Acting*, ed. by Hal Burton, BBC.

GILL, Brendon. "Preachers." *The New Yorker*, March 4, 1967, p. 140.

_____. "Defoliation of a Classic." *The New Yorker*, Nov. 28, 1983, p. 168.

GILLIANT, Penelope. "Peter Brook: A Natural Sabateur of Order." *Vogue*, Jan. 1, 1966, pp. 102–5.

GILMAN, Todd S. "The Textual Fabric of Peter Brook's 'King Lear': 'Holes' in Cinema, Screenplay, and Playtext." *Lit/Film Quarterly*, 1992, pp. 294–300.

GLOVER, William. "Theatre is Becoming More a Place of Violence, Obscenity." *The Shreveport Times*, Feb.13, 1966.

GORDON, Giles. "O Babbling Brook." *Punch*, April 22, 1988, pp. 44–5. [rev of *Shifting Point*]

GOTTFRIED, Martin. "Theatre." *Women's Wear Daily*, Dec. 30, 1965.

GOY-BLANQUET, Dominique. "Slides of the Cortex: 'L'homme Qui'." *Times Literary Suppliment*, May 14, 1993, p. 20.

GREER, Herb. "Credo Quia Contra-Courant Est." [interview] *Transatlantic Review*, Oct. 1976.

GRIFFIN, J. "He Directed the New Version of Faust." *Theatre Arts*, Dec. 1953, p. 71+.

GROWTOWSKI, Jerzy. *Towards A Poor Theatre*. New York: Simon and Schuster, 1968.

HALE, Lionel. "Youth Takes a Bow." *Daily Mail*, April 27, 1946.

————. "Ballet v. the Bard." *Daily Mail*, April 7, 1947.

————. "Shakespeare for the Eye." *Daily Mail*, April 27, 1947.

HALL, Peter. "Avoiding a Method." *RSC: The Crucial Years* (pamphlet), London, 1963, pp. 14–9.

HAMPSHIRE, Stuart. "Sade's Theatre." *The New York Review of Books*, Feb. 3, 1966, pp. 5–6.

HARRIS, L. F. "Peter Brook's 'King Lear': Aesthetic Achievment or Far Side of the Moon?" *Theatre Research International*, Autumn, 1986, pp. 223–39.

HARVEY, Andrew. "Peter Brook Makes Believers of us All." *Vogue*, Oct. 1987, pp. 444–5+.

HAYMAN, Ronald. *Techniques of Acting*. London: Methuen and Co., Ltd., 1969.

————. "Life and Joy." [interview] *The Times*, Aug. 29, 1970.

————. *Artaud and After*. Oxford, 1977.

————. *Theatre and Anti-Theatre*. London: Secker and Warburg, 1979.

————. "Rebel in a Theatrical Cause." *Independent*, April 7, 1988. [*Mahab*]

HEILPERN, John. "Shaman Extraordinary" *The Observer*, Aug. 30, 1970.

————. "Peter Brook's Other Dream." *The Observer*, Nov. 26, 1972.

————. "Peter Brook, the Grand Inquisitor." *The Observer*, Jan. 18, 1976.

————. *Conference for the Birds: The Story of Peter Brook in Africa*. Faber, 1977.

————. "Magic of the Birds." *The Observer*, May 11, 1980.

————. "After-words on 'Carmen'—and Some Backstage Secrets." *East Side Express*, Dec. 1–8, 1983, p. 21.

HENAHAN, Donal. "It's Peter Brook's 'Carmen,' not Bizet's or Mérimée's." *The New York Times*, Nov. 20, 1983.

HENDERSON, Liza. "Brook's Point." *Theatre*, Spring 1988, pp. 35–8.

HENRY, William. A. [Mahab. rev] *Time*, Oct. 19, 1987, p. 85.

_____. "Samovars Without Sterotypes." *Time*, Feb. 8, 1988, p. 84.

HENTOFF, Nat. "Peter Brook: 'Yes, Let's Be Emotional About Vietnam.'" *New York Times*, Feb. 25, 1968.

HERSON, E. J. "La Tragédie de Carmen." [review] *Theatre Journal*, Oct. 1984, pp. 408–10.

HEWES, Henry. "This Other Stratford." *Saturday Review*, Sep. 24, 1955, pp. 24, 26.

_____. "The World of Reasonable Madness." *Saturday Review*, Dec. 8, 1962, p. 51.

_____. "Real Royalty." *Saturday Review*, May 23, 1964, p. 35.

HIGGINS, John. "Peter Brook's reply to the critics." *The Times*, Oct. 18, 1978.

HILTEBEITEL, A. "Transmitting 'Mahabharatas': Another Look at Peter Brook." *TDR*, Fall, 1992, pp. 131–59.

HOBE. "Show on Broadway: 'The Fighting Cock.'" *Variety*, Dec. 16, 1959.

HOBSON, Harold. "And Now Tybalt." *Sunday Times*, Oct. 12, 1947.

_____. "British Talents Combined in Version of Gay's Work." *Christian Science Monitor*, Aug. 25, 1953.

_____. "Happy Return" (on '55 *Hamlet*)

_____. "Close-run Thing in Moscow." *The Sunday Times*, Nov. 3, 1955.

_____. "The Power and the Glory." *The Times*, April 6, 1956.

_____. "The Family Reunion." *The Times*, June 8, 1956.

_____. "A Foretaste." *The Sunday Times*, June 10, 1956, p. 6.

_____. "A View From the Bridge." *The Times*, October 12, 1956.

_____. "National Theatres." *The Sunday Times*, Aug. 18, 1957.

_____. "The Return of The Lunts." *The Sunday Times*, June 26, 1960.

_____. "A Vengeful Universe." *The Sunday Times*, Nov. 11, 1962.

_____. "Out of the Myth." *The Sunday Times*, Dec. 16, 1962.

_____. "The Dirty Plays of London." *Show*, Jan. 1965, pp. 7–8.

_____. "US—A Magnificient Song." *The Christian Monitor*, Oct. 29, 1966.

_____. "A Ritual of Despair." *The Times*, March 24, 1968.

_____. "A Second Look At The Shakespeare/Brook 'Dream'." *Christian Science Monitor*, June 19, 1971.

HODGDON, Barbara. "Two King Lears: Uncovering the Filmtext." *Leterature Film Quarterly*, 1983, pp. 143–51.

HODGSON, Moira. "Theatre." *The Nation*, Jan. 16, 1988, p. 66. [*Mahab.*]

_____. "Theatre." *The Nation*, Feb. 27, 1988, pp. 283–4.

HOPE-WALLACE, Philip. "Novel Reaches The Stage: The Power And The Glory." *Manchester Guardian*, April 6, 1956.

_____. "A View From The Bridge: Mr. Miller's News Play." *Manchester Guardian*, Oct. 12, 1956.

HOUSTON, Penelope and MILNE, Tom. "Interview With Peter Brook." *Sight and Sound*, Summer, 1963, pp. 31–41.

HUDSON, Roger. "Theatre of Cruelty." *Prompt*, No. 4, 1964, pp. 13–8.

HUFTEL, Sheila. *Arthur Miller: The Burning Glass*. 1965. [includes Brook's *View*]

HUGES, Allen. "Ford Foundation Gives $2-Million to Assist the Arts." *New York Times*, Oct. 3, 1970.

HUGHES, C. "Memories and Mistakes." [*Carmen*] *America*, Jan. 21, 1984, p. 34.

HUGHES, David. "Peter Brook: A revolution at the Opera." *Sunday Times*, Nov. 15, 1981.

HUGHES, Ted. *Oedipus*, London: Faber and Faber, 1969.

———. "'Orghast': talking without words." *Vogue*, Dec. 1971.

HULL, David Stewart. "London." *Film Quarterly*, Winter, 1960, pp. 30–5.

HUNT, Albert. "Acting and Being." *New Society*, Feb. 20, 1975, pp. 466–8.

———. "The Trials of working with a Master Magician." *New Society*, Aug. 26, 1982.

———. "Brook's Poem of the World." [*Mahab.*] *New Society*, April 15, 1988, pp. 20–1.

HUSSEY, Dyneley. "Covent Garden Opera." *The Musical Times*, Dec. 1949, pp. 448–9.

INNES, Christopher, *Holy Theatre*, Cambridge: Cambridge Univ. Press, 1981.

IRVING, Clive. "Lively Arts." *World Journal Tribune*, Nov. 6, 1966. [on *US*]

IRVING, Gordon. "The Lark." *Variety*, April 27, 1955, p. 64.

"S. J." "Fry Goes To War." *Liverpool Post*, March 9, 1954.

JELINKOVA, R. "Royal Shakespeare Company on Tour." *Theatre World*, April, 1964, pp. 6–8.

JOHNS, Eric. "Wonder Boy." *Theatre World*, June, 1949, pp. 35, 36.

———. "Experiment." *The Stage and Television Today*, July 18, 1968, p. 8.

JONES, David Richard. *Great Directors at Work*. UC/Berkely Press, 1986.

JONES, Edward Trostle. *Following Directions: A Study of Peter Brook*. New York; Berne; Frankfurt an Main: Lang, 1985.

KAEL, Pauline. *I Lost It At The Movies*. New York: Bantam Books, 1965.

———. "Peter Brook's Night of the Living Dead," *The New Yorker*, Dec. 11, 1971, p. 135.

KALEM, T. E. [review of *Lear* film] *Time*, Nov. 29, 1971, p. 55.

———. "Vacuum Packed." *Time*, May 19, 1980, p. 52.

KALMAN, J. "An Event Stems from Combustion: Actors, Audiences and Theatrical Energy." [interview] trans. by D. Williams, *New Theatre Quarterly*, May, 1992, pp. 107–12.

KANE, John. "When my cue comes, call me and I will answer." *Sunday Times*, June 13, 1971.

KAUFFMANN, Stanley. "The Provocative Marat/Sade." *New York Times*, Jan. 9, 1966.

———. "Empty Space." *New Republic*, Oct. 20, 1973, p. 22.

———. [*mahab.* film review] *New Republic*, May 7, 1990, pp. 28–9.

KENT, Letitia. "The Rule of the Game as Performed by Peter Brook." *The Village Voice*, Feb. 8, 1968.

KERR, Walter. "First Night Report." *New York Herald Tribune*, May 6, 1958.

———. "'The Fighting Cock'." *New York Herald Tribune*, Dec. 9, 1959.

———. "Kerr on 'The Physicists'." *New York Herald Tribune*, Oct. 14, 1964.

———. "Marat/Sade." *New York Herald Tribune*, Dec. 28, 1965.

———. "Marat/Sade: All work and No Play." *New York Herald Tribune*, Jan. 16, 1966.

———. *Thirty Plays Hath November*. New York: Simon and Schuster, 1969.

KING, Francis. "The Rehearsal's the Thing." *New York Times*, Oct. 18, 1987, Book Review, p. 15.

KINGSTON, Jeremy. "Theatre." *Punch*, Sep. 9, 1970, p. 376.

KLEIN, Donald. "The Stage: 'Marat', A Stunning Event." *Long Island Post*, Jan. 6, 1966.

KNAPP, Bettina. *Antonin Artaud: Man of Virtue*. Avon, 1969.

KNIGHT, Arthur. "Filming Marat/Sade." *Saturday Review*, July 30, 1966, p. 43.

KOLODIN, Irving. "The Met's New *Faust*." *Saturday Review*, Nov. 14, 1953, pp. 32–3.

KOENIG, Rhoda. "Blood and Sand." *New York*, Nov. 21, 1983. [*Carmen*, mainly photo essay]

KOSINTSEV, Grigori. *Shakespeare: Time and Conscience*. trans. Joyce Vining, London, 1967.

KOTLOWITZ, Robert. "Nothing But Talent." *Harper's Magazine*, April 1966, pp. 124–5.

KOTT, Jan. *Shakespeare Our Contemporary*. Garden City: Doubleday and Co., Inc., 1966.

———. The Theatre of Essence: Kantor and Brook." *Theatre*, Summer/Fall 1983, pp. 55–8.

KRAMER, M. [*Mahab* review] *New Yorker*, Nov. 2, 1987, pp. 146–8.

KROLL, Jack. "A Dream of Love." *Newsweek*. Feb. 1, 1971, p. 73.

———. "Placing The Living Shakespeare Before Us." *New York Times*, Feb. 7, 1971.

———. "Peter Brook's Volcanoes." *Newsweek*, May 19, 1980, pp. 101–2.

———. "An Epic Saga of India." *Newsweek*, Sep. 21, 1987, pp. 74–5. [*Mahab.* in LA]

———. "Trees Grow in Brooklyn." *Newsweek*, Feb. 22, 1988, p. 72.

KUPFERBERG, H. "Peter Brook's 'Carmen'." *High Fidelity*, March 1984, p. MA25–MA26.

KUSTOW, Michael. "Sovereign of the Enchanted Isle." [*Tempest* in France] *Observer*, Oct. 14, 1990.

KUSTOW, Michael; HUNT, Albert; and REEVES, Geoffrey. *Tell Me Lies*. Indianapolis and New York: Bobbs-Merrill, 1968.

LABEILLE, D. "Formless Hunch: An Interview with Peter Brook." *Modern Drama*, S. 1980, pp. 219–26.

LAHR, John. "We Want To Be Humane, But We're Only Human." *Evergreen Review*, April 1968, pp. 37–40, 73–4.

———. "Knowing What to Celebrate." [interview] *Plays and Players*, March 1976, pp. 17–9.

LAMBERT, J. W. "Plays in Performance." *Drama*, Spring, 1958, p. 16.

———. "Plays in Performance."*Drama*, Winter, 1964, pp. 18–9.

———. "Plays in Performance." *Drama*, Summer, 1968, p. 18.

LANG, C. S. "'Boris Godounov' at Covent Garden." *The Musical Times*, June, 1948, p. 17.

LAWSON, S. R. "Old Vic to Vincennes:Interviews with Michael Kustow and Peter Brook." *Yale Theatre*, Fall, 1975, pp. 87–91.

LEJEUNE, C. A. "The Unpredictable Peter Brook." Spring, 1950, pp. 15, 55. [clipping in Mander & Mitchenson Theatre Collection, magazine unidentified]

LELLIS, George. "Cinema and Arti-facts." *Film Heritage*, Winter, 1968/69, p. 17.

LEVIN, Bernard. "The Visit." *The Daily Express*, June 24, 1960.

———. "The Seeds of Genius: Watch them Grow." *The Times*, April 3, 1980.

———. "Two men on remarkable journeys." *The Times*, June 26, 1980.

LEWIS, Anthony. "Peter Brook's Theater Is a 'Living Event'." *The New York Times*, Jan. 15, 1971.

LEWIS, Theophilus. "Marat/deSade." *America*, Jan. 29, 1966, pp. 181–2.

LEY, G. "The Rhetoric of Theory: The Role of Metaphor in Brook's 'The Empty Space'." *New Theatre Quarterly*, Summer, 1993, pp. 245–54.

LIEBERSON, Jonathan. "Chopping Up 'The Cherry Orchard'." *New York Review of Books*, March 3, 1990, pp. 26–8.

LIEHM, A. J. "The Politics of Sclerosis: Stalin and Lear." [interview] *Theatre Quarterly*, April/June 1973, pp. 13–7.

LITTLE, Stuart. "Brook, at the Martin Beck Lectures Cast on Düerrenmatt's 'Physicists'." *New York Herald Tribune*, Sep. 1, 1964.

———. "Brook Blasts the Marat/Sade First Nighters." *New York Herald Tribune*, Dec. 29, 1965.

LOCKSPEISER, Edward. "Bliss Opera Staged at Covent Garden." *Musical America*, Nov. 1, 1949, p. 6.

LONEY, Glenn. ed. *Peter Brook's RSC Production of William Shakespeare's 'A Midsummer Night's Dream': Authorized Acting Edition*. Dramatic Publishing Co., 1974.

————. "The Carmen Connection." *Opera News*, Sep. 1983, pp. 10–4.

————. "Myth and Music: Resonances Across the Continents and Centuries." *Yale Theatre*, Spring 1988, pp. 21–7.

LONG, Roger. "Peter Brook's The Mahabharata: A Personal Reaction." *Asian Theatre Journal*, Fall 1988, pp. 233–5.

LOTTMAN, H. R. "Peter Brook's Dream." *Saturday Review of the Arts*, Jan. 1973, pp. 7–8.

MACDONALD, Dwight. "Lord of The Flies." *Esquire*, Feb. 1964, pp. 28–9.

MACK, Maynard. *King Lear in our Time*. U. of Cal Press, 1969.

MAGEE, Bryan. "Bomb Shell at the Aldwych." *The Listener*, Nov. 3, 1966, p. 651.

MAMBRINO, Jean. "Une Histoire de L'humanite: Le Mahabharata concu par Peter Brook." *Etudes*, Nov. 1985, pp. 507–13.

MAROWITZ, Charles. "Grappling With a Masterpiece." *Observer*, Dec. 16, 1962.

————. "Theatre Afield." *Village Voice*, Jan. 10, 1963.

————. "Lear Log." *TDR*, Winter, 1963.

————. "Düerrenmatt's Comic-Strip Commitment." *Village Voice*, March 14, 1963.

————. "Notes on The Theatre of Cruelty." *TDR*, Winter, 1966, pp. 152–72.

————. "The Royal Shakespeare Company's US." *TDR*, Winter, 1966, pp. 173–5.

————. "Peter Brook's Oedipus." *Village Voice*, March 28, 1968.

————. "From Prodigy to Profesional as Written, Directed and Acted by Peter Brook." *New York Times Magazine*, Nov. 24, 1968, pp. 62–3, 92–118.

————. "Brook: From Marat/Sade to Midsummer Night's Dream." *New York Times*, Sep. 13, 1970.

————. *Confessions of Counterfit Critic*. London: Methuen, 1973.

————. *The Act of Being*, London: Seeker and Warburg, 1978.

MAROWITZ, Charles; MILNE, Tom and HALE, Owen eds. *The Encore Reader: A Chronicle of the New Drama*. London, Methuen, 1965.

MAROWITZ, Charles and TRUSSLER, Simon, eds. *Theatre At Work*. London, Methuen, 1968.

MARRIOTT, R. B. "... and a 'Tempest' for the actors." *The Stage and Television Today*, July 25, 1968, p. 12.

MARSHALL, Norman. *The Producer and the Play*. Macdonald, 1962.

MATTHEWS, Harold. "The Tempest." *Theatre World*, Oct. 1957, pp. 12–6.

MAVOR, Ronald. "Time and Again Provides a Rewarding Evening." *The Scotsman* (Edinburgh), March 12, 1958.

MCCALL, Anthony. "Heading Towards New Horizons." *Cue*. May/June, 1983. [*Carmen*]

MCCLAIN, John. "'The Fighting Cock:' Harrison's Back in Feeble Work." *New York Journal-American*, Dec. 9, 1959.

MILLER, Arthur. "Introduction." *A View From The Bridge*, New York: Viking Press, 1960, pp. v–x.

MILLER, Jonathan. "Trailing Clouds of Glory?" *The New Yorker*, Aug. 31. 1963, pp. 59–60.

MILNE, Tom. "Cruelty, Cruelty." *Encore*, March/April 1964.

———. "Reflections on The Screens." *Encore*, July/Aug. 1964.

———. "Lord of The Flies." *Sight and Sound*, Autumn, 1964, pp. 194–5.

MISHKIN, Leo. "Peter Brook's 'Tell me Lies'." *The Morning Telegraph*, Feb. 13, 1968.

MISHRA, Vijay. "The Great Indian Epic and Peter Brook." *Meanjin*, Winter 1988, pp. 343–52.

MITTER, Shomit. *Systems of Rehearsal: Stanislavski, Brecht, Grotowski and Brook*, Routledge, 1993.

MOLINE, Karen. "The Magical Mystery Tour Guide: Peter Brook." *Interview*, Feb. 1988, pp. 68–72.

MOREHOUSE, Ward. "'Little Hut' Collapses Without Morley." *New York World-Telegram and Sun*, Oct. 10, 1953.

MORLEY, Sheridan. "Peter Brook: Quarrying theatre in Australia." *The Times*, April 7, 1980.

MULLIN, Michael. "Peter Brook's King Lear: Stage and Screen." *Literature Film Quarterly*, 1983, pp. 190–6.

MULRYNE, J. R. "Anthony and Cleopatra: Penny Plain or Tuppence Coloured" in *Du Texte a la scene: Language du theatre*. ed. by Marie-Therese Jones-Davies. Paris: Turot, 1983.

MUNK, Erica. "Looking for a New Language." *Performance*, Vol. 1, #1, 1971.

———. "The Way's the Thing." *Village Voice*, May 12, 1980.

———. "Western Eyes." *The Village Voice*, March 14, 1989, p. 95+ [*Mahab.*]

MUSICAL AMERICA. "Keep 'em Still." June, 1959, p. 11.

MYERS, Harold. "A View From The Bridge." *Variety*, Oct. 17, 1956, p. 70.

———. "Marat-Sade Complete in 15 Days."*Variety*, June 8, 1966, p. 3. [on making of the film]

NADEL, Norman. "'Physicists' Is Truly Theatre Science." *World-Telegram and Sun*, Oct. 14, 1964.

NADOTTI, Maria. "Exits and Entrances: Maria Nadotti on Two Tempests." *Artforum*, Dec. 1991, p. 20–1. [Brook's compared with Greenway's "Prospero's Books"]

NEW REPUBLIC. "Quest of Peter Brook." June 28, 1980, pp. 27–9.

NEW YORK HERALD TRIBUNE. "Much Ado About 'Romeo'." July 8, 1947.

NEW YORK TIMES. "T. S. Eliot Play Revived." June 9, 1956.

———. "Paris Cool to 'Cat'." Dec. 20, 1956.

————. "Shakespeare Fete In England Opens With The Tempest." April 3, 1963.

————. [letters to the entertainments editor on *Midsummer Night's Dream*— many different opinions] Feb. 28, 1971.

————. [yet more letters] March 14, 1971.

NEW YORKER. "Peter Brook." Nov. 14, 1983. pp. 41–2. [*Carmen*]

NEWMAN, Ernest. "'The Olympians' – I." *The Sunday Times*, Sep. 3, 1949.

————. "'The Olympians' – II." *The Sunday Times*, Sep. 10, 1949.

NEWSWEEK. "Movies: The Film Is Better." Aug. 26, 1963, p. 76.

————. "Theatre: How1! How1!" June 1, 1964, pp. 80–1.

NOBLE, Yvonne and Temperley, Nicholas. "The Beggar's Opera (1953 and 1983)." *Eighteenth Century Life*, May 1985, pp. 109–17.

OAKES, Philip "Something new out of Africa." [interview] Sunday Times, Jan. 4, 1976.

OBSERVER. "Shaman and Showman of Paris." April 10, 1988.

O'CONNER, Gary. "How the Master Magician Casts His Spell." *The New York Times*, Nov. 19, 1989. [Mahab. on tv]

O'CONNER, John J. "Peter Brook's Carmen'." *New York Times*, Feb. 13, 1986. [tv review]

OIDA, Yoshi. "Shinto Training of the Actor." *Darlington Theatre Papers*, Third Series, #3.

OLIVER, Edith. "Theatre: Brook's Orchard." *New Yorker*, Feb. 8, 1988, p. 97.

OPPENHEIMER, George. "Inconsolable and Gay: 'The Fighting Cock.'." *Newsweek*, Dec. 16, 1959.

PANICELLI, I. "Listen Carefully: The 'Mahabharata' on Film." *Art Forum*, Nov. 1989, pp. 122–4.

PANTER-DOWNES, Mollie. "Letter From London." *The New Yorker*, Dec. 3, 1966, pp. 208, 210–11.

————. "Letter From London." *The New Yorker*, Sep. 19, 1964, p. 206.

PARABOLA. "Leaning on the Moment: a conversation with Peter Brook." Spring, 1979.

————. "Lie and Glorious Adjective." [interview] Aug. 1981.

————. "The Fine Art of Tuning, Penetrating the Surface." Sep. 1988, pp. 57–9.

————. "The Sleeping Dragon." Fall, 1990, pp. 52–4.

PARKER, Brian. "Ran and the Tragedy of History." [*Ran* is Kirosawa's film with *Lear* influence] *University of Toronto Quarterly*, Summer 1986, pp. 412–23.

————. "The Use of mise-en-scene in Three Films of King Lear." *Shakespeare Quarterly*, Spring 1991, pp. 75–90.

PEOPLE. [*Mahab* review] Nov. 9, 1987, pp. 134–5.

PICTURE POST. "Theatre's Enfant Terrible." June 14, 1952, pp. 47–8.

PINE, Ralph. "Books." *Theatre Crafts*, May 1988, p. 75. [*Shifting Point*]

PITT-RIVERS, Julian. "Peter Brook and the Ik." *Times Literary Supplement*, Jan. 31, 1975.

POLLACK, Daniel B. *Peter Brook: A Study of a Modern Elizabethan and His Search for New Theatrical Forms*, Unpublished PhD dissertation, New York University, 1979.

PONCE, Fernando. "A la busqueda de un teatro politico perdido." *Arbor: Ciencia, Pensamiento y Cultura*, May, 1982, pp. 57–67.

POPE, W. MacQueen. "The London Theatre." *The Morning Telegraph*, July 7, 1951.

————. [review of *Colombe*] *The Morning Telegraph*, Dec. 14, 1951.

————. "Welcome Tempest in Stratford Show." *The Morning Telegraph*, Aug. 27, 1957.

————. "London Theatre." *The Morning Telegraph*, Dec. 14, 1957.

POPKIN, Henry. "Theatre." *Vogue*, Oct. 15, 1964.

PORTER, Andrew. "Musical Events." [*Carmen*] *New Yorker*, Dec. 19, 1883, pp. 130–1.

PORTERFIELD, Christopher. "Wizard of Anti-Magic." *Time*, Oct. 19, 1970, p. 72.

————. "In Search of the Essence." [*Carmen*] *Time*, Nov. 28, 1983, p. 78.

PRIDEAUX, T. "Circus in the Forest of Arden." *Life*, Feb. 26, 1971, p. 12.

————. "Stage, Screen and Opera—Peter Brook is master of the Daring and Bizarre." *People*, June 16, 1980, p. 108.

PRONKO, Lenoard C. "Los Angeles Festival: Peter Brook's The Mahabharata." *Asian Theatre Journal*, Fall 1988, pp. 220–4.

PUNCH. [*Loves Labour's Lost*] May 22, 1946, p. 446.

PURDOM, C. B. "Stratford's *Measure for Measure*." *Theatre Newsletter*, March 25, 1950, p. 5.

RADCLIFFE, Michael. "Radical Magician." *The Observer*, May 11, 1986 (magazine) pp. 32–3, 35.

RADIN, Victoria. "Theatre—War and Peace." *New Statesman*, April 29, 1988, pp. 32–3.

REA, K. "The Physical Life of the Actor." [interview] *Drama*, 1984, pp. 13–7.

READ, Bill. "Peter Brook: from Stratford-on-Avon to the Gare du Nord." *Boston University Journal* xxiv, #3, 1975.

REESE, Jack E. "The Formalization of Horror in 'Titus Andronicus'," *Shakespeare Quarterly*, Winter, 1970, pp. 77–84.

REEVES, Geoffrey. "Shakespeare on Three Screens." *Sight and Sound*, Spring, 1965, p. 69.

————. "Finding Shakespeare on Film." *TDR*, Fall, 1966, p. 69.

————. "The Persepolis Follies of 1971." *Performance*, Vol. 1, #1, 1971.

RICH, A. "Carmen in the Raw." *Newsweek*, Nov. 21, 1983, p. 105.

RICH, Frank. "Theater: Peter Brook's 'Tragédie de Carmen'." *New York Times*, Nov. 18, 1983.

RICHARDSON, Jack. "The Best of Broadway." *Commentary*, March 1966, p. 76.

ROBERTS, Peter. "'Lear:' Can It Be Staged?" *Plays and Players*, Dec. 1962, pp. 20–2.

_____. "A Midsummer Night's Dream." *Plays and Players*, Oct. 1970, pp. 42–43, 57.

ROBERTSON, Nan. "Making Way for 'Mahabharata'." *The New York Times*, Sep. 30, 1987.

RODDY, J. "Marat/Sade." *Look*, Feb. 22, 1966, p. 110.

ROGOFF, Gordon. "The Carpet Orchard: Brook's Cherry Orchard in Brooklyn." *Theatre*, Spring 1988, pp. 39–40.

RONCONI, Luca. [interview] *Cahiers Renaud-Barrault*, #79, 1972.

RONIN, M. "Lively Arts." [interview] *Senior Scholastic*, March 31, 1967, p. 21.

ROSENTHAL, Harold. *Two Centuries of Opera at Covent Garden*. London: Putnam and Co., 1958.

_____. *Opera at Covent Garden: A Short History* London: Victor Gollancz, 1967.

RYAN, Patricia Louise. *Peter Brook: A survey of his Directorial Achievement*. Unpublished MA Thesis, Wayne St. Univ. 19.

RYLANDS, George. "On Acting Shakespeare." *The Listener*, April 23, 1964, pp. 661–2.

SAINT-DENIS, Michel. "King Lear ad Infinitum . . ." *World Theatre*, Summer, 1964, pp. 135–40.

SANDERS, L. "Barely Bizet." *Saturday Review*, Jan/Feb. 1984, pp. 44–5.

SARRIS, Andrew. ed. *Interviews With Film Directors*. Indianopolis and New York: Bobbs-Merrill, 1967.

_____. "Films." *Village Voice*, Feb. 29, 1968.

SAUVAGE, L. "Beter Brook's 'Carmen'." *New Leader*, Nov. 28, 1983, pp. 17–8.

SCHECHNER, Richard. (ed.) "'Marat/Sade' Forum." *TDR*, Summer 1966.

_____. "Peter Brook's Plastic Theatre." *Village Voice*, Feb. 25, 1971.

_____. "Talking With Peter Brook: Interviews by Richard Schechner, Mathilde La Bardonnie, Joel Louanneau, and George Banu." *TDR*, Spring 1986, pp. 54–71.

_____. ed., Millon, Martine and Husemoller, Anna. "Talking With Three Actors." *TDR*, Spring 1986, pp. 82–91. [previously published in *Alternatives Théâtrales*, July '85.]

SCHLESINGER, Arthur Jr. "Movies." *Vogue*, March 1, 1968, p. 106.

SCHNEIDER, Steve. "Peter Brook's Controversial 'Carmen' Stars Two Casts." *New York Times*, Feb. 9, 1986. [cable tv notes]

SCHONBERG, Harold C. "Peter Brook's 'Carmen' Stirs Lively Debate." *New York Times*, Nov. 27, 1983.

SCURO, Daniel. "'Titus Andronicus:' A Crimson Flushed Stage!" *Ohio State University Theatre Collection Bulletin*. Vol. 1, 1970, pp. 40–8.

SEARS, R. D. "Performing Arts: Peter Brook and the Mahabharata: Critical Perspectives, ed. by David Williams." *Choice*, June 1992, pp. 1553–4.

SEIBERT, G. G. *America*, Nov. 14, 1987, p. 358+. [Mahab. review]

_____. "What the Good Doctor Ordered." *America*, Feb. 13, 1988, pp. 160–1.

SEIDENBERG, R. *American Film*, May 1990, pp. 60–1. [*Mahab.* film rev.]

SELBOURNE, David. *The Making of 'A Midsummer Night's Dream'*. Methuen, 1982.

SENECA. *Oedipus*. Translated by David Anthony Turner, Adapted by Ted Hughes, London: Faber and Faber, 1969.

SERBAN, Andrai. "The Life in a Sound." *TDR*, Dec. 1976.

SHAW, William P. "Vision and Violence in Polanski's 'Macbeth' and Brook's 'Lear'." *Lit/Film Quarterly*, 1986, pp. 211–3.

_____. "Text, Performance, and Perspective: Peter Brook's Landmark Production of Titus Andronicus, 1955." *Theatre History Studies*, 1990, pp. 31–55.

SHEED, Wilfred. "The Stage." *Commonweal*, Jan. 21, 1968, pp. 476–7.

SHEVTSOVA, Maria. "Peter Brook adapts 'Carmen'." *Theatre International*, #10, 1983.

SHORT, Randall. "Movies: The Mahabharata." *Vogue*, March 1990, p. 298.

SHORTER, Eric. "Lost Man of British Theatre." *Daily Telegraph*, Nov. 17, 1974.

_____. "Timon of Athens." *Drama*, Winter, 1974, pp. 21–7.

_____. "Off the Cuff, with Peter Brook and Company." *Drama*, Summer, 1978, pp. 28–33.

_____. "Brook and Others in Avignon." *Drama*, Autumn, 1979, pp. 33–7.

_____. "Lost Man of British Theatre." *Daily Telegraph*, Oct. 17, 1974.

_____. "Paris: Savary and Brook." *Drama*, Spring, 1975, pp. 22–7.

_____. "Gamlets, Gimmicks, Snooks and Puppets in Paris." *Drama*, Winter, 1977/78, pp. 19–24.

_____. "False Prophet?" *Daily Telegraph*, Feb. 12, 1979.

_____. "Chekov Through English Eyes in French, 'The Cherry Orchard'." *Drama*, Autumn, 1981, p. 11.

SHOW. "Moderato Cantabile." Dec. 1961, p. 31.

SHULMAN, Milton. "A Better Look at the Madness of Science." *Evening Standard*, Jan. 10, 1963.

SIEGEL, M. B. [review of *Mahabharata*] *Hudson Review*, Spring, 1988, pp. 180–1.

SIMON, John. "'Lear' Is Not Fit for a King." *New York*, Dec. 19, 1971.

_____. "Avaunt-Garde and Taint Your Wagon." *New York*, May 26, 1980, pp. 79–81.

_____. [*Mahab.* review] *New York*, Nov. 2, 1987, pp. 210–11.

_____. "What Price Majesty?" *New York*, Feb. 8, 1988, pp. 89–91. [c.o.]

SMITH, A. C. H. "Peter Brook's 'Theatrical Yoghourt'." *Daily Telegraph*, Sep. 17, 1971 (magazine) pp. 9–10, 12.

_____. *Orghast at Persepolis*. New York: Viking Press, 1972.

SMITH, Michael. "Theatre Journal." *Village Voice*, Jan. 13, 1966.

_____. "Theatre Journal." *Village Voice*, Dec. 15, 1966.

SMITH, Robert. "Connecting Playscripts and Audiences: The Director as Matchmaker." *Secondary School Theatre Journal*, Sum. 1985, pp. 16–8.

SMITH, Robert M. "Interpretations of Measure for Measure." *Shakespeare Quarterly*, Oct. 1950, pp. 208–18.

SOLICH, Wolfgang. "Prolegomenon for a Theory of Drama Reception: Peter Brook's Measure for Measure and the Emergent Bourgeoisie." *Comparative Drama*, Spring 1984, pp. 54–81.

SONTAG, Susan. "Marat/Sade/Artaud." *Partisan Review*, Spring 1965, pp. 210–19.

SORIA, D. J. "A Question of Style." *High Fidelity*, March 1984, p. MA8-MA11.

SPEAIGHT, Robert. *"The Cycle of Shakespeare Production."* in his Theodore Spencer Lecture, Harvard: Oct. 1969.

THE STAGE AND TELEVISION TODAY. "Peter Brook Lab Will Experiment in Paris." April 25, 1968.

_____. "RSC Presentation Experiment Opens." July 18, 1968, p. 1.

STEPHENS, Frances. "Dark of The Moon." *Theatre World*, April 1949, pp. 11–2.

STODDARD, J. H. [review of *Mahabharata*] *Theatre Journal*, Oct. 1988, pp. 398–400.

STRICK, Philip. "Lord of The Flies and Peter Brook." *Film*, Autumn, 1963, pp. 15–7.

STUART, Charles. "Second Thoughts on *Salome.*" *Theatre Newsletter*, Jan. 28, 1950, p. 5.

STUTTAFORD, Genevieve. "Nonfiction—The Shifting Point." *Publishers Weekly*, Sep. 18, 1987, p. 166.

STYAN, J. L. [review of Theatre of Cruelty season] *Plays and Players*, March 1964.

SULLIVAN, Dan. "The Lengthy But Worthy Trip Of 'Mahabharata'." *Los Angeles Times*, Sep. 7, 1987.

SUMMERS, S. "Brook at Didcot." *Sight and Sound*, Autumn, 1977, pp. 219–20.

SYLVESTER, Robert. "'Flowers' Bloom, 'Stockings' Rip." *The Daily News*, Jan. 24, 1955.

J. T. "'The Fighting Cock.'" *The Village Voice*, Dec. 16, 1959.

TAUBMAN, Howard. "A Challenging 'Lear'." *New York Times*, May 31, 1964.

―――. "Dürrenmatt's 'Physicists.'." *New York Times*, Oct. 14, 1964.

―――. "Theatre: The Assassination of Marat." *New York Times*, Dec. 28, 1965.

TAYLOR, George. "Twentieth Century Theatre: 'Peter Brook and The Mahabrahata,' edited by David Williams." *New Theatre Quarterly*, Aug. 1992, pp. 293–4. [rev of book]

TAYLOR, John Russell. "Peter Brook: or the Limitations of Intelligence." *Sight and Sound*, Spring, 1967, pp. 80–4.

―――. "Theatre and Cinema—Uneasy Neighbors." *Plays and Players*, July, 1968, pp. 54–5.

TDR "'The Mahabharata:' Directed by Peter Brook: Adapted From the Indian Epic by Jean-Claude Carriere." Spring, 1986, pp. 53–99.

THEATRE. "Some Observations on the Theatre of Peter Brook." Fall/Winter, 1980, pp. 72–8.

THEATRE CRAFTS. [Mahab. review] Nov. 1987, pp. 27–31+.

THEATRE WORLD. "The Winter's Tale." Sep. 1951, p. 9.

―――. "The Winter's Tale." Dec. 1951, p. 22.

THOMPSON, Bibi. "Arts and Humanities—Performing Arts: The Mahabharata" *Library Arts Journal*, May 15, 1990, p. 92.

THOMSEN, Christian W. "Peter Brooks Theaterasthetik in The Empty Space und seine Arbeit an Shakespeare." *Maske un Kothurn*, 1981, pp. 231–50.

TIME. "Like the North Pole." Nov. 21, 1949, pp. 81–2.

―――. "Deadly. Rough, Immediate." Nov. 8, 1968, p. 94+.

THE TIMES (London). "Titus Andronicus" July 2, 1957.

―――. "The Tempest at Drury Lane." Dec. 6, 1957.

―――. "Heartbreaking Intensity of Lear." Dec. 14, 1962.

―――. "The Blackest of Black Comedies." Jan. 13, 1963.

TONKIN, Boyd. "The Discovery of Fire." *New Statesman*, April 15, 1988, pp. 38–9. [Shifting Point]

TONKIN, Boyd, and COLVIN, Claire. "Maha Marathon." *Drama*, 1986, pp. 21–3.

TREWIN, J. C. "Saints and Sinners." *The Illustrated London News*, May 28, 1955.

―――. "All the Works." *The Illustrated London News*, Aug. 27, 1955.

―――. "Titus Andronicus' at the Stoll." *Birmingham Post*, (?), 1957.

―――. "'The Tempest' at Stratford." *Birmingham Post and Gazette*, Aug. 14, 1957.

―――. "Curtain Rise." *The Illustrated London News*, July 9, 1960.

―――. *The Birmingham Repertory Theatre: 1913–1963.* Barrie & Rockliff, 1963.

_____. *Shakespeare on the English Stage* : 1900–1964. Barrie & Rockliff, 1964.

_____. "Stratford '70." *Flourish*, Spring, 1971.

_____. *Peter Brook: A Biography*. Great Britain: Macdonald & Co., 1971.

_____. "Brook's Dream Abroad." *Contemporary Review*, Nov. 1972, pp. 244–8.

TRILLING, Ossia. "The London Theatre." *Theatre Newsletter*, Feb. 11, 1950, p. 2.

_____. "The London Theatre." *Theatre Newsletter*, July 7, 1951, p. 2.

_____. "Theatrical Rounds in Paris." *Theatre World*, May 1958, pp. 44–5.

_____. "Peter Brook in Persia: Playing with Words at Persepolis." *Theatre Quarterly*, Jan/March 1972, p. 33+.

_____. "The Shiraz—Persepolis Festival of Arts 1971". *Drama*, Winter, 1971, pp. 45–9.

TRUSSLER, Simon. "Private Experiment in Public." *Plays and Players*, Feb. 1964, pp. 20–2.

_____. "Cruel, Cruel London." *TDR*, Spring, 1965, pp. 207–15.

_____. and ITZIN, C. "Director as Misanthropist: On the Moral Neutrality of Peter Brook." [interview] *Theatre Quarterly*, Spring, 1977, pp. 20–8.

TYNAN, Kenneth. "Chamber of Horrors." *The Observer* (London), Aug. 21, 1955.

_____. "Island Fling." *The Observer*, Aug. 21, 1955.

_____. "Muscovites Find Hamlet Austere." *The Observer*, Nov. 27, 1955.

_____. "King's Rhapsody." *Observer*, Dec. 12, 1955. [*Hamlet*]

_____. "Curtain Time in Moscow." *Harper's Magazine*, March 1956, pp. 61–5.

_____. "The Power and the Glory." *The Observer*, April 8, 1956.

_____. "The Family Reunion." *The Observer*, June 10, 1956.

_____. "The Tragic Sense." *The Observer*, Oct. 14, 1956.

_____. *Curtains*. New York: Atheneum, 1961.

_____. "An Incomparable and Fresh Lear." *New York Herald Tribune*, Nov. 18, 1962.

_____. "A World Without Gods or Hope" *The Observer*, Dec. 16, 1962.

_____. "Prophetic Satire in the Madhouse." *The Observer*, Jan. 10, 1963.

_____. *Tynan Right and Left*. New York: Atheneum, 1967.

_____. "Theatre Abroad." *The New Yorker*, Nov. 9, 1968, p. 144.

THE UNESCO COURIER. [*Mahab.* review] Sep. 1989, pp. 4–9+.

VARIETY. "Tell Me Lies." Feb. 14, 1968, p. 6.

_____. "Peter Brook Organizes Theatre Research Center." June 17, 1970, p. 55.

_____. "Venice Film Fest Reviews: The Mahabharata." Sep. 13, 1989, p. 32.

_____. "Off Broadway Reviews: "The Cherry Orchard." Jan. 27, 1990, p. 100.

VINAVER, Stepven. "The Marat/Sade." *Encore*, Sep/Oct. 1964.

WALLACE, Robert. "A Gamble on Novices Works Almost Too Well." *Life*, Oct. 25, 1963, pp. 97, 100–5.

WALSH, M. and BLAYLOCK, W. "Carmen, But Not Bizet's." *Time*, Dec. 21, 1981, p. 69.

WARDEL, Irving. "Complex Simplicity." *Plays and Players*, Jan. 1963, pp. 50–1.

_____. "Actors at their new Exercise." *The Times*, July 19, 1968.

_____. "The Saint and the Sybarite." *The Times*, Sep. 14, 1968.

_____. "Transatlantic Rituals." *Yale/Theatre*, Summer, 1968, p. 44.

_____. "To The Heights on a Trapeze." *The Times*, Aug. 28, 1970.

_____. "Rituals in the Desert: the Shiraz Festival, 1970." *Gambit*, Vol. 5 #18–9, 1971.

_____. "Selling Shakespeare to Paris." *The Times*, Nov. 20, 1978.

_____. "The Indian Pilgrimage of Peter Brook." *The Times*, May 5, 1982.

_____. "Images of Tenderness, Triumph and Death." [on *Mahab.*] *The Times*, July 13, 1985.

WARRE, Michael. *Designing and Making Stage Scenery*. Studio Vista, 1968.

WATT, Douglas. "Two Big Music Shows with Varied Troubles." *The Daily News*, Dec. 12, 1954.

WATTS, Stephen. "New Approach to Old Drama." *New York Times*, May 17, 1964.

WAUGH, Evelyn. "Titus With a Grain of Salt." *The Spectator*, Sep. 2, 1955.

WEALES, G. "Epic Communication." *Commonweal*, Nov. 20, 1987, pp. 655–6. [*Mahab.*]

WEBSTER, Margaret. "A Look At The London Season." *Theatre Arts*, May 1957, pp. 29–30.

WECHSLER, Bert. "Video Review: Latest Movies." *Video Review*, May 1988, 58. [*Lear* movie]

WEIL, H. S. "The Options of the Audience: Theory and Practice in Peter Brook's 'Measure for Measure'." *Shakespeare Survey* #25.

WEILER, A. H. "The Screen in Review." *New York Times*, Aug. 25, 1953. [*Beggar's Opera*]

WEINTRAUB, Bernard. "Recording the 'Marat/Sade' Madness." *New York Times*, Feb. 12, 1966.

WEISS, Peter. *Marat/Sade* Geoffrey Skelton, trans. Calder, 1965.

WETZSTEON, Ross. "Peter Brook: Breaking the Code." *Village Voice*, Feb. 2, 1988, p. 97+.

WHITEHEAD, Phillip. "Just How Open a University?" *The Times*, June 5, 1984.

WHITTAKER, Herbert. "Horror Play is Based on Greed and Revenge." *The Globe and The Mail* (Toronto), March 2, 1970.

WILLBOURN, Hugh. "The Mahabharata in Avignon." *Plays and Players*, Oct. 1985, pp. 35–6.

WILLIAMS, David. *Theatre of Innocence and Experience: Peter Brook*, 1964–1980, unpublished Thesis, University of Kent, 1983.

————. "A Place Marked by Life." *New Theatre Quarterly*, Vol. 1, #1, Feb. 1985.

————. *In Search of Lost Theatre: The Story of Peter Brook's Centre*, Paris: CICT, 1986.

————. (ed.) *Peter Brook: A Theatrical Casebook*. London: Methuen, 1988.

————. (ed.) *Peter Brook and The Mahabharata: Critical Perspectives*. London; New York: Routledge, 1991.

WILLIAMS, Gary, Jay. "From The Dream to The Mahabharata; Or, Draupadi in the Deli." *Theatre*, Spring 1988, pp. 28–31.

WILSON, David. "Tell Me Lies." *Sight and Sound*, Spring, 1968, pp. 98–9.

WORSLEY, T. C. "Measure For Measure." *New Statesman and Nation*, April 1, 1950, p. 27.

————. "Late Shakespeare." *New Statesman and Nation*, July 7, 1951.

————. "Sentimental Tragedy." *New Statesman and Nation*, May 23, 1953.

————. "Grand Guignol." *New Statesman and Nation*, Aug. 27, 1955.

————. "Realistic Melodrama." *New Statesman and Nation*, Oct. 20, 1956. p. 482.

YARROW, Andrew L. "Transforming a Brooklyn Theater." *New York Times*, Jan. 5, 1988.

ZARRILLI, Phillip. "The Aftermath: When Peter Brook came to India." *TDR*, Spring 1986, pp. 92–9.

————. Neff, Deborah; and Meduri, Avanthi. "More Aftermath after Peter Brook: Comment and Reply." *TDR*, Summer, 1988, pp. 14–9.

ZIEGLER, Wesley J. "Stripping Off The Layers." *Theatre Today*, Spring, 1971, pp. 4–8.

INDEX TO THE PRODUCTION CHRONOLOGY

(Numbers below refer to production number, not page number)

ASSISTANT / ASSOCIATE DIRECTORS

CO-DIRECTORS

DIRECTOR WITH BROOK AS "COLLABORATING DIRECTOR"

FILM "PRODUCTION DIRECTOR"

LANGUAGE RESEARCH (Avesta)

DESIGNERS & TECHNICAL STAFF

COMPOSERS (incidental music)
CONDUCTORS
CHOREOGRAPHERS
"MUSIC DIRECTORS"

MUSICIANS, SINGERS

PRODUCERS (American sense)
ASSOCIATE PRODUCERS
PRODUCING ORGANIZATIONS

INDEX TO THE INTERVIEWS

(Numbers here refer to pages)

Other titles in the Contemporary Theatre Studies Series: